KANT'S WORLDVIEW

KANT'S WORLDVIEW

How Judgment Shapes Human Comprehension

Rudolf A. Makkreel

Northwestern University Press
Evanston, Illinois

Northwestern University Press
www.nupress.northwestern.edu

Printed in the United States of America

10 9 8 7 6 5 4 3 2 1

Library of Congress Cataloging-in-Publication Data
Names: Makkreel, Rudolf A., 1939– author.
Title: Kant's worldview : how judgment shapes human comprehension / Rudolf A Makkreel.
Description: Evanston, Illinois : Northwestern University Press, 2022. | Includes bibliographical references and index.
Identifiers: LCCN 2021025097 | ISBN 9780810144309 (paperback) | ISBN 9780810144316 (cloth) | ISBN 9780810144323 (ebook)
Subjects: LCSH: Kant, Immanuel, 1724–1804. | Judgment (Logic) | Knowledge, Theory of.
Classification: LCC B2799.J8 M35 2022 | DDC 121—dc23
LC record available at https://lccn.loc.gov/2021025097

To Frithjof Rodi

Contents

Acknowledgments ix

List of Abbreviations of Works by Kant xi

Introduction 3

Part 1. Cognizing, Comprehending, and Knowing the Natural World

1 Comprehending the World through Intuitive Assimilation, Conceptual Acquisition, and Rational Appropriation 13

2 Kant on Alexander Baumgarten and Logic: The Aesthetic, Analytical, and Synthetic Distinctness of What Is Empirically Assimilated 26

3 Georg Friedrich Meier on Comprehension and Kant on Its Relation to Cognition and Knowledge 39

4 The Acquisition of Cognition and Its Transcendental Sources 47

5 The Role of Judgment in Validating Cognition as Meaningful and Appropriating Knowledge as True 59

6 The Modal Categories of Empirical Inquiry and the Limits of What Can Actually Be Known: Replacing Prejudices with Preliminary and Provisional Judgments 71

Part 2. Comprehending and Contextualizing the Human World

7 Seeking Practical Resolutions for Irresolvable Theoretical Antinomies 87

8 Law as Legislative and Law as Legitimating: The Role of Feeling and Judgment in Morality 100

9 Aesthetic Communicability and the Medial Recontextualization of Experience 112

10 The Modal Relevance of Reflective Judgment for Kant's Worldview 125

11 What Kant Means by Life 135

12 Comprehending Teleological Purposiveness by Appropriately Contextualizing It 148

13 Kant's Anthropology and Its Strategies for Moving beyond the Inner Sense of Psychology: Reexamining All the Senses 161

14 Vital Sense, Interior Sense, and Self-Assessment 176

15 The Distinction between Kant's Cosmopolitanism and His Cosmical Philosophy 198

16 The Obstacles to Be Overcome in Fulfilling the Goals of a World-Oriented Philosophy 209

Conclusion: Kant's Multifaceted Worldview 228

Notes 247

Bibliography 263

Index 273

Acknowledgments

This is a continuation and expansion of my earlier book on Immanuel Kant. Although that work focused on his aesthetics and his views on the imagination, it was also epistemic and explored the interpretive nature of reflective judgment. In this work, various other contributions of judgment will also be considered to show how Kant augments what is cognized by the understanding with a mode of rational comprehension that is both theoretical and practical. This focus on the overall aspects of Kant's philosophy will also lead me to examine his ethical and sociopolitical, religious, and anthropological writings in order to articulate what could be called his worldview. Beyond recognizing Kant's main stated positions, the general tenor of his mode of thinking will be characterized. Thus, while underscoring what is distinctive about the results Kant achieved in the various disciplines to which he contributed, I will also look for reflective affinities that can disclose his underlying orientation to the world.

One of the virtues of explicating Kant's worldview will be to demonstrate that his idealism incorporates many of the empirical concerns of human beings. Recently there have been attempts to make Kant's thought more relevant by stressing his impure ethics, his non-ideal politics, and his pragmatic tendencies. These efforts will be put in context by showing how his reflective worldview expands on the "world-concept" that directs the *Critique of Pure Reason*. Beyond providing a more coherent overall comprehension of Kant, the theme of worldview thinking is especially timely given that we are facing social and environmental problems that will require unprecedented consensus-building in an age of conflict.

Some of the chapters of this book include revised versions of texts originally published elsewhere. Chapter 3 reproduces some parts of "Kant on Cognition, Comprehension, and Knowledge," in *Natur und Freiheit. Akten des XII. Kant-Kongresses 2015*, ed. Violetta Waibel and Margit Ruffing (Berlin: Walter de Gruyter, 2018). Chapter 8 includes some passages previously published in "Relating Aesthetic and Sociable Feelings to Moral and Participatory Feelings," in *Kant's Observations and Remarks*, ed. Susan Shell and Richard Velkley (Cambridge: Cambridge University Press, 2012), copyright Cambridge University Press, reprinted with permission. Chapter 9 includes some passages recently published in "Kant and the Need for Orientational and Contextual Thinking: Applying Reflective Judgement to Aesthetics and to the Comprehension of Human Life," *Kantian Review*, vol. 1 (2021), copyright Cambridge University Press, reprinted with permission. Chapters 13 and 14 include some passages previously published in "Self-Cognition and Self-Assessment," in *Kant's Lectures on Anthropology*, ed. Alix Cohen (Cambridge: Cambridge University Press, 2014), copyright Cambridge University Press, reprinted with permission; as well as some parts of "Baumgarten and Kant on Clarity, Distinctness, and the Differentiation of Our Mental Powers," in *Baumgarten and Kant on Metaphysics*, ed. Courtney Fugate and John Hymers (Oxford: Oxford University Press, 2018), copyright Oxford University Press, reproduced with permission of the Licensor through PLSclear. Chapter 15 includes some passages previously published in "Differentiating Worldly and Cosmopolitan Senses of Philosophy in Kant," in *Kant und die Philosophie in weltbürgerlicher Absicht, Proceedings for the XIth International Kant Congress*, ed. Stefano Bacin and Alfredo Ferrarin (Berlin/Boston: Walter de Gruyter, 2013).

I would like to express my appreciation of the support of the Heilbrun Fund of Emory University and the encouragement of academic colleagues, graduate students, and friends. Over the years no one has been as supportive of my work as my beloved wife Frances Tanikawa Makkreel. As an intellectual historian, she always knew how to ask the right questions and lead me to clarify things more. Among the many others I would like to thank for rewarding conversations and exchanges over the years are Karl Ameriks, Frans Brom, David Carr, Andrew Chignell, Marcus Duwell, Thomas Flynn, the late Nicholas Fotion who gave me his analytic perspective on some of my writings, Rodolphe Gasché, Catalina Gonzalez, Dilek Huseyinzadegan, Apaar Kumar, Beatrice Longuenesse, Sebastian Luft, John Lysaker, Matthew McAndrew, Colin McQuillan, Jennifer Mensch, Felicitas Munzel, Eric Nelson, Angelico Nuzzo, Onora O'Neill, Richard Parry, Riccardo Pozzo, Tom Rockmore, my longtime Dilthey coeditor Frithjof Rodi, Robert Scharff, my favorite anthropologist Bradd Shore, Kristi Sweet, Simon Truwant, Eric Watkins, Cindy Willett, Eric Wilson, Jeffrey Wilson, John Zammito, and Rachel Zuckert. Finally, I would like to thank Trevor Perri and Anne Gendler at Northwestern University Press for their help.

Abbreviations of Works by Kant

AA	*Kants gesammelte Schriften: Akademieausgabe*
A/B	*Critique of Pure Reason*
AN	*Allgemeine Naturgeschichte und Theorie des Himmels*
AP	*Anthropology from a Pragmatic Point of View*
BE	*Bemerkungen zu den Beobachtungen über das Gefühl des Schönen und Erhabenen*
C2	*Critique of Practical Reason*
C3	*Critique of the Power of Judgment*
"CHR"	"Determination of the Concept of a Human Race"
"FI"	"First Introduction to the *Critique of the Power of Judgment*"
"FS"	"The False Subtlety of the Four Syllogistic Figures"
GM	*Groundwork of the Metaphysics of Morals*
"ICD"	"Inquiry concerning the Distinctness of the Principles of Natural Theology and Morality"
"IUH"	"Idea for a Universal History with a Cosmopolitan Aim"
LL	*Lectures on Logic*
M	Baumgarten, *Metaphysics: A Critical Translation with Kant's Elucidations*
MM	*The Metaphysics of Morals*
MNS	*Metaphysical Foundations of Natural Science*
"MTT"	"On the Miscarriage of All Philosophical Trials in Theodicy"
OBS	*Observations on the Feeling of the Beautiful and the Sublime*
OP	*Opus postumum*
"OT"	"What Does It Mean to Orient Oneself in Thinking?"
PFM	*Prolegomena to Any Future Metaphysics*
PG	*Physische Geographie*

PP	*Perpetual Peace: A Philosophical Sketch*
R	*Religion within the Boundaries of Mere Reason*
RA	*Reflexionen zur Anthropologie*
"RH"	"Review of Herder's *Ideas*"
RL	*Reflexionen zur Logik*
RM	*Reflexionen zur Metaphysik*
RMP	*Reflexionen zur Moralphilosophie*
SIW	*On the Form and Principles of the Sensible and Intelligible World*
"TP"	"On the Use of Teleological Principles in Philosophy"
VA	*Vorlesungen über Anthropologie*
VL	*Vorlesungen über Logik*
VMR	*Vorlesungen über Metaphysik und Rationaltheologie*
"WE"	"An Answer to the Question, 'What Is Enlightenment?'"

KANT'S WORLDVIEW

Introduction

Immanuel Kant recognized that nature as we understand it in terms of the lawful regularities of the *Critique of Pure Reason* nevertheless contains much that remains incomprehensible. The full horizon of human experience is a world that still needs to be comprehended by reason. This leads him to invoke a more inclusive idea of philosophizing according to a world-concept (*Weltbegriff*). But reason cannot simply extrapolate from the ways in which the understanding proceeds to determine lawful order. Kant comes to realize that the speculative projections of reason need to be tamed by our own powers of orientation and judgment. This will mean that the overall worldview that we can actually arrive at will need to include supplementary modes of organizational order that are not determinant but reflective.

To the extent that human experience can make sense of the world and attain a worldview, it will be a layered affair where different modes of reflection and judgment are operative. The nature and role of reflection in Kant is at issue today—especially in ethics and social and political philosophy. There is good reason for this because the meaning of "reflection" varies in the different contexts it comes up. The two terms that Kant uses are *reflectiren* and *überlegen*, the latter of which can also be translated as "to consider or weigh alternatives." More literally, *über-legen* involves the "laying over" of things, or an "overlapping" that suggests the possibility of discerning different levels of awareness and spheres of reality. Kant asserts that even animals can *reflectiren* about things, but only instinctively, and thus not at the level of weighing alternatives (*überlegen*) with the aid of judgment. Indeed, in an early essay Kant claimed that it is the capacity to make judgmental distinctions that allows human consciousness to rise above mere animal sentience, and this conviction leads him to increasingly explore and expand the functions of judgment. Initially, judgment is the analytical power to abstract concepts from perceptual marks and the logical power to distinguish and connect concepts; epistemically, judgment becomes the schematizing power to relate the categories of the understanding to objects, that is, to *immediately infer* how universals apply to particulars; in the *Critique of Judgment* and the two final versions of the logic lectures, judgment is also given the reflective power to make much broader *mediate inferences* that relate things of a particular kind to concerns of a more general nature. Reflective judgment will allow us to discern the kinds of affinities that cannot always be captured by concepts of the understanding.

Whereas the first part of this work on philosophizing according to a world-concept focuses mostly on these and other theoretical issues, the second part will turn to our practical concerns as we act in the world. Here normative considerations will play a central role. In explicating what practical reason adds to human experience, I will also consider what role reflection and feeling are allowed to play, starting with the demand that we respect the moral law. Then, as we deal with aesthetic feeling and the evaluative role of reflective judgment in finding consensus and universal agreement, the various ways in which we contextualize the world will become central. This link between reflective judgment and contextual differentiation will allow us to see that although this orientational mode of judgment is introduced rather late in Kant's career, it could well have its roots in the idea of rational comprehension that he adopted from Georg Friedrich Meier and gradually revised in his lectures on logic. Indeed, I will show that the themes of comprehension and reflective judgment converge in Kant's theory of the sublime, as well as in his characterization of the immanent purposiveness of organisms. Contextual differentiation, reflective judgment, and comprehension are purposive strategies for both specifying our understanding of the cosmos and expanding on it. They will also allow me to develop Kant's still somewhat abstract world-concept into a worldview that emphasizes how humans should relate to the cosmos and its other inhabitants.

Kant's overall project of a cosmical philosophy guided by a world-concept is often equated with cosmopolitanism. However, I will argue that cosmical philosophy requires us to develop all our powers, whereas cosmopolitanism, as Kant defines it in the *Critique of Judgment* and in *Perpetual Peace*, is mostly geared to politically restraining the aggressive instincts of our animate soul and tempering the *animus* of mind that makes us socially competitive. This kind of cosmopolitanism leaves us at the level of the culture of skill, but cosmical philosophy according to a world-concept must move to the higher spiritual level of self-legislating. The culture of skill must be supplemented with the culture of moral discipline.

This is a brief outline of a few defining themes of this work that will highlight some overlooked aspects of Kant's worldview. According to the *Deutsches Wörterbuch*, Kant was the first to use the German term for "worldview": *Weltanschauung*. Because the term occurs only once in his writings, I will treat it as a limit idea that highlights Kant's constant concern to philosophize with the world in mind. Another point that needs to be made here is that Kant's own use of *Weltanschauung* designates a sublime or awe-inspiring viewing of the world that provides a momentary insight, rather than a reflectively thought-out view of life that is developed over time. Although Kant was a systematic thinker oriented by a world-concept, he never fully defined a worldview in the way we think of it now. But this is not all that unusual, for few thinkers articulate their own worldview. Often the term is applied to others in a pejorative sense, as when Hegel dismisses the Kantian "moral worldview" as abstract and removed from the reality of the ethical communal life that the *Phenomenology of Spirit* expects us to partake in. In order to explicate Kant's overall worldview in a more open-minded but critical way, I will bring out the texture of his thinking in following the progress of his work. My aim is to show that despite blind spots in Kant's own outlook, he projects a multilevel worldview that offers philosophical directives for humans to reflectively engage with each other even when consensus eludes them.

In chapter 1 of this book, the three main divisions of the *Critique of Pure Reason*—the Aesthetic, the Analytic, and the Dialectic—are correlated with three more general ways in which we relate to the world: *intuitive assimilation*, *conceptual acquisition*, and *rational appropriation*. What I characterize as "intuitive assimilation" encompasses not only what the senses provide us perceptually, but also those inherited beliefs we allow ourselves to be persuaded of. It is also the level of awareness that is addressed in Kant's lectures on logic, where we see him teaching his students to strive for intuitive clarity and logical distinctness and examine their subjective beliefs for internal consistency and potential prejudices. A shift to the conceptual acquisition of apperception is needed to gain a more determinate cognition which can be understood in lawful ways. This constitutes the central level of the *Critique of Pure Reason*, where Kant provides the categories that make objective experience possible. The function of rational appropriation is different again: it is to dissolve the dialectical antinomies that can result from striving for overall comprehension and to resolve them by means of a canon of knowledge that aims to deliver the certainty of an intersubjective consensus. These are not levels of literal cognitive possession, for we do not actually cognize anything at just one level. Nor do all three levels need to be fully activated in claiming to cognize something. These levels expand on Kant's own spelling, reading, interpreting distinction to provide a better way of delineating and contextualizing the three main divisions of the first *Critique*.

Attitudinally, these levels can be related to (1) how we clarify our outlook on our surroundings based on both the particularity of what is actually perceived and the contingency of what is believed, (2) how we form a more general cognitive world-picture made possible by the relational concepts of the understanding, and (3) how the theoretical and practical necessary norms of reason can expand what we know into a full-fledged worldview. Similarly, in his lectures on anthropology Kant prescribes three analogous levels of human maturation: the technical *cultivation* of *assimilated* dispositions, *civilization* as the pragmatic *acquisition* of social order, and finally *moralization* as the rational and reflective *appropriation* of virtue. These levels that fill in our historical development will be correlated with Kant's essay on religion, where he distinguishes three predispositions to the good that define the animality of the soul, the sociality of the human mind, and the communality of spirit, respectively. Finally, I will relate all this to the three levels of validating human rights in the late *Metaphysics of Morals,* where Kant moves from an initial *unilateral assimilation* of property to its *bilateral contractual acquisition* and finally to a mode of omnilateral *appropriation* that requires universal approval. These same three levels of legitimation can be applied to the way we take responsibility for and own up to our knowledge claims. These initial attempts to position the first *Critique* relative to Kant's corpus more generally will be gradually explicated in terms of more definitive claims as we proceed to the other chapters.

Chapter 2 will deal with Kant's lectures and reflections on logic and how he assimilates Alexander Gottlieb Baumgarten's efforts to supplement logical or analytical distinctness with an aesthetic distinctness in order to then develop his own conception of synthetic distinctness. This third kind of distinctness provides an important background for transitioning to the new standards of mathematical measurability and objective determination in the "Transcendental Analytic." Chapter 3 shows how Kant revises the way that Georg Friedrich Meier defines the levels of cognition and leads up to comprehension. Whereas Meier claims that human comprehension can provide cognition that is objective and absolute, Kant argues that it is always relative to some purpose. Comprehension is a rational mode of cognition (*Erkenntnis*) that is both theoretical and practical, but it falls short of the certainty of knowledge (*Wissen*) demanded by the "Canon of Pure Reason." Chapters 4 and 5 will analyze the *Critique of Pure Reason* in terms of its own transcendental sources. Special emphasis will be given to the revised role of judgment in the second edition, where the general logical power to relate concepts to each other becomes the transcendental power to schematically relate concepts to objects. Schematization is a judgmental function of the imagination whereby abstract mathematical and relational categories obtain their objective meaning. The categories allow us to read natural events as part of a lawfully ordered objective world. Chapter 6 focuses on the last set of categories: the postulates of empirical thinking. These three categories of modality relate what can actually be experienced to what we cognize as possible or necessary. These discussions will be extended to the problem of human prejudices that Kant examines in his lectures of logic. There he considers how prejudices that we contingently believe can be suspended and neutralized into possible preliminary judgments that can serve as hypotheses for further empirical inquiry into what is necessarily the case. The contingency exposed by prejudices will come into focus as a fourth modality when we discuss reflective judgments in chapters 9 and 10.

Part 2 of this book deals with the other two *Critiques*, as well as the writings on anthropology, religion, and cosmopolitanism, to prepare us to further fill in Kant's worldview. Chapter 7 examines the shift from dialectical to practical reason and shows that the antinomies of pure reason have no constitutive solutions and are resolved by regulative principles that guide maxims of judgment. Kant's effort in the third antinomy to reconcile natural determinism with the freedom to unconditionally begin something appeals to the possibility that a noumenal act outside of time can have a phenomenal effect in time. But this speculative rational solution from on high is not all that convincing. Later in his essay on religion, Kant provides a more down-to-earth solution by allowing phenomenal incentives to be incorporated into rational maxims of action as long as they remain subordinate. This again raises questions that can only be resolved by judgment.

Chapter 8 explores the shift in Kant from the idea of law as legislative for nature to the idea of moral law as both self-legislative and as legitimating actions that accord with reason and the feeling of respect for others. This was the first feeling that Kant regarded as pure, and the role of judgment is to consider how far other sociable feelings can be made morally compatible. Aesthetic feelings are examined for their formal purity in chapter 9. This chapter introduces the *Critique of Judgment* and is pivotal because aesthetic judgments are considered to be reflective, unlike the determinant judgments of the first two *Critiques*. In the "Introduction" to the *Critique of Judgment*, Kant lays out four judgmental contexts of *field, territory, domain, and habitat* that expose different modalities of human thinking. Since taste deals with subjective preferences, Kant warns that no domain of lawful *necessity* can guide reflective judgments about beauty. We must therefore orient ourselves to the *actual* territory of experience in new ways. Here Kant makes room for the fourth modality of *contingency* by introducing the habitat where we happen to be located as we relate to the object being evaluated. In order to arrive at a consensus in matters of taste, we must imaginatively transpose ourselves from the contingent local habitat of our psychic state of sensuous pleasure to a *possible* mental *sensus communis* to arrive at an appropriate aesthetic assessment. Whereas the imaginative schematization of concepts of the understanding in the first

Critique served to *prefigure* the objects of experience, the nonconceptual aesthetic schematization of the third *Critique* allows us to imaginatively *reconfigure* our experiential context. A linguistic extension of imaginative schematization is added in §59 of the latter work, where Kant shows how poetic symbolization can create reflective analogies among distinct contexts. The modal shifts in our thinking associated with these judgmental contexts are further explored in chapter 10. There we also see Kant turn from the calm and contemplative state of mind associated with the finite forms of beauty to the more stirring experience of the sublime, where the imagination struggles to survey an immense and formless magnitude. Sublimity confronts us with the problem of comprehension in a new way. Comprehension, which was originally conceived as a function of reason, is now related to reflective judgment. This makes it possible to see that the way judgment shapes comprehension also manifests itself in one's worldview. In chapters 11 and 12, reflective judgment is related to teleological purposiveness and what Kant means by life. This is important because how life is conceived is central to one's worldview about the significance of things. Organisms are delineated as reciprocal systems that are immanently purposive. But whereas aesthetic purposiveness was playful and oriented to the field of the possible, organic purposiveness finds itself contextually bounded by a contingent habitat. Organisms such as plants and animals are only relatively self-sufficient and self-modifying: they depend on external resources.

It is paradoxical that Kant often refers to the ideas of life and enlivenment in the aesthetic part of the third *Critique* and almost never in the teleological part about biology. We can feel what it is to be alive, but we cannot objectively define life. Kant refuses to appeal to a life-impulse to explain natural organisms, but has no hesitation in speaking of a human vital sense in his anthropological lectures. Chapters 13 and 14 will show how Kant replaced introspective psychology with a pragmatic anthropology that conceives of the life of the mind as world-oriented. Now his concern is not just to know the world but to "have the world," which includes having on outlook on it. We are warned not to get lost in the obscurities of inner (*innere*) sense and are offered a new notion of an interior (*inwendige*) sense that does not look or focus inward, but takes our pulse while looking outward. Accordingly, Kant's interior sense can be considered to be reflexively self-aware but not self-consciously reflective. This reflexivity of interior sense involves a mode of self-feeling that is responsive to its contextual situation and can fill in what it means to be engaged with the world. It involves an individual's outlook, but not yet a full-fledged reflective worldview. This is complemented with a fresh examination of the outer senses that is less concerned with them as providing the content for cognitive concepts and more with how they can orient a judgmental assessment of our surroundings.

Increasingly, Kant becomes a contextual thinker who resorts to orientational reflection. We are amphibious creatures who are always in danger of falling into amphibolies, which is to fail to reflect on what differentiates one situational context from another. The problem of how to mediate between different regions will be shown to be central to Kant's version of cosmopolitanism as discussed in chapter 15. He does not propose an overall world government, but a confederation of nation-states with distinctive borders. The task is to make these borders permeable and regulate how we can cross them peaceably. This is also the chapter where I show why the idea of cosmopolitanism does not exhaust Kant's project of philosophizing according to a world-concept. The latter, more demanding project of a cosmical philosophy will provide the proper framework for defining Kant's worldview.

Chapter 16 and the conclusion will attempt to characterize the nature of Kant's worldview. To prepare for this, it was important to weave some of the main philosophical positions he developed over the years into the more topical themes of reflection and judgment, orientation and comprehension that recur throughout this book. Chapter 16 supplements Kant's philosophical views with his perspectives on human culture and the skills it cultivates. However, his concerns for universal consensus and omnilateral legitimacy in matters of ethics and politics led him to overlook the importance of ethnic differences in the development of cultural goals. He accepted the views of the Swedish botanist Carl Linnaeus about racial differences, although he eventually downplayed them in his cosmopolitan political theory. Johann Friedrich Herder made Kant aware of the controversial nature of these views of Linnaeus, but it is not clear how much they would still have figured in Kant's more comprehensive cosmical worldview, had he spelled it out more himself. The conclusion probes the essentials of Kant's idealism of freedom in relation to other types of worldviews that have been distinguished since the rise of historical consciousness starting in the nineteenth century. It also shows how Kant deals with more mundane life-concerns about how to treat animals, the nature of human friendship, and how much reflective judgment can contribute to making practical life-decisions.

The themes of comprehension and judgment, and contextualization and reflective orientation, as well as the modal significance of human thought, which are central to this reading of Kant, intersect with many better-known aspects of his philosophy that I shall of course also take into account. I hope that even these aspects will be illuminated to bring out the critical import of Kant's overall worldview.

Part 1

Cognizing, Comprehending, and Knowing the Natural World

1

Comprehending the World through Intuitive Assimilation, Conceptual Acquisition, and Rational Appropriation

> What we inherit [*ererben*] or assimilate, we must acquire [*erwerben*] for ourselves in order to appropriately own [*besitzen*] it.
> —Goethe, *Faust*

By relating the task of understanding as defined in the *Critique of Pure Reason* to what Kant sometimes refers to as "comprehension," it is my aim to provide an overall characterization of his philosophical project. Since Kant argues that the faculty of the understanding (*Verstand*) proceeds discursively, namely, one step at a time, the very project of a more holistic comprehension (*Begreifen*) could seem to be problematic. As he states in the "Transcendental Dialectic," "concepts of reason serve for comprehension" (A311/B367), but they are purely inferential and are sometimes sophistical. Although comprehension for Kant could never provide anything like a Hegelian experiential grasp of the reason of things, he did continue to explore the relevance of comprehension for experience. To help define what Kant ends up meaning by comprehension, I will reference some important discussions about it in Kant's lectures on logic and in his *Critique of Judgment*.[1] The former kind of comprehension is rational, the latter aesthetic, and it is in the context of his discussion of the mathematical sublime that Kant broaches the idea of an overall "worldview [*Weltanschauung*]" (*AA* 5:255),[2] which would be expanded on by nineteenth- and twentieth-century philosophers to denote a common or generic outlook on life. As it is used in this work, the term "worldview" designates a comprehensive way of characterizing Kant's distinctive philosophical project.

What is at stake in contrasting "understanding" and "comprehension" is the scope of what humans can claim to know. Referring to David Hume's skepticism, Kant complains that he unduly stresses the limits of experience and dismisses any role for reason beyond its empirical use. He classifies Hume among those "geographers of human reason" (A760/B788) who survey the earth solely in terms of its sensible appearances. While it is important to base knowledge claims on the empirical understanding, we must remain open to what could lie beyond the horizon of sense. Critical philosophy must therefore supplement "the *limits* of actual geographical" surveys of the earth with "the *boundaries* of all possible description of the earth" (A759/B787, emphases mine).

Kant briefly explicates this distinction between limits and boundaries in his *Prolegomena to Any Future Metaphysics.* Limits (*Schranken*) are negative empirical markers that do not take into account what could lie beyond them. Boundaries (*Grenzen*) are positive in that they "presuppose a space existing outside a certain definite place and enclosing it" (*PFM* 11; *AA* 4:352). The earthly limits that confine the senses need to be critically re-conceptualized as worldly boundaries that leave room for reason to search further.[3] From this we can infer that whereas earthly limits are imposed from without, worldly boundaries are in some sense self-imposed. Earthly limits are external negative restraints on the understanding, but worldly bounds can be regarded as internal positive constraints on reason as it attempts to comprehend both what we can and cannot know. Comprehension will be shown to be a mode of reason whose bounds must be judgmentally self-binding.

This topological sketch of the scope of worldly comprehension will gradually be filled in to give content to Kant's worldview, and it is important at the start to correlate this with a multilevel approach signaled by his efforts to go beyond traditional academic philosophy. Although much of the *Critique of Pure Reason* is still couched in standard academic terms, in the "Architectonic" near the end, Kant claims that philosophy should no longer restrict itself to some narrow scholastic concept (*Schulbegriff*) but move on to a more inclusive world-concept (*Weltbegriff*). The standard academic problems addressed in the "Analytic" of how the understanding can cognize nature in the universally valid terms that make the sciences possible, must undergo further testing by reason. And when Kant elaborates what is to be included in his world-concept, it turns out to involve not only the scientific cognition of nature, but also our historical cognition of the world. Therefore Kant imposes a "Canon of Pure Reason" on both the conceptual cognition (*Erkenntnis*) of the sciences and the world-acquaintance (*Weltkenntnis*) (A826/B854) that draws from experience more generally. This more inclusive conception of what can be cognized provided near the end of the *Critique of Pure Reason* leads Kant to ask whether cognitive claims have their source in persuasion or in conviction. Persuasion is merely psychological in that "it has its ground only in the particular constitution of the subject" (A820/B848), whereas conviction strives to be rational and aims at universal agreement. Yet both fall short of the certainty (*Gewissheit*) that Kant expects of knowledge (*Wissen*). This means that cognition can attain the certainty of being true knowledge of the world only if it is both formally coherent and in agreement with the overall content of our experience.

The need to overcome beliefs based on persuasion was already a topic in Kant's lectures on logic. They deal extensively with the ways in which prejudices are formed on the basis of pre-given regional influences and how they must be transformed into proper judgments. Kant's admission that from early on we hold many prejudices based on our historical circumstances, means that how we are said to cognize nature in the "Analytic" of the *Critique of Pure Reason* is to some extent an abstraction. We do not start with a blank slate, as this work could suggest. Kant knew very well that what we end up knowing involves the intersection of many influences, and in the lectures on logic he distinguishes as many as seven levels of cognition, the highest of which is comprehension. Whereas cognition as defined in the "Analytic" is a function of intellectual understanding (*Verstand*) for which the givens are particular and sense-based, knowing as defined later in the "Canon of Pure Reason" draws on the more encompassing understanding (*Verstehen*) of reason which attempts to put everything in context. The aim of the present work is to show how the move from cognition to knowledge can be accounted for in a comprehensive interpretation of Kant's theoretical philosophy that will also make sense of his own use of the term "comprehension" in his lectures on logic and elsewhere.

Any attempt to approach Kant comprehensively must also take his practical philosophy into account. Indeed, Kant's moral views may have as much influence on overcoming historical prejudices as his theoretical reflections. Some of the sources of our prejudices are instinctive inclinations, and clearly morality is meant to put a check on actions that are merely in accordance with them. It will be shown that many traditional prejudices about honor and happiness are challenged in Kant's moral writings, even though they are not necessarily addressed as prejudices. The same can be said about his reservations about actions motivated by sympathy. Our sympathies often disclose how provincial we are. Perhaps one of the reasons why Kant does not place that much stress on the overcoming of prejudices in his first two *Critiques* is that he considered his popular writings like the essay on Enlightenment to be more effective venues. Still, the question remains to what extent Kant's critical philosophy, which stresses the a priori conditions that we provide to frame our experience and our responses to it, is able to deal with the prejudices and parochial stereotypes that negatively distort our conception of the world. Both the a priori conditions of cognition and our prejudices have a pre-givenness to them. The first kind of pre-givenness is formal and anticipatory, while the other is rooted in inherited informational content. They affect us implicitly and may not always be distinguished from each other. But we will not be able to effectively communicate what we think about the world unless these distinct influences on experience are untangled. Thus we need a more differentiated account of Kant's critical project than is usually provided.[4]

In pursuing the theme of Kant's world perspective, it will also be important to consider his anthropological lectures because they most fully recognize how we are in fact contextually embedded in the world. These lectures also go into more empirical detail about the contributions of the various senses to what is cognized, and they expose the illusions we must seek to avoid and the prejudices we need to overcome. But most of all, Kant's pragmatic approach to anthropology aims to replace scholastic learning with close-up acquaintance with the world. Here Kant is seeking cognition that is useful for our life in the world. This is where cognitive judgments cross over into evaluative judgments and where theory is related to practice. When this happens, cognition as the production of a world-picture initiates the *formation* of a more comprehensive worldview. Kant is often thought of as a constructionist. However, there is something artificial about construction that he rejects as inappropriate for philosophy. Only mathematicians have the power to mentally construct geometrically ordered configurations by means of pure intuition. Philosophers have the different task of using the understanding to give determinate meaning to a causally ordered given world whose unfolding can only be anticipated in general ways. There will always be unanticipated givens to deal with for a philosopher like Kant as he addresses the problems of the natural sciences and points forward in his anthropology to what would become the tasks of the human sciences in aiding us to cope with the world.

Three Levels of Judging the World

Critics have said that Kant is an old-fashioned representationalist who bases what is cognized on timeless rules. Hubert Dreyfus, for instance, argues that representational approaches cannot adequately account for the way we use information to cope with a changing world. He claims that representations involve general rules for thinking about the world which in turn require further rules to become relevant to actual situations.[5] However, this critique by Dreyfus of representationalism as regressively rule-bound does not get to a core element of Kant's epistemology, namely, the power of judgment. To the extent that cognition involves making judgments about reality, it does not require us to have representational images in our head which must then be related to things outside. To judgmentally represent the world to oneself is not to copy actual things, but to structure their relations. Although the power of what Kant calls determinant judgment appeals to already accepted rules (whether logical or epistemological) to structure the actual world, he also makes room for reflective judgment, which is a rule-creating power. Reflective judgment starts with particulars that cannot be made sense of by our available rules. Because the function of reflective judging is introduced in the *Critique of Judgment,* it is often thought that it is only relevant to aesthetic issues of taste and ascribing purposiveness to organic life.[6] But we will see Kant discuss reflective judgment in the last two versions of his logic too, where it is made use of for cognitive induction. Kant's later writings will make it possible to relate his representational theory of determinant rule-based thinking about the world at large to a more reflective and context-oriented way of making sense of the world we live in. Kant was aware that there are many aspects of our experience that disclose how we are placed in the world, and they go back to what is assimilated from childhood on. This assimilation takes note of what happens to us and the actions and attitudes of those around us. At this level, we attend to the common perceptual marks of things that Kant discusses in his lectures on logic. Much of human apprehension remains at the level of comparative reflection and is not explicated in the universal conceptual terms of the *Critique of Pure Reason,* and Kant acknowledges this whenever he refers to the narrowing effects of the prejudices we inherit. In his lectures on geography, Kant stresses the importance of learning from our fellow human beings and concludes that "every foreign experience imparts itself to us either as narrative or as description" (*PG,* 9:159), which speaks to the need for both comparative history and geographical awareness. Kant considers geographical orientation crucial so that we will not just generalize about the world based on our own locale.[7] He also shows a clear awareness that orientation opens up more than a perceptual take on the world, for it is rooted in feelings of bodily placement and equilibrium (see "OT" 4–5; *AA* 8:134–36). Feelings also play a role in how we use our common sense to evaluate our perspective on the world. These are ways in which our cognitive understanding of the world is fed from the ground up. And to the extent that reason demands an overall perspective, it is clear that Kant is also willing to introduce overarching rational ideas to supplement the discursive universals of scientific experience.

In the *Critique of Pure Reason* itself, Kant gives a more formal acknowledgment of the multilayered ways in which we respond to the givens of sense. First there are the subjective forms of space and time of the "Transcendental Aesthetic" whereby we intuitively "*spell out* appearances," which the concepts of the understanding of the "Transcendental Analytic" then allow us "to *read* as experience" of objects. Finally, in the "Transcendental Dialectic" our "reason naturally exalts itself to modes of cognition that go much further" (A314/B371). Reason can be said to introduce *interpretive* rational ideas to comprehend the overall systematic laying-out (*Aus-legung*) of the world. Or as Kant wrote in one of his metaphysical *Reflexionen*: "nature is our task, the text of our interpretations [*Auslegungen*]" (*RM* 5637; 18:274).

Kant's own way of formulating what these three parts of the *Critique of Pure Reason* contribute to cognition is useful, but it is expressed in an architectonic way that could suggest that the last level is metaphysical. This accords with the way he speaks of reason as primarily speculative in his extensive discussions of the dialectical antinomies of metaphysics. However, as I already indicated, later in the "Canon of Pure Reason," Kant makes it clear that reason also contributes to the more direct and important task of determining whether empirical cognitive claims can count as reliable knowledge. I will therefore reformulate Kant's three-stage account of spelling, reading, and interpreting in a way that is more consistent with the ways in which he refers to layers of awareness and human engagement in his other writings. Instead of merely relying on Kant's somewhat academic language of textual deciphering and reading, I will propose a more inclusive experiential input/intake distinction that goes through stages. Accordingly, my opening thesis, which will be elaborated and justified in the next chapters, is that for Kant experience involves both a passive input—the mere sensations (*Empfindungen*, A167/B209) or impressions (*Eindrücke*, A68/B93) of sense—and three increasingly more active kinds of intake that correspond to those of spelling, reading, and interpreting, namely, *assimilation, acquisition,* and *appropriation.* Instead of gazing at the world as an external textual object to be deciphered, the three processes of assimilation, acquisition, and appropriation place us in the world from the start. Textualization becomes part of worldly contextualization.[8]

The first kind of intake is a process of assimilation: it is receptive rather than passive in that it filters and orders apprehended representations in space and time. And if we consider that much of our everyday experience is also ordered by common sense, we can widen the process of assimilation to include not only the intuitive forms of space and time of the "Transcendental Aesthetic," but also the medial elements[9] assumed by Kant's own spelling/reading metaphor. Assimilation can then be said to survey things spatiotemporally and *spell out* the common "marks [*Merkmale*]" that are conceptually abstracted from perceptual phenomena in Kant's lectures on logic.[10] This broader way of characterizing the aesthetic level of intake will become especially relevant in chapter 5 when we examine how Kant differentiates knowledge from cognition and both from persuasion and opinion in the "Canon of Pure Reason." It will also allow us to diagnose how unreflected beliefs can enter into the body of our cognitive judgments, as Kant acknowledges in his logical reflections. Assimilation is a process that can include obscure modes of awareness, for Kant refers to modes of representation and acquaintance that are not fully conscious. And as Beatrice Longuenesse has pointed out, this is the level where judging remains a mere capacity (*Vermögen*) and is not yet an active power (*Kraft*).[11] What is intuitively spelled out will not always be clear and may need to be made more distinct by means of either a mathematical "deciphering [*entziffern*]" using "signs *in concreto*" or a philosophical use of "signs *in abstracto*" ("ICD" 250; 2:279).

The second or reading level of intake as defined by the "Transcendental Analytic" provides the cognitive sources for more *actively acquiring a determinate objective understanding of the world.* This is where Kant the epistemologist provides transcendental conceptual and judgmental conditions that make possible the transition from perceived commonalities to universally valid apperceptive claims. This more inclusive classification of "cognitive acquisition" allows us to recognize that categorial or connective concepts not only generate a discursive kind of scientific cognition that is readable as a serially ordered set of objective meaning relations, but also perform a synthetic judgmental function. The term "intake" may seem to minimize what the categories contribute to cognitive experience, but as we will see in chapter 4, the categories differ from other concepts precisely by allowing judgment to conceptually "take in" the objective meaning of intuitive content. Here conceptual intake is at the same time schematically projective. What distinguishes conceptual acquisition from assimilation is that concepts become objective: they are no longer representational perceptual marks, but universally apperceptive in their intentional directedness at objects.

Finally, for the more complete world-perspective that Kant develops in the last parts of the *Critique of Pure Reason* and in later works, *a rational appropriation is needed that can interpret how things add up and fit together systematically for us.* This final level of systematization can be applied to the overall organization of scientific cognition to test it as legitimate knowledge in the "Canon" just as much as to the metaphysical speculations of the "Dialectic." The legitimating level of knowledge goes beyond taking formal possession of given sense-contents and understanding determinate conceptual relations among those contents in order to be able to judgmentally affirm that the world has been appropriately structured. Each level appeals to different standards and norms. Assimilation is proto-judgmental in being selective and seeking clear and distinct conceptual order; acquisition uses judgment to project universal determinant propositions; and appropriation will be judgmental in a rational sense that aims to give a systematic completeness to what is known.[12]

These three stages of owning up to the way we structure what is known experientially raise the further question of whether what is understood discursively over time can also be comprehended in one timeless conspectus or orientational worldview. To answer this question, the third level of rational appropriation will need to be considered more closely to see whether it can also satisfy the more reflective human demands for comprehensiveness. The dialectical projections of reason remain speculative and leave many intellectual issues unresolved. However, in his lectures on logic Kant adds a level beyond rational insight that is called "rational comprehension." Rational comprehension does not proceed determinantly to systematize what is known, but ventures more tentatively into what lies beyond its boundaries. This more reflective mode of reason will be relevant to what is considered to be a worldview that indicates our place in the world. And as we proceed, we will find that Kant uses different terms for this more exploratory comprehension that makes room for what he considers to be rational beliefs.

The kind of comprehension that is defined in Kant's lectures on logic will be examined in chapters 3 and 5. This is a rational comprehension (*begreifen* = *comprehendere*) that grasps something which lies beyond what is understood objectively, but only relative to some subjective purpose. Thus rational comprehension is denied absoluteness and remains interpretive. Two other kinds of comprehension—*Zusammenfassung* and *Comprehension*—will be discussed in chapter 10 in relation to the sublime as it is explored in the "Critique of Aesthetic Judgment." They aim at something absolute, but can only access it indeterminately through the imagination and reflective analogies. Finally, Kant opens the "Critique of Teleological Judgment" by stating that "one has good reason to assume, in accordance with transcendental principles," a general "subjective purposiveness of nature in its particular laws for the comprehensibility [*Fasslichkeit*] of the human power of judgment and the possibility of the connection of the particular experiences in one system of nature" (*C3* 233; 5:359). Here comprehension is used to make reflective sense of the ways that organisms function insofar as we do not have the power to explain them mechanistically. It will be shown that comprehension for Kant is either a relative but purposive interpretation of what is phenomenal or an indeterminate glimpse into the noumenal.

The task of the next two chapters will be to provide further textual sources that support this way of explicating Kant's own spelling-reading-interpreting sequence in terms of the just-mentioned levels of assimilation, acquisition, and appropriation. The assimilative aspects of our experience will include not only the synthetic a priori subjective forms of time and space needed for perceptual apprehension as exposited in the "Transcendental Aesthetic," but also the analytic contributions of Kant's lectures on logic that are meant to cope with inherited beliefs and attitudes that could be the source of prejudices. The acquisitive aspects of experience will focus on the transcendental judgmental conditions of Kant's epistemology by which the perceptual constituents of cognition are recognized and attain their justification as aspects of apperception. The shared appropriative aspects of experience include Kant's constitutive systematic aims, but will show the further need for regulative ideas as well as the later refinements of Kant's theory of reflective judgment.

Related Evidence for a Layered Approach to Experience as It Pertains to Human Practices and to Working Out Kant's Worldview

In the anthropology lectures, where Kant examines experience in terms of how we behave socially and should act morally, he refers to distinctive predispositional levels of human animation. In the early *Collins* anthropology lectures of 1772–73, Kant is reported to relate them to three ways of thinking about the life of the soul:

> Insofar as the soul is capable of impressions [*Eindrücke*] that the body suffers passively, it is called *anima*, but insofar as it is capable of self-active action, it is called *mens*. Insofar as both are united and the former capacity stands under the moderating influence of the other, it is called *animus*. (VA-*Collins*, 25:16)

Animus is the intermediate level that characterizes most of our mental and social life. The three levels are then clarified as follows:

> *Anima* is called "soul," *animus* "mind," *mens* "spirit" . . . . In regard to the first way we are passive, in regard to the other [second], passive but simultaneously reactive, in regard to the third way we are entirely self-active. (VA-*Collins*, 25:16)

The passive nature of the lowest level of soul (*Seele*) serves to maintain life and corresponds to what Kant calls our "mechanical" or instinctive "predisposition to animality" (*R* 50; 6:26) in his *Religion within the Boundaries of Mere Reason* of 1793. As with all animals, this level involves the instinct to preserve and propagate ourselves. At this collective level of soul, human beings are passively affected by circumstances and instinctively bound to family and "community with other human beings" (*R* 51; 6:26). However, in the final published version of *Anthropology from a Pragmatic Point of View* of 1798, we read that in human beings this mechanical predisposition to animality can come to manifest itself as a "technical predisposition" (*AP* 226; 7:322) that is not purely passive. This is compatible with the claim I made earlier that the assimilative level of experience is receptive and is more than a passive being subjected to bodily impressions and instincts at the first level of soul. Assimilation is about medial intuitive intake, not passive sense input. This assimilative level of experience corresponds to the "syntheses of apprehension and reproduction" in inner sense of the A edition "Subjective Deduction" and provides the perceptual marks of things that are reflected on and conceptually analyzed in the lectures on logic.

Kant correlates the second level of mind (*Gemüth*) with what he calls the predisposition to humanity. This predisposition "*involves comparison* (for which reason is required)" and "the inclination to *acquire* [*verschaffen*] worth in the opinion of others" (*R* 51; 6:27). Here reason is "pragmatic" in that we judge others as either useful to us or not. At this human level of mind, we begin to act by reacting to others as we compete and socially cooperate with them. This second or human predisposition does not correspond fully with the apperceptive level of cognition in that it does not explicitly call on a priori resources. However, it does seek social recognition and to that extent is comparable to the synthesis of recognition of the "Subjective Transcendental Deduction." Although human or social recognition falls short of the conceptual recognition that makes objectivity possible, it is intersubjective. Both aim at a kind of consensus or universal understanding.

Only at the third, wholly rational level of spirit (*Geist*), which Kant calls the "principle" of the life of consciousness, can we be self-active and be considered as personally responsible for what we know to be true, right, and good. Then we finally take full ownership of our views and actions, that is, reflectively appropriate them. Kant calls this the level of personality; it subjects not just some, but all human actions and interactions to the demands of reason.

Another version of this kind of layering can be found in the *Metaphysics of Morals*, where Kant distinguishes three levels of justification or legitimization for a human stance or position. Applied to the problem of property rights, he refers initially to a *unilateral* claim where one assimilates or selectively "apprehends" what one comes across if it is needed to preserve life without being aware of any counterclaim. A *bilateral* claim becomes necessary to assert oneself against another human being who is directly competing to "acquire [*erwerben*]" the same property or goods. Here the aim is a determinate social contract with that other being. Finally, an *omnilateral* claim is universal and rational in that it assures that what is claimed as appropriately ours "(*appropriatio*)" (*MM* 47; 6:258–59) is compatible with the freedom and rights of all. At this third level, both moral personality and ethical systems aim at the consent of the community as a whole. By gearing my reading of Kant's moral writings to passages like this in the final *Metaphysics of Morals*, I will place special importance on the third co-legislative formulation of the categorical imperative and its further cultural and political elaborations by Wilhelm Dilthey and John Rawls, respectively. At this level, moral judgment becomes juridical and legitimating.

My project is to explore to what extent moral and anthropological normative distinctions reinforce those referring to what is cognized and known at the level of experience. This will be done by cross-referencing Kant's logical, epistemological, moral, aesthetic, and anthropological writings in order to bring out his worldview. My approach to Kant will make the case that his lectures on logic have as their main task a coming to terms with the content of what has been selectively assimilated. The lectures analyze perceptual content for the marks that spell out the common features of things. By contrast, Kant's *Critique of Pure Reason* functions mainly at the second level of acquiring conceptual cognition to synthetically reorder what was intuitively assimilated in determinant universal terms. The third level of appropriating what we know and value about the world is more demanding, and will lead us to balance what reason can do to comprehend overall systematic order in the "Dialectic" and the "Canon" of the first *Critique* with what reflective judgment must do to specify the discrete contextual spheres of organization that define human life. This reflective contextualization affects the formal conditions of human communicability and needs to be addressed if intersubjective consensus about worldly matters is to be possible.

Assimilation is subjective and aims for distinctness, acquisition makes possible objective determination, and appropriation reaches for intersubjective consensus. The various ways in which these levels can intersect may also account for the different worldviews we profess. What has been assimilated conditions one's subjective *world-outlook*, what is acquired will result in a more objective *world-picture*, and what is appropriated aims at an overall normative *world-view* that should have intersubjective legitimacy.

Historical Justification

This layered approach to Kant's experiential worldview is not just a hermeneutical afterthought, for it also has a historical basis. Indeed, in the next two chapters I will bring out how this way of thinking about cognitive levels in Kant can be supported by how he relates himself to his predecessors and contemporaries as he gradually develops his own philosophical positions. It is at the assimilative level of apprehensive intake that we can see Kant respond to the traditional Cartesian concern with clear and distinct ideas in his reflections and lectures on logic. This concern for clarity and distinctness still applies to how perceptual cognition is analyzed. However, the way in which the clarity-distinctness contrast was analyzed both logically and aesthetically by Alexander Baumgarten and Georg Friedrich Meier gradually pushed Kant to the realization that even their refinements about distinctness could not provide the mathematical determinacy required for the apperceptive level of scientific cognition. His so-called Copernican revolution offers a new mode of conceptual acquisition that moves beyond the more established modes of logically assimilating and analyzing the distinctness of things without, however, fully replacing them.

To sum up, the first assimilative level of experience is about gaining formal *distinctness in our thinking*, the second acquisitive level is mainly concerned with the conceptual *determination of meaningful cognitive relations*, and the final, more comprehensive appropriative level aims at *knowing or ascertaining* truth.

Since there are severe limits to what we can know with certainty according to Kant, attempts to either be comprehensive or make things more comprehensible do not entail having a complete or exhaustive understanding. Yet that limitation does not prevent us from appropriating a holistic worldview of how things fit together and an appreciation for contexts and relations that affect how we understand those regions of reality that we are most familiar with. This becomes evident when we see

Kant write about worldly orientation and systematic organization. To orient oneself is to contextualize, and for this work it will also mean placing Kant's main works in the systematic context of his other writings and in that way to find reinforcing tendencies that reflect back on the former. In his 1893 proposal to the Prussian Academy of the Sciences to inaugurate what is now the 29-volume edition of *Kant's gesammelte Schriften,* Dilthey wrote that it would provide an "objective basis" for the task of "elucidating the inner relations among the works, handwritings, and lectures."[13] My goal of comprehensiveness is in this vein: it is more about exploring internal relations among Kant's writings and about orienting our understanding of his works than it is about claiming to have done full justice to their totality.

2

Kant on Alexander Baumgarten and Logic

The Aesthetic, Analytical, and Synthetic Distinctness of What Is Empirically Assimilated

This chapter gives some historical background for understanding how Kant developed his epistemology by showing how he gradually shifts his attention from the traditional standards of clarity and distinctness for what is intuitively assimilated to his own judgmental demands for conceptual determination and objectivity. The Cartesian standards of clarity and distinctness are not often discussed in relation to Kant's epistemological and metaphysical writings. Since these standards were still very much debated by Kant's immediate predecessors, he did indeed think about them and their aesthetic and logical import. To better comprehend Kant's theory of cognition, it is important to recognize how he came to delineate three kinds of distinctness relevant to what can be cognized.

Descartes set the stage for what clarity and distinctness would come to mean for Leibniz, Christian Wolff, and Alexander Baumgarten, and for how these terms were redefined along the way. Descartes expected cognitive judgments to be based on perceptions that are clear and distinct. He wrote in the *Principles of Philosophy* that "a perception which can serve as the basis for a certain and indubitable judgement needs to be not merely clear but also distinct." He continues by calling a perception "clear" if "it is present and accessible to the attentive mind . . . and 'distinct' if, as well as being clear, it is so sharply separated from all other perceptions that it contains within itself only what is clear."[1] A perception is distinct if in addition to being clear, it is sufficiently delineated so as to not be confused with anything else.

Leibniz expands on this with much more detail. He speaks of knowledge being either obscure or clear, confused or distinct, inadequate or adequate, symbolic or intuitive. Some of these added standards will become relevant later in our discussions of Kant. It is interesting that Leibniz makes distinctness the central rather than the final cognitive standard, for he states that knowledge will not be "perfect" until it is "both adequate and intuitive."[2] Adequacy adds a further requirement of distinct composite concepts, namely, that they must be fully analyzed down to primitive distinct concepts that can be clearly intuited.[3] Leibniz admits that this perfection is rarely achieved, and that perhaps only the knowledge of numbers can come close. Even algebra and arithmetic rely on symbolic "substitutes for the objects themselves . . . whose explanation we can omit for the sake of brevity."[4]

At the beginning of his cognitive spectrum, Leibniz seems willing to accept the "obscure idea" of seeing a flower as sufficient for momentary knowledge. For the knowledge of something to be clear it must "enable me, when I am confronted with a new instance, to recognize it or distinguish it from anything similar to it."[5] Christian Wolff also allows the quality of being distinguishable to enter into the idea of clarity. On the topic of perceiving a series of objects, he writes that if "I can cognize each one and distinguish it from others," then I can "say that my present thoughts are clear."[6]

Accordingly, clarity "arises from noting the differences in a manifold."[7] But a thought only becomes distinct, according to Wolff, when we can determine these differences and understand them. A concept is clear if one can recognize its object, and it is distinct if one can also recognize what distinguishes it from other things.[8] Here we could say that clarity involves an implicit awareness of what distinctness makes explicit. Thus Wolff speaks of degrees of cognition, a notion to which I will return in the next chapter. Baumgarten, the father of modern aesthetics, departs from Wolff by arguing that distinctness is just a special kind of clarity. Instead of simply shifting from clarity to distinctness, he thinks that more emphasis needs to be placed on the nature of clarity itself so that we can come to recognize that there are different kinds of clarity.

From Intensive and Extensive Clarity to Logical and Aesthetic Distinctness

In his *Reflections on Poetry* of 1735, Baumgarten writes that for a clear representation of a thing to also become logically distinct, it must be made "intensively clearer"[9] by having its distinguishing marks analytically articulated. This means that logical distinctness requires the explication of marks within marks in order to "deepen" the clarity of a representation. Poets, however, have a different concern, according to Baumgarten, which is to make representations "extensively clearer"[10] by widening their scope to encompass ever more marks.

In the fourth edition of his *Metaphysics*, published in 1757, Baumgarten goes further and qualifies the general assumption of his contemporaries that what is assimilated from the senses cannot be distinct. He claims that there can be "sensible perception to which belongs something of the distinct" (*M* §522, 202). For aesthetics, it will be important to explicate what this sensible counterpart of logical distinctness is. *Metaphysics* §531 suggests that it involves liveliness. There Baumgarten writes that "greater clarity due to the clarity of marks can be called INTENSIVELY GREATER CLARITY, while greater clarity due to the multitude of marks can be called extensively greater clarity. An extensively clearer PERCEPTION is LIVELY" (*M* §531, 204).

Extensive clarity makes use of a multitude of loosely differentiated marks to produce the lively scope of thought and speech that characterizes literature and gives aesthetic pleasure. Intensive clarity, by contrast, provides the analytical depth of internally differentiated marks that is expected of higher or logical cognition. The same perception of an object can be described in an aesthetically lively language as well as with more logically distinct terms.

Kant picks up these themes in one of his *Reflexionen* where he contrasts "extensive clarity through external marks" with "intensive clarity through inner [marks]" (*RL* 2368; 16:334). In *Reflexion* 2377, he writes in the manner of Baumgarten: "Distinctness is a logically greater clarity, liveliness an aesthetically greater clarity" (*RL* 2377; 16:337). Then in the next *Reflexion* Kant explicitly designates what Baumgarten referred to as "something of the distinct" as aesthetic distinctness. Thus Kant contrasts an "aesthetic distinctness [*Deutlichkeit*] of cognition through examples" and a "logical distinctness through concepts" (*RL* 2378; 16:337).

All the Baumgarten passages quoted so far about clarity and distinctness relate to the early sections of the chapter on "Empirical Psychology" devoted to the inferior or sensible cognitive faculty. In the section on the intellect or superior cognitive faculty, Baumgarten begins by speaking of attention, abstraction, reflection, and comparison in ways that will be related to Kant as well. What is also noteworthy is that the extensive-intensive contrast that seemed to be reserved for lower cognition now finds its place in higher cognition as well. In §634 Baumgarten speaks of an "extensively more distinct perception" as having "more, and more lively marks than other distinct perceptions." Just as there are both extensive and intensive kinds of clarity, we find confirmation that there can be both intensive and extensive distinctness at the level of the intellect. Intensive distinctness is directed at internal differentiation and extensive distinctness at external differentiation. By analogy, even extensively clear perceptions of the lower faculty may be assigned, if not a logical *distinctness,* what could be called a "*distinctiveness*" that sets the representation of one thing apart from that of others and what Kant ended up calling "aesthetic distinctness." This potential of sensible cognition is elaborated in Baumgarten's *Aesthetica* of the 1750s, where extensive clarity is described as a "richness" that can create strong aesthetic impressions. By gaining extensive clarity, an aesthetic representation may become less distinct within while gaining a specificity that allows it to become more clearly distinguishable from without, that is, from other representations. This allows Baumgarten to relate the aesthetic richness of extensive clarity to the distinctiveness that singles out concrete individuals. The task of poets is not to describe in terms of abstract universals, but to portray individuals intuitively.

According to Baumgarten, the attentiveness that characterizes the intellect is a function of what can be perceived most clearly from the embodied soul's perspective (see *M* §625, 228–29). The more attentive we are to one thing, the more we must abstract away from other things. Attention and abstraction would not be needed if we were not an embodied intellect coping with sensible cognition for which the overall horizon is filled with obscurities. Thus Baumgarten claims that God, for whom everything in the world is equally clear, need "not pay attention, abstract, reflect, or compare" (*M* §870, 295). For humans, paying attention seems to require an abstractive act that gains clarity about one part of a perception by separating it from its other parts. When this abstractive mode of attention is "successively directed at the parts of a total perception," Baumgarten calls it "REFLECTION." However, "attention toward a total perception after reflection is COMPARISON" (*M* §626, 229). Accordingly, Baumgarten formulates a *rule of reflection* that distinguishes the parts of a whole successively and merely relative to each other, and a *rule of comparison* that distinguishes them simultaneously in relation to the whole to which they belong.

These procedures of abstraction, reflection, and comparison that Baumgarten relates to the attentiveness of the intellect will be important to keep in mind when we discuss Kant's theory of empirical concept-formation in his *Lectures on Logic.*

Subordinative and Coordinative Distinctness

We saw Kant take note of the kind of aesthetic clarity that Baumgarten fostered and how he then pushed it in the direction of aesthetic distinctness. There is also an interesting anthropological *Reflexion* where Kant draws further consequences about the nature of distinctness.

> As to distinctness, it is perfectly compatible with intuition. For distinctness has to do with the differentiation of the manifold in a whole representation. Insofar as these cognitive constituents can be thought through universal concepts, distinctness is a consequence of the understanding; if it comes about through particulars, then it is a form of sensibility. The first occurs through subordination, the second through coordination. (*RA* 643, 15:283)

John Zammito comments on this *Reflexion* from 1769–70 by noting that "Kant quickly threw off the whole language of clarity and distinctness as distracting, though he retained the contrast between coordination and subordination."[11] However, this contrast between coordination and subordination is still about distinctness. That distinctness still matters is made evident in Kant's 1770 Inaugural Dissertation, *On the Form and Principles of the Sensible and the Intelligible World.* There he writes that

> the sensible is poorly defined as that which is *more confusedly cognized,* and that which belongs to the understanding as that of which there is *distinct* cognition. For these are only logical distinctions which *do not touch* at all the things *given.* . . . Thus, sensible representations can be very distinct and representations which belong to the understanding can be extremely confused. (*SIW* 387; 2:394)

Since sensible representations are of "things as they *appear*" and intellectual representations are of "things *as they are*" (*SIW* 384; 2:392), they involve different uses of the understanding. Metaphysics makes a "REAL USE" of the understanding, according to Kant, for which concepts "are given" and "abstract from everything sensible" (*SIW* 385–86; 2:393–94). Such concepts aim at an overall or "complete [*adaequatam*] cognition" (*SIW* 385; 2:393) and do not need to be distinct. But for the phenomenal world, we need to make a "LOGICAL USE" of the understanding which aims at "distinct cognition" (*SIW* 385; 2:393). Here we use "empirical" concepts that are only partially "abstracted from what is sensible" in order to define what is "common" (*SIW* 385–86; 2:393–94) to things as distinctly as possible. But the logical use of the understanding also involves pure concepts such as space. This leads Kant to develop a contrast between an intuitive distinctness that coordinates things in space as "a singular representation embracing all things *within itself*" (*SIW* 396; 2:402) and the subordinative distinctness whereby "an abstract common concept contains [particulars] *under itself*" (*SIW* 396; 2:402). Thus, the standard logical paradigm of subordinative distinctness needs to be supplemented with a new phenomenal or coordinative paradigm made possible by geometry:

> Evidence being the clarity of certain cognition, insofar as it is likened to sensible cognition, is not only greatest in geometry; it is . . . the *paradigm* and the means of all *evidence* in the other sciences. For, since geometry contemplates *relations of space* and since the concept of space contains within itself the very form of all sensible intuition, nothing can be *clear and distinct* in things perceived in outer sense unless it be by the mediation of the same intuition, the contemplation of which is the function of the science of geometry. (*SIW* 396; 2:403)

Thus the need for clarity and distinctness is not dismissed but reiterated by Kant; only some of the rationalists' assumptions about what defines them are questioned. Instead of agreeing with Leibniz, who found cognitive perfection in the serial ordering of arithmetic and number theory concerned with analytic and comparative distinctness, Kant looks to the spatial mode of coordination of geometry to make possible a contextually mediated synthetic distinctness.

In the 1781 "Preface" to the *Critique of Pure Reason*, Kant again speaks of the need for distinctness. He acknowledges that

> the reader has the right to demand first discursive (logical) distinctness [*Deutlichkeit*] through concepts, but then also intuitive (aesthetic) distinctness through intuitions, that is, through examples or illustrations *in concreto*. I have taken sufficient care for the former. That was essential to my undertaking but was also the contingent cause of the fact that I could not satisfy the second demand, which is less strict but still fair. (Axvii–xviii)

The characterization of intuitive/aesthetic distinctness as providing examples recalls his earlier effort to expand on Baumgarten's notions of aesthetic clarity and poetic liveliness. We know, however, that Kant limits his use of examples because he thinks that what they illustrate can distract from subtle logical distinctions and thus mislead. But the Inaugural Dissertation had invoked a more promising idea of exemplifying the sensible distinctness related to geometrically delineated evidence. What is not adequately underscored in the first edition preface is the fact that intuitive distinctness as geometrically ordered in terms of the form of space becomes an important part of a new "Transcendental Aesthetic" that has great cognitive import.

Zammito's claim can now be revised to mean that the concern for aesthetic clarity will become a concern for mathematical measurability and that the idea of conceptual subordination will sharpen the standard of distinctness into that of lawful determination. Nevertheless, the old standard of comparative distinctness is retained as a meta-concern of the *Critique of Pure Reason* and is made a requirement that must apply to the "form of the investigation" (Axv) to be pursued. Moreover, the text itself still refers to the analytical or distinguishing marks of concepts at many places.[12] It is important to attend to how these more traditional logical ways of finding distinguishing marks and of forming clear and distinct concepts continue to provide a background for the new epistemic approach that will be developed by Kant.

Reflection and Comparison in Concept-Formation

Returning to the lectures on logic, it is worth noting that the *Dohna-Wundlacken Logic*, which is as late as 1792, and the *Jäsche Logic* of 1800 still contain many vestiges of the Baumgartian terminology inherited by Kant. They are central texts for the current debates about Kant's theory of empirical concept-formation as examined, for instance, in Beatrice Longuenesse's *Kant and the Capacity to Judge*. In the *Dohna-Wundlacken Logic*, we still read that logical distinctness through concepts "is effected through few marks . . . [while] aesthetic distinctness [is effected] through many marks" (*LL* 446–47; 24:709). Aesthetic distinctness is characterized by "liveliness" and "a swarm of coordinate representations" (*LL* 447; 24:709).

There is a similar mixture of Baumgartian and Kantian language in the final *Jäsche Logic*. In the "Introduction" a mark is described as

> *that in a thing which constitutes a part of the cognition of it or . . . a partial representation, insofar as it is considered as ground of cognition of the whole representation.* All our *concepts* are marks . . . and all *thought* is nothing other than a representing through marks. (*LL* 564; 9:58)

This characterization of a mark suggests that it is derived from our perceptual apprehension of a thing and provides a preliminary *partial content* for thinking about it. A mark is considered sufficient if "it suffices always to distinguish the thing from all others" (*LL* 566; 9:60). Then later, in part 1 of the *Jäsche Logic* entitled "Universal Doctrine of Elements," we are introduced to the acts of the understanding "through which concepts are generated [*erzeugt*] according to their *form*" (*LL* 592; 9:94).[13] These acts are the same three operations that Baumgarten attributed to the attentiveness of the intellect, namely, reflection, comparison, and abstraction. However, the *Jäsche Logic* presents them in a different order by placing comparison ahead of reflection. This is then elaborated in a clarificatory note by Jäsche:

> To make concepts out of representations one must be able to *compare, to reflect, and to abstract,* for these three logical operations of the understanding are the essential and universal conditions for the generation of every concept whatsoever. I see, e.g., a spruce, a willow, and a linden. By *first comparing* these objects with one another I note that they are different from one another in regard to the trunk, the branches, the leaves. . . . *Next I reflect on what they have in common among themselves,* trunk, branches, and leaves themselves, and I *abstract* from the quantity, the figure, etc. of these; thus I acquire a concept of a tree. (*LL* 592; 9:94–95; italics added)

This note added by Jäsche claims that comparison focuses on differences and reflection on commonality. This sharp contrast is not confirmed by all the *Reflexionen* in which Kant addresses the respective roles of comparison and reflection in concept-formation. Jäsche's note is partly supported by the *Vienna Logic* of the early 1780s, for it too places comparison ahead of reflection and claims that "from reflection . . . one cognizes that which many things have in common" (*LL* 352; 24:909). But these Vienna lecture notes do not support Jäsche's further claim that comparison focuses on differences. Instead, we read there that "in one consciousness I grasp many representations, in which I compare what is only a repetition of the other" (*LL* 352; 24:909). If we also consult the *Logik Busolt* of 1790, we find that concept-formation begins with the act of reflection, which attends "to what is manifold in intuition"; the comparison that follows takes note of both "difference and identity"; abstraction then "forgets all differences and considers only the identity" (VL-*Busolt,* 24:654). Since the nature of reflection will be a theme throughout this work, we can note that it provides a vague sense of the interrelatedness of what is represented. This accords with how reflection is defined in the "First Introduction to the *Critique of Judgment,*" namely, as the act of "holding representations together" among themselves or in relation to our "cognitive faculty" in "consideration of a possible concept" ("FI" 15; 20:211).

In three of the five *Reflexionen* where Kant considers the operations involved in concept-formation, reflection precedes comparison, and in the two others comparison precedes reflection. But even when comparison is discussed first it does not look for differences, as Jäsche claims. Thus in *RL* 2854, "*comparatio*" is about "*nota* als *communis*" (16:547). Since Kant varies the sequence in which reflection and comparison are discussed, one could, like Longuenesse, follow the Jäsche order with the caveat that it is not a sequential order, for each of the three operations "depends on the others and all proceed simultaneously."[14] Yet in her further account of their relation, which is also geared to the "Amphiboly" chapter of the *Critique of Pure Reason*, Longuenesse speaks of the need to have "comparison be *supplemented* by reflection on the relation of our representations in general to their sources in our mind."[15] Kant himself, however, says that the "comparison of representations . . . *first requires* a reflection" (A269/B325). This provides evidence that from the critical standpoint there is a right ordering which puts reflection ahead of comparison. The rationale for this can be articulated if what we have learned from Baumgarten's comments about reflection and comparison is related to their treatment in Kant's *Logik Pölitz* of the 1780s. I think these lecture notes offer the most nuanced conception of the respective functions of these two closely related acts. There concept-formation begins with reflection, which is described as a successive process of becoming conscious of representations whereby (1) "I successively [*nach und nach*] become conscious of various representations or compare [*vergleiche*] various representations with [*mit*] my consciousness" (VL-*Pölitz*, 24:566, my translation). Then the same lecture notes add that (2) if I also "compare [*vergleiche*] them among one other [*untereinander*], that involves comparison [*comparatio*]" (VL-*Pölitz*, 24:566, my translation). The first sentence speaks of reflection as a subjective comparing that is "successively directed," just as it was described by Baumgarten. The second sentence moves from this temporal reflective *activity of comparing* representations with one's consciousness to a more *content-directed objective comparison* of these representations among themselves. This same distinction is made in one of Kant's own *Reflexionen* and reinforces the view that the second content-directed comparison is objective. The text of *RL* 2878 starts with the act of *reflection* and defines it as the temporal or "successive [*nach und nach*] becoming-conscious of representations and holding them together with one consciousness [*einem Bewußtsein*]" (*RL* 2878; 16:556). This is followed by a *comparison* of representations based on the atemporal "unity of consciousness [*Einheit des Bewußtseins*]" (*RL* 2878; 16:556) that is the basis for making objective claims. The initial reflective act of temporal or subjective comparing can at best provide an assimilated *differentiation*, and only an "objective comparison [*comparatio mit dem object*]" (*RL* 2876; 16:556) can produce the *logical distinctness* needed for the concept of a tree. What Kant calls "*comparatio*" is an objective comparison that discerns not only the differences among the leaves of spruces and willows pointed to by Jäsche, but also their similarities. A later passage in the *Logik Pölitz* confirms that to distill what is common requires more than the reflection mentioned by Jäsche. To locate what is conceptually common requires not only the "attention" that was Baumgarten's covering term for reflection and comparison, but also abstraction, his condition for paying attention. Thus Kant is recorded as saying:

> Where I find identity of consciousness, I separate or abstract from everything else to attain a concept, e.g., I see a spruce, a willow, or a linden; I see that they have a trunk, branches, and leaves that are different; one has more branches than another, etc.: now I *attend to what they have in common* qua trunk, branches, and leaves by abstracting from their shapes; thus I attain the concept of a tree. (VL-*Pölitz*, 24:566–67)

The commonality that Jäsche ascribes to reflection is purely subjective and insufficient to account for the conceptual unity that also requires comparison and abstraction. This is also reinforced by the "Amphiboly" chapter of the *Critique of Pure Reason*, where Kant himself writes that reflection (*reflexio*) is "the state of mind in which we first prepare ourselves to find out the subjective conditions under which we can arrive at concepts" (A260/B316).

From Logical or Analytical Distinctness to Synthetic Distinctness

The distinct empirical concept that is the product of the attention, reflection, comparison, and abstraction described in the foregoing provides an analytic concept. The resulting concept "tree" represents what the assimilated marks of spruces, willows, and lindens have in common. But with this we do not yet have a universally distinct or rule-giving concept. In the "Introduction" to the *Jäsche Logic*, Wolffian logicians are criticized for assuming that distinctness is always a product of analysis. There is, according to Kant, also a distinctness that arises from synthesis. This claim can already be found in the *Blomberg Logic* from the early 1770s. Since he based his lectures on logic on Georg Friedrich Meier's *Auszug aus der Vernunftlehre* (*Excerpts from the Doctrine of Reason*), Kant sometimes specifically addresses a claim by Meier that he disagrees with. Thus Kant comments on §139 of the *Auszug* as follows: "It is false that our cognition becomes distinct only through analysis, as the author maintains" (*LL* 101; 24:130). He then adds that our cognition can be made distinct either through analysis or synthesis. "We either make *a distinct concept*, and this happens *per synthesis,* or we make *distinct a concept* that was previously confused, and this happens *per analysin*" (*LL* 102; 24:130).

In the *Jäsche Logic,* analysis is said to apply only "to those marks that we already thought in the concept" (*LL* 568; 9:63). In addition to such analytically obtained marks, which are "partial concepts of my *actual* concept," there are also "synthetic marks" that are "partial concepts of the *merely possible* complete concept" (*LL* 565; 9:59). These synthetic marks are important for experience. Whereas analytic marks define an internally directed subordinative series, synthetic marks are coordinative and extend the scope of cognition. All this is summed up in the following passage:

> With the synthesis of every new concept in the aggregation of coordinate marks, *extensive* or *extended* distinctness grows, just as *intensive* or *deep* distinctness grows with the further analysis of the concept in the series of subordinate marks. (*LL* 565; 9:59)

As indicated earlier, Meier's teacher, Baumgarten, introduced the idea of extensive clarity to supplement the inward-looking intensive clarity of logical analysis and make room for aesthetic cognition. But extensive distinctness in Kant is more than aesthetic and has import for conceptual cognition. Whereas the logical analysis of our mental representations serves "the making distinct of *concepts,*" synthesis is said to pertain to "the making distinct of *objects*" (*LL* 569; 9:64). The more one analyzes what is already contained in a concept, the more remote its object tends to become, according to Kant. Synthesis, however, brings us closer to objects.

To make a concept distinct is to deepen it through formal analysis, but to make a distinct concept is to extend it in terms of content. According to the *Jäsche Logic,*

> when I make a distinct concept, I begin with the parts and proceed from these toward the whole. Here there are no marks as yet at hand; *I acquire them only through synthesis.* . . . All distinctness of properly mathematical cognition, as of all cognition based on experience, rests on such an expansion of it through the synthesis of marks. (*LL* 568–69; 9:63–64; emphases added)

With synthesis, we move from the level of logically analyzing what has been assimilated to what can now be called the act of "acquiring" objective cognition. Whereas analytic distinctness articulates the formal relations of subordination among conceptual marks, synthetic distinctness adds measurable intuitive content in order to coordinate conceptual marks with objects of experience. In the *Critique of Pure Reason,* this making of a distinct concept is expanded positively as schematizing its objective meaning (*Bedeutung*) through the imagination (see A146–47/B185–87).[16] However, in the Pölitz logic lectures, Kant contents himself with the negative claim that without coordinatively relating a concept to an object as its mark, the concept "has no meaning [*Bedeutung*] at all" (VL-*Pölitz*, 24:567).

Synthesis "extends my concept as to content through what is added as a mark *beyond* the concept in (pure or empirical) intuition" (*LL* 568–69; 9:63) and is ultimately a "making distinct of *objects*" (*LL* 569; 9:64). Here we seem to be nudged in the direction of an epistemic logic that can judgmentally relate concepts to the objects of experience. But general logic can only "occupy itself" with "the analytic procedure" (*LL* 569; 9:64), and for it judgment remains representational. In the *Jäsche Logic*, judgment is still defined as "the representation of the unity of the consciousness of various representations, or the representation of their relation insofar as they constitute a concept" (*LL* 597; 9:101). Yet a transition from a logic of concept-formation to a logic of epistemic judgment is prepared for by the following sentence: "Through continued logical abstraction higher and higher concepts arise, just as through continued logical determination lower and lower concepts arise" (*LL* 596; 9:99). This makes it clear that concept-formation involves ever more analysis in the service of increasingly distinct concepts, whereas judgmental determination subsumes lower concepts under higher concepts. A "completed determination" (*LL* 596; 9:99) subsumes a particular under a universal and is a synthetic act that requires intuition. In a note we read that "since only single [*einzelne*] things, or individuals, are thoroughly determinate, there *can be thoroughly determinate cognitions only as intuitions*, but not as concepts; in regard to the latter, logical determination can never be regarded as completed" (*LL* 597; 9:99). Here again we see that a general logic of distinct concepts will need to be completed by an epistemic logic of determinant judgments. This will demand a shift from what is analytically assimilated to what is synthetically acquired.

Concept-formation as discussed so far has been about "concepts that are given (a priori or a posteriori)" (*LL* 591; 9:93). A posteriori concepts are abstracted from marks that are given empirically, whereas a priori concepts are given apart from experience and are called "notions" (*LL* 591; 9:93). There is, of course, no discussion of the transcendental categories of the understanding in general logic, but there is a brief mention of "concepts that are made" (*LL* 591; 9:93).

A concept is made when it is neither given a priori or a posteriori, but "invented [*erdichtet*]" and "voluntary [*willkürlich*]" (*LL* 592; 9:94).[17] Here a concept is abstracted "from all matter of thought" and considered purely "in respect of its form, i.e., only *subjectively*; not how it determines an object through a mark, but only how it can be related to several objects" (*LL* 591; 9:94). This would seem to point to general scientific concepts such as "mass" that apply as much to rocks and trees as to particles of matter. Here again we begin to move from what is perceptually assimilated to what will need to be more actively acquired for determinate objective cognition.

Given Kant's main cognitive goal of grounding determinate scientific explanations of the natural world, these preliminary discussions of distinctness relevant to the initial assimilative or perceptual level of experience will become less prominent as we move on. But since determinate explanations are much more difficult to attain when it comes to understanding human life, it should be no surprise to see Kant still speak of kinds of distinctness in his *Anthropology from a Pragmatic Point of View* of 1798. There, where descriptive generalizations about human action and interaction play an important role, he claims that "*clarity* [*Klarheit*] suffices for the *differentiation* [*Unterscheidung*] of one object from another" (*AP* 26; 7:137–38). Distinctness (*Deutlichkeit*), however, is "that consciousness by means of which the *composition* of representations also becomes clear" (*AP* 26: 7:138). This is then explicated as follows: "in every cognition [for which both] intuition and concept are always required, distinctness rests on the *order* according to which the partial representations are combined" (*AP* 27; 7:138). This is the kind of coordinative order that was referred to earlier as "aesthetic distinctness" and can be geometrically delineated when dealing with what is perceptually intuited. Then the text goes on to describe two more kinds of distinctness: that of "a *merely logical* division . . . into higher and subordinate representations" (*AP* 27; 7:138), namely, what has been discussed as analytical or logical distinctness, and "a *real division* into principal and accessory representations" (*AP* 27; 7:138), namely, a synthetic distinctness pertaining to objects themselves. Here distinctness refers not just to aesthetically assimilated content or to logically analyzed concepts, but to synthetic conceptual cognition at the level of substance-attribute determinations. This third kind of distinctness needed to "produce cognition of the object" will require the "faculty of reflecting [*Überlegungsvermögen*]" (*AP* 27; 7:138), namely, the power of judgment. This is because—as will be shown in chapter 5—the imagination that schematizes objects is directed by judgment.

3

Georg Friedrich Meier on Comprehension and Kant on Its Relation to Cognition and Knowledge

So far I have shown how Kant progresses from the conceptual distinctness of representations toward the goal of determinate objective cognition. In the *Critique of Pure Reason*, he speaks mostly of cognition, but also at times of knowledge. Only toward the end of this work in the "Canon of Pure Reason" does it become clear that knowledge (*Wissen*) is cognition (*Erkenntnis*) that is held to be certain (*gewiss*). In this chapter, I will once again examine Kant's lectures on logic to see how they can begin to shed light on how cognition can move in the direction of knowledge. In the early *Blomberg Logic*, we find a lot of attention being given to the contribution that one mode of cognition called "rational comprehension" makes to the final perfection of cognitive certainty. Thus, Kant takes note of the way Meier addresses the problem of "the *comprehensible* [*das Begreifliche*] and the *incomprehensible*" (*LL* 105; 24:134) in §140 of the *Auszug aus der Vernunftlehre* as a way to arrive at the full scope and "certainty of learned cognition" (*RL*, 16:359). Although Kant accepts comprehension as the highest degree of cognition, he will deny it both the fullness of scope that Meier attached to learned cognition and the certainty that he himself will claim for his ideal of knowledge. Theoretically, comprehension falls short of knowledge, but given the limits of what finite humans can actually know, comprehension will be allowed to probe beyond certain knowledge for special purposes and practical reasons.

Levels of Cognition in the *Logic*

In the *Blomberg Logic* from the early 1770s, Kant claims that to "attain a better idea" of what Meier calls the *comprehensible*, it will be useful "to represent the degrees of human cognition" (*LL* 105; 24:134). I think that his main concern here is to address a claim from §67 in the *Auszug* where Meier wrote that "the object of learned cognition is great in scope [*magnitudo eruditae cognitionis obiectiva absoluta*] if it contains much manifold content . . . e.g., God, world wisdom, history, etc." (quoted in *RL*, 16:219–20). This passage about the scope of cognition and its absolute objectivity raises the question for Kant of whether we can comprehend anything absolutely and leads him to consider a progression of degrees of cognition. Commenting on §140 of Meier's text, Kant refers to a mere subjective "knowing [*wissen*]" as the first degree of cognition. It is defined as "representing something to oneself with consciousness [*sich etwas mit Bewustseyn vorstellen*]" (*LL* 105; 24:135). This suggests that this knowing is clear enough to be self-conscious and contains the awareness that a representation is mine. However, Kant's final comments on §140 end up giving a revised gradation according to which the first degree of cognition amounts to a mere "representing [*vorstellen*]" (*LL* 107; 24:137). This change also accords with his own *Reflexion* (see *RL* 2394; 16:343) that it is possible for a representation to be only obscurely felt or even be unconscious. Now it is the second degree of cognition that is designated as knowing or representing with consciousness. Here we move from obscurity to clarity, but as a mode of representing it is still as subjective as the first degree. It is important to recognize that this is a mere colloquial usage of "knowing" or *wissen* that is pre-critical, and it will disappear in Kant's later lectures on logic. And as we proceed, we will learn that the subjective awareness implicit in colloquial knowing will need to be supplemented by an intersubjective certainty in order to actually count as objective knowledge. And that is not a small demand.

The shift to the objective begins with the third degree of cognition, which is "to be acquainted with [*kennen*]" (*LL* 107; 24:136)[1] something "in distinction from other things through comparison with those things" (*LL* 105–6; 24:135). Here we move from clarity to distinctness, although it is merely a comparative distinctness. The next or Kant's fourth degree is to "understand [*verstehen*]" (*LL* 107; 24:136) with a conceptual distinctness made possible by the intellectual faculty of understanding (*Verstand*). The fifth degree is "to have insight [*einsehen*]" (*LL* 107; 24:136) or to cognize through reason (*Vernunft*). The difference between understanding and rational insight is clarified as follows: to understand what gold is one must be able to coordinate its marks of being ductile, yellow, and not subject to rust; but to have insight into the nature of gold, one must also have found the definitive subordinating mark that accounts for its being ductile as well as not subject to rust (see *LL* 106; 24:135).

The sixth and highest degree of cognition is "to comprehend [*begreifen*]" (*LL* 107; 24:136). The aim of comprehensibility is to have "sufficient insight into something [*etwas hinreichendt einsehen*]" (*LL* 106; 24:135) "through reason" (*LL* 104; 24:134). But there is an ambiguity here, for sufficiency could be relative to some particular purpose or it could be absolute, which would mean that it is sufficient "for all purposes" (*LL* 106; 24:135). Kant argues that absolute comprehension is not possible for us: "we never comprehend something *totaliter*" (*LL* 106; 24:135). Since it is the case that "frequently something comprehensible to one man is incomprehensible to another" (*LL* 107; 24:136), it turns out that the sufficiency attained by rational comprehension is always relative. Although comprehension may be the highest degree of cognition, the fact that there may be no consensus about it will disqualify it from being considered knowledge as defined in the first *Critique.*

In the *Dohna-Wundlacken Logic* of 1792, there is a section on the "comprehensible and the incomprehensible" that also speaks of six degrees of cognition: representation, perception, acquaintance, understanding, having insight, and comprehension. The term "perception [*wahrnehmen*]" is now used to designate "representing something to oneself with consciousness" (*LL* 466; 24:730) and replaces the earlier colloquial use of "knowing." When it comes to comprehension, Kant again distinguishes between the kind that provides "sufficient insight into something <for a certain purpose>" and another that is "absolute <in every respect> . . . *comprehendere*" (*LL* 466; 24:730–31).

An example of the former is having the a priori insight into the hydraulic behavior of water that science makes possible. An example of the latter would be to have insight into the essence of water, namely, its fluidity, and this insight into what water is in-itself is denied to us. Kant also offers a better account of the difference between understanding and rational insight. Understanding conceptually explains the possibility of something occurring as the effect of something else, while rational insight cognizes the necessity of this occurrence based on principles.

When we turn to the final *Jäsche Logic* of 1800, we find seven degrees of cognition instead of six. A new degree of "cognizing [*erkennen*] with consciousness" is inserted between acquaintance and understanding. These degrees assess the qualitative perfection of cognition in terms of clarity and distinctness and can be summarized as follows:

1. The list starts with a mere "representing something to oneself [*sich etwas vorstellen*]" (*LL* 569; 9:64), which could amount to no more than obscure awareness. In the *Anthropology*, Kant refers to such obscure representations as a large "field of sensible intuitions and sensations of which we are not conscious" (*AP* 24; 7:135). Replying to the Lockean objection that we should not posit anything that we are not conscious of, Kant sides with Leibniz by pointing out that "we can still be indirectly conscious" (*AP*

24; 7:135) of it. He is not positing a separate region of the unconscious in the way that many later thinkers such as Freud have done. What we are not directly conscious of includes what the soul "passively" receives as "a play of sensations" (*AP* 25; 7:136). We may be unconscious of them in the sense of being only dimly aware of them because they affect us obscurely. These claims about sensations will be further documented when we examine the *Critique of Pure Reason* in chapter 4.

2. Representing "with consciousness" or subjectively "perceiving [*wahrnehmen*]" (*LL* 569; 9:64) provides at least some clarity. In the *Friedländer Anthropology* lectures of 1775–76, it is suggested that representing something with consciousness may coincide with and even rely on representing other things obscurely. Thus, we are told that when a human mind (*Gemüth*) reads words for their meaning, the lower capacity of soul (*Seele*) must still take note (*achten*) of the spelling (*VA*, 25:479).[2] This example is revealing because a literate person can consciously focus on the meaning of the words of a text while obscurely noting the letters they are composed of. However, this only happens if the words are spelled correctly. Once a word is misspelled, we instantaneously stop short and look at the particular letters. Now the letters that are routinely assimilated and which ordinarily remain obscure, must be consciously attended to. This back-and-forth between the light of the conscious mind and the obscurity of soul occurs throughout our experience. The reading example also illustrates that even at the so-called animal level of soul, humans are not reduced to behaving passively or mechanically, but can make technical adaptations by judging that in the sentence "This is a large apple tee," the last word should have been spelled as "tree."[3]

3. Being acquainted with (*kennen*) or learning about (*noscere*) something is to "represent it in comparison with other things, both as to sameness and as to difference" (*LL* 569–70; 9:64–65). To be acquainted with things comparatively produces a degree of sensible distinctness—what was called "aesthetic distinctness" in chapter 2. The Jäsche text says that this comparative acquaintance of level 3 is something that animals are also capable of, which leads Colin McClear to conclude that Kant thinks that animals also have the conscious representations of objects of level 2 and that their acquaintance with them is not merely sensible but perceptual.[4] This may seem like a reasonable conclusion, but it is also problematic because there are *Reflections* where Kant denies nonrational animals consciousness (see *R*1678 and *R*1680, 16:80; and *R*4230, 17:469). Indeed, when we move ahead to the fourth degree of cognition, we will find that becoming acquainted can occur with or without consciousness, just as representing could occur with or without consciousness. This would suggest that degrees 1 and 3 are on the same level of mere obscure

awareness. The former could be what is randomly accumulated in inner sense, the latter what is received comparatively in outer sense. As a consequence, animal acquaintance would be a comparative *awareness* of things that is not yet a perceptual *consciousness.* Similarly, if we consider that in the "First Introduction to the *Critique of Judgment,*" Kant allows animals to reflect, albeit only on the basis of instinct (see *FI* 15; 20:211), it is reasonable to think that he could also allow them an instinctive awareness of sensible distinctness that would correspond to the acquaintance of this third degree of cognition. Again, they would lack the human capacity to consciously relate their representations to themselves as judging subjects. All these deliberations instigated by the *Jäsche Logic* become unnecessary if we consider the *Warschauer Logic* based on lectures from around 1780, where the so-called second stage of representing with consciousness is skipped. This text moves directly from (1) mere representing (*vorstellen*) and (2) comparative acquaintance (*kennen*)—both of which are not yet conscious in Kant's demanding sense of it—to the human (3) "perceptual cognition [*erkennen, percipere*]"[5] that is conscious. By removing Jäsche's level of representing with consciousness of perception (i.e., level 2), the *Warschauer Logic* makes it explicit that animals rise to the level of "acquaintance, but not with consciousness."[6]

4. This is the level at which we transition from being "acquainted [*kennen*]" to "being "acquainted *with consciousness*" or "cognizing [*erkennen*](*cognoscere*)" (*LL* 570; 9:65). The claim that *erkennen* is a kind of *Erkenntnis* sounds tautological. But relative to *kennen, er-kennen* can be conceived as the conscious or explicit re-cognizing something for what it is as appearance. Now what we have claimed so far is reformulated as the statement that animals do not rise to the level of "recognizing objects" (*LL* 570; 9:65). At level 4, sensible distinctness is replaced by intelligible or judgmental distinctness. This accords with what Kant wrote in "The False Subtlety of the Four Syllogistic Figures," namely, that "it is one thing to *distinguish* [*unterscheiden*] among things and something else entirely to *recognize* [*erkennen*] the difference [*Unterschied*] among things. The latter is only possible by means of judgments and cannot occur in the case of a non-rational animal" ("FS" 104; 2:59). At this fourth level we can be said to possess the distinctive marks for identifying objects, that is, partial concepts whereby we begin to cognize the whole of a thing. The first three degrees range over representations that have been *assimilated.* Starting with the fourth degree, the language of representing is dropped, and we are at the level of objective consciousness wherein humans begin the process of *acquiring* cognition of objects. The next degrees are less problematic and can be briefly summarized.

5. "Understanding by means of concepts, or to conceive [*concipiren*]"

(*LL* 570; 9:65) is to make objects intelligible and explain their possibility. Here the perceptual identifying marks of level 2 are replaced by determinate concepts about objects.

6. Cognizing something "through reason [is] *to have insight* into it (*perspicere*)" (*LL* 570; 9:65). The Latin alludes to Baumgarten's definition of reason as "the faculty for perspicaciously perceiving the correspondences and differences of things distinctly" in the "universal nexus" of the world. For Kant, this means having insight into how something fits into the larger scheme of things. Insight is a way of rationally *appropriating* cognition and systematizing it.

7. Rational comprehension [*begreifen*] (*comprehendere*). We read that to comprehend is "to cognize something . . . *a priori* to the degree that is sufficient for our purpose or intent [*Absicht*]. This is because all our comprehension is only *relative*" (*LL* 570; 9:65). I interpret this to mean that at level 6 we use our reason to attain objective insight, whereas at level 7 we also *assess* its significance for our own purposes.

It may seem odd that the last level of cognition adds a subjective component. However, a subjective element is not always detrimental or prejudicial, for we will see Kant argue in the *Critique of Pure Reason* that objective cognition (*Erkenntnis*) can count as knowledge (*Wissen*) only if there is also a subjective judgmental assent. However, if comprehension is relativized by private or selfish purposes, that would be problematic. Let us then see how comprehension measures up against the four kinds of perfection that Kant demands of cognition in his *Logic*: "A cognition is perfect (1) as to quantity if it is universal; (2) as to quality if it is distinct; (3) as to relation if it is true, and finally (4) as to modality if it is certain" (*LL* 548; 9:38).

Cognitive Perfection and Knowledge

Reflection about the quantitative cognitive perfection of universality requires "the determination of the *horizon* of our cognitions" in light of "the capabilities and ends of the subject" (*LL* 550; 9:40). This horizon is determined *logically* "in relation to the interests of the understanding," *aesthetically* "in relation to the interests of feeling," and *practically* "in relation to the interest of the will" (*LL* 550; 9:40). Universality will vary in scope for each of these interests, and comprehension will differ in terms of comprehensiveness. The comprehensiveness test "concerns passing judgment on, and determining, what man *can* know [*wissen*], what he *is permitted* to know, and what he *ought* to know" (*LL* 550; 9:41). This indicates that comprehension is cognition that is in some way normative by taking into account the human standpoint and its interest in attaining knowledge. Comprehension forces us to become self-conscious about the feasibility of attaining knowledge.

The next cognitive perfection that is examined is the relational one of truth. The verbal or "nominal explanation" of truth that cognition must "agree with its object" (*LL* 557; 9:50) demands a comparative definition that pure general logic cannot provide. The latter can only offer the negative formal rules that cognition "*not contradict itself*" and that it "have grounds and not have false consequences" (*LL* 559; 9:51).

A positive standard for truth is indicated in the following section on the qualitative cognitive perfection of distinctness insofar as it moves in the direction of an epistemic logic. Such a logic requires a "synthesis pertaining to the making distinct of objects [*Deutlichmachung der Objecte*]" (*LL* 569; 9:64), which can give concepts of the understanding their objective reference (*Deutung*) and meaning (*Bedeutung*). Here again Kant employs his distinction between analysis to "make a concept distinct" and the synthesis that can "make a distinct concept" (*LL* 568; 9:63). The latter was already referred to as "synthetic distinctness" in chapter 2 and was incipiently "epistemic" because it "pertains to the making distinct of *objects*" (*LL* 569; 9:64). Again we see Kant begin to shift from the language of distinctness to that of determinateness: "Initially it is sometimes necessary to determine a cognition in a broader extension [*late determinare*], particularly in historical things. In cognitions of reason, however, everything must be determined exactly [*stricte*]. . . . Whether a cognition ought to be determined roughly or exactly always depends on its purpose. Broad determination leaves a certain play for error" (*LL* 561–62; 9:55).

Although "truth is an *objective* property of cognition," Kant adds that "the judgment through which something is *represented* as true [in] relation to an understanding and thus to a particular subject, is, *subjectively, holding-to-be-true*" (*LL* 570; 9:65–66). According to Kant, there are three modes of holding a judgment to be true: opining, believing, and knowing. "What I merely opine I hold in judging, with consciousness, only to be *problematic*; what I believe I hold to be *assertoric*, but not as objectively necessary, only as subjectively so (holding only for me); what I *know*, finally, I hold to be *apodictically certain*, i.e., to be universally and objectively necessary (holding for all)" (*LL* 571; 9:66). The perfection of certainty converts objectively valid cognition into a knowing that is confirmed as holding for all. This confirmation comes in the form of "cognition as a system" (*LL* 575; 9:72).

The same three stages of holding something to be true can be found in the "Canon of Pure Reason" of the first *Critique*, and in the next chapter their import for the cognition-knowledge distinction will be explored more fully. However, before moving on to Kant's *Critique of Pure Reason*, I will say a few more things about comprehension as a mode of cognition that is not often discussed in the Kant literature. The most detailed account of comprehension is given in Kant's *Vienna Logic* (ca. 1780), where it is again defined as the possession of "sufficient insight, insofar as something serves a certain purpose" (*LL* 300; 24:846). Comprehension as a mode of rational cognition is thus simultaneously theoretical and practical. Kant also calls comprehension "something requiring much delicateness [*etwas sehr delicates*]" (*LL* 300; 24:846); it can be said to involve tactfulness or reflective discernment in the use of human reason. And he adds that "one must not talk at once of incomprehensibility, even if something cannot possibly be cognized in a speculative respect" (*LL* 300; 24:846). This suggests that comprehension can make things sufficiently distinct and intelligible for human purposes to amount to more than a private assertoric belief without attaining the apodictic certainty of knowledge.[7] Comprehension would seem to include the normative ability to judge what kinds of things we as humans can and should know, and what not. The paradox of comprehension is that it falls short of knowledge because it continues to test and push the boundaries of cognition. This makes it possible to think about comprehension in Kant as a kind of reflective meta-consciousness that can retrospectively assess the different layers of our experience, whether these are measured in terms of clarity and distinctness as suggested by Meier, or conceived more functionally as the modes of intake discussed in chapter 1.

In terms of the functional distinction between what is assimilated and acquired in cognition and then appropriated and assessed, we can say that levels 1–3 of representation, perceptual apprehension, and acquaintance are assimilative, that levels 4 and 5 of re-cognition and understanding manifest acquisition, and that levels 6 and 7 of rational insight and comprehension make appropriatively shared assessment possible. Although comprehension may not attain the certainty of the knowledge that the understanding can acquire when objective cognition is systematized, it functions at the highest level of rational appropriation. Comprehension goes beyond intellectual understanding by recognizing both its limits and weighing its potential import. Ultimately, comprehension will also be acknowledged as a mode of reflective assessment that is a function of judgment. But first we will focus on Kant's main epistemological work, the *Critique of Pure Reason*, which proceeds determinantly.

4

The Acquisition of Cognition and Its Transcendental Sources

Chapter 3 was used to distinguish subjective representational and objective levels of cognition and to highlight the relative purposiveness of rational comprehension. In this chapter, the focus will be on what makes it possible for cognition to be objective and rationally comprehensive. In the "Preface" to the first edition of the *Critique of Pure Reason*, Kant appeals to the related ideas of completeness and thoroughness. He aims at a "completeness [*Vollständigkeit*] in reaching each of the ends" of reason, and a "thoroughness [*Ausführlichkeit*] in reaching all of them together" (Axiv). Thoroughness demands a critical and well-rounded execution of a task. According to Kant, reason has a unified nature which requires that all of its ends be met in a thoroughly coherent manner. Kant's claims for thoroughness and completeness do not, however, entail that we should expect to receive an exhaustive knowledge of reality where everything has been determined. We already saw that human cognitive comprehension (*Begreifen*) is only relatively comprehensive. Critique for Kant projects a systematic completeness by setting boundaries that can distinguish between what we can truly expect to know and what we can merely think about. The first step in that direction is to ask only legitimate questions of nature, which raises the further issue of what makes a question legitimate. That is why Kant speaks constantly of critique as a tribunal of reason that looks for justification. The laws that the sciences aim to discover must be more than observable regularities, and as such they will impose binding constraints on the way we explain the behavior of things. Critique is primarily an inquiry into "all the cognitions after which reason might strive independently of all experience" (Axii). It must explore the feasibility of attaining cognition in terms of its "sources [*Quellen*], scope [*Umfang*], and bounds [*Grenzen*]" (Axii). These are the more fundamental questions that lead me to now examine what Kant means by a transcendental deduction and how it makes the acquisition of objective cognition possible.

The sources of cognition are not to be equated with the empirical inputs that we assimilate in experience and which were analyzed in the earlier chapters on Kant's lectures on logic. There the focus was on how to distinguish between analytic distinctness and synthetic distinctness as two ways of making sense of assimilated empirical content. The task of general logic was to reflect on that content in order to abstract general concepts that no longer refer to particular things. And what we referred to as an incipient epistemic logic was geared to how judgment can make synthetically distinct claims about the various objects that are perceived. However, when Kant speaks of the sources of cognition in the *Critique of Pure Reason,* he is aiming at a new epistemic logic that will provide the transcendental conditions for acquiring a more general objective experiential nexus. The incipient epistemic logic that we discussed in the previous chapters is called a logic of the "particular use of the understanding" which must now be replaced by a logic of the "general use of the understanding" (A52/B76). The particular use of the understanding is redefined as concerning itself with "the difference of the objects to which it may be directed" and can serve as "the organon of this or that science" (A52/B76). This kind of organon would subsequently be developed into methodologies by thinkers such as J. S. Mill, Dilthey, and neo-Kantians like Heinrich Rickert. These methodologies would "offer the rules for how a science [of a specific kind of object] is to be brought about" (A52/B77).

The sources of cognition can only be explicated by further exploring the nature of general logic, which is now divided into two parts: *pure* and *applied.* Pure general logic "has to do with strictly *a priori* principles, and is a canon of the understanding and reason, but only in regard to what is formal in their use" (A53/B77). Applied general logic is called a *cathartic,* which considers any "rules of the use of the understanding under the subjective empirical conditions that psychology teaches us" (A53/B77). It gets rid of psychological impediments and teaches us to be on the lookout for fallacies that can breed in the obscure recesses of the inner sense of the subject. Not only must general logic purify itself of the particularities of objects, but also the peculiarities of thinking subjects.

At this point Kant proposes that there could also be pure a priori logic that thinks of objects in general. This would be a transcendental logic that does not abstract from all content of cognition, but only from empirically derived content. It opens up the prospect of there being "acts of pure thinking" (A57/B81) that can establish an a priori intuitive relation to objects in general. Whereas pure general logic aims to make sure that we think consistently, transcendental logic has the epistemic task of probing what makes it possible for our experience to be purely objective. It is concerned with the judgmental conditions of experience and anticipates the content of possible objects in general ways. Because the truth conditions of general logic are formal and empty of empirical content, they are considered negative (A59/B84). However, transcendental truth conditions are called positive in that they invoke categorial concepts that prepare us to make sense of empirical contents by providing a judgmental meaning framework for experiencing them as objects which can be related to each other.

The first "clue" to all this is given in §10 where Kant writes that transcendental logic "has a manifold of a priori sensibility that lies before it, which the transcendental aesthetic has offered to it as material [*Stoff*] for the pure concepts of the understanding" (A76–77/B102). This material needed for pure concepts of the understanding is said to be contained within the a priori forms of space and time. It is important to recognize that this manifold of a priori sensibility is not the series of discrete perceptual representations that we spoke of earlier in the context of logical analysis. Those sensible representations were assimilated to find the identifying marks of things and bring them "under one concept analytically. . . . Transcendental logic, however, teaches how to bring under concepts not the representations but the pure synthesis of representations" (A78/B104). It teaches us to acquire representations not as a mere associative series, but as an intuitive nexus or manifold that is the product of an imaginative synthesis whose underlying conceptual unity provides judgment with the power to project what it means for thought to determine an object as such (see A78–79/B104–5).

The pure concepts of the understanding which have this power to judgmentally determine objects and define their general relations in nature are called categories. How these synthetic concepts relate to the synthesis of the imagination just referred to differs in the first and second editions of the *Critique of Pure Reason*. This chapter will focus on the imagination and how it weaves experience into a continuous nexus. The next chapter will focus on the way judgment structures and frames experience and gives it meaning.

The Subjective Deduction

The A edition contains a "Subjective Deduction" that refers the manifold of intuition back to a synopsis of sense that was merely assimilated. By itself this synopsis is a mere mode of "receptivity" (A97) and would not be conscious without the spontaneous synthetic operations whereby we "take up" what is provided by the synopsis. Kant writes: "If therefore I ascribe a synopsis to sense because it contains a manifold in its intuition, a synthesis must always correspond to this" (A97). For Kant, sensations are merely momentary modifications of the state of the subject (A320/B376) that can be felt—he speaks of our being affected—but they provide no *lasting* content until they are synthetically acquired. The mind does this by supplying a subjective temporal horizon that gathers a multiplicity of discrete sensations into a manifold continuum. As a momentary modification, a sensation is a mere limit point on the timeline and cannot be consciously represented without a synthesis of apprehension. This is made clear when Kant writes:

> Every intuition contains a manifold in itself, which however would not be represented as such a manifold [*als ein solches*] if the mind did not distinguish the time in the succession of impressions [*Eindrücke*] on one another; for as contained in one instant [*Augenblick*], no representation can ever be anything other than absolute unity. (A99)

We cannot consciously apprehend the absolute unity of a sense impression, for it is like a point that is a vanishing limit of the temporal continuum of consciousness and therefore not a part of it (see A169/B211). Time is a formal continuum that is infinitely divisible and has no smallest part. Thus Kant claims that what we represent as appearances are "continuous magnitudes, either in their intuition, as extensive magnitudes, or in their mere perception (sensation and thus reality), as intensive ones" (A170/B212). Sensations are *subjectively real* and can be felt in terms of their relative intensity, but they cannot provide us with consciousness of anything that is *objectively actual* unless they are synthesized as part of an intuitive manifold or continuum. According to the "Subjective Deduction," we cannot consciously apprehend these instantaneous sensations or impressions without our actively holding onto them and gathering them into the temporal flow of inner sense. Kant calls this a transcendental act of "synthetic apprehension" that unifies discrete impressions of sense as a continuous intuitive manifold. Intuition can be said "to provide a manifold but can never produce it *as* such a manifold . . . without the occurrence of such a synthesis" (A99). Later Kant will expand on this and make it clear that any synopsis of sense is a mere associative "multiplicity [*Vielheit*]" (A168/B210) as distinct from a synthetic manifold (*Mannigfaltigkeit*) of intuitive or perceptual apprehension.

No single apprehended intuitive manifold is adequate for the overall cognition of multidimensional spatial things. To encompass a whole object, I need to also perceptually apprehend its other sides. However, "if I were always to lose the preceding representations . . . and not reproduce them when I proceed to the following ones, then no whole representation . . . could ever arise" (A102). In speaking about this reproductive synthesis of the imagination needed for there to be a continuum of experience that is rule-bound, Kant specifies what differentiates representations as they are now understood from the way they were first treated in the lectures on logic. Then representations were assumed to be units of content that need to be analyzed as parts of perceived particular things. Now representations are schematized synthetically in terms of what it means to apperceive objects in general. Kant's critical philosophy transforms sense inputs into intuitive manifolds that we can imaginatively hold onto and subject to necessary rules which have their source in our mental capacities.[1] The most important of these capacities is the understanding, and the third transcendental synthesis is that of recognition in concepts. Not only must we be able to hold onto past representations through reproduction, but we must also be able to recognize in a concept that what has been reproduced is identical to its original. Concepts of the understanding give an objective unity to what is represented. What was empirically and logically assimilated as representational content must be synthetically "taken up [*aufgenommen*]" (A77/B102) and related to possible objects. The ultimate source for this objective acquisition is the transcendental unity of apperception.

The three syntheses of sensible apprehension, imaginative reproduction, and recognition in the first edition order the temporal manifold of representations as the subjective content of inner sense before subjecting it to universal rules whose objective source manifests itself as the transcendental unity of apperception. This reference to inner sense is stressed at the beginning of the section on the syntheses of apprehension in order to underscore their temporality. Thus, Kant writes that "wherever our representations may arise, whether through the influence of external things or as the effect of inner causes . . . as modifications of the mind they nevertheless belong to inner sense, and . . . the formal condition of inner sense, namely, time" (A98–99).

The Objective Deduction and Transcendental Reflexivity

The second edition of the *Critique of Pure Reason* provides a revised deduction of the pure concepts of the understanding that starts right away with the transcendental unity of apperception as the source of all synthesis. The transcendental unity of apperception is now called a synthetic unity that is self-conscious that all its representations are subject to universal rules of the understanding which can be explicated as the categories. In identifying this self-consciousness, Kant claims in §25 of the second edition "Objective Deduction" that "in the synthetic original unity of apperception, I am conscious of myself, not as I appear to myself, nor as I am in myself, but only that I am" (B157). Kant is claiming here that the unity of apperception involves a transcendental mode of self-consciousness that precedes the empirical self-consciousness of inner sense. To be conscious of how I *appear to myself* is to phenomenally objectify myself in the time of inner sense. To be conscious of myself as I *am in myself* would be to know myself as a noumenal subject out of time. It would be to know *what* I truly am, and this is not directly accessible to us. Instead, the transcendental unity of apperception is the direct but formal consciousness *that* I am. Pierre Keller characterizes this as "an immediate reflexive awareness of self"[2] that precedes the subject-object distinction of "the reflection theory of self-knowledge."[3]

Although this distinction between what is reflexively self-referring and thoughtfully reflective is not generally applied to Kant, it is important and will be expanded on here and later. Before Keller applied the phrase "reflexive awareness" to Kant, I used it to translate Dilthey's conception of *Innewerden* rather than as the "inner awareness" that other translators had employed.[4] I characterized reflexive awareness as the direct self-givenness of consciousness; it is immediately self-referring prior to any mediated reflective subject-object distinction.[5] If we regard Kant's transcendental self-consciousness as formally reflexive in this sense, then it becomes the reference point for what is cognitively acquired through categorial concepts without needing to refer back to what was obscurely assimilated in inner sense. It is this transcendental reflexivity that then allows Kant to dispense with the "Subjective Deduction" in the B edition and no longer appeal to inner sense.

Because the terms "reflexive" and "reflective" are often conflated, it is important to underscore that what is transcendentally "reflexive" is not "reflective." What is reflexive is indexical and is neither the subjective "reflection" that preceded empirical concept-formation in the lectures on logic, nor what Kant would later define as the "reflective" evaluative power of human judgment. The reflection that we spoke of earlier as preceding empirical concept-formation is merely assimilative and comparative, whereas reflective evaluation only comes into focus when we move from the acquisitive level of cognition to the appropriative level of rational comprehension and knowledge. Reflexivity applies to the transcendental awareness *that* I am, while reflection aims at the eventual consciousness of *what* I am.

The transcendental unity of apperception of the second edition is "reflexive" in going behind inner sense and prepares the ground for the "Refutation of Idealism" (B274–79) that Kant now adds in order to demonstrate that inner sense is not more accessible to us than outer sense or more fundamental, as most idealists tend to think. The reason why the section on the three syntheses of the apprehension, reproduction, and recognition of representations in inner sense is dropped in the second edition, is that it is no longer necessary to restrict the temporality of consciousness to inner sense. In fact, the "determination" of representations in inner sense that is needed to have a coherent experience of ourselves cannot occur without reference to outer sense.

Redefining Idealism

The dependence of inner sense on outer sense that is now claimed by Kant is not also a more general call for their interdependence, as I will show later. It is merely a challenge to the psychological assumption of many traditional idealists that what is inner is more reliable than what is outer. Kant's refutation of idealism only rejects those modes of idealism which claim that outer experience is either indemonstrable or illusory. Over against these psychological idealists, Kant still upholds his own more limited or transcendental idealism precisely because he considers it compatible with an empirical realism about outer sense.[6]

Transcendental idealism provides the formal conditions that not only make outer experience possible, but also prove "that inner experience in general is possible only through outer experience in general" (B278–79). Kant writes that "I am conscious of my existence as determined in time" and that "time-determination presupposes something persistent [*etwas Beharrliches*] in perception. This persistent thing, however, cannot be something in me" (B275). Therefore, Kant argues that my consciousness of being determined in time must derive from being able to perceive persistent things outside myself. However, there is an equivocation here. To be aware of temporal persistence does not require me to perceive a persistent external object. I could have an enduring ache that goes on indefinitely. What Kant is really seeking is a persistence that is publicly measurable and which can only be established by relating my temporal consciousness to something that is spatially measurable. The succession of representations in the time-flow of inner experience cannot be measured without reference to the sequence of spatially definable things in outer experience. This means that Kant's own first edition talk of the "determinations of inner sense" (A101) is in effect refuted in the second edition.[7] Time as the form of inner sense cannot be determined without being related to space as the form of outer sense. Indeed, the a priori form of time also applies to outer experience. Thus, the continuum of the manifold of intuition is spatiotemporal.

This further loss of faith in inner sense allows Kant to downplay the still partly assimilative approach of the "Subjective Deduction" and focus on the purely acquisitive approach of the "Objective Deduction," according to which "all the manifold of intuition stand under conditions of the original synthetic unity of apperception" (B136). The downgrading of inner sense also makes the claim that the transcendental unity of apperception is reflexive all the more important, for it opens up a direct albeit formal mode of self-access. Instead of having to introspectively observe the assimilated contents of inner sense, we become able to feel ourselves and orient ourselves in the world. This will be elaborated when we consider Kant's writings on aesthetics and anthropology.

We saw that it is possible to have an assimilative perceptual acquaintance with things that can be logically analyzed. But that was merely a way of clarifying the identifying marks of our subjective representations and making them more distinct. The aim of cognition, however, is to apperceive things objectively by means of a synthetic judgment. Perceptual assimilation only allowed me to claim that "if I carry a body, I feel a pressure of weight" (B142), which is to compare two subjective states. Apperceptive acquisition entitles me to go further and say, "the body is heavy," so that "these representations are combined in the object" (B142) rather than merely in my mind. The objective cognition that this makes possible occurs in what Kant calls the "System of All Principles of Pure Understanding" (A148/B187) in the *Critique of Pure Reason*, where all twelve categories are presented as ways of relating the transcendental unity of apperception to the possibility of experiencing the world objectively.

Acquiring the Continuum for Understanding Interaction

The initial categorial way in which the unity of apperception manifests itself determinately is explicated by the "Axioms of Intuition." They present the quantitative categories of "unity, multiplicity [*Vielheit*], and totality" (A80/B106) intuitively. What was representationally assimilated under the subjective headings of the syntheses of apprehension, reproduction, and recognition is now rendered as capable of being acquired more determinately and ordered mathematically. The "Axioms of Intuition" allow us to order our representations spatially in accordance with the axioms of geometry and temporally by the rules of arithmetic. They frame the measurement of the extensive magnitude of any object as a whole that is the sum of its multiple unit parts. Multiplicity will be reassessed when Kant considers intensive magnitudes.

Whereas the extensive magnitude of what is intuited applies to the apparent surfaces of things, that is, their represented phenomenal outer form, the next section on the "Anticipations of Perception" deals with the intensive magnitude of the intuitive content of objects. Here Kant exposits the qualitative categories of reality, negation, and limitation (A80/B106) that are said to correspond to traditional affirmative, negative, and infinite judgments (A70/B95). Kant considers what is qualitatively felt to be *real* in sensation as an anticipatory affirmation about the *objective content* of what appears. What is initially affirmed in sensible apprehension is "the real of the sensation, as merely subjective representation, by which one can only be conscious that the subject is affected, and which one relates to an object in general" (B207–8). As Kant goes on to point out, sensation as sensation is "capable of a diminution, so that it can decrease and thus gradually disappear" (A168/B210). This qualitative awareness is intuitively "aprioritized,"[8] to quote the neo-Kantian Hermann Cohen, in the second edition formulation that "in all appearances the real, which is an object of the sensation, has intensive magnitude, i.e., a degree" (B207). Because the input of sensation is ephemeral and "fills only an instant" (A167/B209), its magnitude cannot be outwardly extended, but only differentiated from something beyond it. Between it and the perceptually anticipated object "there is a *continuous nexus* of many possible intermediate sensations, whose difference from one another is always smaller than the difference between the given one and zero, or complete negation" (A168/B210, italics added). Here Kant indicates that there must be something there which has a degree of reality that can be located between 0 and 1. One could think of 0 as the sensation as it vanishes with the passing of time and 1 as the object that is perceived. But Longuenesse is helpful in pointing out that objectively the 0 need not mean an empirical lack of reality, but the ideal negativity of the overall forms of pure space and time. She writes that space and time are "metaphysically speaking nothing . . . [and] 'real' only insofar as they are cognized as relations of things, whose reality is 'what corresponds to sensation.'"[9] This means that the reality of particular objects can be approximated by degrees relative to the whole of reality. Now magnitude is not defined by summation, but by means of the internal qualitative differentiation of an overall worldly spectrum. This supports the positive conclusion about which we can agree with Cohen, namely, that the "Anticipations of Perception" make intelligible the infinitesimal delimitation of the objects of Newtonian physics. Traditional infinite judgments[10] can now make way for applying an infinitesimal calculus to the natural world.

Some important conclusions can be drawn from these first two sets of mathematical categories. The axiomatic quantitative categories of unity, plurality, and totality can determine what has been intuitively assimilated from sense. They make what is intuitively represented measurable as extensive magnitude. But the first glimmer of objectivity is acquired with the anticipatory qualitative categories of reality, negation, and limitation. What is intensively felt as the limiting resistance of reality allows us to acquire a sense of being "affected" in a way that "relates to an object in general" (B207–8). Here we approximate multiplicity as a "degree of reality" as in a "moment of gravity" (A168/B210), so that intuition is no longer merely representational but begins to acquire a perceptible objectivity. The mathematical categories also disclose that all appearances are "continuous magnitudes, either in their intuition as extensive magnitudes, or in their mere perception (sensation and thus reality), as intensive ones" (A170/B212). Thus we can say a priori that all sense qualities can be quantified in terms of their degree of intensity and that all mathematical quantities possess one a priori quality, namely, continuity.

The next set of categories provides the dynamical ones of substance-attribute, cause and effect, and communal interaction. They are articulated as the "Analogies of Experience" whose principle is that objective "experience is only possible through the representation of a necessary connection of perceptions" (B218). Here again we cannot a priori anticipate the content of the phenomenal objects of experience, but only the kinds of orderly relations that can arise among them. These three relational categories legislate how objects can be affected and how their states can change over time.

The first analogy of experience formulates the principle of the persistence of substance. The main claim here is that "in all appearances that which persists is the object itself, i.e., the substance [*phaenomenon*], but everything that changes or that can change belongs only to the way in which this substance or substances exists, thus to their determinations" (A183–84/B227). Whereas the states of a substance can change (*wechseln*) and be replaced, the persisting substance can only be said to be altered (*verändert*) (see A187/B230).

The second analogy of experience is formulated in the B edition as follows: "All alterations occur in accordance with the law of the connections of cause and effect" (B232). If all my representations succeed each other in the flow of time, how do I recognize that the alteration of an object is causally necessitated? Kant offers the example of a house that stands before us and can be apprehended part by part by first looking at the roof and then moving down to the ground or vice versa. Here the observed change is due to the way our eyes move. This is quite different from observing a sailboat moving downstream independently of how we shift our gaze. There what is altered is not a product of any act of ours, and we can assume that something is happening independently of our volition. However, since no substance alters itself, we must "presuppose that something else precedes it, which it follows in accordance with a rule" (A195/B240). If something is really happening there, it is an objective alteration that has a necessary external cause.

The category of causal action allows us to read the perception of subjective successive representations as the apperception of objective sequences of actual events or happenings. The next question is how a human being whose representations are assimilated as part of an ongoing time series (*Ablauf*) is able to make sense of things coexisting at the same time. To account for this, Kant posits the category of interaction. His third analogy of experience asserts that "all substances, insofar as they can be perceived in space as simultaneous, are in thoroughgoing [*durchgängiger*] interaction" (A211/B256). To account for the gravitational pull that the Moon and the Earth exert on each other, we cannot appeal to how we apprehend them representationally one at a time. In order to imagine how they can coexist at the same time, we need to appeal to the categorial principle that substances are lawfully connected as part of a community of interaction. Since we apprehend things in temporal succession, the simultaneity of different substances in space could not be recognized by us if there were no interaction among them. Thus, Kant claims that "in our mind all appearances, as contained in a possible experience, must stand in a community [*communio*] of apperception, and insofar as the objects are to be represented as being connected by existing simultaneously, they must reciprocally determine their position in one time and thereby constitute a whole" (A214/B261). Reciprocal interaction is a necessary presupposition for the world to be intuitable as having the spatial depth that can account for coexistence. All experience must be lawfully interrelatable in terms of one spatiotemporal framework.

It is this category of reciprocal community that allows us to apperceive what is successively apprehended in a comprehensive way. Since we cannot cognitively comprehend everything simultaneously, the category of community merely opens up the possibility of some kind of comprehensive understanding as a systematic project that can be filled in only gradually. This will have to be reconciled in chapter 10 with Kant's discussion of the mathematical sublime in the *Critique of Judgment*, which suggests that an instantaneous, aesthetically felt comprehension of the world is nevertheless possible for finite human intellects. However, this will be no more than an ephemeral imaginative awareness, not some overarching objective intuition.

This chapter began with Kant's claim to find a thorough (*ausführliche*) way of executing all the ends of reason together. This hope for convergence seemed rather bold and unrealistic, but if we regard the categories as ways of imaginatively elaborating the transcendental unity of apperception, then the category of community represents a kind of completion of the process. It provides a formal approximation of rational convergence by conceiving a world that is thoroughly (*durchgängiger*) interactive.

There is another set of categories, according to Kant, but they serve a modal function and do not have import for understanding the principled or a priori *bounds* of experience. These modal categories of possibility, actuality, and necessity do not further determine the nature of the objects of experience, for as Kant writes, "if the concept of the thing is already entirely complete, I can still ask about this object whether it is merely possible, or also actual, or, if it is the latter, whether it is also necessary" (A219/B266). I will return to these modal categories in chapter 6, which will discuss the negative or external *limits* that we confront in empirical inquiry.

5

The Role of Judgment in Validating Cognition as Meaningful and Appropriating Knowledge as True

To more intimately relate his a priori categories to a posteriori intuitions, Kant will appeal to the meaning-giving function of judgment. We saw him speak of the meaning of experience as a product of spelling out the manifold of intuition in space and time and reading it as a categorially ordered and lawfully governed nexus. The task of spelling was an assimilative medial skill and that of reading an acquired judgmental skill. Since what relates these two skills is the imagination, those like Peter Strawson who have downplayed the role of the imagination in Kant's epistemology ignore the important ways in which it informs the power of judgment and vice versa.[1]

Before fully explicating the imaginative shift from spelling to reading as a judgmental act of providing objective knowledge, I will briefly note how Kant also frames it in relation to the more comprehensive aims of reason.

> Plato noted very well that our power of cognition feels a far higher need than that of merely spelling out appearances according to a synthetic unity in order to be able to read them as experience, and that our reason naturally exalts itself to cognitions that go much too far for any objects that experience can give ever to be congruent, but that nonetheless have their reality and are by no means merely figments of the brain. (A314/B370–71)

What has been representationally *spelled out* as a successive spatial manifold can be *read* discursively as objective cognition by concepts of the understanding. However, reason wants more. It provides ideas for a systematic *interpretation* that aims to account for the overall coherence of things. Clearly, rational ideas are not constitutive for cognitive experience; only the categories of the understanding are. Kant warns that when ideas of reason lose contact with experience, they can mislead us. To make sure that our rational ideas stay with nature and preserve it as "the text of our interpretation" (*RM*, 18:274), they must be used merely regulatively. They can be heuristic for further cognitive inquiry, but they do not directly add to the fund of what is cognized.

The above passage about reason wanting more than what a reading of the understanding can offer is located in the "Transcendental Dialectic." Reason by itself will inevitably explore the transcendent ideas of freedom, the immortality of the soul, and an omniscient God without, however, attaining adequate theoretical conclusions. Practical reason will be called on to further resolve the dialectical debates of academic philosophy. However, the "Doctrine of Method" which follows the "Dialectic" supplies a more modest theoretical "discipline of pure reason" that establishes a less speculative approach which considers how judgment can employ reason to relate the assimilative and acquisitive aspects of cognition to the final appropriative moment of knowledge about this phenomenal world. Here theoretical reason is allowed to provide us with a "canon" to judge whether the cognition we have acquired passes the test of being true knowledge.[2] To properly bring out this merging of reason with judgment in the "Canon of Pure Reason," we must take note of the increasing role that Kant assigned to judgment when he rewrote his "Transcendental Deduction" for the B edition. It expands the status of the categories from being concepts of cognition to become proto-judgments about objective validity. We will see Kant turning to judgment at both these places in the *Critique*: first to give the categories objective reference in the "Transcendental Deduction," and then to test the intersubjective consensus needed to validate experiential cognition as scientific knowledge.

Schematization as an Imaginative Use of Judgment

Kant's categories are not just universal concepts that relate mental representations to each other; they serve a transcendental function by relating representations in the subject to possible phenomenal objects. From the perspective of general logic concerned with the clarification of concepts, judgments are propositions composed of concepts. But from the perspective of transcendental logic, judgments provide a framing role that gives concepts the power to imaginatively schematize objects. It is no accident that the chapter on imaginative schematization is part of the section entitled "Transcendental Doctrine of the Power of Judgment" (A137/B176).

Categorial judgments make it possible to use concepts not merely to abstractly think of objects, but to intuitively cognize them. This is the significance of Kant's claim in the B edition "Deduction" that a judgment should no longer be considered as "the representation of a relation between two concepts" (B140). Instead, "a judgment is nothing other than the way to bring given cognitions to the objective unity of apperception" (B141). Judgment provides "that unity through which all of the manifold given in an intuition is united in a concept of the object" (B139).

Elaborating the example already cited, this is not just a subjective conceptual association whereby we link an image of a body with the felt pressure of weight that it produces in our inner sense. Instead, we are making the objective judgment that "it, the body, is heavy" (B142). An intuitive manifold is united, not just mentally, but with reference to an actual object. The feeling in inner sense of being weighed down is replaced by the cognition of an object out there whose heaviness can be measured on a calibrated scale for all to verify.

Transcendental logic provides access to physical bodies out there, but even more importantly, its categories make them part of an objective world. Categories are nonempirical concepts that differ from purely formal concepts such as identity and difference by supplying schematic intuitive content. It is this schematic referential function that provides Kant's categories "with sense and meaning [*Sinn und Bedeutung*]" (B149) and refers them to what is perceivable in the world. Categories are universal concepts that refer (*deuten*) to possible objects of experience and are able to anticipate cognition of them that is orderly and meaningful (*bedeutend*). They pre-delineate a world in ways that allow us to structure our experience objectively.

This referential meaning-endowing capacity of the categories is defined in §24 of the B "Deduction" as a "figurative synthesis" (B151) whereby the imagination projects the "objective reality" of the categories (B150). Kant claims that "the transcendental synthesis of the imagination . . . is an effect of the understanding on sensibility and its first application [*Anwendung*] (and at the same time the ground of all others) to objects of the intuition that is possible for us" (B152). The term "application" has been taken to mean that imaginative schematization comes after conceptualization. This has been criticized by Karin de Boer as "the common view that categories are prior to schemata."[3] She argues that schemata should not be regarded as "added onto unschematized categories"[4] and criticizes H. B. Paton and others for assuming this when they speak of "schematized categories."[5] In *Imagination and Interpretation in Kant*, I spoke of schemata as "translating the rules implicit in the categories into a temporally ordered set of instructions . . . [whereby] objects can be determinately related."[6] What distinguishes categories from other concepts is that they are inherently schematizable, and to that extent de Boer has a point. Our experience of the world only uses them as schematized, but Kant also speaks of aesthetic pleasure as having "an *internal* causality (which is purposive) with regard to cognition in general" (*C3* 107; 5:222). Here causality is schematized differently than when we specifically cognize how one moving object *externally* affects another.[7] Since it is the case that schematization is a "hidden art in the depths of the human soul" (A141/B180–81), it is also possible, as Samantha Matherne has argued, that the way each of us imaginatively schematizes "will be guided by a self-given norm"[8] that is left open by the categories. If there can be variation in the way each of us schematizes a category, then it does precede its schema. The issue of imaginative schematization becomes even more complex in the *Critique of Judgment*, where it will become apparent that aesthetic schematization can occur without concepts (see *C3* 167; 5:287). Then the question of a before and after disappears altogether and makes way for the more appropriate question of whether we are schematizing with or without concepts.

This reference forward to the *Critique of Judgment* confirms that imaginative schematizing is above all a function of judging. It was already pointed out that the B edition of the *Critique of Pure Reason* defined categories as more than concepts and judgments as more than conceptual relations. This allows us to rethink both categories and their schemata as embedded in judging so as to make the priority issue moot. Thus, Kant states that "categories are nothing other than [the] very functions for judging . . . the manifold of a given in intuition" so that it "can come together in one consciousness" (B143).

Kant had written in the margins of his own copy of the first edition that "the incomprehensibility of the categories stems from the fact that we cannot have insight into the synthetic unity of apperception."[9] It is thus not unreasonable to propose that the second edition's redefinition of judgment is meant to make the categories more comprehensible. Although Beatrice Longuenesse has also noted the importance of judgment in relation to schematization, she argues for it differently. She regards the figurative synthesis involved in schematization as a mode of "blind" or "sensible synthesis" which must then be discursively analyzed by judgment.[10] Thus she speaks of "the syntheses of imagination that must occur prior to the discursive activity of judgment," so that they can be "reflected under concepts."[11] I am not sure what it means to be reflected under concepts, but I assume that it gives what were called blind imaginative syntheses an analytical distinctness.

We must regard the syntheses of imagination involved in schematization, not as prior to judgment, but as part of it. Judgment in the B "Deduction" involves more than the discursive conceptual analysis that Longuenesse focuses on. In chapter 2, we saw Kant assert in his lectures on logic that there is a "synthetic distinctness" (*LL* 568; 9:63) that goes beyond the logical distinctness of discursive analysis. Whereas logical analysis makes concepts more inwardly distinct, Kant shows that synthetic judgment can make a new distinct concept that extends its content outwards. This synthetic extension of content is exactly what the new definition of judgment in the B "Deduction" brings to fruition, namely, an intuitive making-distinct of objects.

It is through judgmental synthesis, then, that categories can gain a meaningful "grip" on objects and their relations. This judgment-based reading of how the schematizing imagination produces objective cognition differs from the sense-based approach adopted by Eric Watkins and Marcus Willaschek, who claim that intuition "must actually *latch onto an object*" that is given so that concepts can then think it.[12] They admit that their intuitive "latching" language ties cognition to particular sensation-based perceived objects and is merely subjective or "psychological."[13] Imaginative schematization, by contrast, is not about latching subjective sensations onto particular objects, but involves the procedure for recognizing what it means to conceptually represent objects and their conceptual relations.

A judgment-based approach to what it means to cognize objects provides a middle ground between the neo-Kantian downgrading of sensation by Hermann Cohen that derealizes it and the actualizing approach of Watkins and Willaschek, who define a sensation as a "conscious representation."[14] They refer to A320/B376, where Kant describes "representation with consciousness" as "*perceptio*." But there are two kinds of perception: "*sensatio* and *cognitio*" (A320/B376–77). A sensation is merely part of inner sense as a modification of the state of the subject. *Cognitio*, by contrast, is either perceptual intuitive content that immediately refers to a single object, or a concept that refers to many objects by means of a mark common to them. This and other passages which have already been discussed cast doubt on the claim that sensations are fully conscious in Kant's demanding sense of "consciousness." The *Empfindungen* or *Sinneseindrücke* of the *Critique of Pure Reason* are at best ephemeral moments of sentience and are often subliminal, like neurological impulses. The liminal nature of sensation will come up again when we discuss the instantaneous sublime moment in Kant's aesthetics in chapter 10. It is important to pay attention to Kant's terminology on this topic. In chapter 13, I will point to a rare instance when Kant uses the Latinate term "*Sensation*" rather than the usual German "*Empfindung*" to refer to something sensory like an overpowering smell or an explosive sound which cannot be ignored. Here he points to the other liminal extreme of the sensational.

Watkins and Willaschek speak of sensations as the matter of the intuitions that relate to singular objects, but as we just saw, it is not sensation but intuition that defines objects. Cohen even insists that sensations are not to be regarded as givens from which we constitute objects; they are not the "ground" of objective cognition, but the mere effect of objects on our power to represent. If sensations are assumed to be actual, they produce the psychological illusion of "a givenness [*Gegebenheit*]" according to Cohen, instead of referring to "what is objectively given [*das Gegebene*]."[15] Since we have already shown that sensations lie at the limit of consciousness, they can at best be regarded as psychologically real in that they are felt. Sensations are obscure and can only become the intuitive content that informs our cognition of actual objects to the extent that they are assimilated with the aid of syntheses of apprehension, to revive the mixed language of the "Subjective Deduction." Sensations are too ephemeral to constitute the intuitive content of what is perceived, nor is it adequate to regard this intuitive content as the result of "forms determining the sensations,"[16] as Watkins and Willaschek do.[17]

Cohen allows sensations to psychologically "signal or indicate [*bezeichnen*]" objects, but only intuition can "attest to or provide evidence [*bezeugen*]"[18] for them. However, neither can meaningfully latch onto objects apart from concepts, and I therefore propose that it is judgment that gives us a grip (*Griff*) in a way that can approximate what Kant would call having a comprehensive grasp (*begreifen*) of objects. Each of the categories provides a schema for ordering representations in time so that their subjective succession can be judged to constitute an objective sequence. I have already shown how the mathematical categories allow us to think of this world as a continuum in which things can be measured relative to each other. The dynamical categories allow us to explain how things can interact. These were referred to earlier as the "Analogies of Experience" and include the relations of substance and attribute, of cause and effect, and of communal or reciprocal interaction. It is imaginative schematization that allows us to make the judgmental connection between the abstract rule of substantial persistence and actual concrete objects as substrates for their changing temporal states. The schema for causality enables us to judgmentally exemplify the abstract conception of something being subject to a rule-bound change as a necessary objective sequence where one state necessarily follows from another. Causality allows us to posit the existence of events that are not merely contingently prior in time to what is happening, but were necessary to bring it about. Experimentation and observation are still needed, of course, to actually find that antecedent necessary cause. Finally, the schema of community allows us to recognize substances as mutually conditioning each other and therefore to judge them as being simultaneous. Without such inherent schemata, the categories would have a merely abstract logical sense and would lack the objective meaning that structures the intuitive manifold of experience in both time and space. Having characterized schemata as the "true" conditions for the empirical use of the categories, Kant concludes that "transcendental truth . . . precedes empirical truth and makes it possible" (A146/B185).

The transcendental truth-conditions of the "Analytic" provide the general cognitive meaning parameters on the basis of which actual empirical truth claims can be objectively validated. However, as was already indicated, the "Canon of Pure Reason" adds further conditions to test whether cognition (*Erkenntnis*) can also count as knowledge (*Wissen*).[19] These are the judgmental conditions of intersubjective validation that set bounds to what can be known. These bounds which are expected to guarantee knowledge must be self-imposed by us as rational creatures in order to prevent error or mistakes of judgment.

I will summarize all this by reiterating that pure *general* logic sets the formal truth-conditions for all thought and that transcendental logic establishes the cognitive meaning-structures that are *particular* to how thought relates to the limits of human sensibility. Finally, what Kant calls "method" in the "Canon of Pure Reason" locates self-binding rules that *individual* subjects must apply to test what is understood about nature in relation to a comprehensive interpretation of the world. In determining what it is to know, individual subjects must take rational responsibility for their cognitive claims. Knowing is thus assessed in the context of Kant's treatment of reason, but unlike the dialectical speculations of reason, it restricts itself to ascertaining what has been understood.

Whereas *cognizing* aims at general rules that anticipate orderly meaning-relations among objects of experience, *knowing* assesses such objective meaning claims for their truth. In claiming to know, we go beyond cognition by affirming that what was meant is also true. Knowing moves from the reading or acquisitive level of cognitive understanding to the interpretive or appropriative level of reason and holds the outcome to be true (*Fürwahrhalten*) (see A822/B850). No matter how much objective meaning a cognitive claim may provide, it will not amount to an actual truth claim unless it is also supported by "subjective causes in the mind of him who judges" (A820/B848). The cognitive task of judgment is to refer concepts to objects, but knowing demands something more from the judging subject, namely, assent.

The subjective judgmental assent that is a necessary moment in attaining knowledge has not been adequately noted or discussed in the secondary literature. Most accounts of knowledge in Kant focus on objective justification, which is essential, to be sure. But subjective judgmental assent is also needed to ensure individual responsibility in making a truth claim. One possible reason for not taking the assent of the subject seriously is to assume that it is reducible to persuasion, which "has its ground only in the particular constitution of the subject" (A820/B848). Persuasion (*Überredung*) only has a psychological force and must be replaced by a more rational conviction (*Überzeugung*), according to Kant. The conviction of belief that he then goes on to consider is also subjective, as will become apparent.[20] The final commitment to a claim being true will require the responsible subject to reflect and consider the "possibility of communicating it and finding it to be valid [*gültig*] for every human being" (A820/B848). This alone can transform subjective conviction into the intersubjective certainty (*Gewissheit*) that Kant demands of knowledge.

Before indicating how Kant conceives the stages involved in reaching the goal of certain knowledge, I can sum up what we have established about the overall epistemic process. The *assimilation* of sensible intuition in space and time was shown to be *subjectively representational.* Similarly, the logical analysis of what is assimilated remains subjective in that it can only confirm the consistency of what I have in mind. The *acquisition* of cognition made possible by the transcendental unity of apperception and the categories aims to be *objectively meaningful and universally accessible.* We can now add that the subjective judgmental assent needed for the rational *appropriation* of knowledge is really an *intersubjective mode of truth assessment.* According to the "Canon of Pure Reason," individual knowers must test their cognitive results through communication with the whole community of inquirers.

Opinions and Beliefs as Intermediaries between Persuasion and Knowledge

In coming to hold a cognitive claim as true, Kant distinguishes three stages in overcoming psychological persuasion and achieving rational certainty. They are opining, believing, and knowing. In the following passage, these stages are measured by the strength with which a subject takes something to be true:

> *Having an opinion* is taking something to be true with the consciousness that it is subjectively *as well as* objectively insufficient. If taking something to be true is only subjectively sufficient and is . . . held to be objectively

> insufficient, then it is called *believing*. Finally, when taking something to be true is both subjectively and objectively sufficient, it is called *knowing*. (A822/B850)

At first, it may seem that there is not much difference between persuasion and opinion. From the third-person perspective, it is possible to ascribe an opinion to someone and think that he or she is merely persuaded of something. But Kant is speaking from the first-person perspective when he claims that having an opinion brings with it an awareness of its insufficiencies. He places opinion on a reflective level, while persuasion remains unreflective. This is explicitly formulated in the *Jäsche Logic*, where we read that persuasion is "uncertain cognition [that] appears . . . to be certain," whereas "opinion . . . is an uncertain cognition, *insofar as it is held to be uncertain*" (*LL* 577; 9:73). Both persuasion and opinion are uncertain, but only opinion is self-consciously uncertain, according to Kant. And whereas he claims that persuasion is illusory in taking subjective grounds as objective (see A820/B848), no such claim is made about holding an opinion.

Because persuasion is based either on subjective needs and private interests or on historical and cultural influences that are assimilated and taken for granted, it remains unreflective. This same charge will be made later against prejudices, when we come to relate them to what we claim to know. Opining in effect begins the process of reflection by recognizing that much of which we are persuaded lacks justification. Because of this self-awareness, opinion is tentative and suspends the presumption of persuasion. The unusual way Kant characterizes opining makes it a reflective pause on the way to knowing. Here reflection is a preparatory exploratory activity and not the assertion of a point of view, as some have claimed.[21] It is an initial act of orienting oneself.

Believing is the second intermediary step in moving to the certainty that Kant thinks is needed for knowledge. Again, some may regard belief as merely a kind of persuasion. But for Kant there are also more reflective beliefs that bring with them a conviction that exceeds the private presumption of persuasion. Such beliefs should not be dismissed as illusory if they are rooted in the subject's rational capacities. Yet because the conviction of reflective belief is rooted in our own reason, it is still only "subjectively sufficient" (A822/B850). Thus, Kant considers belief in the existence of God reasonable even though no valid rational argument for it is available to us. He refutes all the theoretical proofs for the existence of God, yet claims that there is justification for saying "I am morally certain" (A829/B857) that there is a God. Kant writes that the belief in God "is so interwoven with my moral disposition" that I do not need to worry that this conviction "can ever be torn away from me" (A829/B857).

The conviction of such a rational belief provides a strongly felt moral certainty, but still lacks theoretical certainty because it cannot be communicated to others by means of a rational proof.

It has already been made clear that the theoretical certainty that comes with knowing must be communicable. To know something to be true requires that the subjective sufficiency of "conviction (for myself)" be matched by an objective sufficiency or "certainty (for everyone)" (A822/B850). Thus, the final step in assessing universally valid cognition as legitimate intersubjective knowledge demands that the judgmental assent of one's own conviction be confirmed by the judgmental consent of others. To cite Kant's own words, "knowledge must be communicable and demands concurrence [*Beystimmung*]" (*RL* 2489, 16:391). For objectively meaningful cognition to also count as a truth-claim, it must have been subjected to the scrutiny of the community of human investigators. What defines knowing as the final mode of holding something to be true is that one's own subjective conviction about it has also been recognized as intersubjectively certain through communication.

What we take to be true in knowing is something about which we must be certain that the community of investigators agrees. Kant's theory of truth-assessment (*Fürwahrhalten*) can thus be summarized as follows: knowing (*Wissen*) is cognition that has attained the certainty (*Gewissheit*) of being confirmed by the community of science (*Wissenschaft*). Opining is a kind of problematic judging, firm belief or conviction amounts to assertoric judging, and knowing is apodictic or necessary judging.

Opining, believing, and knowing are the three subjective modes of assenting to or taking something as true, but only the latter adds systematic order to cognition. Knowing is thus cognition that satisfies both the discursive *meaning* standards of the understanding and the systematic *truth* demands of reason. In judgmental terms, we can say that cognition schematizes or imaginatively *realizes* (*realisiert*) meaning claims, which knowing rationally *actualizes* (*verwirklicht*) as truth-claims. The objective validation necessary for meaningful cognition must be supplemented by an intersubjective validation for knowing. For what Kant demands of knowledge is an actual "agreement with the object, with regard to which, consequently, the judgments of every understanding must agree" (A820/B848). Unlike the objective validity of the cognition of the "Transcendental Analytic," the intersubjective validity of knowledge in the "Canon of Pure Reason" cannot be deduced in a priori terms, for it requires the judgmental testing of evidence and communal consent.

Kant's full progression from (1) persuasion as unreflective belief to (2) opinion as a reflective suspension of belief to (3) conviction as rational belief to (4) the final certainty of knowing, will need to be examined further to consider the medial factors that influence the outcome of what we claim to know based on what has been cognized. What Kant describes as the stage of persuasion in the "Canon" is discussed in his lectures on logic under the heading of prejudices that have been assimilated. But before relating what we have learned about overcoming persuasion to the problem of dealing with prejudices, to which we will return in the next chapter, let us conclude by briefly reflecting on Kant's ideal of knowledge and consider where it applies.

So far knowledge has been referred to a cognizable phenomenal world, not to the dialectical speculations of pure reason. Some scholars claim that Kant also allows for knowledge that exceeds sensible experience and is about things-in-themselves. According to Desmond Hogan, "Kant's later writings deny theoretical knowledge of the reality of absolute freedom, but they persistently affirm knowledge of that reality (both '*Wissen*' and '*Erkenntnis*') on practical grounds."[22] Freedom was one of three theoretical ideas outlined in the *Critique of Pure Reason*, the others being God and immortality. The *Critique of Practical Reason* does indeed assert that "among all the ideas of speculative reason, freedom is also the only one the possibility of which we *know* [*wissen*] a priori, though without having insight into it, because it is the condition of the moral law, which we do know" (*C2* 3–4; 5:4). This is an indirect knowing without insight. Our practical knowledge of freedom may have the certainty associated with theoretical knowledge, but not the rational insight that was defined in chapter 3 as the sixth level of cognition. We have access to the subjective reality of our own freedom, but we do not actually experience it in a way that can be explained. The practical knowing of freedom that Hogan points to involves a paradoxical knowing about what is theoretically unknowable about ourselves. Although we can claim to know that we are free because it is a condition of morality, we cannot claim the same about the ideas of immortality and God, for they are not conditions of morality. They would seem to be objects, not of practical knowledge, but of practical belief.

Concerning the idea of God, Andrew Chignell claims that Kant also allows for a "theoretical" belief in his existence that is, however, "non-epistemic" in not being about the phenomenal world.[23] We saw that the discussion of belief in the "Canon of Pure Reason" was mostly about the moral interest that makes it rational to believe in God. But Kant also added that there "is in merely theoretical judgments an analogue of practical judgments" (A825/B853) where belief can arise. Although Kant's example of such a theoretical belief was about possible inhabitants of phenomenal planets, which makes it in principle knowable, Chignell chooses to make it "non-epistemic" by extending it to things-in-themselves. He relates this theoretical belief to what Kant considers the only possible argument for demonstrating the existence of God. Kant acknowledges that the argument is

> not apodictically certain because it cannot demonstrate the objective necessity of such an archetypal being. But it can demonstrate the subjective necessity of *accepting* it. It can in no way be refuted because it has its ground in the nature of human reason which makes it *necessary* that I accept a being that is the ground of everything that is possible. Without it I could not cognize what makes something possible. (*VRT*, 28:1034)

Although such an argument falls short of providing either theoretical or practical knowledge as defined by Kant, it offers something more than the theoretical belief that Chignell assumes it to be. Belief is merely assertoric and "provides a conviction that is not communicable" (*RL* 2489, 16:391). But the acceptance of God as the subjectively necessary ground of everything should be communicable if, as Kant says, it has its ground in the nature of human reason. I therefore propose that Kant's argument for a subjectively necessary ground of everything that is possible can be located at the a priori level of rational cognitive comprehension that we found in the lectures on logic. It was shown in chapter 3 that Kant regards comprehension as the highest degree of cognition. Comprehension can make things sufficiently distinct and intelligible for human purposes to amount to more than the assertoric conviction of belief without attaining the apodictic certainty of knowledge. The supposed claim to comprehend God's existence may be at the level of a mere deistic theoretical principle, but it is universalizable, whereas the more full-blooded practical theistic belief defended in the *Critique of Pure Reason* is not. Since Kant spoke of comprehension as being simultaneously theoretical and practical, it would seem to provide a good middle ground between Hogan's claim that we can *know* our freedom as the *ratio essendi* of the moral law and Chignell's incommunicable theoretical *belief* in God. Comprehension can make sense of both the ideas of freedom and of God by granting them a cognitive basis while delimiting their full knowability. Kant's third idea, of the immortality of the soul, is harder to defend rationally and would seem to remain a moral belief at best.

Kant's conception of comprehension is important because it is not merely a kind of reasoning to be used on the way to knowledge, but also makes possible a mode of judging that can go beyond the bounds of what finite beings can know to chart our wider bearings through a worldview.

6

The Modal Categories of Empirical Inquiry and the Limits of What Can Actually Be Known

Replacing Prejudices with Preliminary and Provisional Judgments

This is the last chapter that will examine how the three levels of cognitive intake contribute to the overall world-picture we form during the course of our lives. I have concentrated so far on how we move up from the assimilative to the acquisitive and appropriative levels. Now I will also show how Kant's claims about the modal categories of acquisitive intake can shed further light on the mistakes we can fall into at the assimilative level.

The nine categories that have been discussed so far place principled bounds (*Grenzen*) on what we can claim to cognitively comprehend and ultimately know. The last three modal categories that I will examine here differ in that they allow us to take into account the empirical circumstances that place limits (*Schranken*) on what we do actually know.[1] The dynamical categories of (1) substance and attribute, (2) cause and effect, and (3) simultaneity and reciprocity discussed earlier as the "Analogies of Experience" set *self-imposed conceptual bounds* on what kinds of relations objects of experience can be subjected to. The final three categories, namely the modal categories of possibility, actuality, and necessity, are called "Postulates of Empirical Thought" and establish the *external limits* of what is cognizable. They do not further determine the meaningful relations that can exist among objects of experience, "but rather express only their relation to the faculty of cognition" (A219/B266). Just as the middle dynamical category of causality was pivotal, so now the middle modal category of actuality is crucial. For objectively speaking, to cite Norman Kemp Smith, all "truth, even that of *a priori* principles, is merely *de facto*. . . . Only by reference to the actual . . . can possibility and necessity be defined."[2] The distinction between the three modal categories turns out to be a merely subjective one. Objectively or cognitively viewed, the categories converge: necessity is defined by the causal determinants of what is actual, and what is experientially possible must also be actualizable. However, in the *Critique of Judgment* we will see that when judgment becomes its own reflective power rather than being determined by the understanding, these three modalities need not hinge as much on actuality. There a fourth modality of contingency will be added, allowing reflective judgment to probe beyond the boundaries of what is known. The three modal categories of the first *Critique* have the mere negative task of defining the fixed limits that are imposed on empirical thought. As was indicated earlier, boundaries are in some sense self-imposed and may therefore be reflectively revisable.

Kemp Smith elaborates as follows on the limits set by the postulates of empirical thought: "Experiences capable of being actual for one individual may be merely possible for another. And what is merely actual to one observer may by others be comprehended in its necessitating connections."[3] Although the first *Critique* does not go into detail about the problem posed by the different exposure that each of us has to the world, it is acknowledged briefly when Kant discussed persuasion as a product of psychological limitations and shortcomings. But the problem of persuasion is more widespread. We are rhetorically persuaded of many things through the social pressures exerted by our surroundings. This more general problem is discussed in some detail in Kant's lectures on logic about the prejudices we inherit. Although this problem is not directly discussed in the *Critique of Pure Reason*, we have prepared for it by characterizing the level of intuitive intake as also involving medial modes of assimilation that make use of different natural languages conveying information.

The prejudices that we assimilate from our surroundings are prejudgments that resemble the private persuasion that was discussed in the "Canon of Pure Reason." Like persuasion, prejudices are unreflective, but there are other reasons why they are problematic. They often narrow our perspective on life by drawing restrictive distinctions, which when applied to human relations can lead to us-them oppositions. Moreover, they become ingrained and accepted as commonplaces that can generate further unreflective beliefs. Prejudices tend to be group-based and are hard to change. There is, however, another type of pre-judgment that Kant contrasts with prejudices (*Vorurtheile*), namely, *vorläufige Urtheile*, standardly translated as "provisional judgments." To bring out the important transitional role of these *vorläufige Urtheile* in empirical inquiry, I will call them "preliminary" rather than "provisional" judgments. Provisionality is really a hallmark of reflective judgments, as we will see later.

The preliminary judgments used in empirical inquiry play a transitional role by allowing us to test prejudices by means of reflection. I already spoke of the logical reflection needed for the formation of empirical concepts. This involved the comparative consideration of our representations both among themselves and with our consciousness. However, preliminary judgments will introduce a slightly different sense of reflection that has to do with a deferral of judgment.

Suspending Prejudices into Preliminary Judgments and the Provisional Inferences of Reflective Judgment

Reflection on the meaning-content of a prejudice can turn a principle that is blindly held to be true into a preliminary judgment which serves as a maxim for investigating the truth. While a principle claims to be generally applicable, a maxim is a rule that directs a particular subject's inquiry into a specific matter. A preliminary judgment "is one in which I represent that while there are more grounds for the truth of a thing than against it, these grounds still do not suffice for a determining or a definite judgment, through which I simply decide for the truth" (*LL* 577; 9:74). A preliminary judgment can transform a state of being persuaded by outside influences into a state of being on the lookout for evidence that is more convincing. It is a neutralizing response to what is initially accepted as plausible on the basis of persuasion and transforms it into a possible hypothesis for investigation. As such, a preliminary judgment is like the opining we discussed earlier, and in the *Jäsche Logic* they are actually equated. An opinion in Kant's neutral sense is like a "premonition of truth" that serves as the basis for empirical inquiry. It suspends the "plausibility [*Scheinbarkeit*]" that is merely a "quantity of persuasion" in order to set the stage for the "probability [*Wahrscheinlichkeit*]" (*LL* 583; 9:82) that we expect from empirical cognition. The prejudices of which we are persuaded have a mere subjective plausibility that investigation then attempts to replace with probability, for which the grounds are "objectively valid," although not objectively sufficient to amount to certainty.

It is important to note that in the lectures on logic, Kant distinguishes between the *rational certainty* of knowledge discussed earlier and *empirical certainty*. Whereas rational certainty in the *Critique of Pure Reason* was apodictic, empirical certainty in the logic lectures is merely assertoric. In explicating the latter, Kant focuses mainly on how empirical investigation settles for conviction in many cases. Thus we read in the *Jäsche Logic* that "to be able to pass from mere persuasion to conviction, we must first of all reflect, i.e., see to which power of cognition a cognition belongs, and then investigate. . . . Many remain with persuasion. Some come to reflection, few to investigation" (*LL* 576; 9:73). The ability to pass from the persuasion of prejudice to the conviction of proper judgment demands that prejudices must first be called into question and neutralized into preliminary judgments. This can be reformulated as a transition from the actual persuasion of prejudice to the reflection of a preliminary judgment that makes empirical investigation possible. This confirms my view that the reflection involved in preliminary judgment is not to be equated with reflective judgment, as is often done. The reflection of preliminary judgment is a process of comparison that puts the claim made in a prejudice into a wider context to prepare for further inquiry. It withholds the assent that normally attaches to judgments, whether they be determinant or reflective. Preliminary judgments can be considered as tentative hypotheses for subsequent investigation. Here reflective comparisons can suffice to test prejudicial generalizations by searching for both confirming and counter-instances. The broader kind of generalizing inquiry associated with reflective judgment is discussed more than fifty pages later in the lectures on logic under the heading of "Inferences of the Power of Judgment" (*LL* 625; 9:131–32). Like reflection, reflective judgment is comparative, but it goes much further by searching for the "common ground" (*LL* 626; 9:132) among similar things. Logically, reflective judgment "infers from many to all things of a kind, or from many determinations and properties, in which things of one kind agree, to the remaining ones, insofar as they belong to the same principle" (*LL* 626; 9:132). In the former case reflective judgment is inductive, while in the latter it specifies by means of analogies.

There is an important late *Reflexion* by Kant where he claims that the determinant judgments of the understanding are *immediate inferences* applying concepts to particulars and that reflective judgments go further and are *mediate inferences* like those of reason (see *RL* 3200, 16:709). Accordingly, reflective judgments are "inferences to what is provisional [*Schlüsse zu Vorläufigen*]," that is, far-ranging inferences with a provisional scope; they "do not aim for determinant judgments" (*RL* 3200, 16:709) but go beyond them. This makes it clear that reflective judgments are not the preliminary judgments (*vorläufige Urteile*) of empirical inquiry that anticipate determinant judgments of the understanding. Instead, reflective judgments can give provisional estimations about overarching principles of classification. Therefore it is misleading for Longuenesse to claim that in reflective judgments "the effort of the activity of judgment to form concepts fails."[4] Reflective judgments involve more than the reflection relevant to the formation of empirical concepts and the reflection needed to suspend and overcome prejudices; they are about conceptualizing a principled way of organizing groups of things. When reflective judgments are applied to the empirical search for truth, they function at the highest level, and in the *Critique of Judgment* their capacity to consider things in wider contexts will be made evident and transcendentally justified.

In the search for "empirical certainty" (*LL* 627; 9:133) we can thus chart a progression from (1) the persuasive force of prejudices and (2) the reflective pause of preliminary judgments to (3) the investigative outcome of determinant judgments to (4) the provisional principles of classification made possible by reflective judgment. It is important to note that Kant wants preliminary judgments to only temporarily defer from making a determinant judgment. Such a temporary deferral amounts to a critical, merely neutral, suspension of judgment. A more permanent refraining is called a negative or skeptical doubt, which Kant does not endorse.

The Sources and Kinds of Prejudice

A prejudice is a belief that has come to be accepted in a noncognitive or unreflective way. So far I have discussed prejudices mainly as obstacles to reliable empirical inquiry about the world. But prejudices can also warp our life-attitudes more deeply. There could be something in the emotional makeup of some individuals that inclines them to be persuaded that an assertion is true. This corresponds to the first of three main sources of prejudice listed by Kant, namely, inclination. The other two sources of prejudice he mentions are imitation and custom. Whereas private inclination is a psychological source of prejudice, both imitation and custom point to external sociohistorical sources. In the *Blomberg Logic,* Kant is quoted as saying that inclination leads us to investigate things "only from the side where we wish that it were so and not otherwise. . . . there is simply no reflection . . ." (*LL* 132; 24:167). Here we see that the subjective comparison of preliminary reflection requires us to critically assess whether our own preferences might have influenced our views and beliefs. If a belief has been held since childhood, our tendency to imitate others might account for it. Thus Kant is quoted as saying, "In youth one does not yet have any skill in judging, hence one allows oneself to be driven by imitation, and one quickly accepts as certain and undoubted what is maintained by others" (*LL* 131; 24:166).

The third source of prejudices, which Kant calls "custom [*Gewohnheit*]," refers to what we assimilate from our local habitat as well as the habits we ourselves develop over time. Concerning the former, Kant says: "Almost everyone, be he who he may, esteems the fashions and customs of his country or his fatherland as the best and most proper" (*LL* 131; 24:165). Here we tend to be quite provincial, preferring what we are familiar with from our local community. But the preferences that we contingently inherit only become prejudices if it is assumed that they should be generally followed. Kant claims that prejudices are more than particular premature judgments in that they tend to impose themselves as "general rules for judging" (*LL* 130; 24:164).

It is important to examine prejudices because they can be deeply rooted persuasions functioning as rules that generate further premature judgments. Just as we saw persuasion to be illusory in holding subjective conditions to be objective, so a prejudice can be illusory in holding something contingently local to be general. But not all illusions can be overcome, for Kant thinks that there are certain unavoidable empirical and transcendental illusions. Therefore, it is mistaken to think that Kant expects to eradicate all human prejudices. Prejudices are so pervasive that it would be unreasonable to expect that they can all be eradicated. The main thing that defines the process of enlightenment is to free ourselves from the "greatest prejudice of all . . . i.e., superstition" (*C3* 174; 5:294). Kant also admits that what "is accepted by means of a prejudice . . . is not yet on that account always false as to its matter" (*LL* 133; 24:168). Therefore he warns against having a "prejudice against prejudices" in such a way as to "reject everything that has arisen through prejudices" (*LL* 133; 24:169). Instead of immediately rejecting each and every prejudice, we should "test them first and investigate well whether there may not yet be something good to be found in them" (*LL* 133; 24:169). But as we will see, this does not mean that there are any good prejudices. Whatever good is to be found in any prejudice must be extracted and converted into an explicit judgment that has been tested.

According to critical philosophy, nothing should be taken at face value or as mere input. In today's digital world, we would need to expand Kant's sense input into a broader medial informational input. Reconciling the way we access informational inputs with the way cognition is constituted and critically justified is a more difficult problem than ever. That is why the sensible content that is assimilated and whose perceptual marks are then representationally analyzed was distinguished from the synthetic intuitive and conceptual modes of acquiring cognition that epistemic scholarship mostly focuses on. Even though the scope of what each of us is exposed to is limited, it is important to logically analyze it for its internal consistency. In order to expand this limited perceptual scope, Kant was not unwilling to appeal to our imagination as a way of questioning provincial habits of belief and our private prejudices. What is imagined can also become a judgmental resource.

Another reason why analysis of the assimilative perceptual level is important is that Kant's assumption of a convergence between our ordinary perceptual experience of the world and the mathematical natural-science conception of nature is no longer accepted. Both were thought to conform to Euclidean geometry in the eighteenth century, but that is no longer the case after the introduction of alternative geometries and the curved spatiotemporal continuum of general relativity. These developments lead many to think that Kant's so-called Copernican revolution has been left behind. It is possible, however, to distinguish between doctrinal aspects of Kant's philosophy and his more general critical approach, which is adaptable to new circumstances.

In fact, Kant never claimed to have instituted a Copernican revolution. Instead, he proposed a general analogue to the general Copernican hypothesis that the apparent movement of the Sun around the Earth is a perceptual illusion created by the way we observers move with the earth (see Bxxii). His counterpart working hypothesis was to propose that our mental activities also affect and shape the way phenomena appear to us. Similarly, we can begin to expose the limiting illusions of our own prejudices by reflecting on our own activity of belief-formation and judging.

This kind of self-reflection comes into focus when we see Kant examining different kinds of prejudices. He distinguishes, for example, between the prejudice of modernity and the prejudice of antiquity. Young people tend to favor what is new and lean toward the prejudice of modernity. Those who pursue the empirical sciences, as well as those who value genius and wit, are also inspired by the idea of modernity. However, the prejudice of antiquity is much more pervasive and can be linked to the other two sources of prejudice: imitation as following the past and custom as continuing the past. Kant defines the prejudice of antiquity as "grounded on esteem toward the *old*. What survives of the old . . . always contains the illusion of being good, for one infers that it would be hard for it to have survived and to have come down to us if it were not good and were of no value" (*LL* 141; 24:179). Traditions can be the repository of important truths, but if we accept any of them on authority, we make our reason passive. This would allow reason as an active principle of conviction to be replaced by prejudice as a blind principle of persuasion. Even if the content of a prejudice were to be true, its form would be false.

These discussions of inherited prejudices, persuasion, and conviction make it clear that we bring both implicit assumptions and explicit presuppositions to what we think about the world. Some presuppositions function formally as a priori cognitive conditions that can be schematized in terms of universally anticipated meaning-structures. But when we assimilate prejudices, they come with more local and concrete assumptions about the content of reality. It was shown in chapter 5 that rationally our judgmental assent to cognitive meaning-structures demands systematic verification and the consent of the scientific community. It is often the case, however, that our judgmental assent allows itself to be influenced by a preexisting consent which derives from inherited prejudices and even from so-called common sense. And as we relate ordinary experience to scientific cognition, some of the assumptions that we draw from the consent based on our life-situation and social involvements will need to be either changed or eliminated.

In chapter 2, I considered how Kant distinguished between an analytical distinctness of logical thought and a synthetic distinctness of experiential cognition. Whereas the latter kind of distinctness provided a model for Kant's new transcendental account of acquiring objective experience and scientific cognition, the traditional Cartesian logical methods of attaining analytical distinctness nevertheless remain relevant for gaining clarity about how our prejudices enter into this cognitive framework. Whereas Kant's transcendental conditions of cognition incorporated a progressive sequence of reflective opining and believing into the trajectory of attaining certain communal knowledge, for individual knowers it is necessary to also submit to a regressive analysis of possible local prejudices in order to clear the way for sound empirical judgments that attain a high degree of "probability" as an "approximation to certainty" (*LL* 583; 9:82). The stages in the empirical process of truth-assessment delineate a movement beyond the mere plausibility of persuasion and prejudice through the preliminary likelihood of opinions and hypotheses to a probability that is high enough to justify conviction, but not certainty.

Kant's extensive examination of prejudices in his lectures on logic reinforces the claim that he acknowledges what I have called an assimilative level of human consciousness. It also explains why some of the functions of logic are considered cathartic. Whatever the peculiarities that affect our sensibility as individual human beings, the task is to minimize their effect on how we come to apperceive the world. This is further confirmed by Kant's own language of the "epigenesis of pure reason" (B167) in the second edition of the *Critique of Pure Reason*: reason must add its own contributions to what is genetically derived.

The Genesis-Epigenesis Distinction

It is important to note that the term "epigenesis" refers to a biological theory that is more thoroughly discussed in the *Critique of Judgment* and which will be examined in chapter 12. As a biological term, "epigenesis" adds a physiological dimension to the levels of sense input and cognitive intake that we discussed earlier. From this perspective, what is assimilated is not merely about how the soul and mind process sensible and other medial inputs, but also about what the physiology of the brain contributes. This opens up the consideration of potential causal pathologies, which Kant worried about often.[5]

By the "epigenesis of pure reason" Kant means that our cognition of the world is "not all borrowed from experience" (B166). There are also elements of cognition that are "self-thought" (B167) or self-acquired. Thus, the categories of the understanding are not mere "subjective predispositions for thinking implanted in us . . . in such a way that their use would agree exactly with the laws of nature along which experience runs" (B167). These contingent natural laws governing the genetic development of the human brain and how it functions do condition us, but they do not ground the critical project of understanding nature as objectively and necessarily lawful. The epigenesis of reason upholds the thesis that however our brain functions in physiologically processing sense data, our mind has the epigenetic power to contribute a spontaneous form to those data.

The genesis-epigenesis distinction brings out that the sensible empirical inputs which we have discussed so far do not reach consciousness directly from our sense organs but are mediated by the brain. What Kant just referred to as the background for his discussion of epigenesis is the way our brains condition our consciousness. The neurological conditions that we are born with provide a kind of hard-wiring, and this will affect the ways in which data come bundled. But all this is subject to further conceptual organization. And although the neural network that processes our sense impressions can be said to provide an intermediary medium that influences our consciousness, it does not enter consciousness itself. Since our sense organs offer us a multiplicity of discrete inputs, what Kant refers to as the original synopsis of sense in the A "Deduction" can be seen as the result of the way our brain processes these stimuli in light of our biological or animal needs. What I have called the assimilative level of cognition could be said to straddle the genesis-epigenesis divide, as when Kant says at A97 that "receptivity can make cognition possible only if combined with spontaneity," namely, synthetic activity. Here he refers to the three subjective syntheses of apprehension, reproduction, and recognition that satisfy the more discerning human needs for clarity and distinctness. The acquisitive level of the apperceptive syntheses of the B "Deduction" that provide an objective and determinate understanding of the world is clearly epigenetic and ultimately invokes the judgmental responsibility of the individual knower.

Of course, the empirical elements of our experience are not limited to the physiological stimuli that our own brains process as we observe the things around us. From childhood on we learn from interactions with our parents, playmates, teachers, coworkers, friends, and our communal surroundings. All this gives us access to opinions, beliefs, and conventions that we assimilate in a not merely passive way. Even children filter out what they are indifferent to and focus on what interests them as being either favorable or unfavorable. Assimilation involves the receptive filtering of what is inherited and the apprehensive intake of what is perceived, which can then be analyzed logically, as was done in chapters 2 and 3. In order to communicate with others, we could still rely on the comparative marks that were perceptually assimilated and relate them to what can be universally apperceived in conceptual terms. This unavoidable dependence on empirical conditions places *external limits* on the scope of what we can actually know.

Regarding the *self-imposed bounds of critique*, we can only claim to intuitively *cognize* phenomenal objects and must restrict ourselves to mere abstract *thought* about things-in-themselves. Kant reinforces this bound by contrasting the human understanding to an archetypal or divine understanding "which through its self-consciousness could supply to itself the manifold of intuition" (B138) without any act of synthesis. For such an intellect, just to think of something would be to bring it into existence. This could be called an intuitive or creative intellect. But the fact that our intellect is not that powerful does not mean that it cannot acquire access to the actual and independent things that appear to us in the physical world. Kant's idealism has sometimes been misunderstood to mean that phenomenal objects are merely mental entities cut off from the things out there in the physical world. This is another version of psychological idealism that conflates the actual things out there in the world with the things-in-themselves which Kant claimed we cannot know. Although he sometimes refers to *Objecte* as representational or mental, the *Gegenstände* of apperception stand over against us. In fact, Kant allows us to distinguish between phenomenal "things themselves [*Dingen selbst*]" (A281/B337) that we can intuitively cognize in experience and what they would be as noumenal things-in-themselves (*Dingen-an-sich*) as projected by our reason. To know things-in-themselves would require intellectual intuition, which we do not possess. But we can cognize things themselves in this world as apperceived phenomenal objects. Because we access phenomenal things themselves from without, they do not count as things-in-themselves whose essence is to be intelligible from within.

When disputing Leibniz, who thought that we could know the inner determinations of a drop of water, Kant is careful to call it a "*Ding an sich selbst*" (A272/B328). Although this is also translated as a "thing in itself" (A272/B328), it would be better to distinguish it as a "thing in and by itself," that is, a phenomenal thing taken out of its spatial worldly context. For Kant, Leibniz's isolated drop is an indiscernible or pseudo-object (*Gegenstand*) of the understanding that falsely "intellectualizes appearances" (A271/B327). There is no reason to search for the inner determinations of phenomenal objects to the extent that we cognize their mechanistic behavior, as in classical physics. Kant will, however, find it necessary to go from the outside in when it comes to organic phenomena and make sense of their immanent purposiveness.

According to Kant, our reason can only think of a noumenal thing-in-itself as a negative or limiting object (*Object*). To positively intuit a thing-in-itself would be to know it *from the inside,* as it were. In line with this metaphor, Kant is willing to speak of God as penetrating the core of our being and knowing more about our inner motives than we do. Only an archetypal or divine intellect could intuit a thing-in-itself apart from any external relations. We can only intuit phenomenal things themselves and cognize them as objects in relation to other objects. No phenomenal *object = thing itself* can be understood *in itself or by itself* because nothing can be sensibly intuited as being self-sufficient or self-caused. All natural objects are conditioned or externally caused.

Thus, the claim that the things themselves as we experience them are phenomenal does not make them privately ours. By cognizing them as objects through relational categories, they become in principle publicly accessible. The shared ways that finite intellects apperceive objects allow the sciences to assign them universally valid formal and relational properties. And to fully know them as defined by empirical judgments requires that we have been in communication with other researchers. For as Kant writes, truth as "agreement with the object" has as its "touchstone" the "possibility of communicating it and finding it to be valid for the reason of every human being to take it to be true" (A820/B848).

It is possible to accept this reading of what knowledge of things themselves entails without endorsing the other half of Kant's account. It is reasonable to dismiss the idea of an archetypal intellect as pure speculation and dispense with the ideal of a noumenal thing-in-itself as well. One could then argue that although we know things in this world only from the outside, we human beings are not mere things and can make sense of ourselves from the inside. There is some truth in that, but insofar as this is the case, Kant's reply will be to reiterate what was claimed earlier about the transcendental unity of apperception, namely, that it ascertains only *that* we are, not *what* we are. Kant would insist that we do not really know ourselves as we are in ourselves. Most of what we know about ourselves is how we appear to ourselves phenomenally, and as we will see in part 2, this leaves room for self-deception and many doubts about the power of introspection. It will lead Kant to insist that we can only come to comprehend ourselves by going from the inside out and regarding ourselves as part of a larger reciprocal context (see chapter 11). And to the extent that we then bring this reciprocal perspective back into ourselves, we can partake of the noumenal in a moral sense. This allows Kant to refashion the phenomenal-noumenal split as two ways of approaching our world. Similarly, he will coordinate the ideas of going from the inside out and from the outside back in when he attempts to characterize the immanent purposiveness of organic reciprocity. But these efforts are heuristic and regulative; they allow us to characterize how organisms function without constitutively explaining their behavior.

We will conclude the epistemological first part of this work with the following summarizing chart of the levels of awareness that are in play in human experience as Kant comprehends it.

Passive Affectedness: animal sentience or awareness / brain processing / sense impressions / synopsis of sense / soul as modifiable by the behavior of others.

Receptive and Selective Assimilation: human perception and acquaintance / representational comparison and logical analysis / formal subjective space-time and medial intuitive content / prejudices and preliminary judgments / the *anima* level of soul capable of modifying itself, and to be heuristically ascribed to organisms.

Active Acquisition: the conscious syntheses of apprehension and reproduction in the "Subjective Deduction" that raise representational intuitive content to the level of objective intuitive content for the understanding / the productive syntheses of conceptual recognition in the "Objective Deduction" / the transcendental unity of apperception / objective cognition / determinant judgments / the reactive human *animus* and the active conscious level of mind relevant to social and moral issues.

Reciprocal Appropriation: comprehension / knowing / reason / *mens* or spirit / being self-active / what will be explored more as reflective judgment and normative questions of legitimacy.

At each of the above levels of awareness—the mere affectedness of input and the assimilation, acquisition, and appropriation of intake—I have added at least one analogue that will become relevant when we come to deal with Kant's writings on morality, aesthetics, anthropology, and cosmopolitanism in the next part of this work. What should be apparent from this summary is that we have only seen Kant develop our initial outlook on life into a kind of cognitive world-picture. An overall world-view will require not just knowledge about the natural world, but also judging how we should respond to it and its other inhabitants. Whereas part 1 of this book focused mostly on the assimilative and acquisitive levels of cognition, the main task of part 2 will be to fill in the last level of reflective appropriation.

A worldview requires a systematic cognitive understanding of the natural world, but it also aims for an evaluative comprehension of it from our standpoint. This is why an orientational approach to the world is needed. We must recontextualize the world as one in which we are involved in practical terms, as Kant makes clear in his lectures on anthropology. A worldview must express how we are engaged with other human beings—not only morally and politically, but also socially and aesthetically. These will become our concerns now.

Part 2

Comprehending and Contextualizing the Human World

7

Seeking Practical Resolutions for Irresolvable Theoretical Antinomies

In the "Transcendental Dialectic" of the *Critique of Pure Reason,* Kant admits that reason aims to comprehend the world absolutely from beginning to end, but in doing so it becomes entangled in antinomies that cannot be positively or objectively resolved. His response is to in effect dissolve these theoretical antinomies and to then seek solutions on the basis of practical reason. But as we follow Kant in this approach in part 2, I will show that practical reason can only solve the problem of completing our worldview by means of subjective maxims that demand resolutions of choice from us. And in setting the right priorities for ourselves, we will need to call for support from judgment to do so. Irresolvable rational antinomies can be replaced by reflective amphibolies that are soluble, but only if we learn to properly contextualize the human world. As I will argue in chapters 10 and 16, amphibolies are orientational confusions that can be resolved through transcendental reflection and good judgment.

The Metaphysical Antinomies

All four of the antinomies of the dialectic of pure reason examine the possibility of arriving at an "absolute completeness" (see A415/B443) that goes beyond the more formal systematic completeness that the canon of critical reason was able to provide. The first antinomy demands a decision about the question of whether the world as a whole is finite or infinite. Did it have a beginning in time, and is it bounded in space, or not? (see A426–27/B454–55). Kant argues that this very question is based on an illusion, namely, that the world as the horizon of all phenomenal objects is measurable as a given totality in the way that objects are. The fallacious assumption here is that if the conditioned is given, then the whole series of all conditions is also "given [*gegeben*]." But this totality of conditions does not coexist in the present and therefore can only be projected through a regress that will always "be posed [*aufgegeben*] as a task" (A508/B536). Kant attempts to resolve the antinomy by dissolving it, that is, by claiming that the question of a finite or infinite regress in the phenomenal series of experiential givens is an inadmissible one. There is no constitutive or objective solution to this antinomy, only a regulative or subjective solution in terms of how we should proceed in aiming to humanly comprehend the world as a whole. "The question is no longer how big this series of conditions is in itself . . . rather, the question is how we are to institute the empirical regress and how far we are to continue it" (A514/B542). Although Kant does not explicitly appeal to judgment here, in effect we have a subjective maxim of judgment to keep looking for further conditions for what is given in experience as long as it seems reasonable to think that we can learn more. For us it is not an infinite, but an "indeterminate kind of regress [*in indefinitum*]" (A513/B541) that makes sense.

The second antinomy seeks an answer to the question of whether composite substances in the world can be resolved into simple parts or not. Although we saw Kant maintain that the regress from the conditioned to its prior conditions can only proceed *indefinitum,* he now points out that any given whole can be infinitely divided because "the conditions of its possibility . . . are all given along with it" (A523–24/B551–52). But this regress *infinitum* means only that the whole is "divisible to infinity," not that it "consists of infinitely many parts" (A525/B553). Infinite divisibility applies to an appearance as a mathematical *quantum continuum,* not to an appearance as an organized body or *quantum discretum.* To assume that the member parts of an organized body can in turn be articulated into simple parts, i.e., "that the whole is articulated to infinity—this is something that cannot be thought at all" (A526/B554). Again, this is an antinomy that can only be negatively resolved by pointing to a confusion that renders as unfounded both the thesis maintaining the existence of ultimate simple parts and the antithesis maintaining that "no composite thing in the world consists of simple parts, and nowhere in it does there exist anything simple" (A435/B463). The notion of ultimate simples or monads is not empirically meaningful—we can only make sense of those member parts of an organized whole body that can actually be experienced.

The third antinomy is the most important because it also has moral import. It concerns the question of whether all appearances in the world occur solely in accordance with the causality of the laws of nature, or whether we must also "assume another causality through freedom in order to explain them" (A444/B472). The first two antinomies were called mathematical and dealt with homogeneous series. There both the proposed alternatives were shown to be false. The third and fourth antinomies are called dynamical and consider appearances not merely as part of a spatiotemporal "world" but as actually existing caused occurrences or events in "nature" (see A420/B448). Mathematical series refer only to what is intuitively given in a spatial field, but dynamical series refer to the phenomenal appearances of things, and to that extent need not abstract from their possible relation to things-in-themselves. Although the negative resolution to the first antinomy was to show that an absolute beginning of the world in time makes no sense, the third antinomy raises the different question of whether "in the course of the world different series may begin on their own as far as their causality is concerned," and whether we can "ascribe to the substances in those series the faculty of acting from freedom" (A450/B478). This would allow, not for an "absolute first beginning" as far as time is concerned, but for an "absolute beginning . . . as far as causality is concerned" (A450/B478). The resolution here is partly negative in that material substances as phenomenal things cannot be thought to affect themselves. On the other hand, it cannot positively be ruled out that they could be affected from outside the phenomenal series of which they are a part. Thus, Kant adjudicates that it is possible to satisfy both the demand of the understanding to explain everything in terms of temporal causal conditions and the demand of reason to appeal to an intelligible cause that "could start to act from itself" (A533/B561). In order to reconcile this transcendental idea of freedom or spontaneous causality with the demand of the understanding that every phenomenal event can be accounted for by empirical antecedents, Kant speculates that intelligible or free causes act outside the temporal series of appearances of natural causality while nevertheless having an effect on this series. The causality of freedom offers itself "in two aspects, as intelligible in its action as a thing-in-itself and as sensible in the effects of that action as an appearance in the world of sense" (A538/B566). But it is not made clear why the effects of intelligible action on appearances do not constitute a superfluous or miraculous interference in the natural course of events. Noumenal freedom and phenomenal determinism are both allowed to be true or compatible: coexisting in their respective spheres, as it were. But as Henry Allison acknowledges, their so-called compatibility involves an "incompatibilist conception of freedom"[1] that somehow violates the natural causal continuum.

Although the question of freedom is superfluous when explaining the behavior of material objects, it is essential for understanding the behavior of human subjects. In an attempt to address this, Kant switches from transcendental "freedom in the cosmological sense" (A533/B561) to the idea of an "intelligible cause" (A537/B565). The intelligible is defined as "that in an object of sense which is not itself appearance" (A538/

B566). It is this shift that allows Kant to now supplement the language of appearances and objects with a discourse of "subjects" that have both an "empirical character" and an "intelligible character" (A539/B567). The actions of the former "as appearances, would stand through and through in connection with other appearances in accordance with constant natural laws" (A539/B567). The actions of the latter, that is, our intelligible character, "would not stand under any conditions of time" (A539/B567) whose causality is freedom. The Guyer/Wood translation informs us that in his own copy of the first edition, Kant added a note here asserting that the transcendental "causality" of this intelligible subject's representations derives from "life" as found in the "faculty of desire" or "pure will" (A538/B566n). This shift to a living subject would seem to go beyond the level of a mere mechanical substance without invoking some supervenient thing-in-itself affecting it. Now Kant only needs to appeal to the intelligible will of a living subject. The idea of such an intelligible or noumenal will allows us to "say quite correctly that this active being begins its effect in the sensible world *of itself* [*von selbst*], without its action beginning *in it itself* [*in ihm selbst*]" (A541/B569). Because our intelligible character is not in time, it cannot begin anything, yet Kant thinks that its effect can. "Thus freedom and nature, each in its full meaning, would both be found in the same actions, simultaneously and without any contradiction" (A541/B569). Rather than being an explanation of human freedom, this invocation of simultaneity makes room for the possibility of an instantaneous convergence of the intelligible and empirical. Whether this suffices to overcome the incompatibility of freedom interfering in the natural course of things is not clear, but it allows us to imagine noumenal freedom as reinforcing the temporal processes involved in our decisions and actions. It also sets the stage for moving from transcendental freedom to practical freedom and the power of choice (*Willkühr*).

Before we move on to the practical choices we make in our phenomenal life, there is one more aspect of Kant's appeal to our intelligible character that needs to be considered, namely, the normative dimension that it adds to our self-understanding. It brings out that the causality of reason is really about imposing an ought on us. Thus Kant writes that

> however many natural grounds or sensible stimuli there may be that impel me to *will*, they cannot produce the *ought* but only a willing that is yet far from necessary but rather always conditioned, over against which the ought that reason pronounces sets a measure and a goal, indeed, a prohibition and authorization. (A548/B576)

On this basis, one could say that the causality of our intelligible character does not "work down" from on high to interfere with the causal nexus that conditions us, but allows us to "look up" by means of a "mode of thought" that can judge what ought to happen and what ought not to happen (see A550–51/B578–79). Here judgment serves to bridge the divide between the phenomenal and the noumenal. It makes it possible for our empirical character to not give in to the instinctive mechanisms of its inclinations and resist the temptation to be self-indulgent.

Reconciling Sensible and Intelligible Considerations in Moral Decisions

For a more successful way of thinking about how sensible and intelligible considerations can be reconciled morally, let us look at what Allison has called the "incorporation thesis" that Kant introduces in *Religion within the Boundaries of Mere Reason*. This incorporation thesis allows us to reconcile phenomenal and noumenal considerations by showing how they should function in our decision-making. Instead of attempting to somehow incorporate a noumenal causality into the worldly phenomenal causality without being able to understand it, Kant now considers what goes into human decision-making. No attempt is made to explain what caused someone to act in a certain way. What is at stake here is a judgmental assessment about human intentionality and what enters into a maxim of action. Accordingly, a sensuous inclination to act can determine the rational will (*Wille*) only insofar as it has been incorporated into a chosen maxim of action. That is, as Allison writes, a natural incentive (*Triebfeder*) "is denied any causal efficacy apart from the adoption of a maxim by an agent to act on the basis of that incentive."[2] If we are moved by inclination, it is because we "allow ourselves to be so moved."[3] This is the point where the transcendental freedom to understand what is possible crosses over into the practical freedom to act on the basis of what our reason allows us to project about what ought to be.

Human beings have already been considered in terms of their theoretical transcendental capacity to transform their sense impressions into a manifold of appearances which can be meaningfully structured as an objective world. But at the same time, the categories of the understanding objectify the phenomenal manifestations of ourselves as causally conditioned. As embodied, we are finite phenomenal beings who are limited by the very lawfulness that our mind has the power to legislate formally and fill in empirically in terms of content. Thus we understand that if a bus hits us, our body will be badly injured and we could even die as a result. What our reason adds to this understanding is an awareness of alternatives to what is the case, namely, what could be. It also allows us to judge how best to avoid being hit by buses and cars before we cross the street. Most importantly, it makes it possible for us to call out for help when injured. And as J. S. Mill has pointed out, the fact that we accidentally swallowed a poison does not prevent us from intentionally seeking an antidote. These are undoubtedly the kinds of considerations that led Kant to claim that even though human beings will always be "pathologically *affected* by the moving causes of sensibility," they need not be "pathologically *necessitated*" (A534/B562). As children we are tempted to eat every sweet that comes our way, but as we eventually learn that sweets are bad for our health, we can decide to resist. Thereby we have the ability to limit the natural process of determination to one of conditioning. The empirical conditions that come our way can be countered by other conditions. To return to more Kantian language, reason gives us the power of choice (*Willkühr*) to be watchful and avoid getting in the way of dangerous moving objects, but also to counteract injuries resulting from having been distracted. This more than reactive way of responding to the world is based on the ability to "determine oneself from oneself, independently of necessitation by sensible impulses" (A534/B562). It is to attempt to replace what is with what could be.

So far, I have considered how the empirical and intelligible aspects of human action may be reconciled in prudential terms. The incorporation thesis, however, attempts to reconcile them in the moral terms demanded by practical reason: rethinking what could be with what should be. The incentives that are incorporated into a maxim of action will refer both to our natural predispositions concerned with human self-love and to our recognition of the moral law. Now according to Kant,

> the difference, whether the human being is good or evil, must not lie in the difference between the incentives that he incorporates into his maxim (not in the material of the maxim) but in their subordination (in the form of the maxim): *which of the two he makes the condition of the other.* (*R* 59; 6:36)

Our practical freedom lies in the capacity to recognize that respect for the moral law should take priority over our natural inclinations. Setting priorities lies at the heart of Kant's transcendental philosophy. It also entails that despite what Friedrich Nietzsche claims, Kant does not mandate that we annihilate our inclinations, but that we place some bounds on them.

In chapter 2, reason was contrasted with understanding by its perspicacious capacity to discern systematic relationships among our phenomenal experiences. But for reason to be self-determining, it must go deeper than the phenomenal consciousness that characterizes both our inner and outer sense. One of the distinctive features of Kant's transcendental idealism is that it does not grant inner sense an advantage over outer sense. Both are merely phenomenal. Indeed, inner sense is less reliable than outer experience because it cannot be mathematically measured and objectively verified. Kant thinks that most inner experience is obscure and that introspection is unreliable and can easily turn pathological. Since it is difficult to be sure of what exactly motivates us in our behavior, the incorporation thesis cannot expect us to exclude all inclinations of self-love. To root out all such natural tendencies, many of which are obscure, would be an endless and hopeless task. Thus, the incorporation thesis prescribes that our natural inclinations must be held in check so that they do not take priority over our respect for the moral law.

Inner experience cannot probe the noumenal ground of our being. Yet if we are to determine ourselves, as demanded by practical reason, we must be able to have some transcendental access to our noumenal nature in order to initiate an action outside of the temporal causal series of phenomenal events that defines our everyday experience. It is this noumenal nature that was called our intelligible character, and we will have to see whether Kant's moral and religious writings can be of further help in comprehending it.

Kant's main result in attempting to resolve the third antinomy is to claim that it is *not inconsistent* to claim that there can be events—and more specifically actions—that are both physically conditioned and rationally determined. Since he is here broaching the noumenal ground of what we cognize phenomenally, he cannot arrive at anything beyond a double negative. The same is true for the fourth antinomy, which concerns the question of whether there can be an absolutely necessary being either as part of the world or outside it as its cause. Here Kant considers not only whether there can be a cause that is unconditioned, but also whether there can be a being whose existence is unconditioned. We know that there cannot be such an unconditioned existing being as part of the phenomenal world, but we cannot refute the belief that such a being could exist as "an *ens extramundanum*" (A561/B589). Thus there could be a being like God that necessarily exists. Since Kant denied the validity of all the arguments for the existence of God, including the most rational ontological conception of God as an absolutely necessary being, it is clear that he rules out our knowing that there is such a being with theoretical certainty. But neither can God's existence be refuted, which leaves moral rather than theoretical certainty as a fallback position. Unfortunately, moral certainty is a mode of belief that cannot be shared. According to Kant, our moral disposition may entitle each of us to say, "I am morally certain" that there is a God, but not that "it is morally certain that there is a God" (A829/B857). Moral certainty is really only a private conviction. What made the idea of God's comprehensibility in chapter 5 attractive was the claim that it is rationally sharable—to be sure, only intersubjectively rather than objectively. The question to be dealt with now is whether Kant's practical philosophy can find something that transcends moral belief and religious comprehensibility.

Practical Reasoning

The main difference between theoretical and practical reason is that the latter is purely self-determining. The practical use of reason "is concerned with the determining grounds of the will, which is a faculty either of producing objects corresponding to representations or of determining itself to bring about such objects (whether the physical power is sufficient or not)" (*C2* 12; 5:15). This heightened power of self-determination does, nevertheless, acknowledge a limit. Practical reason can determine our will to choose something that goes against the way we are naturally inclined to act. But it does not have the power to ensure that its decision can physically override the way we are empirically conditioned to act. The practical freedom of the will is self-legislative, but not absolute in executive terms.

There is, however, another advantage that practical reason has over theoretical reason. Since theoretical reason makes determinations about the world that we observe outside ourselves, these determinations are merely formal in nature. They legislate how the natural world is lawfully ordered. Practical reason is more than formal in that it can judge the worth of the content of the maxims that we choose to act on. Maxims are subjective rules whereby subjects set themselves specific material goals. The task of practical reason is to determine whether such maxims of action can be universalized.

This universal test is expressed in Kant's *Groundwork of the Metaphysics of Morals* of 1785 as his categorical imperative: "*act only in accordance with that maxim through which you can at the same time will that it become a universal law*" (*G* 31; 4:421). This rational imperative is then given various formulations that clarify how our moral duties are to be defined. They take what can be understood by the imperative and aim to comprehend how it is to be applied practically. Since there are three formulations, it makes sense to ask whether they conform in any way to the three experiential levels of part 1. The first formulation requires us to take responsibility for our decisions by being formally consistent. It reads: "*act as if the maxim of your action were to become by your will* a universal law of nature" (*G* 31; 4:421). This formulation expects me to imagine what would happen if everyone acted as I plan to act in a particular situation. If I decide that it is useful to make a false promise about repayment in order to get a loan, I need to also consider what would happen if everyone did this. Just the economic chaos that would result makes it obvious that it would be irrational for me to will this. The first formulation does manifest the analytical aspects of the assimilative level of experience and shows that we would be "contradicting our own will" (*G* 34; 4:424) by making exceptions for ourselves and thus undermine the objective *formal nature* of the categorical imperative.

The second formulation of the categorical imperative introduces the synthetic *content* of ends (see *G* 39; 4:431). Whatever material end I intend to pursue, it must be kept in mind that both self and others must be respected as ends in themselves. This translates respect for the law into respect for the dignity of other human subjects as autonomous persons: "*So act that you use humanity, whether in your own person or in the person of any other, always at the same time as an end, never merely as a means*" (*G* 38; 4:429). We may use the help of others in attaining our ends, but there are bounds that do not allow us to use them in a way that reduces them to mere means. Moreover, since the natural end that human beings have is their own happiness, Kant elaborates that this formulation also commits each of us to further the ends and happiness of any other human being as far as we can. In engaging with another person for a project of mine, I must be sure to preserve the dignity of each of us.

The first formulation of the categorical imperative considered the contradictions that could follow from making a self-serving maxim universal. It was *assimilative* by making distinct some of the negative consequences that could accrue to me from a false promise of repayment. The second formulation is more determinant and requires us to more actively *acquire* a sense of the standpoint of others. Now Kant demands that we put ourselves in the place of others, and determines that they may not be treated as objects. When we turn to the third formulation of the categorical imperative, we will find it to be *appropriative* in that it leads us to think of ourselves as participating members of a moral community. This is the most comprehensive formulation and translates respect for the law and for other human subjects into the recognition that it is not just my reason that legislates by deciding the form of the moral law; I must regard "every rational being as *a will giving universal law*" (*G* 40; 4:432). This prepares the ground for what Kant calls the "kingdom of ends" in which we are all co-legislators of the laws. This accords more with the actual world, in which no one can anticipate all possible moral issues that need to be resolved.

Morality becomes a shared project in which we participate: each member can prescribe its laws and must also be subject to them. In the domain of morality, no human being is sovereign and exempt from moral laws. Kant summarizes the third formulation by calling it "a *complete determination* of all maxims," namely, that "all maxims from one's own lawgiving are to harmonize with a possible kingdom of ends" (*G* 44; 4:436). Then he characterizes the three formulations as "progressing from the *unity* [*Einheit*] of the form of the will (its universality), the *multiplicity* [*Vielheit*] of the matter (of objects, i.e., of ends), and the *allness* [*Allheit*] or totality of the system of these" (*G* 44; 4:436). Thus Kant ends by projecting a communal and systematic conception of reciprocal moral legislation.

An interesting variation on these three formulations of Kant's legislative categorical imperative can be found in Dilthey's Inaugural Dissertation of 1864 and again in his *System of Ethics* of 1890. This is worth considering because it shows how Kant's idealism can be historically amended and has ramifications for our efforts to define his worldview. And in that regard, Dilthey's reformulations point to some blind spots in Kant's worldview that I will consider more extensively in chapter 16. First of all, Dilthey attempts to wean ethics away from Kant's abstract *legislative* model and move it toward a more concrete *formative* approach that relies on all our human capacities. Thereby he also aims to show how Kant's moral insights can be extended from a morality of individual duties to one of social responsibilities and obligations. Dilthey's ethical approach is social from the start and empirical enough to consider feelings of group solidarity while also taking synthetic a priori ethical norms seriously. Solidarity is explicated as a fellow-feeling (*Mitgefühl*) that works from within the members of a group and is more likely to activate us to do good than the reactive sympathy (*Mitleid*) which Hume and Adam Smith had relied on and Kant had already found inadequate.[4] But Dilthey acknowledges that this more powerful feeling of solidarity is limited in scope and needs to be expanded to include a concern for those who are different. Whereas a legislative ethics commands us from on high, a formative ethics works from the ground up and replaces the constraint of law with that of self-control. With this aim, Dilthey proposes three ethical principles that revise and reorder Kant's three formulations of the categorical imperative.

Dilthey's first ethical principle demands from each of us an unconditional commitment to do what is right or just based on respect for other human beings as ends in themselves. Dilthey sees no need to derive this respect for others from the respect for universal law of Kant's first formulation. Dilthey's commitment to what is right or just (*Rechtschaffenheit*) is now made the *a priori synthetic principle of unity (Einheit)* and replaces Kant's first legislative formulation.[5] Dilthey's second ethical principle is not just about the equal rights of all, but adds the benevolent concern for the well-being of all. Benevolence "does not place us into that rigid chain of mutual obligation through the will's sense of what is right or just, but rather in a free reciprocal relation of human sentiments which, without a feeling of compulsion, pervades the whole moral world."[6] This second principle of benevolence transforms respect for the rights of others into a felt identification with their fate. It adds a more free and open-ended *synthetic principle of multiplicity* (*Vielheit*) that encompasses both what unites and differentiates human beings. Although benevolence was also a Kantian virtue, Dilthey's affirmation of it seems to be more in the spirit of another Enlightenment thinker, namely, Gotthold Ephraim Lessing, who encouraged a tolerance of difference.

Only in his third ethical principle does Dilthey invoke the universal validity that Kant demands of all three formulations of the categorical imperative. It moves beyond both the initial homogeneous unity of commitment and the "unsurveyable multiplicity"[7] of benevolence to project a universally valid ideal of perfection. But this is not the Enlightenment universality of a uniform consensus for all time, but a universality that is historically developmental. According to Dilthey, the attempt to create a universally valid morality must produce different forms over time. He writes:

> The urge toward perfection, like benevolence and fidelity to mutual justice, involves a creative synthesis of our moral organization; however, its conception and clarification in consciousness is obtained in combination with the theoretical content of human spirit. Thus, there are as many different ways to understand the nature and basis of this urge for perfection and value as there are cultural stages.[8]

Dilthey's ideal of perfection produces a *synthetic plurality* of articulations over time, some of which may be religious and some of which strive to remain purely secular. They replace the systematic "*allness* [*Allheit*]" or totality of Kant's kingdom of ends with a "*plurality* [*Mehrheit*]"[9] of culturally appropriate ethical systems. Kant's sequence of unity, multiplicity, and allness is replaced with a non-totalizing sequence of unity, multiplicity, and plurality. "Plurality" may seem like a synonym for "multiplicity," but it is a differentiated and organized mode of multiplicity—not just an undifferentiated aggregate.

Dilthey conceives of morality as a process of human improvement that expresses itself in three kinds of synthesis: most basically as the *unity* of a commitment to what is right and treat others justly; more humanely as an open-ended *multiplicity* of benevolence; and finally historically as an articulated *plurality* of culturally ethical systems that aim to perfect the "striving for inner worth."[10] Whereas Kant's ethics located the ideal of inner worth in individual character, Dilthey projects this same ideal of inherent worth onto the historical world of cultural development for the sake of developing a more inclusive social ethics. Here we find an ethical paradox that Kant never confronted: the very attempt to perfect a universally valid form of morality produces historically distinct ethical systems, each claiming to possess its own inner worth. The formation of ethical systems cannot be separated from the formation of cultural institutions and must confront the problem of pluralism. When we come to discuss the nature of human culture later, we will return to this problem.

The above comparisons and contrasts allow us to see that respect for others as ends in themselves must lie at the heart of any moral system. It is not surprising, then, that many scholars favor Kant's second formulation of the categorical imperative. Yet the most consequential and controversial formulation is the third systematic one that Dilthey historicized. It is the most challenging version because the more comprehensive an ethical system claims to be, the more human differences need to be factored in. It is also the formulation that John Rawls focused on. The good intent of acting only on maxims which can be universalized as lawlike still needs to be tested for its unintended effects on others.

According to Rawls, laws will only be just if they can be accepted as fair by means of public agreement. Thus he points out that Kant's initial standard of universality is less important than his demand that laws "be agreed to under conditions that characterize men as free and equal rational beings."[11] It is interesting that Rawls assumes that Kant's noumenal self is a "collective one. The force of the self's being equal is that the principles chosen must be acceptable to other selves."[12] Thus, like Dilthey, Rawls pays more attention to the third level of Kant's moral philosophy and less to its initial insistence on legislating universal laws. Rawls writes that "those who think of Kant's moral doctrine as one of law and guilt misunderstand him. Kant's main aim is to . . . [work toward] an ethic of mutual respect and self-esteem."[13] It is placing this stress on the third appropriative or collective level of morality that allows Rawls to indicate that he regards his own conception of "the original position" with its veil of ignorance as "a procedural interpretation of Kant's conception of autonomy and the categorical imperative."[14] As we proceed to follow the development of Kant's thought, further reasons for this comprehensive assessment of his moral philosophy will be given as we see him broaden the abstract demand for lawfulness into that of legitimacy in subsequent chapters. Rational lawfulness will be reconciled with juridical legitimacy so that more emphasis can be placed on judgment.

Since the *Groundwork* provides Kant's first critical treatment of morality, it is the usual place to begin examining his moral philosophy. However, the primarily legislative and determinant aspects of the *Groundwork* present a rather abstract view of morality because of its initial focus on the duty to obey laws. Only a more reflective approach to ethics can be comprehensive without submerging individuality. It is unfortunate that Kant's moral philosophy is best known through this work because some of the rigid views expressed there, especially about not lying under any circumstances, seem exaggerated. And because decisions based on feelings are criticized as irrational, Kant has often been regarded as a cold-hearted legalist when it comes to morality. But a fuller interpretation that also takes account of the *Critique of Practical Reason* and the "Doctrine of Virtue" from the *Metaphysics of Morals* can put some of this in context and allow us to comprehend where subjective feeling and individual judgment may enter into the picture.

8

Law as Legislative and Law as Legitimating

The Role of Feeling and Judgment in Morality

In this chapter I will consider to what extent feelings can play a role in a philosophy which teaches us that morality is primarily about our duty to obey universal laws. This will require some reflection about what law means in human affairs and a recognition that Kant came to distinguish a wide range of feelings, some of which we are naturally disposed to have and some of which can be cultivated to broaden our horizon.

While it is true that the themes of legislation and law are central to Kant's philosophy, our layered approach to his thinking can contextualize them. Each of his three cognitive faculties—understanding, reason, and judgment—legislates in some way, but it is the understanding that is given the widest legislative scope. The understanding is the theoretical faculty that prescribes the formal lawfulness for the way we all experience nature. It provides us with the a priori categories that are needed to structure and give meaning to the sensible manifold of our phenomenal consciousness. Our experience can be objective and universally valid because we all apply the same formal categorial rules to the contents provided by the senses.

In the *Critique of Practical Reason*, Kant spells out why theoretical reason should not also legislate like the understanding, when he writes that it has a tendency "to lose itself beyond its boundaries among unattainable objects" (*C2* 12; 5:15) and therefore needs to be curbed. Reason's theoretical task is not so much to legislate as to determine whether the laws of the understanding can be related to each other in an orderly way to constitute a coherent system. In doing so, reason begins to take on a judiciary role. It moves from the concept of natural law that the understanding uses to order the world to that of judicial law concerned with legitimation. This move from law as legislative to lawful legitimacy is captured by Kant's image of the tribunal of reason. The systematic order aimed at by reason must be self-legitimating.

Although theoretical reason is not allowed to go beyond what the understanding legislates, we can allow practical reason to legislate its own laws, but only insofar as we prescribe them to ourselves. Thus, Kant writes that practical reason "can at least suffice to determine the will and always has objective reality in so far as volition alone is at issue" (*C2* 12; 5:15). He writes that these objective laws "must sufficiently determine the will as will, even before I ask whether I have the ability required for a desired effect" (*C2* 18; 5:20). Practical laws apply to us insofar as we are free rational beings who are capable of self-determination in deciding how to act. This is a formal determination that abstracts from actual outcomes. Regarding the subjective maxims we adopt relative to achieving desired effects, we saw that Kant expects us to evaluate their content in order to determine whether they can stand the test of universalization. Kant speaks of this as a "rule of judgment under laws of pure practical reason" which is to "ask yourself whether, if the action you propose were to take place by a law of nature of which you were yourself a part, you could indeed regard it as possible through your will" (*C2* 60; 5:69). The rule requires you to imagine yourself as both a legislator of a law and as a subject of that law.

On the basis of the earlier engagement with Rawls about the *Groundwork*, this would mean that one can only legitimately legislate the moral law to oneself as a co-legislator with others. But the *Critique of Practical Reason* raises a deeper concern not only about what I actually legislate to myself and others, but also about the spirit in which I do so. This is the problem of the good will, or my attitude toward the law. It raises not just the question of whether I followed the rule that determines what I should do, but the more profound question about the legitimacy of how I decided to do it. This also involves what Kant would later call "reflective judgment," but now it is left as the question of whether I did what I did out of a genuine feeling of respect for the law. This raises the more general question of the role of feeling in morality.

What Gives a Feeling Moral Legitimacy?

Kant makes it very clear in the *Groundwork* that charitable acts based on the feeling of sympathy have no true ethical worth. He calls such acts "amiable" and acknowledges that they may deserve "praise and encouragement," but not our moral "esteem" (*G* 11; 4:398). Kant also expresses doubts about actions performed with the hope of gaining honor. Like sympathy, the feeling of honor has social merit, but may not be truly moral. In both cases, the emotional involvement that is exhibited in doing good works seems to detract from their moral worth. This, together with the great emphasis that Kant places on the duty to obey the moral law, readily gives the impression that he does not want feelings to play any role in his moral philosophy. Is morality then just a matter of applying practical reason for Kant, and is he a cold legalist?

Paradoxically, it is the very attempt to forestall legalism that makes Kant suspicious of those who rely on feelings like sympathy in morality. One of his most explicit negative statements about the role of feeling is revealing because he thinks that decisions based on mere feeling will accord with the moral law in a mere legal sense. This is what Kant writes about feeling in chapter 3 of the *Critique of Practical Reason*:

> What is essential in the moral worth of actions is that the moral law should directly determine the will. If the determination of the will occurs in accordance with the moral law but only by means of a feeling of any kind whatsoever, which must be presupposed in order that the law may become a determining ground of the will, and if the action does not occur for the sake of the law, it has legality but not morality. (*C2* 62; 5:71)

The proper determination of what is in accordance with the law must have recourse to reason and not just to feeling to gain our acceptance. Yet in explicating what it means for an action to occur for the sake of the law, Kant begins a more extended examination of a special feeling that we must develop for the moral law. The respect for the law that was discussed in relation to the *Groundwork* was a feeling of "subordination" (*G* 14n; 4:401n) imposed by the law. In the *Critique of Practical Reason*, respect becomes a more heartfelt feeling toward the moral law. It turns out that for the moral law to become an incentive to action in a sensuous being, some special feeling is needed that is not rooted in our natural inclinations. It must be an a priori feeling that freely assents to reason. To the extent that it places a check on other feelings which have their source in the body and its inclinations and emotions, the feeling of respect for the moral law is negative, but as an incentive to make the moral law a maxim of action it is positive.

What is distinctive about this a priori feeling of respect for the moral law is that it is a subjective incentive to action that coincides with the required objective agreement of our reason with the law, and this overlap is essential for judging our moral worth. Kant writes:

> The concept of duty thus requires of action that it objectively agree with the law, while of the maxim of the action it demands subjective respect for the law as the sole mode of determining the will by the law. And on

> this rests the distinction between consciousness of having acted *in conformity with duty* and *from duty*, that is, respect for the law. The former, legality, is possible even if inclinations alone are the determining grounds of the will, but the latter, morality or moral worth, must be placed solely in this: that the action takes place from duty, that is, for the sake of the law alone. (*C2* 69; 5:81)

The last clause could be seen as more demanding than the incorporation thesis discussed in the previous chapter. There it seemed that acting from duty only requires us to give respect for the law priority over self-interested incentives that might have been incorporated in our maxim of action. Here it might seem that respect for the law must be the only consideration. Since Kant himself thinks it is impossible for us to rid ourselves of incentives based on self-love in our lifetime, one possible resolution would be to posit an instantaneous limiting moment in which only the feeling of respect for the law is decisive and moves us.[1]

We can conclude that the usual emphasis that is placed on Kant's categorical imperative—that we must act only on maxims that can be universalized—is a necessary condition for being moral, but not the sufficient condition. This is because one can act on the commendable maxim not to lie for nonmoral reasons, namely, from fear of being caught and exposed. Then the action of truth-telling would be in conformity with the moral law to be truthful, but it would be merely legally right. In that case, inclination based on the feeling of self-love would be the incentive or subjective determining ground of our will. Fear of punishment or embarrassment at being caught in a lie or in another kind of violation of the moral law would diminish our sense of self. It is not enough, then, to act merely *in conformity with duty*, but *from duty* or respect for the law. When Kant writes "it is of the greatest importance in all moral appraisals to attend with the utmost exactness to the subjective principle of all maxims" (*C2* 69; 5:81), he means for us to make sure that the maxim is based on the feeling of respect. A maxim is only truly moral for Kant if it is adopted out of genuine respect for the law. This feeling of respect is also a necessary condition for having a moral character.

We can now see that this account of the feeling of respect is not incompatible with Kant's initial attack on feelings such as sympathy. Respect is not a feeling that influences the will to accept the moral law. Rather, it is a feeling which confirms that the will has already accepted the law. What Kant worried about at first was the will being influenced "only by means of a feeling." Respect, however, is a feeling that is at the same time a consciousness of the law. It is a nonempirical feeling "produced solely by reason" (*C2* 65; 5:76) and which has been assented to. It expresses an active commitment from the individual agent. This felt commitment affirming the law is hardly legalistic. In fact, what Kant is rejecting as having mere legality are actions that meet the universalizability test but are chosen primarily on the basis of empirical feelings and inclinations rooted in self-love. They may follow the letter of the law, but not its spirit. Feeling as such cannot be a sufficient condition for making a moral decision, but there is one special feeling—respect for the moral law—that is a necessary condition.

Edifying Aesthetic Feelings

There may be only one truly moral feeling, but are there any other feelings that have a moral relevance? To answer this question, I will now return to the social feelings of sympathy and honor we started with. What about them is incompatible with morality, and is there anything in them that could be made compatible with morality? This is important for understanding Kant's practical philosophy because he actually started as a moral sense theorist. In the early essay *Observations on the Feeling of the Beautiful and Sublime* of 1764, Kant spoke of certain aesthetic feelings that can uplift us. The appreciation of beauty is claimed to evoke the feelings of sympathy and agreeableness. For its part, the sublime magnificence of great art arouses a sense of human honor. These refined natural feelings are edifying and are recognized by Kant as making us more humane.

According to Kant the feelings of sympathy and agreeableness associated with beauty are admirable for showing a concern for others. Sympathy is rooted in an immediate upwelling of love, and agreeableness arises from the bonds of family and friendship. However, they are not reliable sources of moral action, for they are partial rather than universal affections. Sympathy can produce generous acts, but it is not a moral incentive because it leads us to be moved by a particular situation without putting it into the larger context of our overall duties to others. On the basis of sympathy, we are inclined to favor those who are similar to us and ignore others who are more remote from ourselves. Kant's terms for "sympathy" in the *Observations* are *Sympathie* and *Mitleiden* and evoke a sense of passivity or suffering.

But there is a broader feeling "that lives in every human breast and extends itself much further than over the particular grounds of sympathy and agreeableness [*Gefälligkeit*]" (*OBS* 31; 2:217, translation amended). The feeling that Kant has in mind here pertains to "the dignity of human nature" and involves a "well-disposedness [*Wohlgewogenheit*]" (*OBS* 31;

2:217, translation amended) to all human beings. This feeling of being universally well-disposed is a virtuous attitude because it allows us to evaluate our responses to others in a balanced and principled manner.

Kant does admit, however, that because of the weakness of human nature, we cannot expect everyone to develop this feeling of well-disposedness in the principled manner that is needed for moral action. Therefore "providence has placed . . . helpful drives [such as sympathy and agreeableness] in us as supplements for virtue" (*OBS* 31; 2:217). These are, however, "adopted" rather than "genuine" virtues (*OBS* 31; 2:217). One could say that an adopted virtue is one that has been instinctively assimilated, not actively acquired or reflectively appropriated. Unfortunately, not even the adopted virtue of sympathy suffices to stimulate our inert human nature to more generally useful (*gemeinnützigen*) actions. According to Kant, it needs to be supplemented by "a feeling for honor [*Gefühl für Ehre*]" to uplift us, that is, to counterbalance our "cruder self-interest and vulgar sensuality" (*OBS* 32; 2:218). Here Kant invokes the feeling for honor associated with the sublime magnificence that an imposing cultural artifact such as a pyramid or a cathedral can inspire.

Of all the refined feelings that can motivate us to do good, the feeling for honor seems to inspire us the most. Yet this feeling is also claimed to be morally problematic in the *Observations*. It is edifying in that it addresses our sense of worth, but it does so on the basis of how we appear to others. Instead of deciding to do what we ourselves judge to be right, we allow the judgments of others to determine our course of action. As Kant writes:

> What a good part of humanity would have done neither out of an immediately arising emotion of good-heartedness, nor out of principles happens often enough simply for the sake of outer appearance, out of a delusion that is very useful although in itself very shallow [*seicht*]—as if the judgment of others determined the worth of ourselves and our actions. (*OBS* 32; 2:61–62)

Individuals motivated by a feeling for honor may do good deeds merely to avoid the censure of others or to gain their praise. But then they are not acting as autonomous persons.

If a good deed is based on moral principles, it is of course virtuous, but if it is done out of the sympathy of good-heartedness, then it is merely an adopted virtue. Deeds motivated by a feeling for honor seem even less desirable because they merely possess the "sheen of virtue [*Tugendsschimmer*]" (*OBS* 32; 2:218). A feeling for honor leads us to do things that have the outward appearance of virtue. It resembles virtue but has merely what

Kant calls the "appearance of propriety [*Anstand*]" (*OBS* 32; 2:218). Propriety is quite superficial and is really about respectability or rank (*Stand*). The human feeling for honor uplifts us in social status, but it need not be morally motivated. These comments about honor have led Allen Wood to consider the concern with honor as the source of human evils.[2]

Kant's reservations about the feeling for honor do not mean, however, that we should not prize our honor. It is thus important to recognize that Kant calls noble human beings who are virtuous on principle "worthy of honor [*ehrwürdig*]" (*OBS* 31; 2:218). Our behavior should be honorable but not aim at public recognition of it. What Kant has called the "feeling for honor" seems to be the felt need for the glory and magnificence that attaches to public honor. The aesthetic magnificence of honor can be seen as a surface manifestation of the "desire for honor [*Ehrbegierde*]" (*OBS* 39; 2:227), which is normally translated as "ambition." Kant warns that it is foolish to make this desire for honor "the rule to which one subordinates the other inclinations," but adds that "as an accompanying drive it is most excellent" (*OBS* 39; 2:227). Indeed, beyond the aesthetic feeling *for* honor and the ambitious passion or desire *for* honor there is an admirable cognate, namely, the love *of* honor. According to Kant, this "*love of honor* [*Ehrliebe*] is distributed among all human hearts, although in unequal measure, which must give to the whole a beauty that charms to the point of admiration" (*OBS* 39; 2:227). The whole that is meant here is the great stage of society where "different groups unite themselves in a painting of magnificent expression" (*OBS* 39; 2:227). The love of honor is admirable when it expresses itself in proper measure. Indeed, this love of honor directs us to the beauty and dignity of human nature that inspires individuals to be worthy of honor (*ehrwürdig*).

It was made clear in the *Groundwork of the Metaphysics of Morals* that there are two kinds of worth: relative worth and inner worth. "Relative worth or value" (*G* 42; 4:435) can be measured and has a price that can be matched. Inner worth, however, is immeasurable and cannot be matched by an equivalent. The human dignity that is worthy of honor involves this kind of inner worth or value. This indicates that it is possible to distinguish between honor that is externally measured and honor that is inherently deserved.

Such a distinction can actually be found in the remarks that Kant entered into his own copy of the *Observations* around 1765. In these remarks we read that although the love of honor makes us competitive, it can have the effect of improving human beings. But ultimately, Kant wants individuals to develop a feeling of "inner honor" (*BE*, 20:130) that can dispense with the need to measure themselves relative to others. This allows for a sense of one's own dignity. Inner honor presupposes a capacity for judgmental self-assessment. If inner honor involves the belief that it is possessed "without measuring oneself with others" then it "is called pride [*Stoltz*]" (*BE*, 20:130). Pride is not usually admired, but Kant seems to accept its appropriateness as long as it does not turn a person into someone who is arrogant (*hochmüthig*) (*BE*, 20:130). Arrogance is an excessive pride that results from measuring oneself against others and despising them. Inner honor is a measured pride that dispenses with comparisons.

We saw that in the *Observations* and in Kant's *Remarks* about them, sympathy was associated with beauty and the feeling for honor was associated with sublime magnificence. But we also saw that sympathy is a blind inclination and is therefore unreliable as a moral incentive. Similarly, the aesthetic feeling *for* honor tends to be unprincipled and merely concerned with outer appearance. Neither obeys the moral law out of respect for it. Accordingly, the superficial feeling *for* honor was replaced by a genuine love *of* honor, and sympathy by a well-disposedness which is not a temporary feeling but an enduring attitude toward the human species in general guided by a "principle" (*OBS* 30; 2:216) of action.

Although these reflections on human feeling dating from the time that Kant held a moral sense theory are ignored in his *Groundwork*, it will be shown that he reintegrated some of these feelings into his final theory of morality. Thus some pre-critical views are made critical, albeit in a qualified way.

Cultivating Aesthetic Receptivity to Transform Edifying Social Feelings into Active Participatory Feelings

In *The Metaphysics of Morals* (1797), Kant actually goes so far as to introduce a felt counterpart of sympathy that we should cultivate for moral purposes. He returns to the question of sympathy and considers it as part of a larger examination of "shared feeling [*Mitgefühl*]" (*MM* 204; 6:456).[3] Nature has implanted in us a "*receptivity* [*Empfänglichkeit*]" for the feeling of sympathy as part of our disposition to humanity, but we can also cultivate this disposition as the "*capacity* [*Vermögen*]" and willingness to share in the feelings of others at the level of personality. To the extent that we are merely receptive to others, we feel sympathy. The moral challenge is to develop a more active counterpart to sympathy, namely, "a participatory feeling [*theilnehmende Empfindung*]" (*MM* 204; 6:456).[4]

The German word used for sympathy here is *Mitleid*, which literally means "suffering with." It can also be translated as "pity." Sympathy and pity as modes of suffering are unfree and can even become contagious and generate a more reified mode of compassion (*Mitleidenschaft*). The passive root of sympathy is as objectionable to Kant as ever and entails that there can be no duty to feel sympathy for others or act on its basis. The new expression "*theilnehmende Empfindung*" introduced in *The Metaphysics of Morals* is often translated as "sympathetic feeling," but this risks confusing it with the sympathy that Kant finds inadequate. I am translating it more accurately as "participatory feeling" to bring out its more active character. A participatory feeling is a free feeling that is not passively received, but a spontaneous expression of our "practical humanity" (*MM* 204; 6:456).

Thus, Kant goes on to claim that we should be involved in the well-being of others through "an active moral participation [*thätige Theilnehmung*]" (*MM* 205; 6:457)[5] and we can do so by means of a duty to cultivate shared feelings that are aesthetic in nature. This very late position about a participatory moral feeling resembles the viewpoint in the *Observations on the Feeling of the Beautiful and the Sublime* that local sympathy must be replaced by a broader attitude of being generally well-disposed. But the feeling of moral participation invoked in *The Metaphysics of Morals* goes beyond being well-disposed by also requiring active cultivation.

Having supplemented the feelings of sympathy and being well-disposed with the more active counterpart of a love of human beings that should be cultivated, we can now also ask how Kant's early concerns with honor fare in *The Metaphysics of Morals.* We find that he no longer speaks of the questionable feeling *for* honor, but he does invoke the "feeling *of* honor [*Ehrgefühl*]" (*MM* 108; 6:336) when he discusses the problem of how to punish the deed of killing someone in a duel. Since both parties consented to the duel to defend their honor, Kant claims that the one who kills his opponent cannot strictly be accused of murder. Here a court of law must either "declare by law that the concept of honor (which is here no illusion) counts for nothing and so punish with death, or else it must remove from the crime the capital punishment appropriate to it, and so be either cruel or indulgent" (*MM* 109; 6:336). Kant describes this legal quandary as a

> discrepancy between the incentives of honor in the people (subjectively) and the measures that are (objectively) suitable for its purpose. Accordingly, the public justice arising from the state becomes an *injustice* from the perspective of the justice arising from the people. (*MM* 109; 6:337)

Even though it is in the interest of the state to punish the surviving duelist in order to discourage other duels, the subjective need of individuals to defend their honor should temper the punishment. Kant praises the man of honor as valuing something even "more highly than life" (*MM* 107; 6:334). He should therefore not be punished for the crime of killing someone in the same way that a scoundrel is punished. Thus the feeling of honor is not always illusory, and the individual who acts on it is no longer accused of being mainly concerned with appearances.

In fact, the love of honor is now equated with an "inner honesty [*honestas interna*]" (*MM* 175; 6:420) that resists vices such as lying, which compromise human dignity. Love of honor becomes a "mode of thinking" that is directed at "the dignity of humanity" in one's own person (*MM* 175; 6:420). Kant is more clear than ever that he regards the love of honor as a "virtue [*Tugend*]" (*MM* 175; 6:420). Accordingly, he strengthens the moral legitimacy of this feeling. The love of honor is more than a subjective concern to defend one's own dignity, and is "a right to which [an individual] cannot renounce his claim" (*MM* 210; 6:464). Honor and respect are melded in the concept of being honorable or respectable.

Kant also reiterates his position that love *of* honor constitutes a proper pride, which is a "concern to yield nothing of one's human dignity in comparison with others (so that the adjective '*noble*' is usually added to 'pride' in this sense)" (*MM* 211; 6:465). What honorable pride means must be assessed in relation to another virtue that Kant expects us to possess, namely, humility. Neither of these qualities requires us to compare ourselves with others and then judge ourselves as better or worse. Humility for Kant does not mean that we should humble ourselves before others; it primarily involves having respect for the "holiness of the moral law" (*MM* 187; 6:436).[6] From the more comprehensive reflective perspective that will be developed in the next section, it will become possible to reconcile the language of pride with humility through the virtue of self-esteem.

If the feelings of honor and active participation can be validated as having moral worth, it should be made clear in what sense. They are discussed in the second part of *The Metaphysics of Morals* entitled "The Doctrine of Virtue" and belong to what Kant calls "Preliminary Aesthetic Concepts Concerning the Mind's Receptivity to Concepts of Duty as Such" (*MM* 159; 6:399). We again see Kant correlating aesthetic feeling with moral attributes. But the difference between the *Observations* of 1764 and "The Doctrine of Virtue" of 1797 is that thirty-three years later Kant distinguishes between pathological and moral modes of aesthetic receptivity. A feeling that "precedes the representation of the law" is empirical in origin and therefore merely "pathological," but a feeling "which can only follow upon" the law as its effect on the mind is called "moral" (*MM* 160; 6:399). Moral aesthetic receptivity is not passive but involves an openness to our rationality. In addition to the feeling of respect for the moral law, Kant also lists other aesthetic moral feelings: pangs of conscience, the love for human beings, and respect for oneself. These are all moral virtues that should be cultivated.

Moral Virtues Encompass Both Imperfect and Indirect Duties

When discussing these moral virtues, Kant moves beyond the domain of the perfect duties governed by the categorical imperative. Perfect duties must be fully complied with. Thus we have a perfect duty to never kill or harm human beings. In contrast, imperfect duties are duties of virtue where a "failure to fulfill them is not in itself a culpability" (*MM* 153; 6:390). Imperfect duties are also called "wide duties" because they give us some latitude in how far to fulfill them. Kant clarifies this by warning that a wide duty is not one that allows us to "make exceptions" for ourselves, but only "to limit one maxim of duty by another" (*MM* 161; 6:401) that is also relevant to the situation we are in. Wide duties to cultivate our moral feeling and to subject our decisions to the verdict of conscience are not about maxims of action directed at some single end and therefore cannot be determinantly tested. Kant writes that conscience "is not directed to an object, but merely to the subject (to affect moral feeling), and so it is not something incumbent on one, but rather an unavoidable fact" (*MM* 160; 6:400). Our conscience points to "the voice of the inner judge" to whom we have an "indirect" (*MM* 161; 6:401) duty to pay attention rather than ignore. Adding the adjective "indirect" is due to the fact that the voice of conscience is often related to a higher being like God. As we will see later, Kant thinks that we have direct duties not to all living beings,[7] but only to human beings, including ourselves. Concerning the direct but wide duty to love human beings, we can see it as a specification of what was said earlier about supplementing the provincial affection of sympathy with a broader participatory engagement with humanity. When this is related to the welfare of other human beings, Kant speaks of benevolent conduct. Since we cannot will ourselves to feel love for others, Kant writes "a *duty to love* is an absurdity. But *benevolence* [*amor benevolentiae*] as conduct can be subject to a law of duty" (*MM* 161; 6:401). Benevolence (*Wohlwollen*) replaces the well-disposedness (*Wohlgewogenheit*) of the early *Observations* as a universal attitude to others that we should always try to cultivate. But there can be no determinant rule to instruct us how far to practice benevolence or goodwill to others. It is an imperfect duty whose execution requires the kind of reflective thinking that we related to comprehension and that will be more fully explored as reflective judgment throughout the rest of this work.

In all cases of judgment, there is a need to relate particulars to a universal. In the case of a determinant judgment, there is already a relevant universal rule that can be appealed to in deciding a particular case. In the case of reflective judgment, the available rules do not suffice to guide us in deciding what is appropriate. Here feeling may play a role in establishing what is legitimate, as we will see when we discuss Kant's theory of aesthetic judgment. Aesthetic receptivity or openness is important not just in matters of taste, but also when it comes to making sense of what Kant calls the duties of virtue.

Respect as such is the last of the four aesthetic moral endowments exposited by Kant in *The Metaphysics of Morals*. However, it should be made clear that what is at issue here is really the feeling of "self-esteem [*Selbstschätzung*]" or a person's "*respect* for his own being" (*MM* 162; 6:403). Here too, Kant thinks that self-esteem cannot be a perfect duty. It is instead the basis for recognizing a duty as a duty. Rather than *having* a duty to esteem themselves, human beings must *embody* "respect for the law within [themselves] in order even to think of any duty whatsoever" (*MM* 162; 6:403). In effect, the feeling of self-esteem is the transcendental condition which makes it possible to conceive ourselves as constrained by a duty. The respect for the law that was invoked as the necessary subjective incentive in the *Critique of Practical Reason* is now internalized as a participatory esteem for the law within ourselves. Our maxims of action must be consistent with the "*dignity* of humanity in our own person" (*MM* 175; 6:420).

I have argued for the moral import of the feelings of respect, benevolence, conscience, and honor, among others. Sympathy remains problematic insofar as it tends to be provincial. But instead of replacing it with an innate feeling of well-disposedness, Kant ends up supplementing sympathy with the imperfect duty to cultivate a participatory love for others. We have fully rehabilitated the love of honor by linking it to the dignity of our humanity. Cultivating the love of honor and the love of others are moral virtues. They involve feeling and should not unduly influence the objective decision as to what is the right course of action, but like the feeling of respect, they are essential in how we execute our decisions. They make the difference between acting according to the mere letter of the moral law and acting in accordance with its spirit.

9

Aesthetic Communicability and the Medial Recontextualization of Experience

In the *Critique of Pure Reason,* the "aesthetic" referred to the formal relations of the space-time continuum that frame our assimilation of the contents of sense and make them objectively measurable. These contents of sense are not just passively received, but are given an apprehensible form. In the *Critique of Judgment,* the aesthetic is contextually expanded to encompass a responsiveness to what is represented, namely, "what I make of it in myself" (*C3* 91; 5:205). Representations are still judged in relation to objects in the world, but not for what they teach us about how these objects exist in the natural world and are causally related to each other, but for how these objects relate to us as individuals. Now the way sensations (*Empfindungen*) as sense impressions affect us is measured in terms of the pleasure or pain we feel (*empfinden*). Since sense assumes a different medial significance, the aesthetic question becomes: What do I make of sensuous pleasure, not as a sensible bodily state, but as a mental state that reflects my relation to these objects?

In chapter 2, we saw Kant transform the extensive or aesthetic clarity that Baumgarten had made relevant to the appreciation of beauty into an aesthetic distinctness relevant to logic. This underscores the fact that prior to the *Critique of Judgment,* Kant had refused to correlate the aesthetic with the appreciation of beauty and the arts. The aesthetic clarity that Baumgarten had related to a poetic liveliness that expands the mind was reduced by Kant to the intensity of sense-content. In his early *Reflections on Logic,* liveliness was said to pertain to "intuition, strength, sensation" (*RL* 2370, 16:335), that is, to how "greatly we are changed" (*RL* 2366, 16:334) or affected. But in the *Critique of Judgment,* liveliness is redefined as the response of our faculties to what is judged to be beautiful. What is represented as beautiful "directly brings with it the feeling of the promotion of life" (*C3* 128; 5:244). Beauty produces aesthetic pleasure, which enhances our "feeling of life" (*C3* 90; 5:204). But this pleasure is not just *assimilated* as a sensible stimulus. Nor is Kant's pure aesthetic judgment interested in *acquiring* a cognitive understanding of its object.

To comprehend the full significance of the aesthetic judgment, it must be conceived as a kind of *reflective appropriation* of something more. To judge that a flower is beautiful is not to add another objective property that extends our cognition of it, but to discern a relational quality that defines our attitude to it. The aim is to attain a state of mind that can appropriately contemplate the flower. The task here is to relate to the object in a way that is also communicable to other human beings. Aesthetically apprehending the object puts us in an enhanced state of mind that we aim to share with others. What is reflectively *appropriated* here is an affinity with other human beings. Once this expansive pleasurable state of mind has been attained, we can attend to the formal properties of the object and judge them, so that the aesthetic experience can no longer be misconceived as being purely subjective and private.

Paul Guyer has claimed that there are "two kinds of reflective judgment"[1] operative in Kant's aesthetics—one about "the estimation of the object"[2] for its capacity to produce a valid feeling of pleasure, and the other which claims that the pleasure is universally valid because it was "produced by the harmony of the faculties in the perception of its object."[3] There are indeed different kinds of reflective judgment, as we saw in chapter 6, where we distinguished between inductive reflective judgments that proceed "from many to all things of a kind" (*LL* 626; 9:132) and analogical reflective judgments that infer from partial agreement among things of a kind to more complete agreement. But what distinguishes aesthetic reflective judgments is an orientational shift that is needed to properly evaluate what makes it possible for a pleasure to be shared. What Guyer refers to as an estimation of the object is not just a theoretical assessment but a normative evaluation (*Beurtheilung*) (*C3* 102; 5:216). The aesthetic judgment is a third, but single kind of reflective judgment. Yet Guyer is right to suggest that there are preparatory stages involved in making a valid intersubjective judgment of taste.

In his first attempt in §8 of the *Critique of Judgment* to move the aesthetic beyond private feeling, Kant speaks of a judgment of taste as "generally valid [*gemeingültig*]," by which he means it is a "public [*publike*]" (*C3* 99; 5:214) judgment. If one considers this claim in relation to his lectures on logic, it becomes clear that this could only produce the aesthetic consensus of popular taste. At this level we merely *assimilate* the fashions of the people around us. This leaves this first attempt at reaching an aesthetic consensus at the level of what Kant called "a prejudice of taste" in his lectures on logic (*LL* 135; 24:172).

To move beyond this level of assimilation so that we can *acquire* good taste, we must aim for a consensus that is "universally valid [*allgemeingültig*]" (*C3* 100; 5:215). Aesthetic pleasure can only be pure if it is referred not to our bodily satisfaction or to the content of the tastes of those around us, but to the formal harmony of our own cognitive faculties. This harmony is then more fully explicated in §9 as a reciprocal interplay of the imagination and understanding, or as a reflective appreciation of beautiful form. It is this level of "sharable attunement [*Zusammenstimmung*]" (*C3* 104; 5:219) applicable to "us human beings in general" (*C3* 327; 5:462) that lies at the heart of Kant's aesthetics. However, sometimes Kant also points to a stronger consensus that would produce a universal voice (*allgemeine Stimme*) and claim the concurrence of everyone (*jedermanns Beistimmung*) (*C3* 104; 5:219). This third mode of consensus can be linked to what Kant sketches in the appendix of the "Critique of Aesthetic Judgment" as "a culture of the mental powers . . . aimed at the highest degree of perfection" (*C3* 229; 5:355). However, aesthetic purposiveness is a purposiveness without a purpose and is therefore not about perfection. Kant's third kind of consensus represents a regulative ideal that points ahead to the theory of culture in the "Critique of Teleological Judgment." This will be the universal voice of a more determinate communal *appropriation* that is grounded in Kant's moral writings.

To elucidate what is involved in the intermediate but pure aesthetic consensus that Kant is mainly concerned with in the first half of the *Critique of Judgment*, we must consider what it means to actively acquire good taste. The crucial insight to be gained from §8 is that the universality of an aesthetic judgment "must be of a special kind, since the predicate of beauty is not connected with the concept of the object considered in its entire logical sphere and yet it extends the predicate over the whole sphere of those who judge" (*C3* 100; 5:215). This involves a shift in the sphere or context of our attention, the significance of which needs to be clarified. To do so I will look at sections II and III of the "Introduction" to the *Critique of Judgment*, where Kant indicates that when we think of or attend to an object, we can consider it as part of either (1) a field *(Feld)*, (2) a territory (*Boden*), (3) a domain (*Gebiet*), or a habitat (*Aufenthalt*) (*C3* 61; 5:174).

To consider an object in terms of a field is to leave it open whether it can be experienced or not. The object could be something that is merely logically or imaginatively *possible* relative to "our faculty of cognition in general" (*C3* 61; 5:174). Kant also speaks of the sphere of the supersensible as a field for ideational thought that is important for "the practical use of reason" but which can in no way "extend our theoretical cognition" (*C3* 63; 5:175). A territory denotes the this-worldly context "within which cognition is possible for us" (*C3* 61; 5:174), given our actual human capacities, sensibilities, and dispositions. This would be the sphere of phenomenal objects that we can *actually* experience and understand. When we think about this territory, we rely on empirical concepts and common sense. Then Kant proceeds to distinguish those parts of a territory of experience for which our cognitive faculties are legislative. These are domains governed by *necessary* lawful relations. There are two such domains for us: that of the theoretical laws of nature as dealt with in the first *Critique*, and the domain of the moral laws of the second *Critique*. The third *Critique*, however, also considers those parts of the territory of experience where we have not discovered universal laws and where even common sense may fail us. These are local habitats where order is "*contingent*" (*C3* 62; 5:174). Habitats exhibit what I would call the order of familiarity, or what we happen to be acquainted with. Although Kant does not assert this, each of these contexts exhibits a different modality of order. An analysis of how Kant uses these terms here indicates that a field is a sphere of mere possibilities; a territory defines what is possible for us, and thus actualizable; a domain is governed by necessary laws; and a habitat is a local sphere of contingent but familiar order.

Before showing how these modal distinctions can serve to clarify the scope of the reflective judgments that define aesthetic debates about the beautiful and the sublime, I will refer briefly to the insightful way in which Uygar Abaci has recently characterized the modalities of determinant judgments. He claims that the three "modal categories" of the first *Critique* are "second-order or concept-level predicates" that do not "purport to express features of objects themselves but of our representations of them in relation to our cognition in general."[4] According to Abaci, each modality extends the scope of what is posited about the world by relating it to a different cognitive faculty. Beginning with Kant's own claim that "while possibility was merely a positing of a thing in relation to the understanding . . . actuality is at the same time in connection with perception" (A235/B287), Abaci adds that "when this connection with perception is established through a causal inference, the object is posited in the context of actual experience as determined by its thoroughgoing causal unity; that is, the entire actual world or cosmology of objects is added to it."[5] This is meant to ground the necessity of a causal claim in the faculty of reason. To be sure, Kant says at B100 that we can think of apodictic judgments "as if" they were a function of reason, but Abaci goes too far by incorporating reason directly into a cognitive claim of the understanding that something is necessitated by a relevant law of nature. Causal claims do not need to be justified by what Abaci refers to as the thoroughgoing "construction of a system" of "experience as a whole."[6] That task is considered in the "Dialectic of Pure Reason," and not even to Kant's own satisfaction. The system of knowledge that Kant defends in the subsequent "Canon" is only what the community of scientists has been able to agree upon.

Despite this disagreement with Abaci, I think that his more general "subjectively synthetic"[7] characterizations of modality can be usefully extended to reflective judgments in the *Critique of Judgment*. I indicated in chapter 6 that according to Kant, the determinant judgments of the understanding are *immediate inferences* applying concepts to particulars and that reflective judgments go further and are *mediate inferences* (see *RL* 3200, 16:709). Accordingly, reflective judgments can go beyond determinant judgments, even if only provisionally. Now that it has also been made clear that causal determinant judgments are contextually circumscribed by a lawful "domain [*Gebiet*]," which is a mere "part of the territory [*Boden*]" (*C3* 62; 5:174) of experience, I propose that a rational use of reflective judgment can help us to comprehend this larger sphere. This can further extend Kant's modal approach and assess what we think relative to "cognition in general" (*C3* 102; 5:217). Although what we determinantly cognize to be necessarily true about a set of natural events fails to give us a rational access to nature as a whole, Kant points to reflective aesthetic judgments as giving us figurative ways of "deciphering the *Chiffreschrift* of nature" (*C3* 180; 5:301).

Since aesthetic reflective judgments are both orientational and evaluative, they must also consider our contingent location (*Aufenthalt*) in the world in order to take our attitudinal standpoint into account. And since the second half of the *Critique of Judgment* reflects on organic purposiveness as the lawfulness of the contingent, Abaci's rationally filled-in "context of actual experience as a whole" turns out to have pockets of contingency that cannot be fully explained by finite subjects and require reflective interpretation. Contingency needs to be added as the fourth modality in order to recognize the way that reflective teleological judgments can further decipher nature.

Although aesthetic judgments do not add to our already existent cognition of things, their modality is to add to our cognition of the world in general by recognizing how our place in it affects our response to things. Their function is not just to widen the scope of our overall worldly context, but to imaginatively recontextualize how we see things within this world. Clive Cazeaux also takes note of the contextual spheres delineated in the "Introduction" to the *Critique of Judgment* in an effort to characterize aesthetic consciousness in Kant as a metaphorical mode of thought. His claim is that none of these spheres really applies because metaphor is "*the disrespecter* of domains" (Cazeaux 2004: 11).[8] But precisely because metaphors disrespect the determinacy of domains, they can traverse the other three worldly contexts. I will employ them as transitional locational horizons against which to explore what Kant means by "the whole sphere" of those who judge aesthetically. Aesthetic judgments are reflective judgments because they are not content to rely on the concepts already made available by either our understanding or our reason for cognitively determining what is being represented. Here feelings and attitudes cannot be excluded in coining new words, concepts, or ideas to express our assessment of things.

While determinant cognitive judgments are directed by the rules of the available spheres of discourse and the domains of scientific inquiry, reflective judgment must seek its own rules to orient itself in its estimation of objects. Or as Kant says, only the reflective power of judgment can "give itself . . . a transcendental principle" (*C3* 67; 5:180) in evaluating things. Rather than being directed or necessitated from without, reflective judging can be considered to be self-orienting. Just as bodily orientation combines perception and feeling, mental orientation cannot afford to exclude feelings in establishing what is worth exploring and in finding the words or concepts to express our appreciation of things. Before we can expect to find anything approximating a concept to assess an aesthetic object, we need to properly contextualize it.

In section III of the "Introduction" to the *Critique of Judgment,* Kant writes that as a reflective power on its own, aesthetic judgement "can claim no field of objects as its *domain,* yet it can have some *territory*" (*C3* 64; 5:177). Domains are too well defined and conceptually ordered to do justice to spontaneous aesthetic representations. Since Kant indicates that there is always something unexpected about something that strikes us as beautiful, we can add that we come upon it as part of a contingent habitat that we are then expected to relate to the larger territory of human experience. The predicate "beautiful" is a mere placeholder for a more considered assessment that needs to be made in conjunction with those who experience the world like us. It invokes a human communicability without appealing to ready concepts. Here our imagination "schematizes without a concept"' (5:287) as we apprehend the play of forms in objects without fully determining them. Kant regards schematization as the core function of the imagination, namely, to project a figurative meaning onto things. In the *Critique of Pure Reason,* the task of the imagination was to mediate between the conceptual universality of the categories and the empirical particularity of sensible intuition. There the function of schematization was to explicate the timeless rules of a priori categories as a lawful temporal ordering of experience. To schematize the concepts of the understanding is to *prefigure* the objective scientific "meaning [*Bedeutung*]" (A146/B185) of the causal course of events. In the *Critique of Judgment,* however, aesthetic schematization occurs without the guidance of concepts and allows the imagination to formally *configure* states of affairs and playfully *reconfigure* things we have already experienced. Aesthetically, the form of the objects of outer sense is enjoyed as a "play of shapes (in space, mime, and dance)," and the contents of inner sense can be rhythmically conveyed in music as a "mere play of sensations (in time)" (*C3* 110; 5:226). Although Kant places priority on figurative form in the visual arts, he allows that color can be an important supplement in that it can reinforce our attention to form and enliven its enjoyment. This leads him into an interesting discussion of *parerga* or addenda that are not inherently part of the *ergon* or work proper, yet frame it in important ways so as to not indifferently fall outside it either. *Parerga* are thus the borderline or contextual features of a work of art that "belong to it externally" like "draperies on statues" (*C3* 111; 5:226) to make them more socially acceptable. A *parergon* is an ornamentation that fortuitously embellishes an artwork and is contrasted with a distractive, decorative "golden frame" (*C3* 111; 5:226) that the proud owner of a painting adds to flaunt his possession of it. Contextualizing ornamentation is acceptable if it evokes more than what is given and makes the content of the work more humanly attractive. Kant objects to the golden frame, however, because it is the kind of hard border that draws attention to itself. As an arbitrary decoration, the frame is limiting and cuts the painting off from its intersubjective human context.

Borders are important orientational markers as we move through the world, but they should be permeable boundaries rather than reduced to limits. This is indeed true for the four horizonal judgmental contexts that Kant delineated. Domains and habitats are both parts of the territory of human experience, and fields can be said to border on its edges. The local region in which we feel at home counts as a habitat. Similarly, what is obscurely felt in inner sense can be regarded as a private habitat. However, not all feelings are so delimited in scope. Indeed, the feelings aroused by beauty can transpose us outside ourselves.

Thus, Kant claims that it would be "self-contradictory" to assign the communicability of aesthetic pleasure immediately to "the representation through which the object *is given*" (*C3* 102; 5:217). Instead, the universal communicability of aesthetic beauty pertains to "the state of mind in the given representation which, as the subjective condition of the judgment of taste, must serve as its ground and have the pleasure in the object as a consequence" (*C3* 102; 5:217). As immediately given to me, a beautiful object refers to the limited *habitat* of how I am affected, namely, the pleasurable psychic (*seelische*) state of my soul. But to aesthetically apprehend this object is to imaginatively schematize it onto the larger *territory* of what can be humanly shared and produce a reflective pleasure that pervades one's mental state (*Gemüth*). Whereas in the first *Critique* the imaginative schemata inherent in pure concepts of the understanding linked them to objects in a law-bound domain, in the third *Critique* "schematizing without a concept" has no predefined boundary and allows for a change of context. Here the imagination recontextualizes objects so that we can adopt a proper attitude toward them that allows our pleasure to be enhanced by being shared. Whereas the cognitive mode of schematization was said to *prefigure* objects, the aesthetic mode of schematization *reconfigures* them in a broader medial context so that we can evaluate them intersubjectively. Kant has often been criticized for focusing too much on the subjective aspects of aesthetic judgment and too little on the objective aspects. But the Kantian idea of schematic reconfiguration modally expands aesthetic awareness into something intersubjective and worldly. Aesthetic judgments can bring out the worldly import of a thing of beauty.[9] Or as Karl Ameriks has argued, Kant expects an aesthetic judgment to be "attuned to how *normal* human beings in general should be ready to react to the public appearance of a relevant object."[10]

By relating a judgment of taste to "the whole sphere" of those who judge aesthetically, we make beauty and sublimity modal or contextualizing predicates that widen our horizon based on playful borderline shifts in attitude. Aesthetic pleasure is shared not by discursive communication through concepts, but by a felt communicability of a state of mind that can navigate among the judgmental contexts delineated in sections II and III of the "Introduction." What was a mere private sensation is transformed into a communal sentiment that Kant calls a *sensus communis.* We do this by comparing "our judgment not so much to the *actual* as to the merely *possible* judgments of others" (*C3* 174; 5:294; italics added). This means that in approaching the actual territory of human experience from the standpoint of our contingent habitat, we must also imagine this territory as surrounded by the field of the possible. In a proper judgment of taste, my relation to the represented object is mediated by the way my cognitive faculties function in attunement with human beings in general. Insofar as the harmonious interplay of my imagination and understanding in appreciating a beautiful painting also evokes the state of mind minimally necessary for cognition as such, Kant holds that aesthetic pleasure is in principle universally communicable. And if my pleasure possesses this communicability, I will be judging the aesthetic object not just through its effect on me, but through my attitude of engagement with others. Thus the felt pleasure has been reflectively recontextualized as a sharable state of mind, and the assent that I give to a thing of beauty or a work of art will be a product of my engagement with other human beings and their expected consent.[11] The initial local sense of public (*publike*) consensus of §8 is replaced in §9 with a broader consensus that in some sense approximates the more open-ended "public [*öffentliche*] use of reason" ("WE" 56; 8:37) that Kant thinks will result from enlightened political debate. Yet we should no more expect to reach final rational guidelines for good taste than we can rely on traditional standards of taste. Being even more suspicious of mere current popular taste, Kant is willing to acknowledge that we may look to the tradition to provide "precedents" of admired art. But he warns that

> emulation [*Nachfolge*] of a precedent, rather than imitation [*Nachahmung*], is the correct expression for any influence that products of an exemplary author may have on others; and this means no more than drawing on the same sources from which the predecessor himself drew, and learning from him only how to go about doing so. (*C3* 164; 5:283)

To regard a historical precedent as exemplary is not to appeal to it as an example that is to be blindly followed or imitated. Its exemplariness lies not in being a determinate standard or ground, but in serving as a medial reference point to orient oneself by. To emulate what is exemplary is to bring out the normative nature of the aesthetic judgment. In §17 Kant begins to explore this when he discusses how "normal ideas" of beauty relate to the normative ideal of beauty. Normal ideas of human beauty are originally based on regional familiarity, and Kant accepts that they will differ for Europeans, the Chinese, and Africans. These contextualized normal ideas are mere empirical averages and are unable to provide the imagination with the determinant rules for schematizing the normal idea of a more general human beauty. Only as part of the ideal of beauty, which must also include the rational idea of the purposes of humanity, can we fashion "the image of the whole species, hovering among all the singular and multiply varied intuitions of individuals" (*C3* 119; 5:234). An ideal of beauty may be aimed at in the production of art, but it is not essential for the pure judgment of taste.

Before turning to Kant's views on artistic creativity, we can conclude that "the modality of the satisfaction in the object" (*C3* 121; 5:236) of an aesthetic judgment has a kind of necessity. Kant starts the modality scale by saying that it is possible for any representation to be combined with pleasure, and if a representation actually produces pleasure, it counts as being agreeable. "Of the beautiful, however, one thinks that it has a necessary relation to satisfaction" (*C3* 121; 5:236). Yet the necessity is distinctive in that it cannot be conceptually demonstrated: it is not apodictic but "exemplary" (*C3* 121; 5:237). Apodicticity can only be attained in a well-defined domain. In the territory of aesthetic engagement with others, we can only expect the pleasure to have an exemplary validity. What this means is that we cannot conceptually demand or command that others agree with our evaluative judgment that something is beautiful. We can only "ascribe assent to everyone" (*C3* 121; 5:237) because of a felt ideational sense of the communicability of the satisfaction.

Artistic Creativity and Symbolic Presentation

Pure aesthetic purposiveness is content with the suggestive play of aesthetic ideas and is not directed at an ideal cultural end or moral purpose. An aesthetic idea is a representation of the imagination that "occasions much thinking" (*C3* 192; 5:314), although there are no available conceptual or linguistic expressions to communicate it to others. What distinguishes artists from aesthetic spectators is what they do with their aesthetic ideas to fashion something ideal out of them. In §49 Kant speaks of aesthetic ideas that can take root in an artistic genius from "undeveloped material of which the understanding took no regard in its concept" (*C3* 194; 5:317). However, if the power of genius is to be more than idiosyncratic, it must be made communicable by "expressing what is unnamable in its mental state" (*C3* 195; 5:317). Now the implicit communicability of the aesthetic judgments of spectators crosses over into a more explicitly suggestive communicability. What is needed for the expressive power of artistic genius is the spirited capacity to "apprehend the rapidly passing play of the imagination" involved in an aesthetic idea and "unify it into a concept" (*C3* 195; 5:317). Genius is thus the power to imaginatively go beyond the determinant concepts of the understanding by means of schematic aesthetic ideas that suggest a field of possibilities, some of which are then expressed in a new concept that is in some sense "reflective" and "ideal." Such a concept "discloses a new rule, which could not have been deduced from any antecedent principles" (*C3* 195; 5:317). As distinct from determinant concepts of the understanding that are derivable from the scientific principles governing the necessary domain of nature, these new expressive concepts serve reflective judgment in expanding the actual territory of human experience.

Finally, in §59 the discussion of schematization is expanded by means of the idea of *hypotyposis*, which also makes room for linguistic symbolization. *Hypotyposis* as the medial process of giving presentational (*darstellend*) content to representational (*vorstellend*) thought can produce either a schematic mode of intuition which is "direct" and "demonstrative" or a new mode of ideational symbolization which is "indirect" (*C3* 226; 5:352). By calling the conceptual schematization of objects "direct,"

Kant seems to contradict the first *Critique,* where schematization was considered indirectly intuitive, in contrast with the direct intuitive demonstrative power of mathematical constructions. To save Kant from contradicting himself a further distinction needs to be added, namely, that conceptual schematization was about prefiguring objective relations *in our experience,* whereas ideational symbolization is about configuring relations among various contexts that allow artists to make interpretive claims that go *beyond our experience.* What is suggested now is that the new symbols created by the expressive power of genius have a linguistic resonance that evokes analogues of sense. Symbolization adds a presentational medial dimension to aesthetic schematization that allows artists to discern analogous relations among different modal contexts. Thus Kant shows how reflective judgment can apply a rule that makes sense of how things are related in a familiar and intuitable context in order to illuminate how things of a more ethereal nature can be related in a different, less familiar context. An example of this is Kant's effort to exhibit the political differences between despotic and constitutional governments by comparing the former to machines that are controlled from without and the latter to organisms that are organized from within. There is no one-to-one intuitive correspondence between political and organic systems, merely a symbolic analogy that empowers the imagination. The contexts being compared are quite different; only the rules for reflecting about them are similar. A case could be made that the symbolic elaboration of this kind of reflection amounts to a further aesthetic mode of reflective judgment. This is because symbolic relations go beyond merely recontextualizing things by allowing structural resemblances among different contexts to be expressed. We will confront similar questions about other applications of reflective judgment when we consider what is reflective about teleological judgments and how they relate to what I have called reflective comprehension. My main concern is to show the richness of the idea of reflective judgment rather than to make an exhaustive list of all its modes. They all develop the relation between imaginative orientation and judgmental contextualization.

Reassessing the Artistic Relevance of Kant's Aesthetics

Based on his theory of genius, Kant has most often been recognized as a proponent of the expression theory of art. However, in terms of his influence on modern art criticism, he has also been related to the advocacy of formalism by Clement Greenberg and others. While it is true that Kant prizes the formal aspects of the arts, he can hardly be recommended as a formalist art critic. Kant's more lasting contribution to the appreciation of art does not lie in his visual and musical discernment, but in opening up what an aesthetic judgment and symbolization can contribute to our state of mind and to expansive modes of thought. In my interpretation of what is entailed by aesthetic schematization, Kant has an even more contemporary relevance. I showed that for something to be aesthetically appreciated, we should imagine a new context for its contemplation. We must be able to take it out of the familiar local habitat where we find it and reframe it in relation to a larger territory where a new attitude of human engagement can be fostered. If aesthetic schematization is a modal recontextualizing in terms of our attitude and a medial reconfiguration in terms of a work's symbolic mode of presentation, then this also makes room for the more recent view that art can be the "transfiguration of the commonplace."[12] This claim by Arthur Danto and the similar claim by Jacques Rancière that photography is "the appropriation of the commonplace"[13] are also about recontextualizing. The main difference is that for them recontextualization pertains not only to the Kantian aesthetic response to things, but also to their material transformation into works of art. These contemporary conceptions of art as transfigurative designate a movement beyond traditional representational and expression theories of art toward what I would call a presentational and articulative approach that is medium-focused from the start. While poets do indeed express their emotions through ideas, their influence relies on the vivid imagery of their language. Expression becomes more modulated when we turn to music.[14] Composers do more than find sounds and rhythms to express mute inner feelings, for they already experience the world in terms of its tonalities. Their work becomes part of a tonal medial context that preexists them and involves conventions about harmony and dissonance that are transmitted and transformed over time. Similarly, art historians have focused on the ways that painters have generally used their medium to create special visual effects. The realization that they can present things in a linear or painterly manner[15] makes it possible to see painters as part of a shared medial context in which certain styles of seeing are passed on and modified. But, starting with the Cubists who used collage and other techniques to focus our attention onto the canvas itself, the medial plane of visibility has become increasingly prominent in modern art. And how artistic medial contexts serve to recontextualize things has become most radically evident in the work of artists like Marcel Duchamp and Jasper Johns, who remove things from their normal functional contexts and reposition them in newly organized presentational contexts.[16] Their efforts to materially recontextualize things such as urinals and flags also decontextualize them and force viewers to adopt a disinterested attitude toward their normal reactions and expectations. Whereas Kant thought it was up to each viewer to adopt a neutral, open-minded, or disinterested response to works of art, modern artists often use medial techniques to impose a more negative or skeptical disinterestedness on us.

10

The Modal Relevance of Reflective Judgment for Kant's Worldview

The thematization of judgmental contexts opened up by the third *Critique* provides an important way to critically assess the worldly relevance of Kant's philosophy. It adds a new dimension to the important theme of modality in his thinking. In the previous chapter I agreed with Abaci that the modality of a judgment can disclose something about how we represent things in relation to the whole of our cognition. Modality indicates the comparative range of confidence or certainty we can have about our cognition. I also showed that the *Critique of Pure Reason* sets certain bounds on this range which Abaci's expansive reading does not take into account. Similarly, he trivializes the Kemp Smith claim discussed in chapter 6 that in the first *Critique* the modal categories of possibility and necessity obtain their sense from what can actually be experienced and cognized.[1] As Kemp Smith argued, objectively or cognitively viewed, the three modalities converge: what is experientially possible must also be actualizable, and necessity is defined by the causal determinants of what is actual. Since what each of us knows to be actual on the basis of outer experience is limited, this will lead us to form many hypotheses that are false. If these hypotheses are distinctly formulated, they can be objectively tested as determinant judgments. But when it comes to relating our ideational representations among each other as part of cognition in general, no such determinacy is available. Ideationally, we must consider not only the contents of outer sense but also those of inner sense, as well as imaginative representations generated by reason and desire. Then the problem of modal order becomes more complex and must cope with potential illusions and resulting prejudices. Modality will no longer be merely a cognitive index of what actually or materially exists in nature, but a more general measure of the value that our representations can have for us.

In the first *Critique*, Kant writes that the modality of a judgment "concerns only the value of the copula in relation to thinking in general" (A74/B100). Here modality measures how strongly we assent to what is being asserted in a judgment. What reality-value do we attach to a proposition? Is what it asserts possibly real for us, actually real, or necessarily real? Later in the same work, Kant returns to the problem of finding our modal bearings in the "Appendix" to the "Analytic of Principles" of the first *Critique* that is entitled "On the Amphiboly of Concepts of Reflection." Here he considers what mode of reality our ideational representations can have for us based on what cognitive faculty they derive from, and then he issues certain formal cautions that Abaci does not mention. What Kant does in the "Amphiboly" is to provide a "transcendental topic" that establishes "the place where the representations of things that are being compared belong, thus of whether they are thought by the pure understanding or given in appearance by sensibility" (A269/B325). Such a transcendental topic requires a mode of "reflection [*Überlegung*] (*reflexio*)" (A260/B316), which is not about "objects themselves, in order to acquire concepts directly from them, but is rather the state of mind in which we first prepare ourselves to find out the conditions under which we can arrive at concepts" (A260/B316). Here Kant is not just interested in the reflection and comparison of perceptual marks needed to arrive at empirical concepts as discussed in chapter 2 on Kant's logic, but in how to use certain contrastive concepts to orient our cognition in general. Whereas the categories are universal concepts that relate intuitive representational content to phenomenal objects, Kant also identified four sets of contrastive "concepts of reflection" (A260/B316) that indicate how any representational contents can be related to each other as we think about them. He considers whether our representations are in agreement or are opposed. Do they point to identity or difference? Are they of an inner nature or an outer one? Finally, do they pertain to matter or form?[2] These concepts of reflection are modally transcendental in that they require us to establish "which cognitive power" representations can be "objects for, whether for the pure understanding or for sensibility" (A269/B325). Thus Kant argues that if representations have their source in outer sense, then their conceptualization will need to prioritize form over content, difference over identity, and so on. This is because the material content of actual phenomenal objects is initially impenetrable. But if representations have their source in the understanding or reason, then the identity of inner conceptual content takes precedence. From the way Kant applies these distinctions in his "Amphiboly of the Concepts of Reflection," it becomes clear that his main concern is to show that this kind of transcendental reflection can forestall a Leibnizian conflation between the phenomenal world that belongs to our empirically focused understanding and the noumenal world of pure reason. Thus, the rational judgments that Abaci used to fill in the whole context of the world of cognition may not belong to the phenomenal world that we can understand, but to the noumenal world that we can only think of in the abstract. Kant introduces "transcendental reflection" (A269/B325) in the first *Critique* to force us to recognize that these two worlds must be approached differently. Transcendental reflection discerns further conditions affecting modality that must be acknowledged when deciding in what sense something can be real for us.

Distinguishing between the phenomenal and the noumenal worlds is no longer the main issue in the third *Critique*, where reflective judgments are solely about the human phenomenal world. Here the question of reflective placement is not which faculty or world is primary, but which this-worldly context is primary. Now reflection is no longer preliminary to the empirical concept-formation relevant to determinant judgment, but a supplement to conceptual judgments as we proceed to make reflective normative judgments about our proper placement in the world. Looking back at Kant's initial definition of modality as a reality-index of our thinking and his claim that the progression from problematic to assertoric and apodictic judgments comprises the basic "moments of thinking in general" (A76/B101), we can now see that modality is also a way of orienting our thoughts and contextualizing our judgments.

Whereas in the first *Critique* transcendental reflection required us to think differently about the phenomenal and the noumenal world, in the third *Critique* transcendental reflection is about how to properly orient ourselves within the phenomenal world we inhabit. Kant's four contexts of field, territory, domain, and habitat specify the empirical world in modal terms but still belong to it. While the field of the merely possible will diverge from the territory of what actually exists, the domains of necessary laws and the habitats of contingency will overlap with what is actual. Since these contexts can intersect and partly converge, the problem for judgment becomes that of asking what each context can add to our comprehension of the world. Each can specify a distinctive kind of value or significance. What we learn from our local habitat may be useful for our everyday survival, but at times we will also need the expertise of outsiders who draw on the domains of scientific inquiry. The extent to which our overall experience should rely on each of these contexts is an interpretive problem. At different moments in our lives, different priorities will have to be set. This has pragmatic consequences for Kant's worldview, as we will see later. To have a worldview is to have worked out a certain modal perspective on the world. It is not just to build up a cognitive picture of the world, but also to be prepared to respond to it appropriately.

The judgmental contextualization that the third *Critique* introduces is philosophically significant for Kant's project of doing philosophy in accordance with a world-concept. And whereas the primary concern of the first *Critique* was the subordinative form of determinant judgment, the specifying procedure of reflective judgment is coordinative. The former legislates from on high, the latter works from the ground up to navigate among intersecting contexts.

Reflective judgment is not merely the power to find a universal concept for a particular that is hard to define because it is unfamiliar or complex. It is also the more comprehensive power to compare and contrast contexts so that we can properly frame particulars to define their individuality. When Kant refers to "a principle of the power of judgment for providing concepts in the face of the excessive diversity in nature (in order to be able to *orient itself* in this diversity)" (*C3* 78–79; 5:193), he is pointing to what reflective judgment and rational comprehension have in common. If the power of reflective judgment is to orient itself, it needs a principle for contextualizing the world. Insofar as we need to adopt an orientational stance on the world, Kant compares us to amphibious creatures who move back and forth between land and water. This comes with the warning not to fall into amphibolies or confusions of thought as we navigate among different contexts. Here I would add that judgmental contextualization is ultimately about how to assess the most relevant factors in a situation. As will become evident in subsequent chapters, it concerns not only how to adjust to other regions of the world, but also how to recognize the different contexts that intersect where we happen to be.

Reflective contextualization is in effect a hermeneutical orientational strategy for comprehending philosophical issues that need to be both understood theoretically and evaluated normatively.[3] This broader relevance of judgmental contextualization will also show itself when we explore Kant's later writings about cosmopolitanism and when the question of moral amphibolies arises in relation to the scope of our duties. Although Kant presented his four contexts rather abstractly, their importance can be illustrated more concretely by imagining how they can be applied to human history, which is about as complex a subject matter for interpretation as any.[4] Thus, in gathering the various accounts and documents that are left to us of past wars, historians can contextually frame them in terms of the actual territorial disputes at stake, and the contingent local habitats that may have sparked the conflict. Local newspaper reports about battles and casualties will have a different status than the legal papers that document the outcome of the war. The latter will have to be made sense of in terms of the respective laws of the governmental domains involved. The various contextual discourses distinguished here intersect and are all relevant, but they do not have equal force or validity and must be weighed reflectively in historical interpretation. Each sphere may demand its own norms of assessment.

Having claimed that the power of reflective judgment searches for new insights to characterize objects by way of appropriately contextualizing them, we can now characterize the *Critique of Judgment* as a whole by also pointing to its overall contextualizing role in Kant's corpus. Although the third *Critique* tries to mediate between the earlier two *Critiques*, it is not to be regarded as their synthesis. This is because Kant does not use the power of judgment to integrate the results of the theoretical understanding and practical reason. The third *Critique* offers no intermediary domain and provides no doctrinal metaphysical foundation like the first two *Critiques*. However, Kant does point out that judgment can orient us as we make "the transition from the manner of thinking in accordance with the principles of the one to that in accordance with the principles of the other" (*C3* 63; 5:176). What is offered here is a kind of harmonization of the theoretical and the practical. This still allows us to regard the third *Critique* as relating the other two, but it does so by providing a broader orientational or reflective framework for comprehending them. Reflective judgment frames the two kinds of determinant judgment defined in the first two *Critiques*. They delineated two systematic domains, one of the laws of nature and the other of moral laws. The third *Critique* provides an orientational framework for reassessing them that also allows certain formal feelings to play an evaluative role, but only if they have been distanced from the content of our emotions.

Orientation and Reflective Specification

Even prior to the 1790 orientational distinction between field, territory, domain, and habitat as judgmental contexts, orientation was the topic of the 1786 essay "What Does It Mean to Orient Oneself in Thinking?" in which Kant points out that spatial orientation is just as much a function of feeling as of perception. We cannot orient ourselves in our perceptual worldly surroundings without at the same time feeling the difference between the left and right sides of our own body (see "OT" 4–5; 8:134–36). Similarly, we cannot, according to Kant, orient ourselves to the supersensible world without the "felt need of reason" to "*presuppose* the existence of a highest being" ("OT" 8, 10; 8:139, 141). Kant clarifies that strictly speaking reason cannot feel, yet through "insight into its lack" it phenomenally "effects the feeling of a need" ("OT" 8; 8:139n). And tellingly, Kant relates this felt need to the fact that "we have to judge" ("OT" 8; 8:139). Speculative thought cannot know that there is a God, but for human judgment, a limited formal use of speculation can foster a rationally felt faith that there is some highest being as a "signpost or compass by means of which to orient [ourselves] . . . in the field of supersensible objects" ("OT" 10; 8:142). This formal signpost may seem too abstract, but it was meant to assuage the heated religious debates in Germany at the time and counter dogmatism. Instead of authoritatively directing us from above, Kant seeks orientational pointers for human reflective comprehension. Especially important is his appeal here to healthy reason rooted in common sense:

> A human being who has common but (morally) healthy reason can mark out his path, in both a theoretical and a practical respect, in a way which is fully in accord with the whole end of his vocation; and it is this rational faith which must also be taken as the ground of every other faith, and even of every revelation. ("OT" 10; 8:142)

Reason should mark out our path, but it can only do so if we also orient ourselves through the kind of alliance of judgment and reflective feeling that the third *Critique* opens up. In the longer "First Introduction to the *Critique of Judgment*," Kant was able to expand on the need for this worldly orientation in comprehensive terms. There he writes that "the reflecting power of judgment, given its nature, could not undertake to classify the whole of nature according to its empirical differences if it did not presuppose that nature itself specifies its transcendental laws in accordance with some sort of principle" ("FI" 18–19; 20:215). All judgment involves "reflection [*Reflexion*]" ("FI" 15; 20:211) and uses comparison in an attempt to classify actual things in terms of determinate concepts, many of which are already empirically available to us. To also understand nature in terms of necessary laws, judgment must also be guided by the a priori concepts called the categories. But when we are exposed to things that are unfamiliar, as when we explore distant terrains or see something unexpected, such as a beautiful object, judgment becomes reflective (*reflectirend*) and searches for new concepts. In this inductive classifying procedure we start with particulars and aim at a new universal, moving from some to all. But in the attempt to comprehend the whole of nature, reflective judgment also appeals to an orientational specifying principle. The initial classifying task of judgment could produce an infinite number of classes that would be difficult to survey. To counteract this, Kant goes on to appeal to a transcendental principle of reflective judgment which considers the possibility that nature is a whole that specifies itself into parts with a "kinship among them" ("FI" 19; 20:215). Although the idea of reflective specification is new, I do not think that this introduces a further kind of reflective judgment. It is an elaboration of the kind of thinking that discerns symbolic analogies and indirect affinities among things that have not yet been more directly related conceptually.

Whereas conceptual classification proceeds mechanically, reflective specification proceeds by means of an art or technique of judgment. Kant speaks of "specifying a general concept by adducing or taking into account [*anführen*] the manifold under it" ("FI" 18; 20:215, translation revised). This specifying principle of reflective judgment is not explanatory for it has "no objective determining ground," yet it reflects "in accordance with its own subjective law, in accordance with its need" ("FI" 17; 20:214). Here, the felt orientational need of reason discussed earlier is replaced by a felt need of judgment that allows for a regional or contextual specification of nature. The *Critique of Pure Reason* was about one overarching domain of nature governed by the mechanical laws of physics. In the *Critique of Judgment*, we see Kant distinguish between inorganic and organic nature. Indeed, in an organic habitat, Kant speaks of "a thing existing as a natural end if it is cause and effect of itself" (*C3* 243; 5:371). This internal causality suggests that although the mechanical causality of physics that proceeds through external force may be the most pervasive kind of natural causality, it is not the only one. Reflective specification indicates that certain general concepts can be internally differentiated on the Aristotelian model, where the genus is the matter that is given form by means of its subspecies (see "FI" 18n; 20:215n). The transcendental principle of reflective specification allows us to judge different species of things as variations of a common genus. In the *Critique of Pure Reason*, Kant spoke of specification as a principle for determining "the homogeneity . . . of forms," where different things are nevertheless marked by a "sameness of kind" (A657/B685). In the *Critique of Judgment*, reflective specification serves as an orientational principle for finding contextual family resemblances. General concepts are made into generic forms whose "inner structure" ("FI" 20; 20:217) can be articulated. Whereas determinant judgment aims to explain through available laws, reflective judgment is interpretive and on the lookout for formal organizational contexts.

The Challenges of the Sublime and How to Contend with Our Limits

So far I have discussed aesthetic judgment and reflective judgment more generally as a comparative operation that includes contextualization. But when Kant shifts from the theme of beauty to that of the sublime, we confront something incomparable, which would seem to place it beyond our power to judge and contextualize. Because the sublime tends to be formless, it can blur the modal and medial contextual distinctions that were relevant for appreciating the beautiful. This formlessness leads Kant at times to suggest that the power and magnitude of what strikes us as sublime threaten to overwhelm us. But we also see him focus the infinite horizon evoked by the sublime into a comprehensive "worldview or intuition of the world [*Weltanschauung*]" (*C3* 138; 5:255, translation revised) which can align the phenomenal world with the "supersensible (the intelligible substratum of nature outside us and within us)" (*C3* 220; 5:345). Note that now the supersensible is not conceived as a transcendent world set apart from us, but as an intelligible substratum that is at least partly within us. The sublime is not merely some overpowering force outside of us, but discloses an infinity within ourselves.

Both the beautiful and the sublime enliven the imagination, but in the first case it is related to the understanding, and in the second to reason and its aim for completeness. This leads to a most interesting treatment of aesthetic comprehension that supplements Kant's already discussed claims about rational comprehension. In chapters 3 and 5, we saw Kant speak of comprehension (*Begreifen* = *comprehendere*) as a rational mode of cognition that reflects on the overall bounds of what can be known. But when discussing the mathematical sublime in the *Critique of Judgment*, Kant adds two other kinds of comprehension (*Zusammenfassung*): *comprehensio logica* and *comprehensio aesthetica* (see *C3* 135; 5:251). When perceiving the magnitude of phenomenal objects we can intuitively apprehend (*auffassen*) them part by part, but as we keep on moving to further parts, we lose the intuitive awareness of the first parts, which puts a limit on the process of intuitive comprehension (*zusammenfassen*). Logical comprehension makes up for this loss by using numerical concepts to measure and record what was initially represented. But the aesthetic comprehension that is needed to behold the immense magnitude of a sublime mountain range relies solely on the imagination and does not appeal to numerical concepts. As a consequence, we reach a limiting point at which we become *extensively overwhelmed* by an earthly scene. Yet our overall relation to the world allows us to make an instantaneous contextual shift that releases an *intensive feeling of sublime awe* that discloses another mode of assessment. Although we register a "displeasure from the inadequacy of the imagination in the aesthetic estimation of great magnitudes" (*C3* 141; 5:257), there is "at the same time, a pleasure aroused" by the recognition that it is our reason which can attain an overall idea of "something absolutely great" (*C3* 141; 5:257–58).

Most commentators content themselves with the incapacity of the imagination to encompass great magnitudes in order to immediately focus on the greater power of reason.[5] But Kant later makes it clear in the small print of the lengthy "General Remark" at the end of §29 that in recognizing this limit of its "empirical use," the imagination "acquires an enlargement and power which is greater than that which it sacrifices, but whose ground is hidden from it" (*C3* 152; 5:269). This hidden ground can be located if we consider what Kant says about the life of the mind, which will be one of the themes of the next chapter. For now, we can say that with the sublime, the imagination is inspired by the feeling of respect for reason to expand its scope and provide an instantaneous glimpse of the infinite. Logical comprehension is both intuitive and conceptual; it serves the understanding by adding determinateness to our perceptual survey of the phenomenal world. The aesthetic comprehension of a sublime expanse, by contrast, dispenses with the determinacy of concepts and numbers. Here intuition and feeling merge into an indeterminate viewing of the world (*Weltanschauung*) where things are too far away to be perceptually inspected as an intuition of the world (*Anschauung der Welt*).[6] When we judge the immense ocean to be sublime, it "appears to the eye [*Augenschein*]" in an "instant [*Augenblick*]" as "a clear watery mirror bounded only by the heavens" (*C3* 142, 153; 5:258, 270). All at once we imaginatively behold an all-embracing worldly expanse.

In the "Anticipations of Perception" of the first *Critique*, Kant acknowledged that the real in appearance is encountered "by means of mere sensation in an instant" (A168/B210) which measures a degree of *existence* in terms of an intensive magnitude that approximates 0 and therefore cannot be quantified extensively. It can only be intensively felt to exist. In the discussion of the sublime, this felt intensity is expanded from 0 to 1: it proceeds from an "immediate prehension [*fassen*]" (*C3* 135; 5:251) of *existence* that is sensible and ends with an aesthetic comprehension that provides a supersensible awareness of *coexistence*. Here we have the supersensible not merely as thought by reason, but as a felt oneness of simultaneous coexistence. At one point Kant distinguishes between two kinds of sublimity: an aesthetic kind that manifests itself like a sudden "affect" of enthusiasm for the good, and a more noble "affectless" kind (see *C3* 154; 5:272) where the mind pursues principles informed by reason. Since affects are "blind" they cannot "merit a satisfaction of reason" (*C3* 154; 5:272). Nevertheless, an affect that "arouses the consciousness of the powers to overcome any resistance" can be considered sublime in that it produces "a stretching of the powers through ideas" (*C3* 154; 5:272). The aesthetic sublime may not be fully guided by reason, but it is clearly inspired by reason to stir the imagination to instantaneously comprehend everything that coexists, albeit not determinately as through logical comprehension.

An eloquent characterization of the expansiveness of the noble sublime can be found in the conclusion of the *Critique of Practical Reason*, where Kant wrote:

> Two things fill the mind with ever new and increasing admiration and awe, the more often and more steadily one reflects on them: the starry heavens above me and the moral law within me. . . . I see them before me and connect them immediately with the consciousness of my existence. The first begins from the place I occupy in the external world of sense and extends . . . into an unbounded magnitude with worlds upon worlds. . . . The second begins from my invisible self, my personality, and places me in the presence of a world [*stellt mich in einer Welt dar*] which has true infinity . . . (*C2* 133; 5:161–62)[7]

Here again the expansion of our worldly context is not just a stepwise succession, but evokes a simultaneity that I see as the basis for developing a more comprehensive worldview. To recapitulate what has been proposed about aesthetic recontextualization, we can specify that the beautiful does so in intra-worldly ways, whereas the sublime does so by also projecting a provisional horizon for the world as we know it. I have used the orientational framework of the *Critique of Judgment* to indicate in what respects Kant thinks it is possible to comprehend more than we can understand. With the sublime, however, comprehension is somewhat speculative and evokes paradoxical aperçus about states of mind encompassing both pain and pleasure, frustration and exaltation. Such aperçus will need to be reflectively specified if they are to become useful in filling out a worldview. In any case, Kant's views about the sublime can be useful in pushing us to go beyond not only our individual standpoint, but also our common animality. Thus, he claims that "the judgment on the sublime requires culture (more so than that on the beautiful)" (*C3* 148–49; 5:265). This appeal to culture is not rooted in mere social conventions but "in human nature," or its "predisposition to the feeling for practical ideas, i.e., to that which is moral" (*C3* 149; 5:265).

Because the sublime can also be aroused by violent situations that are overpowering and potentially threatening to us, Kant supplements the mathematical sublime that we have focused on so far with a dynamical mode. The dynamical sublime invokes the idea of life in the most existential sense and will be examined in the following chapters on the feeling of life and teleological purposiveness. They will provide a better framework for differentiating between mathematical and dynamical sublimity.

11

What Kant Means by Life

One way to develop the idea of what a more comprehensive Kantian worldview will look like is to examine what Kant says about the nature of life. After all, a worldview is expected to elucidate what a world-concept means for our life. It is generally thought that the themes of life and purposiveness come together in the second half of the *Critique of Judgment* about teleology. But in fact, Kant already explores the idea of life in the first half of that work. It is thus more accurate to say that the first half is about the enlivening subjective purposiveness of aesthetic judgment, and the second half is about the objective purposiveness of living organisms dealt with by teleological judgment. It is worth noting in this regard that the terms "life" and "enlivenment" are much more prominent in the first aesthetic half of this work than in the second teleological half about organisms, which raises the question of whether Kant is aiming at a naturalistic definition of life at all. Since he also hesitates to define life metaphysically, I will consider to what extent the aesthetic feeling of life evoked by beauty and sublimity can orient us in comprehending how organisms function.

The Shifting Meaning of the Term "Life" in Kant

Perhaps Kant's earliest published definition of human life is in "Dreams of a Spirit-Seer" of 1766, where it is said to be 'the inner capacity to determine one's self by one's free choice" (2:327n). In the *Metaphysical Foundations of Natural Science* of 1786, Kant refers to life in a note as "the capacity of a substance to determine itself to act from an inner principle, of a finite substance to determine itself to change" (*MNS* 105; 4:544). He then adds that "we are not acquainted [*kennen*] with any other inner principle of a substance to change its state other than desire and no inner activity whatever other than thought about what depends on such desire, namely, the feeling of pleasure or displeasure, and appetite or will" (*MNS* 105; 4:544). From this he argues that material substances are inherently lifeless. This means that the primary sense of life for Kant refers to mind as an immaterial substance, and that he is not making any cognitive claims about the nature of biological life.

Two years later in the *Critique of Practical Reason* of 1788, there is another footnote in which Kant refines this mental sense of "life" within the moral context as "the capacity of a being to act in accordance with the laws of the faculty of desire" (*C2* 8n; 5:9n). Pleasure is then briefly referred to as "*the representation of the agreement of an object or an action with the subjective conditions of life*" (*C2* 8n: 5:9n). Since pleasure is merely considered as a gauge of how our relation to the world affects the well-being of our life, Kant considers it as only relevant to matters of prudence and of no further concern for matters of morality proper.

The *Critique of Judgment* of 1790 is the first of Kant's main works to repeatedly refer to the idea of life in the text itself. In §1, he writes that what is represented in an aesthetic judgment

> is related entirely to the subject, indeed to its feeling of life, under the name of the feeling of pleasure or displeasure, which grounds an entirely special faculty for discriminating and judging that contributes nothing to cognition, but only holds the given representation in the subject up to the entire faculty of representation, of which the mind becomes conscious in the feeling of its state. (*C3* 90; 5:204)

Our awareness of life is disclosed in an overall state of mind, and it is made clear that feeling rather than cognition provides our primary access to life. The felt pleasure of aesthetic appreciation is not determinantly cognitive, yet it should be acknowledged that it enlivens the overall play of our cognitive faculties and contributes to the life of the mind by expanding the scope of our thinking. The feeling of life can be said to evoke something akin to the transcendental "reflexive" awareness involved in the consciousness "*that* I am" which was central to the *Critique of Pure Reason*.[1] The difference in the *Critique of Judgment* is that now the feeling of life reflexively gathers our representations into an overall state of mind which can be aesthetically enjoyed. And if this aesthetic appreciation crosses over into a judgment of taste that reflectively takes into account the attitudes of others as well, it could be one of the rare instances in which reflexivity and reflectivity coexist and we feel fully alive.

Aesthetic pleasure is subjectively purposive, but it is disinterested in not satisfying any prudential or moral interests of the subject. It may inspire thought but is not aimed at a specific intellectual or moral purpose. Aesthetic purposiveness serves to "preserve [*erhalten*] our representational state" as we "*linger* in our contemplation [*Betrachtung*] of the beautiful" (*C3* 107; 5:222). And whereas ordinary perceptual representations need synthetic acts of the understanding to be reproduced, the aesthetic representational state has the power to "strengthen and reproduce itself" (*C3* 107; 5:222). This language of preservation and self-reproduction resembles that of biologists when they describe how organisms function. This, together with the fact that Kant speaks of the aesthetic mental state as a cooperative interplay among the faculties that produces equilibrium, raises the possibility that the first half of the *Critique of Judgment* can prepare us for and illuminate Kant's treatment of the purposiveness of organisms in the second half.

Whereas the enlivening pleasure of pure beauty remains at the mental level of the play of the imagination and the understanding, the more complex pleasure of the dynamical sublime can be initiated by the displeasure of bodily fear or fright. When discussing the dynamical sublime instigated by a violent storm, Kant acknowledges an actual disruption of our vital powers, but his focus is mostly about how this convulsion can be resolved by reminding us of our power of reason and by reorienting ourselves to our supersensible moral destination. All that we learn here about our sensible life is that it can be deeply stirred by emotions (*Rührungen*). Most scholarly discussions of the Kantian sublime focus on the dynamic sublime because it can more readily be explored for its moral and religious import, but the mathematical sublime that we referred to earlier is just as significant because it allows us to relate the aesthetic feeling of life to the more spiritual feeling of theoretical respect for what surpasses human measurement. We can experience the mathematical sublime whenever we confront something we cannot immediately survey, so that it overwhelms the imagination. This could be the mountain peaks and the wide ocean mentioned earlier, or a vast edifice such as a cathedral. According to Kant, this produces a regress of the imagination that transforms it from a sensible power in the service of the understanding to a power that bows to reason. In §27 this regress is described as "a comprehending in one instant [*Augenblick*] of what is [normally] apprehended successively . . . it cancels the time-condition in the imagination's [empirical] progression and makes *simultaneity* intuitable" (*C3* 142; 5:258–59). This again undermines the widely held view that the mathematical sublime represents merely a defeat of the imagination over against our reason. The passage about the regress, together with the already quoted comment that the imagination acquires an expansion beyond what it sacrifices, opens up a sudden "glimpse [*Augenschein*]" (*C3* 153; 5:270, translation revised) of simultaneity, as when the heavens offer us the "sight [*Anblick*]" of an "all-embracing vault" (*C3* 152; 5:270).

According to the *Critique of Pure Reason*, the simultaneity of things cannot be determinately *perceived* in the successive timeline of human apprehension. We can only *conceptually account* for things being objectively simultaneous or coexisting by means of the third relational category of "the reciprocity among that which acts and that which suffers [*zwischen dem Handelnden und Leidenden*]" (A80/B106). For "substances in appearance" to be cognized as being simultaneous, they must be located in the "pervasive [*durchgängiger*] community of interaction with each other" (A213/B260). This cognitive systematic context is only "mediately" (A213/B260) accessible, but in the sublime regress of the imagination, simultaneous coexistence is immediately *felt* in an instant, which is a vanishing limit point of the timeline. The displeasure of being perceptually frustrated by what is physically overwhelming impels our imagination to feelingly project the "*overall vocation* of the mind" (*C3* 142; 5:259). The ordinary sense-based and sequential gathering mode of "comprehension [*Zusammenfassung*]" of the perceptual imagination is replaced by a flash-like imaginative "comprehension [*Comprehension*]" (*C3* 143; 5:259) that opens up the supersensible potential of the life of the mind. The causal reciprocity that allows for action at a distance between the Earth and the Moon is now internalized as the more intimate, mentally felt reciprocity of enlivenment. There is no contradiction here: scientific experience requires that a determinate extensive perceptual manifold (*Mannigfaltigkeit*) be connected; aesthetic consciousness is content with an indeterminately felt harmony of an intensive multiplicity (*Vielheit*).[2]

Whereas the purposive aesthetic play of the beautiful gave us some formal clues about the self-preservation and harmonious equilibrium that can be ascribed to healthy organisms, the sublime discloses that life coexists with an environment that can be hostile and disruptive. The sublime offers the paradoxical aperçu that even when life is constrictively contextualized, the very displeasure that seems unpurposive can be made purposive, just as pain can become a warning signal to an animal organism to protect itself from external harm. Despite the more exalting tendencies of the sublime in the direction of the supersensible, it also provides insight into the reciprocity of the acting and suffering that define us as animal organisms. Whereas in the mechanistically conceived world of the first *Critique* causal efficacy is manifested in the surface-suffering of impact and reaction, in the third *Critique* we discern the more animated agency of human creativity, as well as the more deeply felt pain of suffering that stems from the limits of our creativity. We respond to beauty by celebrating the harmonious equilibrium of undisturbed contemplative life, whereas sublimity aims to restore a harmony that has been disturbed. These analogies are suggestive for describing organic behavior but remain vaguely formal, to be sure.

It is with the discussion of music, which Kant unfortunately regards as the lowest of the fine arts, that he begins to directly bring in a more concrete sense of life, namely, our bodily feeling of well-being or health. He acknowledges that the tones of music manifest a "language of affects" that has a pervasive power that "communicates . . . aesthetic ideas" (*C3* 206; 5:328–29). Although aesthetic ideas are prized by Kant for stimulating a shared kind of attitude, he thinks that this communicative effect is very transitory for the sensual tones of music, and therefore it does less to cultivate the life of the mind than of our bodily health. In a long note, we are told that music generates sensuous "gratification (even if its cause happens to lie in ideas)" in that it promotes "the total life of the human being, including the furtherance of bodily well-being, i.e., of health" (*C3* 207; 5:331). Thus, the benefit of music descends from the level of the life of the mind and its play of ideas down to the body to encompass "the feeling of health resulting from an intestinal agitation . . . This vibration of our organs . . . helps restore their equilibrium" (*C3* 208–9; 5:332). Similarly, the play of thought that leads to laughter rather than cognition is said to promote the vital processes of the body. Laughter is described as "*an affect resulting from the sudden transformation of a heightened expectation into nothing*" (*C3* 209; 5:333). Both music and humor can "generate [*hervorbringen*] an equilibrium of the vital powers [*Lebenskräfte*] in the body" (*C3* 209; 5:333) and instruct us "that we can get at the body even through the soul and use it as the physician of the body" (*C3* 209; 5:332).

These discussions of life and vital processes in the "Critique of Aesthetic Judgment" can be seen as a kind of preparation for the later discussions in the "Critique of Teleological Judgment" about how organisms function, but they fail to help us understand how organisms, especially plants that do not seem to feel, are generated and how they fit into a mechanistically conceived world. Since according to that world-concept, matter is inert and dead, what is it that enables material organisms to move themselves? The *Critique of Pure Reason* could only explain the movements of material bodies and changes in them as mechanically caused from without. This billiard-ball notion of change cannot account for self-initiated movements. For its part, the *Metaphysical Foundations of Natural Science* could only account for the appearance of life in matter by seeking its cause "in another substance different from matter, although bound up with it" (*MNS* 106; 4:544). This other substance is the soul. But in the "Critique of Teleological Judgment," Kant will not appeal to the life of a soul in describing how organisms function. Such an appeal would be especially inappropriate in the case of organisms like plants.

This hesitation to ascribe a soul to an organism should be seen in the context of an interesting feature of Kant's philosophy, namely, that its appeal to the traditional metaphysical postulate of the soul recedes over time. We see this especially in the evolution of his lectures on anthropology, where he increasingly supplements references to the soul with references to mind and spirit when describing human life. The final published *Anthropology from a Pragmatic Point of View* of 1798 replaces psychological introspection of the soul with observations that correlate both "the inner as well as the outer aspects of human beings" (*AP* 13; 7:125). The goal of correlating our inner life with our surrounding context so as to effectively interact with it leads Kant to also reject a mere physiological anthropology, because that would study human beings only in terms of their animal nature and their earthly origins. Instead, he proposes an anthropology that is worldly and cosmopolitan. It considers human beings not only in terms of what nature has made of them, but also according to what they can make of themselves as persons with practical reason. Although the nature of our humanity is at the heart of Kant's anthropology, what makes us human cannot be understood without reference to both our animal nature and our moral destination. In his writings on anthropology and religion, Kant offers three ways of explicating what life means for us on the basis of the predispositions to animality, humanity, and personality that were briefly discussed in the "Introduction."

Soul, Mind, and Spirit as Three Levels of Life

Kant's approach in his writings on anthropology and religion is to break up the monolithic idea of the soul as a kind of substance into a more variegated consideration of three functional levels at which life manifests itself. This can be seen as another illustration of what Ernst Cassirer considered to be one of Kant's main contributions to modern philosophy, namely, the transition from substantial to functional thinking. The functions of the soul are recontextualized in relation to those of mind and spirit. As was pointed out in the "Introduction," we find the beginnings of this new way of speaking about life in a passage from the early *Collins* anthropology lecture notes from 1772–73, where Kant distinguishes between lower and higher powers of the soul. The lowest power *of* soul that we share with animals is "the capacity to be modified [*modificirt*]" or to have "impressions that the body suffers passively," and it is called "*anima* (*Seele*) [*soul*]" (VA-*Collins*, 25:16). We humans also have what Kant calls "*animus or Gemüth* [*mind*] and *mens Geist*) [*spirit*]" (VA-*Collins*, 25:16). He then adds that soul, mind, and spirit "are not three substances, but *three ways we feel ourselves living.* In regard to the first way we are passive, in regard to the other [second] we are passive but simultaneously reactive [*reagirend*], in regard to the third way we are entirely self-active" (VA-*Collins*, 25:16).

This way of delineating the lower function of the soul related to the body would allow Kant to acknowledge that all mammals may have the modifiable aspects of a soul while lacking the other aspects that define human beings, namely, the higher functions assigned to mind and spirit. But even this is not certain because most of Kant's references to animal life are contained in the lectures on anthropology and refer to it as one aspect of our own human nature. In the *Metaphysik L1* of the mid-1770s, he spoke of plants as manifesting "a beginning of life" and of the animal kingdom as disclosing "small degrees of life" (28:205). These remarks, and the claim that nonrational animals cannot experience the true "spontaneity" of life (see 28:249), show a reluctance to fully apply the idea of life to organisms.

Kant's uses of the term "soul" are surprisingly noncommittal but are useful for pointing to the assimilative level of experience. Anthropology is chosen as an alternative to psychology because at the time psychology was considered a part of metaphysics and thus forced to posit a soul. Kant's anthropology is ultimately a "pragmatic" discipline "where we abstract from the question of whether the human being has a soul or not (as a special incorporeal substance)" (*AP* 53; 7:161).

Kant's anthropology suggests that at the initial stages of our lives when the predisposition to animality dominates, we rely mainly on the lower soul-like power to register sense impressions rather than on the consciousness related to mind.[3] Merely being alive is about coping with how we are affected. In *Religion within the Boundaries of Mere Reason* (1793), Kant writes that our predisposition to animality defines us as a mere "living being" (*R* 50; 6:26) who behaves on the basis of "physical or mechanical self-love, i.e., a love for which reason is not required" (*R* 51; 6:26). Our "predisposition to animality" is needed for "self-preservation . . . the propagation of the species, [and] for community with other human beings" (*R* 51; 6:26). What Kant calls mechanical self-love at the modifiable level of "soul" is not necessarily egoistic, for it extends to one's family and local community. We could thus say that at the stage of animality, self-love encompasses a sense of solidarity with those akin to us. As long as children are dependent on their parents, they will tend to comply with their demands. Although these demands come from without, they are consented to because of a natural family bond.

Gradually we are expected to rise above this natural life of familial love, but to the extent that it involves basic instincts of survival it can be accepted as one of the "original predispositions to good in human nature"

(*R* 50; 6:26). Kant claims that if there are vices associated with this level of animal self-love, they are grafted onto it. Since at this level reason is not in play, evil as the perversion of reason is not yet possible. Kant is generally accused of wanting to negate our sensuous animal nature as much as possible, but as is made clear later in the same *Religion* text, "incentives of self-love" may be "incorporated" (*R* 59; 6:36) into the maxims of action of adults if they do not claim priority over the way respect for the moral law is incorporated as well. Even when Kant is judging moral goodness, he is willing to acknowledge man's dependence on "the incentives of his sensuous nature because of his equally innocent natural predisposition . . . (according to the subjective principle of self-love)" (*R* 58–59; 6:36).

It is at the level of the second predisposition to humanity that the more lively acquisitive powers of mind manifest themselves, and only the third predisposition to personality can express a fully self-active spirit. In elaborating what is involved in our predisposition to humanity, Kant claims that it exhibits another form of self-love. It too is "physical," but not merely as mechanically caused from without; it introduces a judgmental "*comparison* (for which reason is required); that is, only in comparison with others does one judge oneself happy or unhappy" (*R* 51; 6:27). This mental form of self-love is more egoistic because it is concerned to gain worth in the opinion of others in society at large. We feel ourselves as being in competition with others and want to maintain our standing and honor. To again make use of the language of the *Collins* anthropology lecture notes, the predisposition to humanity involves a state of mind (*animus*) that is reactive to threats from without.[4] But animals also react to their surroundings, which again raises the question of why there are passages in Kant where he does not admit that animals can be conscious. After all, in the "First Introduction to the *Critique of Judgment*," Kant goes so far as to say that nonhuman animals can reflect, which is commonly regarded as a conscious activity of comparing things. We are told there that "reflecting [*reflectiren*] . . . goes on even in animals," though not in an attempt to attain a new concept, but "only instinctively" ("FI" 15; 20:211) to determine an inclination. Nonrational animals are able to reflect *that* one sensible representation differs from another, but Kant thinks that they cannot consciously hold the representations together and judge *how* they can be conceptually distinguished. Because they relate to things instinctively, nonhuman animals are thought to remain at the level of mechanical movement that is either activated from without or from within by an impulse or drive that is irresistible. What characterizes the human power to react to things is that it can be responsive in a more lively or conscious manner, and as we already saw in "The False Subtlety of the Four Syllogistic Figures" of 1762, what makes our reflecting a conscious activity is the ability not just to differentiate things, but to also "judge" what those differences mean ("FS" 104; 2:60).[5] Clearly the power of judgment is essential for cognitive consciousness. This is then developed further in the lectures on logic where we saw that the comparative representational "acquaintance [*kennen*]" with things that animals possess falls short of the "conscious cognition [*erkennen*]" of judgmental distinctions and connections that only humans are capable of (*LL* 569–70; 9:65).[6]

In the *Critique of Pure Reason*, Kant sketches a progression (*Stufenleiter*) of representations that recalls the seven levels of cognition discussed in chapter 3, but differs in focusing on what a representation is referred to and how it is to be designated. For a representation to reach the level of "consciousness," according to Kant, it must be "perceptual," by which he means that it is either a "sensation that modifies the state of a subject" or an "objective perception" that is cognitive (A320/B376). Like other animals, human beings have sense impressions at the modifiable level of "soul" that can provide what was already referred to in chapter 4 as "the real of sensation" by which "the subject is affected" (A165/B207). But a "sensation in itself is not an objective representation" (A165/B208) of the world. Sensations are neither cognitive nor conscious, according to Kant. They are, as I said earlier, subjectively real, but not objectively actual. Sensations exist as "instantaneous" (A99) limiting points on the timeline of our consciousness. What is instantaneously given by sense affects us at the lowest level of the life of "soul," whereas cognition begins at the level of the conscious mind and representational apprehension.

A sensation is thus comparable to what Kant calls "*prehension* [*fassen*] in one glance [*Blick*]" (*C3* 137; 5:254, translation revised) in the *Critique of Judgment*. In the "Subjective Deduction" of the first edition of the *Critique of Pure Reason*, Kant had made it clear that for sense to be intuitable as a manifold representational content, it must be "run through" over time by a synthetic act of *apprehension* (*auffassen*). But what is distributively run through mentally must also be taken together in an act of "*Zusammennehmung*" (A99). This requires the perceptual imagination to reproduce what was initially run through in order to allow the understanding to gradually *comprehend* (*zusammenfassen*) the unity of the apprehended manifold over time.

We can now supplement our earlier discussion of the mathematical sublime by more fully contrasting its instantaneous regressive comprehension (*Comprehension*) with the gradually accumulated progressive account of representational comprehension (*Zusammenfassung*). Whereas our passive being *affected* by sensations occurs at the lowest prehensive limit of awareness, the sublime discloses a more "vigorous *affect*" or "agitation of the mind" (*C3* 154; 5:272, translation revised) aimed at the highest comprehensive limit of consciousness. Thus, life can be said to hover between the capacity to instantaneously register how the human body is affected at the sensible level of soul and the sublime state of mind that is instantaneously enlivened by the imagination. Finally, it is worth noting that Kant speaks of the sublime not as providing a cognitive representation (*Vorstellung*) of something finite, but as providing a "*negative* presentation/exhibition [*Darstellung*]" of the "infinite" (*C3* 156; 5:274, translation revised). If life is to be more *positively* represented, mind must be related to the next level of self-activating spirit.

I have compared the ways in which the imagination functions perceptually in the "Subjective Deduction" and feelingly in the mathematical sublime in order to sketch the wide range of the life of the mind. But the "Objective Deduction" made it clear that determinant cognition cannot be acquired at the level of perceptual apprehension and requires the transcendental unity of apperception, which is at the same level of the life of spirit that was referred to earlier as the power of moral personality in the *Religion*. The only difference is that the transcendental unity of apperception manifests spirit at the level of theoretical understanding (*Verstand*), whereas moral personality expresses spirit at the level of practical reason (*Vernunft*).

The rational predisposition to the good that pertains to personality is defined as "the susceptibility to respect the moral law *as of itself a sufficient incentive to the power of choice*" (*R* 52; 6:27). Here reason is self-actively alive in the sense that only spirit can be for Kant. We saw that the predisposition to animality did not make use of reason, but only of sense and instinct and therefore could merely generate natural goods. The second level of the predisposition to humanity "is rooted in a reason which is indeed practical, but only as subservient to other incentives" (*R* 52; 6:28). This humanity is displayed in how we apprehend others in our social and political dealings and by the incentive to reproductively reinforce our own standing while maintaining civil relations in our prudential affairs. Finally, our personality is "rooted in reason practical of itself, i.e., in reason legislating unconditionally" (*R* 52; 6:28). It is the spiritual source not only of our moral life, but also of everything that we productively strive for in communal life. This corresponds to the third level of the reflective appropriation of experience.

That our thinking about life must ultimately have a spiritual source is made most clear in §49 of the *Critique of Judgment*:

> Spirit [*Geist*] in its aesthetic sense is the enlivening [*belebende*] principle in the mind [*Gemüthe*]. But what this principle uses to enliven the soul, the *material* [*Stoff*] which it uses for this purpose, is what purposively sets

the mental powers into motion, i.e., into a play that is self-maintaining and even strengthens these powers to that end. (*C3* 192; 5:313, translation revised).

The material alluded to here is not physical, but representational. Kant is referring to how aesthetic ideas as representations of the imagination can "occasion much thinking, but to which no determinate thought whatsoever, i.e., no concept, [can] be adequate" (*C3* 192; 5:314). Kant gave our capacity to conceptually understand nature a formal grounding by means of the transcendental unity of apperception. But the "imagination (as a productive cognitive faculty)" can take this formal spontaneity of the understanding a step further "in the creation [*Schaffung*], as it were, of another nature out of the material that the actual [*wirkliche*] one gives it" (*C3* 192; 5:314).

The human, aesthetic imagination is creative in transforming our ordinary experience of the natural world into "something wholly different" and allowing us to "feel our freedom from the law of association (which attaches to the empirical use of the imagination)" (*C3* 192; 5:314). It can creatively transform mechanical nature as we know it into something else, but as Kant later makes clear in his *Anthropology*, this transformative power of our imagination must be distinguished from a divine-like creative power called "*Schöpfung*" (*AP* 61; 7:168). Our imagination can be creative or *schaffend* in being "poetically inventive [*dichtend*]," but it is "not exactly *schöpferisch*, for it is not capable of producing a sense representation that was *never* given to our faculty of sense" (*AP* 61; 7:168). This means that we humans cannot ex nihilo create anything, and certainly not any living creature (*Geschöpf*). Yet, the transformative *Schaffung* of the aesthetic imagination can produce things that are lifelike and thus serve as a kind of model for reflecting on what life means. We already saw that the aesthetic play of the imagination at the level of mind can enhance our feeling of life to maintain itself, and this is more significant than the instinctive feeling of life at the lowest level of "soul," which merely provides instantaneous, ephemeral impressions. And at the level of the life of spirit, the imagination produces aesthetic ideas that can prefigure/configure what Kant will say about organisms in the "Critique of Teleological Judgment" as systems that preserve themselves and procreate. But these intimations will only be regulative and reflective, as will be made clear later.

In one of his *Reflexionen zur Metaphysik*, Kant takes a step further by characterizing life as movement conceived transcendentally (*RM* 4786, 17:728). And in the *Opus postumum*, we read that the a priori capacity of the subject to initiate movement involves at the same time the capacity to "anticipate the counteracting moving forces of matter" (*OP,* 22:506). These claims make it possible to regard life as the transcendental condition for both the power to move and be moved. By analogy, we can say that it is the human/mental feeling of life associated with reflective judgment that provides the transcendental point of unity for both the spontaneity of the understanding and the passivity of sense. And at the level of spirit, the feeling of life allows us to not just be reactively responsive, but to be self-activating and anticipate the kind of reciprocity that Kant finds in organic nature. He is careful, however, not to claim that our feeling of life can define what life is in the biological sphere of nature. The aesthetic feeling of life is mental and was shown to be capable of working its way down to the body as we saw in the case of the enjoyment of music. But the fact that we can feel our body being enlivened does not help us to understand life physiologically. Nevertheless, the realization that this mental feeling is holistic and that its cognate of vital sense pervades our whole body, provides a source of orientation to supplement our *determinate understanding* of the mechanisms of nature with what will be shown to be an *indeterminate comprehension* of organic reciprocity.

We have seen that orientation serves an important function in relating living human subjects to the world. To the extent that human beings have the capacity to move, they need to be able to orient themselves in the world around them in order to avoid obstacles and attain their aims. The power to orient oneself enhances the feeling of life, since it relates to how we move our body. Kant calls orientation an a priori feeling whereby on the basis of distinguishing the left and right sides of one's body, one can perceptually find one's way in unfamiliar territory (see "OT" 4; 8:135). In her book *Ideal Embodiment: Kant's Theory of Sensibility*, Angelica Nuzzo claims that because this capacity to orient oneself engages the body, it is transcendentally embedded there and makes the body itself alive from the start.[7] But Kant says that it is the "subject" that makes this felt distinction about its body. Since he adds that "these two sides outwardly display no designatable difference in intuition" ("OT" 4; 8:134–35), it is judgment that allows us to feel the difference. Because I have argued that Kant locates both the capacity to orient ourselves and our aesthetic enjoyment of life at the level of mind and judgment, Nuzzo asserts that my "interpretation commits Kant to the dogmatic claim that the body is 'lifeless.'"[8] Although Kant's mechanistic philosophy of science does indeed regard our bodies as material objects (*Körpern*) that are inert, I have also shown that aesthetic pleasure can stir the body and that Kant allows for bodily instinctive drives. The feeling of enlivenment is at the level of mind, but Kant does not restrict our sense of life to this level. The way we experience ourselves as having a lived body (*Leib*) is now often highlighted, and Kant himself sometimes uses the latter term, as in the following early passage: "we want to merely investigate whether the capacity to think rationally and the movement of the lived body [*Leib*] that belongs to it" is also affected by "the warmth of the sun that enlivens everything" (*AN*, 1:355). Nuzzo thinks that her theory of ideal embodiment allows Kant to overcome the Cartesian mind-body dualism. Although Kant never dissolves that gap as such, his three-level approach of bodily *anima*, mental *animus*, and spiritual *mens* is an improvement.

There is no doubt that Kant attaches the most significance to life at the level of mind and spirit when it approaches the spontaneity of freedom. He even wrote that "freedom is original life" (*RMP* 6862, 19:183). When it comes to organic nature, he finds that what constitutes life is more difficult to define, as will be shown in the next chapter.

12

Comprehending Teleological Purposiveness by Appropriately Contextualizing It

I have shown that because human beings are acquainted (*kennen*) with their own life through feeling, they find it difficult to conceptually cognize (*erkennen*) life in other forms. Humans are constituted with the power to understand the causation of mechanical motion, not of self-initiated movements. Mechanical causes as we can understand them must have sensible confirmation, which means that they are necessarily external to what they affect. But if there is a self-initiated movement in some organism, it is by nature internal and its mode of operation cannot *receive* sensible confirmation from without. This entails that any study of organisms prior to the availability of X-rays can only proceed indirectly by means of provisional judgments, and teleology will need to be comprehended by means of functional descriptions.

Categorial judgments concerning mechanical causation are determinant or explanatory because they appeal to universal laws of nature from which particular cause-effect relations can be derived. The provisional judgments that Kant calls on to supplement our understanding of mechanism are reflective and proceed inductively from the particular to the general. They reflect on particular organisms as individuals that develop a self-contextualizing identity relative to their environment. These judgments reflectively characterize particular beings whose behavior manifests changes that are not predictable from known laws and thus seem to be contingent. If those observed changes nevertheless further their well-being, we may judge them to be purposive, according to Kant.

This ascription of purposiveness renders an organism an internally ordered system whose parts are judged to be reciprocally related. Plants and animals can be judged to be organic systems that cause changes which affect themselves in terms of their own growth. Each such organism is assumed to "generate [*erzeugt*] itself as an *individual*" (*C3* 243; 5:371) and be its own end. Kant writes that some parts in an

> animal body (such as skin, bone, or hair) could be grasped as accumulations governed by merely mechanical laws. Yet the cause that provides the appropriate matter, that *modifies and forms* it in that way, and that deposits it in the pertinent locations must always be judged teleologically. Hence everything in such a body must be regarded as organized, and everything is also, in a certain relation to the thing itself, an organ in turn. (*C3* 249; 5:377)

Here Kant describes an internal power whereby an organism modifies (*modificirt*) and forms itself, which contrasts nicely with the external way in which the lowest level of soul was said to be passively modified (*modificirt*). *Formative modification* rather than *motion* becomes the appropriate way to describe how organisms function. Organisms manifest "a self-propagating formative power [*fortplanzende bildende Kraft*], which cannot be explained through the capacity for movement alone (that is, mechanism)" (*C3* 246; 5:374). The shift from movement to formative modification is important in that it makes room for plants as organic beings. But the assignment of purposiveness to plants and nonhuman animals that lack reason must be clarified. This teleological purposiveness is not like the conscious, and possibly rational, intentional purposes that humans project for themselves. Organic purposiveness is not projective in that way. Describing an organism as internally organized is technically purposive for our way of judging. The descriptive concept of a formative purposive power is regulative or hypothetical, but it can be reflectively justified "as benefiting [*zum Behuf*] our capacity to cognize nature" ("FI" 8; 20:202). Although such a judgment about purposiveness is subjective, Kant speaks of it as "a priori" and "special" ("FI" 8; 20:202) for our human way of thinking. I thus regard his reflective principle of judgment as an intersubjective transcendental condition for empirical human inquiry in contexts where mechanistic explanations are not available.[1] As long as the ideal of a universal legislative order of nature cannot be fully filled in, Kant considers it appropriate to explore organisms as intermediate regions of organizational order.[2]

Just as the aesthetic purposiveness of the imagination in the first half of the *Critique of Judgment* is a purposiveness without a determinate purpose, so the immanent purposiveness ascribed to organisms discloses no intentional purpose and seems to be primarily self-furthering. Aesthetic purposiveness is about feeling oneself into a context of *possibilities*, whereas organic purposiveness is about being adaptive to an immediately surrounding *actual* context.[3] For Kant, the reciprocal causality of the parts of an organism is not just about its organs mutually affecting each other. They are also "reciprocally the cause and effect of their form" (*C3* 245; 5:373). This is the "basis on which someone judging this whole cognizes the systematic unity of the form and the combination of all of the manifold that is contained in the given material" (*C3* 245; 5:373). An organism can be judged not just in terms of its causal antecedents and constituents, but as a reciprocal system in which actions and reactions are in play, including from its surrounding context. This points back to Kant's third relational category of community that was referred to when explicating the simultaneity of the sublime. It is worth commenting that in a note, the idea of a contextually organized system is compared to the coordinative *organization* of a "body politic" (*C3* 246–47n; 5:375n). What is at stake is the reflective comprehension of what is simultaneously co-generated. In §59 Kant already prepared us for this kind of comparison in symbolic terms by speaking of an "animate body [*beseelten Körper*]" as a reflective analogue for his ideal of a republican state that is self-governing on the basis of laws and resists being controlled from without. Kant acknowledges that there is no one-to-one correspondence between organisms and law-governed nation-states. Yet they exhibit a functional analogy that makes them reflective counterparts. To comprehend these reflective analogues is to draw on one of the formative functions of the imagination that can be called analogue-formation (*Gegenbildung*) or the power to produce a "*Gegenbild: symbolum*" (*RA*, 15:123). *Gegenbildung* is the imaginative power to discern symbolic rather than literal counterparts in different contexts.[4] These comparisons lead me to suggest another counterpart pairing. Organisms for Kant are self-organizing wholes whose parts possess *systemic* internal functions, but whose overall *systematic* formation must counter what could resist them from their surrounding context. The immanent purposiveness of organisms is contextual and not immune from external influences. No matter how healthy a plant is in its internal functions, it will not be able to withstand an extended drought. This bordering relation also points to the possibility that both determinant and reflective judgments may come to intersect in our comprehension of organisms.

I think that this way of contextualizing organisms by moving beyond the second relational category of causality to the third relational category of community provides a way to both acknowledge and deal with the "two kinds of mechanical inexplicability" of organisms that Hannah Ginsborg carefully lays out. The first kind of inexplicability points to the causal limits of *matter* which cannot account for the well-structured arrangement of the parts of individual things such as artifacts and organisms. The second kind of mechanical inexplicability pertains to what makes organisms *natural* rather than *artifactual*, namely, their display of certain ongoing "regularities."[5] Yet by dwelling on this difference at the level of causality and not adequately considering the communal level of interaction, Ginsborg comes to place undue stress on what she calls the design-like nature of organisms. For her, an organism is an object that must be regarded "as if it had been designed, yet without committing ourselves to the claim that it was designed," which "is just to judge that the object conforms to a concept of how it ought to be."[6] In explicating what she means by the "standards"[7] of what a natural product ought to be, Ginsborg turns mainly to Kant's "First Introduction to the *Critique of Judgment.*" But even there Kant wrote that "if we think that a product of nature ought to be something . . . then we are already presupposing a principle that could not have been derived from experience" ("FI" 40; 20:240). The example that Ginsborg then focuses on concerns the purposiveness of a specific organ like the eye, whose "perfection"[8] is measured by an external task. However, what especially characterizes the purposiveness of whole organisms for Kant in the "Critique of Teleological Judgment" is the internal purposiveness among their various organs. This involves a reciprocal organizational adaptation that need not be governed by the normative standards associated with design, for as Kant writes, we often find "certain parts" in organisms that "on account of chance defects or impediments, form in an entirely new way so as to preserve what is there, and so bring forth an *anomalous* creature" (*C3* 244; 5:372). This accommodation to contingent or chance imperfections is not just accepted by Kant, but embraced as "among the most wonderful properties of organized creatures" (*C3* 244; 5:372).

We can provisionally agree with Ginsborg that if the heart fails to pump blood to certain parts of the body, it is not functioning as we think it ought. But this could also be explained by the calcification of the arteries caused by too much ingestion of saturated fats. Which part of an organism is deficient is not always readily apparent. Before we take the invasive action of operating on the heart, it might be worthwhile treating the calcification with dieting and medications. Here we have several provisional strategies that need to be considered. Kant's anomalous creatures show that the immanent purposiveness of an organism is not merely about the inner adaptations among its parts, but also about how the organism as a whole adapts itself to its context where there are no clear oughts at work. What Kant calls the "inner natural perfection" (*C3* 247; 5:375) of an organism does not exhibit the design-like perfection of an intended end. There is something pre-fixed about executing an overall design, which goes against the self-modificatory powers of an organism. These reservations about appealing to the idea of design will be reinforced when we turn to Kant's response to the biological theory of preformationism. What Kant calls the inner natural perfection of organisms is at best a self-modifying and adaptive perfection in which different coexisting contextual forces converge and intersect. The justification for adding the natural-history language of contextual adaptation to the terminology used up to now will become more evident in the next section, where organic epigenesis is discussed. In sum, I think the normativity that Ginsborg discerns in organisms is reducible to the question of what is normal and what is not normal or anomalous. The role of normativity will be redefined in the last section of this chapter, about the relation of reflective judgment to human comprehension and contextual understanding.

Just as the aesthetic purposiveness of appreciating the beauty of a flower or a landscape is not an intellectual pleasure in the perfection of some artistic design, so the organizational purposiveness of an organism is not the manifestation of some self-contained design that predetermines an outcome. Kant's immanent purposiveness points to an organizational functioning that is somewhat metaphorical and figurative, to be sure, but so is the current genetic language about cells of organisms exchanging signals and about neurons in the brain transmitting information to each other. Just as we must not conflate purposiveness with design, so we must realize that the neural transmission of signals falls short of the conscious communication of meaning. And when Kant says that although the composition of the bones in our bodies can be causally explained, they must also be judged teleologically, we should read this heuristically as framing further questions about how these bones can continue to function properly in our bodies. Or to elaborate on Kant's own description, it is to make sure that the "appropriate" minerals are obtained to be transmitted to the "pertinent locations" in the bones. Kant's teleological judgments about the immanent purposiveness of organisms are not themselves supplementary explanations, but merely establish the appropriate meaning framework for pursuing further inquiry and eventual explanations.[9]

In the same vein, the feeling of life and the holistic self-enhancing frame of mind that were explored in the "Critique of Aesthetic Judgment" have no explanatory value for the "Critique of Teleological Judgment." All that I have claimed for them is the orientational function of providing some imaginative *augenscheinliche* clues, or even an instantaneous transcendental glimpse, into what it means for an organism to be in a general state of equilibrium or to adapt to disturbances caused by a more encompassing context. They guide us in describing how organisms function physically in light of the fact that metaphysical efforts to ground life and make organisms less causally "inscrutable" have failed, according to Kant. Speculative metaphysicians who determinately assign organisms "the property of life" are accused of "hylozoism" (*C3* 246; 5:374) in that they would attribute life to matter itself, which is self-contradictory, according to Kant. Equally unacceptable is the "alien principle of a soul standing in communion [*Gemeinschaft*]" (*C3* 246; 5:374) with matter. Even those who appeal to this principle to account for the life of human consciousness would not need it for organisms that lack consciousness. To appeal to a soul in order to explain the self-organizing power of material organisms is to move outside of nature. The formative power that is reflectively ascribed to organisms must be "imparted [*mitgetheilt*] to their material" (*C3* 246; 5:374) by nature itself, not by a speculative principle of life or by "theism" (*C3* 263; 5:392). Hylozoism and theism acknowledge the purposive behavior of organisms, but make assumptions that are either self-contradictory or speculative.

Another approach that Kant finds unacceptable is to altogether dismiss the idea that organisms are purposive. Philosophers who have done this either followed Epicurus, who starts with "lifeless matter" and regards organisms as mere contingent aggregates resulting from mechanistic laws; or they moved in the direction of Spinoza, who posited a "lifeless God" (*C3* 263n; 5:392n). If everything in the world is permeated by an overarching order or fatalistic *architectonic*, then the contingency associated with the generation of organisms is simply explained away. What Kant proposes instead is a more limited *tectonic* of nature that acknowledges the contingent shifts involved in organic processes, but nevertheless looks for a lawfulness even there, which may not be determinant but is at least reflective. The purposiveness that Kant tries to manifest in his exposition of organic processes of formative modification is a "lawfulness of the contingent" (*C3* 274; 5:404). It is the lawfulness of a coordinative functional order rather than of a subordinating predictive order. It inserts a provisional tectonic of organic nature into the architectonic of mechanistic nature. Instead of imposing the idea of life onto organisms or skeptically denying it of them, Kant explores how much sense we can make of the way organisms function by in effect suspending the idea of life. He only refers to the idea of life once in the context of his extensive discussions of how organisms are generated and how they function, and it is a dismissive reference. Thus, he claims that the explanation provided by hylozoism moves us in "a circle: we try to derive the natural purposiveness in organized beings from the life of matter, while yet we are familiar [*kennen*] with this life only in organized beings" (*C3* 265–66; 5:394). His first point is that we should not expect to conceptually cognize what "life *in* matter" is by appealing to the "life *of* matter." The second point is that the life we are familiar with in everyday terms is not scientifically definable. He also casually refers to beasts of prey who "can only be nourished by what lives" (*C3* 294; 5:426), but that is merely by analogy with what it feels like to be alive. Those who use the Meredith translation of the *Critique of Judgment* may not have noticed Kant's hesitancy to directly endow organisms with life, because Kant's neutral term *Geschöpf* is not properly translated as "creature," but as "form of life." Similarly, when Kant speaks of "organized [*organisirte*] creatures" (*C3* 244; 5:372), Meredith substitutes "organic life." Meredith may have felt justified in using the phrase "form of life" because Kant had just claimed that the repeated defoliation of a tree "would kill it" (*C3* 244; 5:372). In response, I would say that while we are acquainted (*kennen*) with trees as "living and dying" on an everyday common-sense basis, from the scientific or philosophical standpoint of cognizing (*erkennen*) the immanent purposiveness of organisms, we should avoid any explanatory principle or unifying idea of "life." Even when discussing our own internal sense of life, we saw Kant speak of three ways in which we feel ourselves to be "living."

Organic and Mental Epigenesis

Kant finds support for his standpoint in Johann Friedrich Blumenbach's theory of epigenesis, which starts with "organized matter" (*C3* 292; 5:424) rather than with living matter. This is elaborated in §81, "On the Association of Mechanism with the Teleological Principle in the Explanation of a Natural End as a Product of Nature" (*C3* 290; 5:421), in an attempt to find a middle ground between natural epigenesis and preformationism.

Although Kant's conception of the immanent purposiveness of organisms ascribes a kind of inherent form to them, it should not be confused with early eighteenth-century preformationism. The ovist version of this theory claimed that the embryo is pre-formed in the mother and that the male's semen only mechanically stimulates its growth. With the aid of the microscope, it became possible to observe the movement of sperm cells in semen and discover that they fuse with egg cells, leading to the epigenetic theory that the embryo forms and differentiates itself after conception. Accordingly, Kant rejected the Malebranchean belief that the form of each animal is divinely pre-formed and developed. He replaced that theory of individual preformation with a "system of generic preformation" that applies to a whole zoological species. This new system conceives form "virtually [*virtualiter*]" as a "predisposition imparted to the stock" (*C3* 291; 5:423). This reduced mode of preformationism is meant to leave room for the theory of epigenesis that Kant prefers scientifically. For in considering those things "that can initially be represented as possible only in accordance with the causality of purposes," this theory "considers nature, at least as far as propagation is concerned, as itself bringing them forth [*hervorbringend*] rather than merely developing them, thus making the least possible appeal to the supernatural" (*C3* 292; 5:424). The simplest way to conceive of Kant's immanent purposiveness of organisms is in terms of growth and differentiation, self-preservation and resisting external harm, all of which involve contextual adaptation. The first epigenetic manifestation of the growth and differentiation of mammals occurs in the enclosed context of the mother's womb. After birth, they are usually nurtured in a protected environment and gradually learn to protect themselves in order to gain a relative independence from the larger world.

In the second edition of the *Critique of Pure Reason*, Kant also speaks of the "epigenesis of pure reason" (B167). By this he means that our cognition of the world is "not all borrowed from experience," for there are elements of cognition that are "self-thought" (B167). Thus, the categories of the understanding are not mere "subjective predispositions for thinking implanted in us . . . in such a way that their use would agree exactly with the laws of nature along which experience runs" (B167). These would seem to be the laws of nature that govern the processes of the human brain. The epigenesis of reason upholds the thesis that however our brain functions in processing the physiological stimuli we receive after our release from the womb, our mind has the power to contribute spontaneous forms to them. We can thus formulate the following parallel: the immanent purposiveness of organisms points to centers of self-organization in a mechanistic world, and the spontaneous epigenesis of reason involves a "self-birth [*Selbstgebärung*]" (A765/B793) of the categories that first give meaning to our sense impressions. It is thus not surprising that Kant speaks of reason as its own organic power or organ.[10] But whereas an organism adapts to contingently given contexts, reason can adopt new possible contexts.

Instead of determinantly attributing life to organisms, we saw Kant reflectively ascribe a "self-propagating formative power" to them. Contextualizing functional descriptions based on objective observation provides the basis for reflective judgments that are purposive from the human standpoint. Kant asserts that for an archetypal intellect that proceeds from the whole to the parts, nothing would be contingent and no special appeal to purposiveness is necessary (see *C3* 276: 5:407). But for our ectypal or discursive intellect that proceeds from part to part, a special regulative principle of overall purposive connectedness is needed for a reflective comprehension of what is observed. This can provide clues for further inquiry into how all organisms function in a way that can also have the reciprocal effect of contributing to a better understanding of human life itself.

Comprehending Purposiveness Reflectively

In the "Critique of Aesthetic Judgment," Kant distinguished two modes of comprehension: the temporal *Zusammenfassung* of representations by the visual imagination, and the instantaneous *Comprehension* of a presentational visionary *Augenschein.* In the "Critique of Teleological Judgment," there is another mode of comprehension (*Begreifen*) that is more intellectual and can be related to the *Jäsche Logic* which was examined in chapter 3. There the cognitive sequence went from sensible acquaintance (*kennen*) and conscious cognition (*erkennen*) to the conceptual cognition of understanding (*concipiren*). Beyond these rungs in the stepladder we discussed rational cognition, which can either constitute objective insight (*einsehen = perspicere*) or relative comprehension (*begreifen = comprehendere*) (*LL* 570; 9:65) that could be either subjective or intersubjective. The relativity of rational comprehension does not make it arbitrary: it only means that it is reflective rather than determinant, and is not to be confused with an objective or absolute encompassing comprehension for which nothing is contingent.

I pointed to an instructive explication of this rational but relative mode of comprehension (*Begreifen*) in the *Vienna Logic,* where it was defined as the possession of "sufficient insight, insofar as something serves a certain purpose" (*LL* 300; 24:846). Comprehension as a mode of rational cognition is thus simultaneously theoretical and practical and requires that we use our reason with tact. This reinforces the conclusion that the purposiveness of rational comprehension is reflective, and indeed we see it applied as such in the second half of the *Critique of Judgment.* Kant first points to this kind of comprehension when discussing the purposiveness that geometrical figures such as circles and ellipses can have for projecting the trajectories of celestial bodies (see *C3* 236; 5:363). But this is a formal a priori purposiveness rather than a real teleological purposiveness. This formal purposiveness makes "comprehensible [*begreiflich*] the unity of many rules resulting from the construction" (*C3* 237; 5:364) of a single geometrical figure.

This is how Kant opens §62: "All geometrical figures that are drawn in accordance with a principle display a manifold and often admired objective purposiveness, namely that of serviceability for the solution of many problems" (*C3* 235; 5:362). What matters here is the suitability of a figure for the generation of many shapes in accordance with a single rational principle. The figure becomes a medial schema for solving as yet unspecified problems. It is a purposiveness that is "objective and intellectual" (*C3* 235; 5:362), and because it is only potentially purposive, it is not called "teleological." It involves a mode of rational comprehension (*Begreifen*) that is a priori and can aid the understanding in attaining mathematical exactitude for its objective causal explanations.

In the rest of the "Critique of Teleological Judgment," Kant moves from the formal objectivity of mathematical purposiveness to consider whether "an objective and material purposiveness" (*C3* 239; 5:366) can be attributed to organic life to make it "comprehensible [*begreiflich*] to us" (*C3* 233; 5:360). Whereas geometrical purposiveness is formal in a general schematic sense, we can comprehend teleological purposiveness as formal in a specifying sense. Here experience leads us to comprehend the material organization of certain things as being end-directed within certain specified contexts.

We can now reassess Kant's discussions about organic functions as a specifying mode of rational comprehension. To comprehend purposiveness in nature requires us to distinguish between a "relative purposiveness" where something is thought to serve as a means to some external end and "an immanent purposiveness of a natural being" as itself an end. While it is true that grass can be useful in providing food for cows, this external purposiveness of grass relative to cows does not explain its existence as an end of nature. We are only entitled to comprehend a product of nature as an end of nature to the extent that it exhibits an immanent form of purposiveness. This means that we must be able to regard it as both "an organized and self-organizing being" (*C3* 245; 5:374). A thing is *organized* if "each part is conceived as if it exists only through all the others . . . and on account of the whole" (*C3* 245; 5:373). As such, a thing could still be a product of the external purposiveness of human design, such as clockmaking. But for something to be one of nature's ends, we must judge it to also be a *self-organizing* adaptive product of nature that produces its own parts to form a reciprocally functioning whole. As a physical thing, a clock's internal motion requires an initial impetus from without, but organisms can be seen to organize and transform themselves and are therefore defined as having an adaptive, self-propagating, formative power.

We saw Kant acknowledge that any claim that organisms function teleologically must be thought of as being merely regulative. By contrast, the physical laws of mechanism were validated as being constitutive for our understanding of all of nature in the *Critique of Pure Reason*. However, if we allow the rational purposiveness of comprehension to encompass reflective judgment, on the grounds that I have given, then the above contrast can be specified to mean that while distributively every part of an organism is subject to the external mode of causality of the mechanical laws of motion and impact, the immanent purposiveness of the whole provides them with a temporary and relative contextual independence. Although this immanent purposiveness is imputed as a hypothetical claim about objective reality, Kant concludes near the end of the "Appendix" to the "Methodology of Teleological Judgment" that it is intersubjectively valid "for us (human beings in general) according to the necessary rational principles for our judgment" (*C3* 327; 5:462). This approach allows us to organize our experience of certain aspects of nature "in analogy with causality according to ends . . . (like the kind we encounter in ourselves) . . . without presuming thereby to explain it" (*C3* 234; 5:360). Kant's teleological claims are organizational and expositional rather than legislative and explanatory. Another way to formulate this is to say that Kant's claims about natural purposiveness enable us to interpret the world in various contextual terms. Indeed, Kant's innovative idea of immanent purposiveness was applied to psychic and historical life in more specific ways by Dilthey in his writings on the methodology of the human sciences in the 1890s.[11]

Dilthey considered Hegel's attempts to explain the purposiveness of history by means of an overall telos that unfolds itself dialectically to be overly speculative. He acknowledged that Hegel deepened our understanding of history by approaching it as a medium of objective spirit whereby past achievements can be transmitted and either rejected or built upon. But Hegel rationalized and homogenized this dynamic medium by imposing a dialectical logic on it. According to Dilthey, a more reliable way to understand the forces and movements of history is to focus on the way the medium of objective spirit can be specified into distinct temporal sociocultural systems that are centered in themselves. It is the task of the various human sciences to articulate the immanent purposiveness of each of these organizational systems. They are "productive systems [*Wirkungszusammenhänge*]"[12] that can have economic, political, educational, or other cultural functions. And because these productive systems are formed by human beings, their immanent purposiveness is not merely regulative but constitutive. This more pluralistic approach to history can also better account for conflict in that different systems can either cooperate or compete when they intersect.

Although Kant did not seem very confident that we humans could find lawlike explanations for the inner workings of organisms, Dilthey thought that explanatory laws specific to sociocultural systems could be found. Thus he pointed to laws of language formation and lawlike patterns of development in certain modern economies and political systems. In any case, the common insight that results from these considerations is that both Kant's comprehension/*Begreifen* and Dilthey's historical understanding/*Verstehen* depend on proper contextual delimitation. Even if our intellectual understanding/*Verstand* cannot causally explain the way organisms modify themselves in any determinant manner, we can, according to Kant, judge them normatively as organisms whose parts are organized to function well together. This is to reflectively comprehend them as organized and self-adjusting beings without appealing to a generic principle of life. In the *Metaphysik Volckmann* of 1784–85, Kant is most explicit about curtailing the appeal to life by circumscribing it as a kind of "representational power" (*VMR*, 28:448–49). Since we cannot assume that organisms such as trees and plants have any representational powers, we cannot explain the way they function by any generic principle of life. However, we may regard animal organisms as being alive insofar as we can ascribe to them "the power to change their own state as a consequence of their own representations" (*VMR*, 28:449).

This is followed up in a note in the "Appendix on the Methodology of Teleological Judgment," where Kant writes that "we can quite correctly infer *by analogy* . . . that animals also act in accordance with *representations* . . . and that in spite of their specific difference, they are still of the same genus [*Gattung*] as human beings (as living beings)" (*C3* 328; 5:464n). And because animals like beavers can be shown to have building skills resembling human technical skills, Kant rejects the Cartesian assumption that they are merely well-coordinated "machines" (*C3* 328; 5:464n) or *automata*. This reflects a change from *RM* 3855, which Erich Adickes places anywhere between 1764 and 1770, where Kant referred to animals as *automata* (17:313). Now animals such as beavers can be called "living beings" to the extent that we see an analogy with the human purposive skill to produce things external to ourselves. We saw that we are entitled to consider all organisms as purposive because they can modify themselves from within. But if beavers can build dams and dig canals to supply water to their dome-like lodges, then we can also ascribe to them something akin to our representational power to produce artifacts that advance our lives. However, the fact that our representational power to produce can be guided by reason does not entitle us to also attribute anything approximating rational consciousness to beavers, for as we saw Kant claim earlier, the power of animals to reflect allows them to differentiate representations merely to use them instinctively. Kant doubts that they can be conscious of what it is that distinguishes these representations, for that would require judgment and reason. Ultimately, Kant seems to place skillful animals at the level of the life of the mere soul, as distinct from the more human levels of mind and spirit. But more generally, since the inherent purposiveness of organisms is only self-organizing and self-modifying, Kant would not need to ascribe any soul-based life to plants, trees, and insects. Although all organisms are generative and organizationally adaptive, only animals with productive skills can be judged to be living beings.

Summarizing Thoughts

I started with Kant's cautions about the idea of the life of the soul as a metaphysical substance that can determine itself to move itself. He abandoned this traditional substantial notion of soul in favor of reflecting about the three more functional ways in which human beings can be represented as living. Anthropologically, the life of the soul is merely about how we are modified and how we feel ourselves to be alive. Kant's main interest is in how the mind acts by reacting and how spirit becomes self-active. The purposiveness of the mental feeling of life central to the "Critique of Aesthetic Judgment" was explicated as an active responsiveness that mediates between the pure spontaneity of the intellect and the passivity of sense. Both the enjoyment of beauty and the imaginative comprehension inspired by the sublime are still in accord with the autonomy of human understanding and reason. However, human efforts to reflectively comprehend organic purposiveness are said to be "heautonomous" (*C3* 72; 5:186) in that here we do not prescribe anything to our understanding of nature overall, but only to how our judgment can organize parts of it. Heautonomy applies to judgment as a reflective principle for the teleological and contextual specification of nature and reminds us that judgment has no overall legislative domain. As a consequence, the most generic form of teleological purposiveness is not the capacity for self-movement aimed at an external end, but that of self-modification as displayed in contextually organized matter.

13

Kant's Anthropology and Its Strategies for Moving beyond the Inner Sense of Psychology

Reexamining All the Senses

Although the feeling of life can stimulate our state of mind, it does not really provide self-cognition, according to Kant. Similarly, we can feel bodily health without any assurance that we really are in good health. These and other problems about human self-knowledge will be related in this chapter to Kant's growing doubts about the reliability of inner sense and his attempts to explore the outer senses more deeply for what they can teach us about ourselves. Going beyond the way the outer senses affect our soul, he looks for how they can develop our mental outlook. Kant addresses these aspects of sensibility extensively in the lectures on anthropology that he gave regularly from 1772 until his retirement in 1796. In light of the fact that many of these lectures as recorded by students at various times have been made available in the 1997 Academy edition volume 25 and then in the Cambridge translation edition of 2012, it is possible to more adequately understand the final 1798 version that Kant allowed to be published as his *Anthropology from a Pragmatic Point of View*. Some of these earlier lectures give more detailed examples to support his views about human nature. There are many positions that Kant holds throughout, but there are also shifts of emphasis that indicate important developments in his thinking.

Only in his early lecture courses on anthropology does Kant seem confident that we can directly intuit and know ourselves. The *Collins* lectures of 1772–73 espouse the view that we can intuit ourselves in a non-phenomenal way. "We have no intuition in the whole world except the intuition of our self; all other things are appearances" (VA-*Collins*, 25:14). The *Friedländer* and *Pillau* lectures, which are from the 1770s as well, also mention our ability to intuit ourselves. But subsequently Kant goes to great lengths to stress the difficulties of observing oneself as one is. The alternative that he proposes is to cognize oneself in terms of what one can make of oneself.

The reason that Kant gives for his increasing doubts that we can objectively intuit ourselves is the unreliability of inner sense. The inner sense that psychology examines is obscure, and this leads Kant to recommend a different anthropological approach that relies less on introspection and also considers what the outer senses can teach us about ourselves. The *Anthropology from a Pragmatic Point of View* is about "cognizing the interior as well as the exterior of the human being" (*AP* 13; 7:125). It is thus important to observe the behavior of human beings and how they interact with each other. For Kant, anthropology is not just a theoretical or observational science that aims to determine what nature has made of us; it should also show us what we can potentially make of ourselves in the world around us. Thus, it will not be a universally valid (*allgemeingültige*) and predictive natural science like physics or chemistry, but a "generally useful science [*gemeinnützige Wissenschaft*]" (*AP* 6; 7:122) that leaves room for human freedom. This kind of anthropology is therefore akin to what have come to be known as the human sciences as they arose in the nineteenth and twentieth centuries.[1] Just as Kant started with the commonly valid (*gemeingültige*) judgments of taste that represent regional fashions in order to aim at the universally valid judgments of good taste which aesthetics should strive for, he is now willing to acknowledge that anthropology will often have to content itself with claims that are merely commonly valid. In his *Prolegomena to Any Future Metaphysics*, Kant was critical of Thomas Reid and John Beattie because they relied too much on common sense. Common sense should always be kept in check by critical reason, but it is perfectly serviceable for "judgments which apply immediately to experience" (*PFM* 33; 4:260). We will see that Kant's anthropology appeals to commonplaces and common sense and goes much deeper into what all the senses can contribute to human comprehension than most of his other writings.

Another strategy used by Kant is to shift our attention from the *inner sense* that traditional psychology had located at the level of the life of the soul toward the higher levels of the life of the mind and spirit. One of the consequences of this shift is to propose the idea of an *interior sense* that allows us to assess our situation in the world. It turns out that Kant's anthropology is essentially about extending our powers of judgment based on a closer investigation into the nature of human sensibility.

The Problematic Nature of Inner Sense

Initially, Kant did turn to inner sense in order to ascertain what is going on in the human psyche. Thus, in the preamble of the extensive *Friedländer* lectures of 1775–76 we read: "The world as an object of outer sense is nature, the world as an object of inner sense is the human being" (VA-*Friedländer*, 25:469). In these lectures, inner sense is still conceived as our capacity to intuit ourselves. Inner sense is not yet dismissed as being unreliable, but attentiveness to it is said to be "wearisome and forcible, although it is necessary for reexamination; it only must not be continuous" (VA-*Friedländer*, 25:492). In the *Mrongovius* lectures of 1784–85, Kant begins to cast doubt on inner sense by speaking of delusional sensations of inner sense (see VA-*Mrongovius*, 25:1256). This reflects the position that Kant articulated in the *Critique of Pure Reason*, namely, that inner sense is purely phenomenal and should not be confused with apperceptive self-consciousness. This position is more fully acknowledged in the final *Anthropology* where Kant complains about the "passivity of the inner sense of sensations" (*AP* 29–30; 7:141).

The main problem with inner sense is that it offers a stream of obscure rather than clear representations. Sometimes Kant speaks of obscure (*dunkle*) representations as being in the shade, as it were, so that we can only be dimly aware of them, but at other times he says we are not conscious of them. What is given in inner sense need not, however, be unconscious because "we can still be *indirectly* conscious of having a representation, even if we are not directly conscious of it" (*AP* 24; 7:135). There are also obscure representations of outer sense, but they can more readily be referred to external objects which have spatial determinacy. The *Anthropology* then expands on this by describing the obscure representations in the human being as a "field [*Feld*]" that is "immeasurable [*unermeßlich*]" (*AP* 24; 7:135) and in which only a few points are clear: "only a few places on the vast *map* of our mind are illuminated" (*AP* 24; 7:135). A clear representation is defined as one that enables us to distinguish one object from another, and therefore it must already belong to outer sense. The representations of inner sense cannot be objectively defined. They constitute an indeterminate temporal stream, or, as the final text reads, "inner sense sees the relations of its determinations only in time, hence in flux, where the stability of observation necessary for experience does not occur" (*AP* 23; 7:134).

Introspective observation of this flux of inner sense is difficult because it interrupts the ongoing processes of experience as we are doing things. Already in the *Friedländer* lectures, Kant is reported to have said that self-observation is more arduous than the observation of things in the external world and should only be done rarely. Then, in referring to a human being who wants to study himself, Kant notes in the *Menschenkunde* of 1781–82 that "when the incentives are active, he does not observe them . . . But if he does observe himself, then all of the incentives are at rest and he has nothing to observe" (VA-*Menschenkunde*, 25:857). This language about the difficulties of introspection is almost identical to that of the final published *Anthropology* (see *AP* 5; 7:121). In the latter, the limits of successfully observing others are discussed as well: "If a human being notices that someone is observing him and trying to study him, he will either appear embarrassed (self-conscious) and *cannot* show himself as he really is; or he dissembles and does not *want* to be known as he is" (*AP* 5; 7:121).

What is recommended as a more reasonable alternative to direct human self-observation (*Beobachten* = *observare*) is a less direct but more reliable "taking note [*Bemerken*] (*animadvertere*) of oneself" (*AP* 20; 7:132).[2] This shift from introspective observation to "taking note of oneself" will become central in the rest of this chapter. Initially, it suggests that an indirect, retrospective taking-note of how I have been affected by inner sense will distort less and at least capture the mood one was in. But this taking-note of inner sense still has its limits and must be kept within bounds. To dwell in any way on these obscure representations of inner sense is to subject ourselves to an overwhelming play of sensations. This is unhealthy and can lead to hypochondria. From early on, Kant indicates that one should not attend to one's *person* as the hypochondriac does, but to one's *activities* in engaging others and the world around us (see VA-*Collins*, 25:23). Thus empirical psychology, which reifies the immeasurable field of inner sense by positing a soul as the habitat of inner sense, is not only suspect as a science, but potentially pathological. By replacing empirical psychology with his own anthropology, Kant makes it clear that we should not study the soul by itself, but attend to how our mental capacities relate us to the territory of the world. What Kant is proposing is an anthropology that leaves the obscurity of the soul behind and focuses on correlating mind and spirit with the world.

Shifting from Soul to Mind: Replacing the Introspective Observation of Inner Sense with a Taking-Note of the Other Senses

Kant used the "Empirical Psychology" chapter of Baumgarten's *Metaphysics* as the text for his lectures on anthropology, and the early lectures reflect this by making more references to the soul than the later lectures do. In the final published version of the *Anthropology*, Kant refers to the soul only in passing as the so-called organ of inner sense. It was shown earlier that there is a metaphysical sense of soul that encompasses all three ways or levels of being alive, but strictly speaking "soul" (*Seele*) now comes to stand for the mere passive capacity to be affected by sense. The intermediate level of mind (*Gemüth*) is more important because it allows us to become active, even if only in a reactive way. Enlivened by spirit (*Geist*), mind can also become self-active. To dwell on the contents of inner sense provided by the soul leads us to attend to how we are affected, which goes against the grain. The basic tenet of Kant's anthropology from a pragmatic point of view is to see us as active participants in the world. Thus, we are expected to move from the obscure habitat of inner sense and turn our attention to the territory of the outer senses.

The *Friedländer* anthropology still claims that the possession of inner sense "gives us an advantage over nonrational animals" (VA-*Friedländer*, 25:492) in that it allows us to be self-aware. Although too much attention to inner sense can make us morbid, it "is needed for revision" (VA-*Friedländer*, 25:492). These notes do not say what needs to be revised, but the example that follows in them, of a farmer who is so occupied by his tasks that he does not realize he is becoming ill, suggests that inner sense should still be used as an index to our bodily condition. Inner sense as the repository of our reactions to things can be useful for self-auditing and some retrospection.

Kant's minimization of inner sense leads him to pay a considerable amount of attention to the outer senses and their proper use. And what is interesting about the *Friedländer* anthropology lectures is their stress on what the outer senses allow us to note about ourselves not just at the level of soul, but at the level of mind. At first, we read that some of the outer senses "affect us externally, others internally. The former are the senses of intuition [*Anschauung*], the latter the senses of feeling [*Empfindung*]" (VA-*Friedländer*, 25:493). The intuitive senses are touch, sight, and hearing; the senses of feeling are smell and taste. "The former present objects to us, the others consist in the way in which we are affected by them. For example, when seeing I perceive objects, but when smelling I feel an impression" (VA-*Friedländer*, 25:493). Later Kant calls the three intuitive senses the "senses of judgment or evaluation [*Beurtheilung*]" (VA-*Friedländer*, 25:495) that teach us about objects, whereas the felt senses of smell and taste lead us to attend to how we are affected. These felt or subjective senses "have more of the sensory [*Sensation*][3] than of reflection" (VA-*Friedländer*, 25:495). Smell and taste are the lowest of the outer senses, and since they are said to affect us internally, they would seem to be absorbed into inner sense at the first level of soul.

But with this we have skipped over a sentence which acknowledges that in all the outer senses we can "distinguish the two aspects of the intuitive and the felt" (VA-*Friedländer,* 25:493). Even the intuitive or objective senses have a feltness to them, and this feltness need not be merely sensory as with smell and taste, but can engender reflection, which is the alternative mentioned in the quote above. This can be shown even for what seems to be the most intuitive or objective sense of "touch (*das Fühlen = tactus*)" which he distinguishes from "subjective feeling (*dem Gefühl*)" (VA-*Friedländer,* 25:493). In touching we not only have a tactile or direct contact with an object, but we may also feel pain at the level of soul if we touch it carelessly. Touch itself can produce a more reflective feeling of pleasure at the level of mind if in stroking the surface of an object, we appreciate its smoothness and note its sheen. Although the sense of sight is a less directly intuitive sense than touch, it is more important because of its broader scope. It is useful in determining and sharing the cognitive properties of objects, but it is also the sense that allows us to take subjective pleasure in the formal relational qualities of things as exhibited in aesthetic appreciation. This formal pleasure is clearly mental and is not absorbed into inner sense at the passive level of soul. Kant is most explicit about the subjective significance of the outer sense of hearing. It provides "no object but presents (*darstellt*) only an impression of it" (VA-*Friedländer,* 25:493). Most importantly, hearing has an intersubjective usefulness: "it is a social sense, and serves to communicate the signs of thoughts, thus it is a means of speech" (VA-*Friedländer,* 25:493).

Since the outer senses directed at the world can also affect our subjective state, it could be argued that it is possible to have inner experiences that are not all that obscure if inner sense were to be correlated with the outer senses. Indeed, it is the defining feature of Dilthey's efforts to supplement the Kantian theory of experience (*Erfahrung*) with a conception of lived experience (*Erlebnis*) in order to bring the inner and the outer closer together. To illustrate this, Dilthey gives an example of a lived experience that is both emotional and directed at the external world: he speaks of looking at the picture of Goethe in his study, but calls it an inner experience because it reminds him of the fact that it used to hang in his father's house and that it was later given to him. This outer perception of a picture on the wall in his study becomes an inner experience to the extent that it recalls the past and arouses emotions that bring about a kind of self-awareness. Precisely because introspective acts of attentive self-observation tend to interrupt the activities of the mind, Dilthey attaches importance to the way consciousness can both attend to something outside it and still take note of itself. Even when I am totally absorbed by what I see around me, it is always still possible to recall that I just had this experience. This is a reflexive awareness (*Innewerden*)[4] that is implicitly self-referential. As was indicated in chapter 4, reflexive awareness is not yet the explicit and reflective self-consciousness of self-knowledge, but it is like Kant's "I think" in being "able to accompany all my representations" (B131). Whereas Kant's "I think" mainly supports outer experience, Dilthey's reflexive awareness supports the merging of inner and outer experience.

Although Kant himself sometimes distinguishes between inner sense and inner experience, he seems to regard the latter as merely the accumulation of the obscure contents of inner sense, which he dismissively consigns to psychologists to worry about. He leaves it to them to study the "sum of all perceptions under laws of nature" (*AP* 30; 7:141). What inner experience amounts to epistemically for Kant was made clear in the "Preface" to the B edition of the *Critique of Pure Reason*, where he reduces inner experience to the "empirical consciousness of my existence" (Bxl). This consciousness of "my existence in time" is "only determinable through a relation to something that, while being bound up with my existence, is outside me" (Bxl). Inner experience for Kant is merely the temporal consciousness that I exist and only adds to the transcendental formal consciousness that I am, an awareness *that* I exist inside a world. Unfortunately, Kant's inner experience does not synthesize the contents of inner sense with the contents of outer sense to give inner sense enough determinacy to define *what* I am. This is where the three-level approach of Kant's epistemology becomes rigid and betrays a prejudice: inner experience seems condemned to stay at the lowest level of soul.

Kant shows no interest in enriching or refining inner sense by correlating it with outer sense in order to raise it to the mental level at which Dilthey filled it in as lived experience. In chapter 1, I treated the three levels of experiential intake that are evident throughout Kant's corpus as flowing into each other, but here Kant seems to assume that inner sense can only passively register that we are affected by outer sense without recognizing what that influence is. His strategy in the pragmatic anthropology is to become aware of ourselves by using outer sense less to fill in inner sense and more to establish our outlook on the world. The outer senses must be geared not just to the objects around us, but also to help us respond to those with whom we interact. As we begin to form a worldview from our particular perspective, this surrounding world becomes the context for coming to know ourselves. While it was obvious that objects cannot be known from within, Kant now wants us to acknowledge that we cannot know ourselves from within either and that inner sense is just as phenomenal as outer sense. Only by going outside ourselves can we hope to eventually cognitively "take in" who we are. He advises us to abstract as much as possible from the passive soul life of inner sense and to focus instead on how we must actively take command of our states of mind by gearing them toward the world. This is perhaps most clear in the *Anthropology Parow* of 1772–73, where we again see the shift from Soul in the broad metaphysical sense to Kant's more narrow sense of soul that belongs to our physical body and can be left behind by focusing on mind and spirit.

> Insofar as the Soul is thought of as connected to the body and cannot prevent what affects the senses from being communicated to it, it is soul, and there it is merely passive. But insofar as the Soul reacts to sensible impressions and proves itself active, it is *animus* [mind], and to the extent that it is entirely independent of all sensibility and represents something to itself, it is *mens* [spirit]. (VA-*Parow*, 25:247)

Instead of focusing on a soul inside the body, Kant's anthropology teaches us to take note that our mind functions inside the world and that our spirit extends into and hovers over this world. This means that a physical pain affecting the soul (*Seele*) in the passive sense (*anima*) can be reassessed by the more active *animus* of the mind (*Gemüth*). With this expansive state of mind, human beings can respond to the pain that the soul suffers by redirecting their attention to the world at large. One can dwell on the pain and feel sorry for oneself, or one can try to ignore the pain as much as possible by refocusing and attending to broader concerns. To truly rise above the pain requires an act of spirit (*Geist* = *mens*), which is self-active and supposedly independent of all sensibility. At this third level of spirit, Kant considers a person's attitude to be under the control of his or her free will, which makes it possible to adopt the Stoic ideal of being in possession of oneself (*Selbstbesitz*). This is equivalent to taking responsibility for one's attitude to life and tantamount to what I have called the level of reflective appropriation. Accordingly, Kant concludes that "the soul can be swimming entirely in pain, and yet in the spirit there can be great gladness" (VA-*Collins*, 25:17).

To be in possession of oneself in this full Stoic sense is not to dwell on the contents of inner sense or even the resulting state of mind, but to rise to the serene level of spiritual composure. The Stoics arrived at this serenity through their principle of apathy. Kant does not, however, adopt this Stoic principle of apathy wholesale, mainly because it is too negative. It involves the activity of abstraction, which, although important according to Kant, is not yet a positive worldly attitude. Despite initially endorsing the principle of apathy as correct, he later qualifies that endorsement. Thus we must be cautious in ascribing a Stoical worldview to Kant.

In the published 1798 version of the *Anthropology*, we read at first that "the principle of *apathy*—namely that the wise man must never be in a state of affect, not even that of compassion with the misfortune of his best friend, is an entirely correct and sublime moral principle of the Stoic school; for affect makes us (more or less) blind" (*AP* 152; 7:253). Kant considers an affect as a sudden feeling that disrupts the mind's composure and "makes reflection impossible" (*AP* 150; 7:251). An extreme case is Kant's example of a rich man who "feels as if his entire happiness were lost" (*AP* 153; 7:254) when he discovers that his servant has broken a rare crystal goblet. In her recent thought-provoking book *Kant on Reflection and Virtue*, Melissa Merritt makes this example central to her analysis of what moral reflection means for Kant. What the rich man could not do is to "compare" this unfortunate loss to the "broader whole" of his life of fortune.[5] The overpowering affect of shock and anger makes the rich man incapable of reflecting on his overall situation.

Affects render us blind in moral situations, but they are momentary. Kant draws an illuminating contrast between the affect of anger and the passion of hatred. Anger is a sudden natural affect and is often quickly forgotten. However, when anger turns into the hatred of something, it becomes a destructive passion that bores into us and lasts. An affect is compared to "*drunkenness* that one sleeps off," whereas passion is like "*dementia* that broods over a representation which nestles itself deeper and deeper" (*AP* 151; 7:253). Affects are like temporary aberrations that one can get over, and they can even be put to good use. Enthusiasm is an example of an affect that can be of value when it becomes allied with reason. The feeling of sublimity is often considered to be such an affect: it stimulates the mind and may even grant us an instantaneous glimpse of the noumenal. What is dangerous is fanaticism, which is the demented, passionate consolidation of enthusiasm and leads to dogmatism.

We can now return to Kant's rich man venting his affect of anger at his servant. Merritt proposes that this act lacks reflection in its basic *constitutive* sense. But if the anger goes over into a passionate hatred that leads the man to fire his servant, then he also lacks reflection in a *normative* sense that is morally culpable. Now the rich man is subject to the blindness of passion, which is not just a sudden inclination but one that has become a "prejudice" and amounts to an inability to judge properly.[6] I agree with Merritt that such a distinction is valid, but I do not agree with her definition of the constitutive sense of reflection, when she claims that to reflect is "to have some (typically tacit) handle on oneself as the source of a point of view on how things are or what is worth doing."[7] For Kant, reflection is often more tentative and is still looking for comparisons to already indicate a point of view. If it did, it would determine our worldview from the start. Whereas Merritt focuses mostly on the normative sense of reflection as it applies to ethical issues, I will continue to explore both the theoretical and practical aspects of reflection, just as I did with comprehension. Both have a wide range of uses.

Returning to the Stoic worldview and its principle of apathy that discourages strong affects such as compassion, we can see Kant qualify his support of its adequacy when he adds in one of his more relaxed states of mind that "the wisdom of nature has planted in us the predisposition to compassion in order to handle the reins *provisionally*, until reason has achieved the necessary strength" (*AP* 152; 7:253). An action will not be moral unless it is based on a rational principle, but we should not be inhibited from using feelings such as compassion and affects such as enthusiasm to "produce an enlivening of the will (in spiritual or political speeches to the people, or even in solitary speeches to oneself)" to create "the preliminary resolve [*Vorsatzes*] to do good" (*AP* 152; 7:254). To be sure, once reason reinforces the enthusiasm of such a resolve, it must be attributed to the faculty of desire and no longer to affect as a momentary feeling.

Apart from being a principle to be adopted, apathy can also be considered as an inherent attitude, and as such it is designated a "natural gift" that some have as a "fortunate phlegm" (*AP* 152; 7:254). This natural temperament may make the transition to acting on principle easier, but it is hardly a moral achievement. For as Kant indicated in the *Friedländer* lectures, temperament is merely "the proportion of feelings and desires" that we inherit. "With temperament we do not act according to principles and dispositions as with character, but according to inclinations" (VA-*Friedländer*, 25:636). What Kant aims for in his philosophy is the transformation of a natural temperament such as apathy into the development of character as a second nature. Whatever good qualities we have assimilated from our temperament must still be actively acquired and reflectively appropriated as character.

The importance of character for Kant's moral philosophy will be discussed later, but for the moment, I propose that apathy at the level of soul can degrade into cold indifference and should be replaced at the level of mind with what Kant calls "equanimity [*Gleichmüthigkeit*]" in the *Mrongovius* lectures. "Equanimity is the firmness of our mental disposition" (VA-*Mrongovius*, 25:1320) that is to be distinguished from the "indifference [*Gleichgültigkeit*] [which] comes from temperament" (VA-*Mrongovius*, 25:1319). Equanimity does not leave us apathetic or unconcerned about what is happening to us and the world around us, but involves a composure that keeps us from lashing out unthinkingly: "to be equanimous one needs only to consider that nothing in our life is as important as our good conduct alone. . . . The equanimous person always has a cheerful heart, and that is the pleasure that Epicurus praises" (VA-*Mrongovius*, 25:1320). Ultimately, Kant accepts the Stoic principle of apathy as a warning not to merely act on the basis of sudden affects, but the attitude of apathy is acknowledged to resemble indifference and should be replaced with Epicurean equanimity. Kant can acknowledge equanimity as a better outlook without endorsing the worldviews of either Epicureanism or Stoicism.

Appropriate Ways of Attending to Oneself

As was indicated at the outset, anthropology from the pragmatic point of view goes beyond what nature has made of a human being to consider "what *he* as a free-acting being makes of himself or can and should make of himself" (*AP* 3; 7:119). This means that instead of introspecting, human beings should be engaged with others and learn what is required to become a good citizen of the world. Kant's anthropology aims to study human beings as both engaged in the world at large and in relation to others up close. Pragmatic anthropology for Kant is essentially a prudential project. When the term "pragmatic" is introduced in the *Friedländer* anthropology lectures, it is said to consist "in the power of judgment to avail ourselves of all kinds of skill" (VA-*Friedländer*, 25:469). In the final *Anthropology*, we read that pragmatic anthropology is not concerned with *knowing* the world, but with what it means for us "to *have* the world" (*AP* 4; 7:120). The former involves understanding what is at play in the world, while the latter teaches how to be a co-player in the world. The Kantian watchwords here are cooperation (*mitspielen*) (see *AP* 4; 7:120) and active engagement.

It is this shift from theoretical philosophy in the academic sense to practical philosophy in the worldly sense that needs to be made before self-consciousness becomes appropriate. It was already pointed out that introspection or observing oneself in isolation from others can become unhealthy, according to Kant. Any intense focus on inner sense can lead to egoism, hypochondria, and even madness. In addition to the less intense "taking note of [*bemerken*]" of ourselves, Kant also speaks of an indirect "attending to [*aufmerken*] oneself," which becomes necessary "when one is dealing with others" (*AP* 20–21; 7:132). I propose that we make a distinction here between a theoretical *self-consciousness* that remains formal and relates to the world as such, and a practical *self-awareness* that we gain through our relations to other human beings. It is this self-awareness that is to be developed by means of a pragmatic anthropology, and its proper cultivation requires tact. This becomes evident right away when Kant warns that "in social interchange, it [attending to oneself] must not become visible; for then it makes conversation either *awkward* [*verlegen*] or *affected*" (*AP* 21; 7:132). Attending to self must be adjusted in accordance with one's social context and should not have to rise to the level of attentive self-observation.

Whereas psychology is dismissed as a theoretical discipline interested in describing *inner sense*, pragmatic anthropology aims to characterize our dispositions. Kant is not interested in "a description of human beings, but of human nature" (VA-*Friedländer*, 25:471). Even when description is unavoidable, it must provide an external context. Kant makes this especially clear when he speaks of the importance of description in geography. When doing earth-writing or describing a place, its "topography" must be framed by a "description of its region [*Gegend*] . . . chorography" (*PG*, 9:159).[8] Similarly, self-awareness and self-description can only become reflective when they are related to how we perceive other human beings in our surroundings.

However, Kant's advice not to dwell on the involuntary *contents* of inner sense that come to us unbidden, does not mean that we should not at times observe our cognitive *activities* involved in representing the world. Indeed, he says that "to observe the various acts of representative power in myself, *when I summon them*, is indeed worth reflection; it is necessary and useful for logic and metaphysics" (*AP* 22; 7:133; italics added). We should take notice of how the cognitive powers function and learn their scope and limits. Anthropology thus has relevance to what was called "applied general logic" in the *Critique of Pure Reason*, namely, the study of how the understanding operates "under the contingent conditions of the subject, which can hinder or promote this use" (A54/B78–79). The main use of applied general logic is negative by pinpointing sources of fallacious reasoning, and it was therefore called "a cathartic of the common understanding" (A53/B78). We can make a comparison between this kind of applied logic and the doctrine of virtue, which assesses the laws of morality relative to "the hindrances of the feelings, inclinations, and passions to which human beings are more or less subject" (A55/B79). As such, pragmatic anthropology serves as a theory of education that teaches us to be aware of the weaknesses of the cognitive faculties that stand in the way of a healthy understanding, and of the hindrances that our inclinations and passions pose for successful action and human interaction. Indeed, the concluding section of the *Friedländer* lectures is entitled "On Education" (see VA-*Friedländer*, 25:722–28).

We can follow this up with an unpublished note for the final *Anthropology* which asserts that "cognition of oneself according to the constitution of what one is in oneself cannot be acquired through inner experience . . . but is simply and solely the consciousness of one's freedom, which is known to him through the categorical imperative of duty, therefore only through the highest practical reason" (*AP* 32n). This means that for anthropology, the cultivation of our cognitive powers must be assessed in terms of how we affect each other through our actions. And because our true self must have a practical relation to the world, the outer senses are needed to inform us about the world and help shape our outlook. The final *Anthropology* thus provides an extensive "defense of sensibility" (*AP* 35; 7:144) when it comes to the outer senses. We saw Kant downgrade sensations as passive material inputs that are liminal, but sensibility remained important as the assimilative intake of perceptual content. Even though the outer senses are part of the lower cognitive faculty, they are not to be despised if they are placed under the control of the "I" of apperception and its spontaneity. The sense of sight provides what comes to be apprehended as the intuitive content for the formal functions of the understanding. It was shown in the opening chapters that although sensations (*Empfindungen*) as physical impressions are at the lower limit of consciousness, the sensible (*sinnliche*) apprehension of conscious perception can attain distinctness. Confusions and deceptions derive from incorrect ways of relating and contextualizing representations of sense. They are errors of judgment, not errors of sense. Kant concludes that the rationalists were wrong to think that the senses confuse and deceive on their own.

Nevertheless, the senses may at times produce a *Blendwerk* of semblances.[9] These can create illusions which need not deceive us. Kant's suggestions about semblance and illusion (*Schein*) have engendered a whole aesthetic tradition, starting with Friedrich Schiller, that includes Susanne Langer's explorations of aesthetic semblances.[10] In the *Critique of Pure Reason*, Kant already indicates that there are many natural optical illusions that cannot be avoided, yet they need not deceive the understanding. He gives the example that "the sea appears higher in the middle than at the shores" (A297/B354). The understanding knows that this is not really the case, so we learn not to be fooled by this illusion produced by light rays. Having said earlier that the senses as such do not deceive, Kant goes on to mention that sometimes a sensible illusion (*Sinnenschein*) may be deceptive. However, to say as Kant does that the use of makeup (see *AP* 41; 7:150) deceives the senses is not convincing. To be sure, we may be deceived by those who apply makeup to cover facial blemishes such as wrinkles. But Kant fails to point out that the smooth facial surface that is perceived is really there, it is just not the natural skin we normally expect to see. The deception is not really due to the senses, for it results from the faulty judgmental assumption that we are seeing a person's unadorned face. Certain contextual conditions have been overlooked. A less neutral kind of artificial semblance is called "bewitchment," which can be caused by the passion of love. With bewitchment the imagination seems to be a contributing factor.

Kant follows the section on sensible illusion with one on "moral illusion" (*AP* 42; 7:151). Here he argues that a part of being a civilized human being is to "adopt the illusion [*Schein*] of affection, of respect for others, of modesty, and of unselfishness without deceiving anyone at all" (*AP* 42; 7:151). These are artificial forms of politeness that make it easier to deal with others. Bowing and courtly gallantry were part of the decorum of Kant's day that may seem insincere to us now. But Kant thinks that no one expects all such sensible signs of politeness to be sincere, and that the semblance of benevolence and respect evoked by them may eventually produce the real thing. Whereas makeup is considered deplorable because it is used to make oneself seem better than one is, certain forms of flattery seem to be acceptable because they make others seem superior.

Finally, Kant makes it clear that sensibility also includes the power of the imagination. The senses provide intuition in the presence of objects, while the imagination provides it even without their presence. In this broader context of sensibility, Kant adds a new mode that stirs the imagination:

> A representation through sense [*Sinn*] of which one is conscious as such is said to be especially sensory or sensational [*heißt besonders Sensation*] when the sensation [*Empfindung*] at the same time arouses attention to the subject's own state. (*AP* 45; 7:153)

Whereas mere sense impressions are not really conscious according to Kant, now he points to instances when sensibility can lead us to attend to our state of mind. This indicates that what is ordinarily an obscure sensation (*Empfindung*) at the level of soul can at times become a conscious "*Sensation*" at the level of mind. Later it is suggested that this could be a strong smell that disgusts us or a loud "stentorian voice" (*AP* 50; 7:158) that disturbs our concentration. This seems to be the only place in his own writings that Kant uses this Latinate term *Sensation*. But earlier I cited a passage from the *Friedländer* anthropology student notes where that Latinate term was also used. Three other uses of this term in the Academy edition are found in letters written to Kant; for example, one by Daniel Jenisch informing Kant that discussions in the literary *Merkur* about his philosophy had created a "most powerful *Sensation*" (*Briefwechsel,* 10:485) or public stir. A *Sensation* is thus a sensory effect that is potentially sensational by stirring attention to how our state of mind is affected. It can evoke an attitudinal response and disclose something about our outlook on the world.

With this sensory effect of sensibility, Kant is adding to something that had already been broached in his "Critique of Aesthetic Judgment" where the subjective aspects of sensations (*Empfindungen*) were first explored. There it was a matter of distinguishing the sensuous pleasure of the agreeable at the level of body and soul from the formally felt pleasure of a judgment of taste at the level of mind and spirit. Whereas the lively state of mind of appreciating beauty was contemplative and self-activated, the *Anthropology* now considers how the awareness of our state of mind can be stirred from without by something that strikes us as sensory. The *sensuous* pleasure of an agreeable or tasty meal is referrable to *inner sense,* and the pure pleasure of a judgment of taste is referrable to a *communal sense.* But to prepare for the state of mind evoked by a *sensory* effect, Kant introduces an "*interior sense*" (*AP* 45; 7:153) in §15 of the *Anthropology.* I think the notion of the sensory that I am teasing out here was anticipated in the discussion of the dynamical sublime, when the fear aroused by a violent storm stirs the imagination to recall that we are more than natural beings and consider our overall state of mind from the perspective of reason. Now in the *Anthropology,* Kant hints that there may be other effects of sensibility that lead us to attend to our state of mind. In the next chapter, I will examine this reactive conception of an interior sense introduced in §15 in relation to another new conception of sense introduced in §16, namely, that of a holistic vital sense. On the basis of this relation, it will be argued that what is special about Kant's interior sense is its contextualizing mode of sensibility.

14

Vital Sense, Interior Sense, and Self-Assessment

The earliest indication that Kant saw a connection between our interior sense and what he would later call our vital sense can be found in one of the *Reflections on Anthropology* from the 1770s. There he writes: "The interior [*inwendige*] animal sense (of feeling one's body) refers to heat and cold, weariness (relaxation) and exertion (tension)" (*RA* #290, 15:109). The interior sense may seem to go *deeper* than inner (*innere*) sense by feeling or probing the general state of one's body and its vitality. However, we will see that in the final *Anthropology*, the interior sense will instead go *higher* than inner sense by reaching up from the obscure level of soul to the more lucid and broader level of mind. The interior sense no longer functions merely at the *anima* level of soul and will acquire a mental *animus* that is directed at the world.

When speaking earlier about how the senses were treated in the *Friedländer* anthropology lectures of 1775–76, we saw that Kant distinguished between the objective senses of sight, hearing, and touch that are intuitive and the subjective senses of smell and taste that provide us with sensory impressions. In the 1798 published *Anthropology*, these senses are no longer distinguished in this qualitative way but in terms of degree, namely, as more or less objective. Moreover, we find a new distinction between specific organ-based senses and a pervasive vital sense that was introduced in the *Mrongovius* lectures of 1784–85 (see VA-*Mrongovius*, 25:1242). The organ-based senses are the five outer senses already referred to. The most objective sense of sight affects the nerves of the eye as a sense organ, just as the most subjective sense of smell affects the nerves of the nose.

The vital sense is distinctive in that it registers how the whole body is affected. In the *Mrongovius* notes we read that "through the vital sense the entire nervous system is disturbed, as for example with horror, which is elicited by ideas as well as outer objects" (VA-*Mrongovius*, 25:1242). The final *Anthropology* elaborates this as follows:

> A sensuous feeling [*Empfindung*] of warm and cold, even one that is aroused by the mind (for example, by quickly rising hope or fear),

> belongs to the *vital sense* [*Vitalsinn*]. The *shudder* that seizes the human being to the core in the representation of the sublime, and the *horror* with which nurses' tales drive children to bed late at night, are of the same kind; they penetrate the body as far as there is life in it. (*AP* 45–46; 7:154)[1]

Whereas the early *Reflexion* about the interior sense referred only to the vitality of our animate body, now Kant refers the vital sense both to the body and to how we are affected by ideas, as when we represent the sublime to ourselves. The sublime involves a state of the body's nervous system but is ultimately a state of mind. In the *Critique of Judgment*, we saw Kant speak of the sublime as an emotional state of being stirred by something overwhelming, like the sight of a threatening volcanic mountain that initially challenges our own vital powers only to release a stronger outflow of them. Something physically overpowering would leave us in a state of terror were it not for the recognition that as human beings we also possess a higher power of reason in which we can find relief. The sublime involves "a subjective movement of the imagination, by which it does violence to the inner sense" (*C3* 142; 5:259) by not allowing us to determinately perceptually comprehend the full scope of the massive mountain. A feeling of awe interrupts the gradual progression of sensible apprehension in time and collapses it into an instantaneous or momentary glance that "makes simultaneity intuitable" (*C3* 142; 5:259). We can now see that the successive or linear time associated with inner sense and outer perception is transformed into a state of mind in which we instantaneously feel the vitality or sublime purposiveness of our "overall vocation of the mind" (*C3* 142; 5:259). Although Kant does not use the term "interior sense" in the *Critique of Judgment*, this is clearly a case of inner sense giving way to something like the vital and interior sense now being explored.

Kant's "vital sense or feeling [*Vitalempfindung*] (*sensus vagus*)" (*AP* 45; 7:153) is not adequately captured by the successive representational flow of "inner sense [*innerer Sinn*] (*sensus internus*)" that he ordinarily speaks of. Feeling cold or hot leaves its mark in what he identifies in the final *Anthropology* as a presentational "interior sense [*inwendiger Sinn*] (*sensus interior*)" (*AP* 45; 7:153). The adjective *inwendig* is normally translated as "interior" to correlate with Kant's Latin, but it also suggests the self-referential reflexivity of *Innewerden* that we discussed in chapters 4 and 12. Whereas the psychological introspection of what occurs in inner sense seems like a futile attempt to look inside ourselves, the reflexivity of interior sense is primarily a feeling of what it is to be ourselves. I will therefore at times also translate "*inwendig*" as "reflexive." Inner sense partakes of the indeterminacy and obscurity of the soul, whereas interior sense has to do with our state of mind, or as Kant puts it here, with "the feeling of pleasure and displeasure, that is, the receptivity of the subject to be determined by certain representations to *preserve or reject the state of those representations*" (*AP* 45; 7:153). What is of anthropological interest concerning vital sense, both in the case of the merely physiological state of feeling uncomfortably hot and the mental state of fear, is the capacity of interior sense to assess what to do about these states. Assuming that the states are felt to be unpleasant, we want to be able to take action to be released from their hold on us. The interior sense, then, is the capacity to preserve or reject a state of mind based on whether it is worth preserving or not. It involves a "mode of thinking [*Denkungsart*]" or taking one's "interior pulse [*tactus interior*]" (*Vorarbeiten zur Tugendlehre,* 23:410). Following up on the relation between self-feeling and self-consciousness, we can say that the interior sense is not merely the reflexive awareness *that* I am, or *what* my state of mind feels like, but also the capacity to assess myself contextually. I would even ascribe a second-order reflexivity to the interior sense that sets the stage for reflective judgment, but Kant himself makes no such claim.

There is also a cryptic allusion to music in a *Reflection* where Kant writes that the "*sensus interior,* the reflexive [*inwendige*] sense, is the feeling of pleasure and displeasure. And this refers to an inner organization. Music" (*RA* 605, 15:260). Both the reference to inner organization and the allusion to music support the above translation of "*tactus interior*" as "interior pulse." It accords with how musicians use the term *tactus* to measure the tempo and beat patterns of a musical composition. Thus, the interior sense can order our mental life just as music organizes sounds into melodic and rhythmic patterns. Whereas inner sense is passive and at the level of soul, the interior sense can more actively order and assess the life of the mind. Interior sense takes the pulse of our life by means of a kind of self-contextualization and assesses whether to accept or reject our worldly situation. Interior sense is not a sense of being inside ourselves, but of how we feel ourselves inside the world.[2]

Here again the relevance of contextualization to Kant's philosophy comes out. In chapters 9 and 10 we saw that reflective judgment is important for properly contextualizing our thinking. This contextualization applies most obviously to how we assess ourselves relative to our circumstances. And for a pragmatic approach to life, this also entails orienting ourselves to the world at large. It is important that we distinguish between domain-like contexts where necessity reigns and other contexts where we must content ourselves with mere facticity or even contingency. And to reinforce the claim that the interior sense is a world-oriented mode of self-assessment, it can be compared to what was said earlier about conscience as a moral self-assessment that refers us beyond ourselves. Conscience can refer us to a noumenal standard or a higher being who serves as an omniscient judge. However, we can ascribe meaning to our relation to such a being only if we acknowledge that this involves a counterpart sphere that can only be made sense of by the symbolic power of *Gegenbildung*, or analogue-formation. We can have only indirect duties to a higher being; direct duties apply only to other human beings. These kinds of *reflective contextual differentiations* are crucial to avoid theoretical and moral amphibolies. In the next section, it will be shown that human sensibility itself demands *reflexive self-contextualization.*

Sensibility and Reflexive Self-Assessment

I have pointed to some similarities between a bodily vital sense and a mental interior sense. However, it should be noted that whereas the vital sense was anticipated in the *Mrongovius* notes, the interior sense was not. All earlier uses of the term "*inwendig*" were found in Kant's *Reflexionen.* He does not seem to have further developed this late conception of an interior sense beyond the passages I have quoted, but its introduction sheds light on how we can attend to ourselves or take our pulse despite the limits of introspection. When we attempt to observe inner sense, we think of the life of consciousness in terms of representational *contents* that are obscure and readily distorted by our imagination. But there is a pragmatic way of thinking about the life of consciousness in terms of *states of mind* that allow us to assess ourselves with reference to the things around us as part of the anthropological project of "having the world" or asserting our standing in it. I propose that Kant's notion of an interior sense can provide a reflexive contextual assessment that signals a transition from self-cognition as a project of introspective self-description to one of sensible self-evaluation that will ultimately require judgment and reflective comprehension. The interior sense of §15 of the *Anthropology* can provide a felt assessment of our overall state of mind, just as the vital sense is said to register our overall bodily state in §16.

Then, beginning with §17, the organ-based senses are reassessed. Kant starts with touch (*Betastung*) as providing direct external perception, which makes it "the most important and most reliably instructive" (*AP* 47; 7:155) sense. Touch is the only sense that gives an immediate external perception. It immediately informs us of the shape of objects and provides the basis for the mediate objective senses of hearing and sight as sources of cognition. As an organ-based sense, touch is considered purely in terms of its objective spatial import. Kant acknowledges that touch can also inform us how an object "feels [*anzufühlen sei*]," that is, "whether its surface is soft or rough, warm or cold" (*AP* 47; 7:155). But he considers such content only of interest to our vital sense.

The sense of hearing contributes nothing to further determining the shape of objects and little about their spatial location. However, because the sounds we utter and hear do not directly point to objects, they are considered to be "the best means of designating concepts" (*AP* 47; 7:155). The use of articulated sounds in speech allows us to reason with others about how we represent objects in order to conceptually define their rule-bound behavior. However, when we listen to sounds in terms of their tonal qualities, then we have music that moves our vital sense. Music is now defined as "a language of sheer sensations [*Empfindungen*] without any concepts" that allows "a communication of feelings at a distance to all present within the surrounding space" (*AP* 47; 7:155). For music to not merely affect our vital sense at the level of soul, but also inspire our interior sense, it would have to produce the aesthetic ideas discussed in the *Critique of Judgment* in order to stimulate the mind. But without the use of words, music is purely tonal and can only generate aesthetic ideas that are as short-lived as sensations and affects, according to Kant. Nevertheless, music can generate rhythmic tonal patterns that are playfully varied and enjoyed with others. The outer sense of hearing has many significant social ramifications.

Sight is a sense of mediate perception, as is hearing. Its importance lies in its capacity to discern matter in motion—not just in the space of touch, but also in the time of hearing. Sight is evaluated as the noblest sense because it has the widest spatial scope and represents objects as intuitively as possible with the least admixture of self-feeling. In other words, sight allows us to forget about ourselves—both in terms of the obscure contents of inner sense and the interior state of our feelings—and become absorbed in the world around us.

Kant also expands on the more subjective senses of taste and smell. Whereas the first three organ-based senses are based on mechanical influence, these last two organ-based senses of taste and smell are said to involve chemical influences which can strongly affect our feeling of pleasure and displeasure, that is, our vital sense. Smell is the one sense that it does not pay to cultivate because "there are more disgusting objects than pleasant ones" (*AP* 50–51; 7:158). Yet we cannot dispense with its medial power because it can warn us of dangerous gases and fumes around us. Taste can warn us that food is spoiled, but it is also the medium for the enjoyment of good food. For Kant, taste "has the specific advantage of promoting sociability in eating and drinking, something the sense of smell does not do" (*AP* 51; 7:159). This will happen if we eat with others and also use our tongues for dinner conversation, as was Kant's practice. The taste of the tongue can bring friends together, which aesthetic taste can then broaden by cultivating the higher senses as well.

Even the noblest sense of sight may affect the interior sense, as Kant admits when he speaks of how "in the strongest light we *see* (distinguish) nothing" (*AP* 50; 7:158). This is a case of being blinded by the sense of sight and frustrated because we cannot clearly see the objects before us. More generally, Kant concludes that "given the same degree of influence on them, the senses *teach* less the more strongly they feel themselves being *affected*" (*AP* 50; 7:158).

The following paragraph in the text confirms that even the most objective organ-based senses may affect our state of well-being, and if they do, it is indirectly by way of the vital sense.

> The more susceptible to impressions the vital sense is (the more tender and sensitive), the more unfortunate the human being is; on the other hand, the more susceptible he is toward the organ-based sense (sensitive) and the more inured to the vital sense, the more fortunate he is—I say more fortunate, not exactly morally better—for he has the feeling of his own well-being more under his control. (*AP* 50; 7:158)

Our fortune depends on not allowing the interior sense to be unduly swayed by the vital sense as it is medially affected either by surrounding conditions like intense heat or by overly stimulated organs of sense. Those persons who do not let the intensity of sense impressions affect their sense of well-being are strong enough to develop a "delicate [*zarte*] sensitivity," but a person who cannot "withstand satisfactorily the penetration of influences on the senses into consciousness, that is, attending to them against his will," is condemned to a weak or "tender [*zärtliche*] sensitivity" (*AP* 50; 7:158).

Delicate sensitivity is more active than the tender kind because it involves a judgmental discernment about what surrounds us by focusing on the details of what the organ-based senses teach us about the world and being willing to face any negative effects on our vital sense. At the level of interior sense, one could learn to abstract from these negative effects as much as possible, not unlike the way Kant suggested in the *Collins* lectures that we should move from the passive level of mere soul to the responsive level of mind and the self-activating or spontaneous level of spirit. Of course, the senses can also have a pleasant enlivening effect on our vital sense, and then we naturally wish to preserve this effect rather than overcome it. If the felt pleasure reaches a reflective level and puts our cognitive faculties into a purposive harmony, then the positive assessment of it at the level of interior sense can be affirmed at the level of aesthetic judgment. In contemporary terms, one could say that Kant's delicate sensitivity is really about responding to our surroundings with discernment.

What characterizes weak or tender sensitivity, as distinct from delicate sensitivity, is the inability to abstract from the negative effects that the vital sense can have on us. Tender souls tend to seek out what is pleasant and avoid what is challenging or threatening in any way. In matters of taste, they would opt for easy beauty or even prettiness and stay clear of the sublime. Tender sensitivity is thus sensibility in retreat. It is the reluctance to suffer potential negative effects on the vital sense and the incapacity to properly respond to them through the interior sense.

Vital sense indicates that our overall physical state of being may be beyond our control, whereas the interior sense, as I am elaborating it here, signals the ability to take control of our overall state of mind through judgmental self-assessment. This is reminiscent of what Kant said about the aesthetic assessment of whether to linger in our present state or to alter it. And in the case of the sublime, we saw that a negative state of vital sense can be transformed into a positive state of interior sense. The self-assessment that results from the sublime invokes our practical vocation and is a special case of the generally more pragmatic self-assessment made possible by our interior sense.

These discussions about the effects of the senses on us and on how we should respond to them and our surroundings reinforce my earlier claim about the reflexive nature of the *inwendige Sinn*. Kant's interior/reflexive sense is not self-observational in an interruptive way, but involves a kind of felt self-awareness that supports the kind of judgmental reflection that is important in ethical and evaluative situations. Merritt too argues that the reflection essential to moral reasoning is not usually "a perception trained on inner goings-on."[3] On the other hand, she allows that when a person pays attention to her feelings in deciding, she is being introspective. However, we need not assume that feelings are always introspective. The feelings relevant to reflecting about what to do are oriented to the world. I therefore propose a link between the reflexivity of the interior sense and moral reflection in order to bring out an important function of reflection that may readily be overlooked. We reflect normatively when we feel the need to pause and assess our situation and find the proper framing context to consider our alternatives.

Merritt's normative definition of reflection is that "all judgments require reflection."[4] Although it is true that for judgments to not be prejudicial they require reflection, it is even more essential that judgments carry forward the preparatory comparative work of reflection (as discussed in chapter 2 about concept-formation) in order to orient our thinking more broadly to its proper context. This was the task of reflective judgment as it was applied to aesthetics and to other evaluative situations in chapters 9 and 10. We saw that determinant judgments are essentially legislative to all rational intellects for how things are and what is worth doing. Reflective judgments, however, take the human standpoint into account and require individuals to evaluate their situation. This is when thinking becomes contextual and human comprehension integrates reason, reflection, and judgment.

Developing Character by Cultivating Our Sensible Faculties

The "interior sense" of part 1 of the *Anthropology* anticipates what Kant refers to as "character" in part 2 of that work. The importance of human character is stressed in all the lectures on anthropology, but we first find a separate part devoted to it in the extensive *Friedländer* lectures. Character represents a principled way of life whereby persons make something of themselves. To develop character means to acquire the resolve to act on moral principles and "not to fly off hither and yon" (*AP* 192; 7:292), like those who subject themselves to the obscure and involuntary contents of their inner sense. What was referred to earlier as "equanimity" seems to be an important constituent of the resolve that is needed to build moral character.

I have interpreted what the *Anthropology* says about the interior sense as the capacity for reflexive or felt self-assessment. The overall self-determination involved in the development of moral character goes further by moving to the level of reflective judgment and rational comprehension. To possess character is to have "inner worth" by living according to the maxim of reason which is to be consistently true to oneself.

With the aim of developing persons with a good character who exhibit wisdom in their everyday life, even the lower or sensible faculties need to be properly cultivated. Since he used Baumgarten's "Empirical Psychology" as the text of his anthropology, it is worth noting how Kant refines Baumgarten's advice. The best way to improve our sensible faculties is to consolidate them and bring out their productive potential. To do so, Kant reduces Baumgarten's list of eight distinct sensible faculties—*imagination, perspicaciousness, memory, invention, foresight, judgment, anticipation, and characterization*—to five. First of all, judgment is not listed as a distinct sensible faculty by Kant. It is really one of the higher faculties, but we will see that the need for its guidance will become apparent at times.

Secondly, he says nothing about what Baumgarten calls perspicaciousness, and he makes invention part of the imagination. Similarly, when Kant goes on to define memory, foresight, anticipation, and characterization, he is more explicit about how they make use of the imagination. This is important because Baumgarten did not attribute any productive powers to the imagination. Baumgarten wrote that "since my imaginations are perceptions of things that were formerly present, they are perceptions of the senses that, while I imagine, are absent" (*M* §558). For him, the imagination reproduces perceptions that have become "obscure" or "covered up" (*M* §559). Therefore, "nothing is in the faculty of imagination that is not first in the senses" (*M* §559). When Baumgarten later speaks of invention as the separating and combining of images, this involves merely rearranging the parts of what has been perceived. His rule of invention is that "parts of images are perceived as one whole" (*M* §590). This would account for the classical image of a centaur that combines the lower limbs of a horse with the upper body of a man.[5]

Kant agrees that the imagination cannot create its own content, yet he expects it to do more than mechanically rearrange the givens of sense. The imagination can be a power that engages the world in an inventive and productive way. In the pre-critical writings, Kant distinguished multiple imaginative formative powers (*Bildungskräfte*) that guide us in ordinary perception.[6] In the *Critique of Pure Reason*, this formative productivity of the imagination becomes the power to synthesize representations in the ideal forms of space and time and schematically project concepts onto apperceived objects. In the *Anthropology*, Kant differentiates three kinds of "inventive faculties [*Dichtungsvermögen*]" belonging to sensibility: "the *forming* of intuitions in space [*imagination plastica*], the *associating* of intuitions in time [*imagination associans*], and that of *affinity* based on the common origin of ideas from each other [*affinitas*]" (*AP* 67; 7:174). The first kind of invention is the common visual formative power. The second kind is a temporal associative power. Although imaginative associations may be useful in shaping certain habits, they remain subjective. Because associations may not be rule-bound, they need to be tamed by "sensibility's productive faculty of affinity [*Verwandschaft*]" (*AP* 70; 7:176), which is the most important inventive power. Kant defines an affinity as "the union of a manifold in virtue of its derivation from one ground" and advises that "in silent thinking as well as in the sharing of thoughts, there must always be *a theme* on which the manifold is strung" (*AP* 70; 7:177; italics added). This imaginative faculty of affinity provides "rules of sensibility" (*AP* 70; 7:177) which can be called *thematic* or *topical* in that they fall short of the *conceptual* consciousness of a rule as a rule. Only the understanding can provide a consciousness of rules as universal. Accordingly, the imaginative union of affinity produces a mere thematic generality or topical commonplace which seems to be "*in conformity with* the understanding although not derived *from* it" (*AP* 70; 7:176). What is imaginatively produced here is more than a mechanical rearrangement of parts. Here judgment is needed to discern something akin to a chemical reaction in which new properties emerge. Another aspect that is added to Baumgarten's account of the imagination is the effect that emotions and passions can have on it. Thus, Kant acknowledges that seeing someone suffer can arouse the sympathetic power of imagination, and he keenly notes that "when a passion appears on the scene, the power of imagination is more enlivened through the absence of the object than by its presence" (*AP* 73; 7:180).

Kant moves directly from his discussion of the imagination to memory and skips over Baumgarten's intervening discussion of perspicaciousness as the capacity to "perceive the correspondences and differences" (*M* §572) that are already inherent in what is given. The capacity to perceive these correspondences prepares for Baumgarten's account of memory. Baumgarten defines memory as the reproduction of past representations, namely, as the faculty of "recognizing" reproduced representations. The "inability to recognize reproduced perceptions" as corresponding to past perceptions is "forgetting," and the faculty of overcoming it is called "recollection" (*M* §582). To recollect is to perspicuously call back something to memory through associated ideas.[7]

Kant's richer conception of imagination makes room for both memory and foresight in that both involve "the faculty of visualizing or imaginatively making present [*Vergegenwärtigung*]" (*AP* 75; 7:182)[8] something that is absent. But more than that, they do so deliberately. Kant writes that

> memory is distinguished from the merely reproductive power of imagination in that it is able to reproduce the former representations *voluntarily*, so that the mind is not just the plaything of the imagination. Fantasy, which is the creative power of imagination, must not mix in with it, because then memory would be *unfaithful*. (*AP* 75–76; 7:182)

Memory is a volitional use of the imagination in an effort to produce coherence in experience. Thus, Kant says that both memory and foresight "are based on the *association* of representations of the past and future consciousness of the subject with the present" and "serve to connect in a coherent experience what *no longer exists* with what *does not yet exist* through what *presently exists*" (*AP* 75; 7:182).

The cultivation of memory is important, according to Kant, because of the way it supports our capacity for foresight. He goes so far as to claim that "recalling the past (remembering) occurs only with the intention of making foresight of the future possible by means of it" (*AP* 79; 7:186). This nicely crystallizes the difference between Baumgarten's metaphysically informed empirical psychology and Kant's pragmatic anthropology. Kant makes memory subservient to the practical need for foresight, or to quote him, foresight "interests us more than any other [faculty], because it is the condition of all possible practice and of the ends to which the human being relates the use of his powers. Every desire contains a (doubtful or certain) foresight of what is possible through it" (*AP* 79; 7:185). Foresight helps to give direction to our desires and can thus provide insight into our character. It is thus important that foresight be grounded in a reliable memory.

Baumgarten assigned the task of perfecting memory to a mnemonic art, which he describes briefly as that "part of aesthetics that prescribes the rules for extending, confirming, conserving, exciting, and restoring a larger and more faithful memory" (*M* §587). Kant's *Anthropology*, by contrast, offers a full three-page account about the urgency of cultivating memory. Developing the power to recall is not just an aesthetic enrichment of the present, but serves an essential life-function as we face the future. Kant replaces Baumgarten's mnemonic art with a more methodical approach. He claims that "there is no *mnemonic art* . . . in the sense of a general doctrine. Among the special tricks belonging to it are maxims in verse . . . since the rhythm has a regular syllabic stress that is a great advantage to the mechanism of memory" (*AP* 77; 7:184). As we will see, Kant distrusts special tricks to unleash the mechanism of memory. And concerning prodigies of memory and literary types who "carry around in their heads . . . a load of books," Kant balances admiration on the one hand with the worry that they may "not possess the power of judgment suitable for choosing among all this knowledge in order to make appropriate use of it" (*AP* 77–78; 7:184).

Kant seeks methodical ways of cultivating memory called "memorizing" and classifies them as either "mechanical, ingenious, or judicious" (*AP* 76; 7:183). Mechanical memorizing is based on "frequent word-for-word repetition" in the way that children are initially taught things. Kant compares it to a rote reciting of a sequence, which if interrupted must be started over from the beginning, and manifests merely the rudiments of understanding. Then there is ingenious memorizing, which he calls "a method of impressing certain ideas on the memory by association with correlative ideas that in themselves (as far as the understanding is concerned) have no relationship at all with each other" (*AP* 76; 7:183). This second so-called method draws Kant's contempt and he calls it an "absurd . . . ruleless procedure of the power of imagination in pairing together things that cannot belong together under one and the same concept" (*AP* 77; 7:183). Kant suggests that this ingenious method appeals to people who like to show off their wit, but it really makes memorizing more difficult by burdening us with an unnecessary association of quite disparate representations.

The method recommended by Kant is that of judicious memorizing. Here judgment is used to create a "table of the divisions of a system" (*AP* 77; 7:184) that puts things in their overall context by making a kind of mental map. This leads the imagination to seek aid from the higher faculties of understanding and judgment. Kant sums up this section as follows: "Most of all, the judicious use of topics, that is, a framework for general concepts, called commonplaces, facilitates remembering through class division, as when one distributes books in a library on shelves with different labels" (*AP* 77; 7:184). Such a topical framework provides a medial orientational system in which a part that has been forgotten can be found by locating it with reference to other thematically related parts which have been retained. Similarly, in his lectures on geography, Kant speaks of the importance of sketching a kind of "encyclopedia" (*PG*, 9:158) that gathers information into an orderly worldly whole. These recommendations can be seen as further elaborations of the way in which human comprehension must be judgmentally specified.

Baumgarten proceeded from memory to a consideration of invention in order to generate foresight, but Kant proceeds directly from memory to foresight. He does not trust invention as a transition from memory to foresight. This is because foresight is conceived not as freely extrapolating beyond past experience, but as a more reflectively considered judgmental extension. Kant proposes two conceptions of foresight. The first is an empirical foresight that "requires no rational knowledge of causes and effects, but only the remembering of observed events as they commonly follow one another" (*AP* 79; 7:186). This mode of foresight as the expectation (*Erwartung*) of more of the same is based on association only. A stronger version of foresight is called "prescience [*Vorhererwartung*]" (*AP* 80; 7:187). This prescience is "a consciousness of the future produced by reflecting on the law of succession of events (the law of causality)" (*AP* 80; 7:187) and replaces expectation based on common sense with expectation based on science.

Both Baumgarten and Kant end their examination of the lower cognitive faculties with our use of signs. For Baumgarten, the "faculty of joining signs together in a representation with the signified" (*M* §619) is called the faculty of characterization. To characterize is to access part of the "nexus of signification in this world" (*M* §619) by using a sign as a means of knowing the existence of another thing (see *M* §347). When the sign is perceived more clearly than the signified, then we have mere symbolic knowledge, according to Baumgarten, but if the signified is perceived more clearly than the sign, then we attain intuitive knowledge (see *M* §620). The science of sensible knowledge concerned with signs is called the "aesthetics of characterization" and it includes "both heuristics and hermeneutics" (*M* §622). Kant calls the faculty of using signs the *facultas signatrix* rather than *facultas characteristica.* Instead of accessing a timeless metaphysical nexus, signifying brings about a temporal worldly nexus. Kant claims that we use signs to cognize "the present as the means for connecting the representation of the foreseen with that of the past" (*AP* 84; 7:191). A present sign can imaginatively or medially fill in the abstractness of what is merely foreseen by connecting it to something remembered from the past. This temporal dimension of signification makes it important for human consciousness because it represents everything distributively over time. Kant distinguishes between two kinds of signs that can hold our representations together: characters and symbols. Characters are "signs which in themselves signify nothing, but only signify something through association with intuitions and then leading through them to concepts" (*AP* 84; 7:191). This was already claimed in the *Critique of Judgment,* where Kant wrote that characters "contain nothing at all belonging to the intuition of the object" (*C3* 226; 5:352) and are only associated with them "as a means of reproduction" (*C3* 226; 5:352). Characters can be words or visible algebraic signs which can express concepts but cannot give them intuitive content. They are externally related to concepts by mere convention. This means that characters only abstractly represent (*vorstellen*) concepts without intuitively presenting (*darstellen*) them. Symbols, however, can intuitively present or exhibit concepts, even if only indeterminately.

Kant's more favorable attitude toward symbolism derives from his skepticism about Baumgarten's claim that a "conception" of the intellect can provide "distinct perception" (*M* §632). Kant argues that logically concepts belong to thought alone and lack intuitive perceptual content. The categories of the understanding and the ideas of reason are special concepts that only become intuitively meaningful when judgment directs them at the world. Whereas imaginative schemata bring out the objective meaning of the categories of the understanding, artistic and aesthetic symbols can bestow an intersubjective meaning on abstract ideas of reason. There is, however, still something lacking in the intuitive nature of symbolism in that it is indirect and based on analogies. This lack becomes more evident when Kant goes on to suggest that ordinary language can be cultivated to provide a provisional symbolism for the distinct concepts needed for adequate human communication. Thus, he writes that "he who can only express himself symbolically still has only a few concepts of the understanding" (*AP* 84; 7:191). To express oneself symbolically would be like relying on Baumgarten's extensively clear or *distinctive* marks rather than on intensively clear or *distinct* concepts (see chapter 2). Although the symbolic use of marks falls short of true conceptual understanding, Kant indicates that the symbolic intuitive presentation offered by the colloquialism "we want to bury the hatchet" can prepare the way for the political concept of peacemaking. Symbols can thus have a pragmatic function of using ordinary language to initiate conceptual thought in spheres where the available concepts fail us. Symbols thus become the medium of reflective judgment.

In the *Busolt* lectures on anthropology of 1788–89, Kant spoke of imaginative symbols as being representative (*stellvertretend*), but in the final *Anthropology* they are called presentational (*darstellend*), as in the *Critique of Judgment*. This is the new formulation: "symbols are mere means used by the understanding to provide its concept with meaning [*Bedeutung*] through the intuitive presentation [*Darstellung*] of an object for it. But they are indirect means only, owing to an *analogy* with certain intuitions to which this concept can be applied" (*AP* 84; 7:191). Symbols are imaginative representations that are not used to directly refer to (*deuten*) a particular thing, but to give multiple things meaning (*Bedeutung*) by indirectly presenting them in relational terms.

The symbolic extension of the imagination produces linguistic characterization and allows us to converse with ourselves in a thoughtful way, instead of vainly trying through introspection to visualize ourselves perceptually. This is summed up nicely in §39 of the *Anthropology*: "All language is a signification of thought and, on the other hand, the best way of signifying thought is through *language, the greatest instrument for understanding ourselves and others*" (*AP* 86; 7:192; italics added). Thinking is then characterized medially as both "speaking with oneself" and "listening to oneself inwardly" (*AP* 86; 7:192).[9] Just as the power to signify puts things in the past and in the future on the same level of thought, it puts the self and others in communion. We can learn about ourselves and assess our character through linguistic comparison with others.

What Kant expects from his pragmatic anthropology, then, is not a mere description of human beings, but a characterization that goes beyond what is directly given. Just as according to his theory of signs, a "character" is a letter that signals something other than itself, so according to his approach to life, "the character of a living being is what enables us to know its vocation or destiny [*Bestimmung*] in advance" (*AP* 234; 7:329). Characterization allows us to be prepared for the future and is thus more pragmatic than description.

Ultimately, a person's character is defined by Kant "as a way of thinking [*Denkungsart*]" (*AP* 191; 7:291) that involves self-prescription, namely, the binding of one's behavior by means of practical principles. What a person "has pre-scribed [*vor-geschrieben*] to himself" (*AP* 192; 7:292) as his character is a way of thinking that at the same time requires linguistic characterization to be communicable.[10] The determination of character seems to require a communal context, and this will be confirmed in what follows.

Using Our Higher Faculties Pragmatically

When it comes to our higher faculties, Kant starts with the same three maxims of thinking in the *Anthropology* that he also prescribes in other works. They are to employ (1) our understanding to "think for oneself," (2) our judgment to "think into the place of the other (in communication with human beings)," and (3) our reason to "always think consistently with oneself" (*AP* 95; 7:200). However, since pragmatically the formation of character as a consistent mode of thinking is central, the last maxim of reason will warrant special attention. Indeed, Kant reformulates the three maxims in a way that expects understanding and judgment to already anticipate the interests of practical reason. The maxims are revised as three pragmatic demands on our cognitive capacities. They can be reconstructed as follows:

1. At the level of understanding, I should be able to think and determine "what I want" (*AP* 123; 7:227n).

2. At the level of judgment, I should be able to discern "what is at stake [*worauf kommts an*]" (*AP* 123; 7:227, translation revised).

3. At the level of reason, I should be able to infer "what comes of it [*was kommt heraus*]" (*AP* 123; 7:227).

The first demand, to determine what one wants, "requires only a clear head [*Kopf*] to understand oneself" (*AP* 123; 7:227). Pragmatically, the responsibility to think for myself and not let others think for me translates into the responsibility to understand my standpoint and role in the world. Thus Kant ends book 1 of the *Anthropology* with the claim that "the most important revolution from within the human being is 'his exit from his self-incurred immaturity'" (*AP* 124; 7:229). Maturity requires me to begin taking charge of myself through self-assessment.

Becoming mature requires moving to the second level of developing good judgment, which pragmatically is the talent for deciding on an appropriate goal and the best means to accomplish it. Anthropologically, this means the capacity to decide what to do in the particular context we find ourselves in. Good judgment is a crucial capacity that we must develop because it can focus on what is essentially at stake in a given life-situation. Kant acknowledges this importance of judgment when he says that once a lawyer has discerned what is really at stake in a legal dispute, "the verdict of reason follows by itself" (*AP* 123; 7:228). To the extent that judgment is governed by the maxim of expansive thought, it should be able to comprehend and justify its own position relative to the overall scheme of things.

The third task is for reason to conclude what comes of it all after we have comprehended and judged; reason must appropriate those results in a principled manner and transform the temperament we inherited into a self-consistent character. Judging allows us to expand our mode of thinking in a communal way, but reason must bring it back to ourselves.

Having surveyed the evolution of Kant's anthropology lectures, it becomes increasingly clear that self-cognition is not learning what inner sense has assimilated, but establishing what reason can actively appropriate as part of a project of comprehensive self-assessment and character formation.

Ethico-Religious Reflections on Conscience as Human Self-Assessment

Although we have focused on the anthropology lectures to highlight the task of human self-assessment, Kant also offered some ethico-religious reflections on this topic that are relevant. In the *Critique of Pure Reason*, he made a troublesome admission about our ethical self-comprehension when he wrote the following footnote:

> The real morality of actions (their merit and guilt), even that of our own conduct, therefore remains entirely hidden from us. Our imputations can be referred only to the empirical character. How much of it is to be ascribed to mere nature and innocent defects of temperament or to its happy constitution [*merito fortunae*], this no one can discover, and hence no one can judge it with complete justice. (A551/B579n)

However, from the perspective of practical reason, we cannot remain within this theoretical limit because we are expected to judge not just whether we have obeyed the moral law, but also whether we have done so based on an inner commitment to the law. This problem is exhibited most acutely in judgments about moral character. In a sense, this could be thought to require a speculative or regulative solution, because as Kant already suggested, only an omniscient God could truly be said to penetrate the intelligible ground of our heart. Objective determinate knowledge of our inner disposition is not possible for us. Nevertheless, Kant indicates that we do have a degree of subjective, reflective cognition of ourselves, as in the case of conscience. Conscience does not provide direct introspective self-certainty (*Selbstgewissheit*), but an indirect self-cognition (*Selbsterkenntnis*) that is reflective.

In the second part of *The Metaphysics of Morals* devoted to virtue, there is a section in which Kant attempts to conceive of conscience together with moral feeling, love of our neighbor, and respect for ourselves as aesthetic modes of moral receptivity that we all have to a certain extent. He writes:

> There is no obligation to have these [moral endowments] because they lie at the basis of morality, as subjective conditions of receptiveness to the concept of duty, not as objective conditions of morality. . . . To have these predispositions cannot be considered a duty; rather any human being has them, and it is by virtue of them that he can be put under obligation. (*MM* 159; 6:399)

Here I will just focus on the first two modes of receptivity: moral feeling and conscience. Moral feeling is what was earlier called respect for the law. No human being can be entirely without this feeling, according to Kant. It is an aesthetic-moral "susceptibility on the part of free choice to be moved by practical reason (and its law)" (*MM* 160; 6:400). Since any consciousness of obligation assumes moral feeling, we can have no duty to acquire it but only an obligation to cultivate it.

Conscience is considered next and is defined as "practical reason holding the human being's duty before him for his acquittal or condemnation in every case that comes under the law" (*MM* 160; 6:400). To judge whether we have performed our duty could be seen as the objective assessment of whether our deeds accord with the law. Such a judgment can be made in a court of law when it comes to duties of right. But here Kant is speaking of duties of virtue that have to do with our inner disposition. Conscience is really the consciousness of whether we have paid heed to our moral feeling in performing our duties. There is also a later section entitled "On a Human Being's Duty to Himself as His Own Innate Judge," where Kant writes that "every human being has a conscience and finds himself observed, threatened and . . . kept in awe (respect coupled with fear) by an internal judge" (*MM* 189; 6:438). Conscience thus converts moral feeling into the kind of awe that we have for a court of law. What is paradoxical about the predisposition called conscience is that "although its business is a business of a human being with himself, his reason constrains him to perform it as at the bidding of another person" (*MM* 189; 6:438). This other person can be thought of as an ideal moral being or "a scrutinizer of hearts" (*MM* 190; 6:439). The moral being who could serve as an ideal interpreter of character is to be thought of as an omniscient judge of conscience. However, Kant warns that if we do appeal to the idea of God as an ideal judge, it is not to be taken dogmatically or doctrinally. We are not entitled "to assume that such a supreme being actually exists . . . for the idea is not given . . . objectively, by theoretical reason, but only subjectively, by practical reason" (*MM* 190; 6:439–40). This means that the regulative idea of a transcendent interpreter must be internalized as an ideal judge. The perfect judge is "distinct from us yet present in our inmost being" (*MM* 190; 6:440). The hypothetical regulative dimension must find its baseline in what is reflectively comprehensible. God as ideal judge is really the product of the analogical or "symbolic cognition" (*C3* 227; 5:353) proposed in the *Critique of Judgment*, which results from "following out the analogy with a lawgiver for all rational beings in the world" (*MM* 190; 6:440). Although reflective judgments of conscience are heuristically oriented by an ideal lawgiver, they are owed to no one but ourselves. Thus Kant warns that we should not treat any of our duties as divine commands. If our duties were determined by God, we would lose our autonomy. "As far as reason alone can judge, a human being has duties only to human beings (himself and others)" (*MM* 192; 6:442). To think otherwise is to commit an "amphiboly in moral concepts of reflection" (*MM* 192; 6:442). A moral amphiboly is a hermeneutical confusion whereby I extend a duty that is valid in one sphere to another. The duty involved in being conscientious is thus rarely determinate and is ultimately reflective in having to decide the extent of our obligation.

Kant sometimes contrasts duties of virtue with duties of right, which are said to pertain to our outer freedom. This suggests that duties of virtue coincide with our inner freedom. But before deciding whether that is the case, we must ask what Kant means by the notion of outer freedom. He writes that it is "limited only by the formal provision of its compatibility with the freedom of all" (*MM* 158; 6:396). At this point the rights of others assert themselves, which leads Kant to admit that while all duties are part of ethics, "it does not follow that the lawgiving for them is always contained in ethics" (*MM* 21; 6:220). The lawgiving of outer freedom is juridical and "formal" (*MM* 146; 6:380) and aims at constraining our inclinations for communal reasons. The inner freedom of morality "goes beyond this and provides a *matter* (an object of free choice), an end of pure reason which it represents as an end that is also objectively necessary" (*MM* 146; 6:380). Whereas outer freedom is constrained by juridical laws, inner freedom is defined as the "capacity for self-constraint . . . by pure practical reason" (*MM* 158; 6:396). The inner freedom of the ethical prescribes that all the ends of our maxims of action possess the universality of lawfulness. Duties of virtue go beyond this demand in that they refer to the "highest, unconditional end of pure practical reason," namely, "that virtue be its own end and . . . its own reward" (*MM* 158; 6:396). To be virtuous is not merely to assert one's inner freedom of self-constraint in acting morally, but to also show "moral strength" (*MM* 158; 6:397) as an individual human being. To become virtuous, we must supplement outer and inner freedom with individual freedom.

One of the duties of virtue is to perfect oneself, but Kant recognizes that "it is a human being's duty to strive for this perfection, but not to reach it (in this life)" (*MM* 196; 6:446). This leads him to make a distinction between perfect and imperfect duties, which is relevant to our earlier question of whether respect for the moral law should be the only incentive or the primary incentive in acting. Concerning the duty to perfect oneself, Kant writes that although it is "narrow and perfect with regard to its object (the idea that one should make it one's end to realize), with regard to the subject it is only a wide and imperfect duty to himself" (*MM* 196; 6:446). As such, it leaves a certain "latitude for free choice" and "reflection" (*MM* 195; 6:445–46) in terms of how to approximate this perfection. That is the nature of duties of virtue: they leave our reflective judgment some latitude. Rationally, objectively, and noumenally, respect for the law must be the only incentive, but when it comes to our subjective and phenomenal existence, respect for the law can only be the first among several incentives. It is left open how far we should extinguish natural self-interested incentives.

Because the depths of the human heart are unfathomable, and can only be plumbed reflectively as oriented by analogies, Kant is forced to express doubt that a person can really know "when he feels the incentive to fulfill his duty, whether it proceeds entirely from the representation of the law or whether there are not many other sensible impulses contributing to it" (*MM* 196; 6:447). Here, then, we see Kant acknowledging the possibility broached earlier that as long as respect for the law is the primary incentive that requires a "revolution in thought," other, more strategic incentives may need to be cultivated as part of the reformatory trajectory of progressing toward perfection. If human beings have heeded their moral feeling and consulted their conscience, this does not mean that they can be certain they are virtuous, but they have at least established a basis for respect for themselves. Of all the subjective conditions of receptiveness to morality, it is conscience that is most hermeneutically revealing.

Although it is sometimes said that some human beings have no conscience, Kant contends that this is not really the case: conscience involves a susceptibility that cannot be eradicated. Those who seem to have no conscience merely have a "propensity to pay no heed to its judgment" (*MM* 161; 6:401). They allow themselves to be distracted, as it were. Conscience seems to be a predisposition to goodness like the predisposition to responsibility, and its suppression seems like a propensity for evil. Just as Kant thinks that it is impossible to fully extinguish the voice of conscience, he also thinks that it is impossible to have an erring conscience. Actually, he says an erring conscience is *ein Unding* (*MM* 161; 6:401), which can be translated as "absurdity," as Mary Gregor does, but it could also be rendered as "monstrosity." This would rule out an erring conscience and unconscientiousness from human nature, but not the possibility of monstrous exceptions. This could have been the way for Kant to go if he had been exposed to the outrageous deeds of recent historical figures guilty of genocide.

Actually, what Kant means by an unerring conscience is quite limited. It does not mean that conscience is infallible, for he admits that "I can indeed be mistaken at times in my objective judgment as to whether something is a duty or not" (*MM* 161; 6:401). However, "I cannot be mistaken in my subjective judgment as to whether I have submitted it to my practical reason (here in its role as judge) for such a judgment; for if I could be mistaken in that . . . there would be neither truth nor error" (*MM* 161; 6:401). Paying heed to our conscience is an act of truthfulness which is a precondition for our ability to separate truth from falsity.

In the essay "On the Miscarrage of All Philosophical Trials in Theodicy," Kant finds this truthfulness in the "formal conscientiousness" ("MTT" 27; 8:268) of authenticity. He sets out to replace traditional doctrinal theodicies claiming to be true with an "authentic (*authentische*) theodicy" ("MTT" 24; 8:264) aiming at truthfulness. Any attempt to interpret the meaning of human existence authentically must also be sincere[11] and may make no pretense to know more than what we can reflectively comprehend. The heart of authenticity or formal conscientiousness is "not pretending to hold anything as true [that] we are not conscious of holding as true" ("MTT" 27; 8:268). Conscience seems to deliver an ultimate subjective reference point for judging our "guilt or innocence," so that if a person has heeded it, "nothing more can be required of him" (*MM* 161; 6:401).

But is conscientiousness as the basis for self-respect tantamount to knowing whether we are good in the more robust sense of being virtuous? If only an ideal interpreter can truly know whether a person has made the revolutionary decision to place respect for the law above all other incentives, then the answer is no. Recognizing our virtue or our purity of incentive demands knowing the truth about ourselves. It seems that conscience only provides a felt truthfulness. Conscience as a mode of feeling may give us a nagging sense that what we have done so far is not enough and that we should do more. If we listen to that reproachful voice and let it reform our ways, then we have started a gradual process of raising our consciousness. Perhaps this is all that Kant can ultimately demand of us in this life.

The assessment of individual virtue is difficult and would seem to require reflective judgment. Kant introduced reflective judgment as an aesthetic mode of comparing subjective and perspectival assessments of beauty, but ultimately it can expose something incomparable, namely, the sublimity of individual character. Judging virtue involves more than a formal determination from without; it demands reflection on the inner worth of one's character. With this we reach the heart of morality, but even here Kant keeps us humble by insisting on the indirectness of reflective judgment. And to the extent that conscientiousness plays a role in this process of self-assessment, namely, being oriented to an ideal judge or interpreter, self-understanding becomes a mode of reflective comprehension. What is interesting here is that in the final parts of the *Critique of Judgment*, the human relation to God comes to be located somewhere between the two poles laid out in the *Critique of Pure Reason*: universally sharable knowledge and private belief. In 1781 Kant denied human beings the theoretical certainty of universally valid metaphysical knowledge of God and allowed them merely the individual moral certainty of religious faith. In 1790 he endorses a mode of holding to be true (*Führwahrhalten*) that assents to God's reality as something that can provide "moral conviction [*Überzeugung*]" (*C3* 327; 5:463) which holds not just for individuals but for "*for us* (human beings in general)" (*C3* 327; 5:463). If morally informed religious awareness is to become helpful in orienting human self-assessment, it must be made clear that it cannot be in the mode of determinant knowledge that metaphysics strives for, but in the reflective mode of "symbolic cognition of God" (*C3* 227; 5:353) which Kant introduced in §59 of the *Critique of Judgment*. It is important here to acknowledge that symbolic cognition is only quasi-intuitive and makes use of linguistic analogies that relate things from different contexts. Although any human faith that relates to God in a noumenal domain remains conceptually abstract, it can be symbolically presented (*dargestellt*) by analogies such as the parent-child relation in the phenomenal terrain. Such a reflective analogy can be comprehensively presentational and supplement what our understanding represents conceptually. Paradoxically, presentational symbols can bring what is objectively remote subjectively close to us, whereas representational concepts create a subjective distance between us and the things around us. Similarly, I have attempted to explicate the notion of an interior sense in the final *Anthropology* by describing it as a reflexive counterpart to Kant's reflective moral conscience. Both contribute to what I have called cognitive self-assessment and can make use of reflective symbolic relations. And to the extent that they help us cultivate our character, they can contribute to an appropriative comprehension of our world.

15

The Distinction between Kant's Cosmopolitanism and His Cosmical Philosophy

In this chapter, I will argue for an important distinction between the oft-referred-to cosmopolitanism of Kant's philosophy and a more general cosmical philosophy that brings out the full scope of Kant's world-concept. The distinction between them has been overlooked, but will be defended based on the fact that they appeal to two different senses of culture. In chapter 1, we saw Kant distinguish two kinds of philosophy: (1) the traditional kind which is in accordance with an "academic or scholastic concept [*Schulbegriff*]," and (2) a more adequate kind in accordance with a world-concept [*Weltbegriff*] (*conceptus cosmicus*) (A838/B866). The first, academic kind of philosophy concerns "a system of cognition that is sought only as a science without having as its end anything more than the systematic unity of this knowledge" (A838/B866). Its aim is thus primarily theoretical and school-based. The other or world-oriented philosophy, which can also be called "cosmical," concerns "the science of the relations of all cognition to the essential ends of human reason [*teleologia rationis humanae*]" (A839/B867). A philosopher of the academic kind is merely skilled in the use of reason, while the philosopher who is world-oriented or cosmical strives to be more; namely, "a legislator [*Gesetzgeber*] of human reason" (A839/B867). What Kant is aiming for is a philosophy that can legitimate itself.

We could say that cosmical philosophy completes the *Critique of Pure Reason* by pointing forward to the *Critique of Practical Reason*. However, the clarification that Kant goes on to give of cosmical philosophy is that it concerns "what necessarily interests everyone" (A839/B867). Thus, the concept of what is worldly seems to encompass more than our moral ends and will include prudential ends as well. It also considers how contiguous disciplines such as psychology relate to philosophy. Thus at the end of the architectonic of pure reason, Kant strives to overcome "the customary academic" conception of psychology, which saw it as part of metaphysics, and find for it a new "habitat" or contextual home in the world of human inquiry (A849/B877). This becomes a part of Kant's overall project to relate "philosophy in a genuine [*ächten*] sense to wisdom [*Weisheit*]" through the path of science which will include not only mathematics and natural science, but also anthropology as the new science that can provide "empirical cognizance [*Kenntnis*] of humankind" (A850/B878).

We find more details about Kant's distinction between the academic and the worldly senses of philosophy in the *Jäsche Logic* of 1800. Academic or scholastic philosophers are said to possess the skill of giving "rules for the use of reason for any sort of end one wishes" (*LL* 537; 9:24). They manifest what Socrates called the *philodoxical* skill to systematize what has been cognized in accordance with their own opinions. By contrast, those who philosophize according to the worldly concept have the wisdom to "show us the ultimate ends [*letzten Zwecke*] of human reason" (*LL* 537; 9:24, translation revised). They are practical philosophers who aim at the "highest maxim for the use of our reason, insofar as we understand by a maxim the inner principle of choice among various ends" (*LL* 537; 9:24). This requires the true philosopher to make reference to the "final end [*Endzweck*]" (*LL* 538, 9:24, translation revised)[1] to which all other ends are subordinated. It is at this point that philosophy in the "cosmical sense" (*LL* 537; 9:24) is also assigned a "cosmopolitan sense or significance" (*LL* 538; 9:25).

The problem that I want to focus on in this chapter is, what happens to cosmical philosophy when it takes on this cosmopolitan significance? I have already raised questions about the *Jäsche Logic* because it claimed things about reflection that were not fully supported by any of Kant's own writings. It could be that here too Jäsche was careless and linked them more closely than Kant intended. Many translators have even merged them by translating both *weltlich* and *weltbürgerlich* as "cosmopolitan." *Weltlich* simply means "worldly" or "cosmical." Only the latter German term, *weltbürgerlich,* pertains to being a cosmopolitan world-citizen. Readers of the otherwise excellent Cambridge translation of the *Critique of Pure Reason* may not realize that Kant's German term *Weltbegriff* is translated as "cosmopolitan concept" instead of "cosmical concept."

So what is the difference between Kant's philosophy according to a cosmical or worldly concept and his thoughts about cosmopolitanism as it can be found in his own writings? While looking for possible differences between the terms "cosmical" and "cosmopolitan," we should also take note of a third variant. In a recent essay, Robert Louden points out that Kant also spoke of a "world-acquaintance [*Weltkenntniß*]" that is "cosmological [*cosmologisch*]" (25:734) in the *Pillau* anthropology lectures of 1777–78. There Kant is said to distinguish between a specific world acquaintance of merchants who exchange regionally and a more general cosmological acquaintance of those who travel in the world. Since only the first kind of world acquaintance is empirically grounded, we are left to conclude that cosmological acquaintance is superficial and unreliable. We are urged to test the anthropological opinions of thoughtless travelers by means of reflection. Thus *cosmological* anthropological acquaintance is clearly not at the level of Kant's ideal of *cosmical* philosophy. Nor does Louden equate cosmological acquaintance with *cosmopolitan* thought. Although he does allow for some "overlap" between cosmological and cosmopolitan considerations, he says that there are "distinct political, legal, and moral overtones in Kant's anthropological use of the term 'cosmopolitan' that are absent in the term cosmological.'"[2] This is no doubt true, but there are also expectations about cosmical philosophy that neither cosmological acquaintance nor cosmopolitan cognition satisfy; namely, true knowledge and the comprehension of what it is to be wise.

In his writings on justice and cosmopolitanism, Otfried Höffe distinguishes between "cosmo-logical" and "cosmo-political"[3] philosophy. And by arguing that the *Critique of Pure Reason* is implicitly political through its reference to a "government of reason (B860),"[4] Höffe would seem to have no objection to calling Kant's philosophy "cosmopolitan" in an overarching sense. I, however, will assign cosmopolitanism an important role that is nevertheless subordinate to cosmical philosophy. Whereas Louden and Höffe favor the cosmopolitan conception of philosophy because of its political, legal, and moral ramifications, I will raise questions about the depth of the philosophical and moral commitments involved in cosmopolitanism.

There is a passage near the end of *Religion within the Boundaries of Mere Reason* where Kant speaks of "the idea of a cosmopolitan *moral community*" (*R* 190; 6:200), which might seem to diminish the differences I see between the cosmical and the cosmopolitan. But as part of his efforts to define the ideal of a true spiritual religious community, it becomes clear that this idea of a cosmopolitan moral community is merely "a good means of enlivening a community to the moral disposition of brotherly love" (*R* 190; 6:200). The label "cosmopolitan moral community" is used to describe the Christian sacrament of holy communion, namely, "a ritual communal partaking at the same table" (*R* 190; 6:199) that is open to all. But Kant warns that we should not attach too much weight to this symbolic ritual: "to boast that God has attached special graces to the celebration of this solemn ritual . . . is a delusion of religion which cannot but work counter to the spirit of religion" (*R* 190; 6:200). By adding the adjective "cosmopolitan" to the moral community, Kant is institutionalizing it and disassociating it from his ideal of the "church invisible" (*R* 111; 6:101).

Anthropological Cosmopolitanism

Louden stresses the anthropological use of the term "cosmopolitanism," which can be made sense of by the fact that the *Jäsche Logic* adds a fourth question to the three that were used to define philosophy in the first *Critique*. To the initial three philosophical questions, What can I know? What ought I to do? and What may I hope? a new question is added, namely, What is man? We need to consider the significance of adding this fourth question about the nature of man to the first three that were already part of philosophy in the *cosmical sense*. Does this fourth question transform cosmical philosophy into *cosmopolitanism*?

Metaphysics is said to answer the first question of what I can know, morals answers the second question of what ought I to do, religion answers the third question of what I may hope, and anthropology answers the fourth question about human nature . Actually, the religious idea of hope is geared to the themes of community and communion, which are not all that different from the aesthetic promise of communicability and the anticipation of consensus. Indeed, Kant attaches special importance to the way we experience beautiful forms in nature by comparing them to a "cipher code [*Chiffreschrift*] by which nature figuratively speaks to us" (*C3* 180; 5:301) and gives us the hope that the world is more orderly than we can understand.

If, as the Jäsche text suggests, the next question about the nature of man relates cosmical philosophy to cosmopolitanism, then we should look to Kant's anthropology for further clues about what this relation means. If cosmopolitanism is about getting humans to cooperate, then the results of anthropological studies are indeed relevant. The first three questions relevant to cosmical philosophy were already about human goals, but they were couched in individual terms. The fourth question is expansive in that it shifts our attention to humans as a species. But the further question to be asked is whether that makes cosmopolitanism the culmination of cosmical philosophy or merely an empirical application of it.

The cosmical questions about what a human being ought to do and what to hope for are couched in moral and religious terms that evoke the abstract language of the kingdom of ends. Cosmopolitan thought, however, is concerned with results and looks for a political counterpart for the kingdom of ends. Cosmopolitanism is thus very much compatible with the outlook expressed in the opening paragraph of Kant's *Anthropology from a Pragmatic Point of View*, where he writes:

> All cultural progress by means of which the human being advances his schooling [*seine Schule macht*] has the goal of applying this acquired cognition and skill for the world's use. But the most important object in the world to which he can apply them is the human being: because the human being is his own ultimate end [*eigener letzter Zweck*]. (*AP* 3; 7:119, translation revised)

The task of a pragmatic anthropology is to inquire into what human beings as free-acting beings can and should make of themselves on this earth. We saw that Kant's anthropology was quite empirical and was largely elaborated in prudential terms. Thus, it is worth asking whether pragmatic anthropology oriented by a cosmopolitan framework can also cultivate the moral wisdom aimed at by cosmical philosophy. A clear answer is not available in Kant's *Anthropology* because it does not discuss wisdom very much. But when Kant relates human skillfulness (*Geschicklichkeit*) as acquired through schooling to the prudence (*Klugheit*) needed for "using other human beings for one's purposes" (*AP* 95; 7:201), he does briefly refer to wisdom (*Weisheit*) (see *AP* 94; 7:200). This could suggest that a pragmatic anthropology can school us not only in developing our technical skills to use things and our prudential capacities to use other human beings, but also in our search for wisdom. However, there is no schooling for wisdom. Indeed, we read in the *Anthropology* that "wisdom, as the idea of a practical use of reason that conforms perfectly with the law, is no doubt too much to demand of human beings" (*AP* 94; 7:200). This is followed up by the claim that we reach the full use of our reason with respect to skill around age twenty, with respect to prudence around age forty, and with respect to wisdom around age sixty. However, in this last period, wisdom is conceived somewhat *negatively*: "it sees the follies of the first two periods" (*AP* 95; 7:201). Kant does not explicitly say so, but it is clear that near the end of our lives, we can no longer be fully active participants in the *cosmopolitan* aims of public life and should redirect our lives to the attainment of a wisdom directed at both the world and ourselves, which I consider to be part of the more elusive *cosmical* project.

Although wisdom is not something that can be taught and must be brought forth from ourselves (see *AP* 94; 7:200), Kant's *Anthropology* does mention that wisdom can be attained by means of the three maxims of thinking that we discussed in the previous chapter and saw him apply pragmatically for cosmopolitan ends. However, the *Critique of Judgment* provides another formulation of the three maxims of thinking that can shed more light on how Kant himself conceived of the relation between cosmical philosophy and cosmopolitanism. But before leaving the *Anthropology*, let us see what Kant says about cosmopolitanism there. He warns that human beings cannot progress

> without being together peacefully, and yet cannot avoid constantly being objectionable to one another. Consequently, they feel destined by nature to [develop], through *mutual compulsion* under laws that come from themselves, into a *cosmopolitan society* [*cosmopolitismus*] that is constantly threatened by disunion. . . . In itself it is an unattainable idea . . . only a regulative principle: to pursue this diligently as the vocation of the human race, not without the grounded presumption [*Vermuthung*] of a natural tendency toward it. (*AP* 236–37; 7:331)

This speaks to an important aspect of Kant's cosmopolitanism; namely, that it is not solely something that we make of ourselves, but something that we are also compelled to submit to. Thus, the concluding sentence of the *Anthropology* states that we cannot expect to progress toward the good "by the free agreement of individuals, but only by an increasing organization of citizens of the earth into and toward the species as a system that is cosmopolitically united" (*AP* 238; 7:333). Cosmopolitanism reveals something about the external organization of the human genus and cannot represent the interior nature of human personality as it is expressed in the moral wisdom of cosmical philosophy.

Let us now compare the three maxims of thinking as they were formulated pragmatically in the *Anthropology* with the way they are formulated in the *Critique of Judgment*. In §40 of this *Critique*, Kant elaborates the three maxims of thinking by placing special emphasis on how judgment lies at the heart not only of good taste, but also of the wisdom and sense of legitimacy that cosmical philosophy aims at. Whereas in the *Anthropology* the second maxim of judgment is to "think into the place of the *other* [*Stelle des Anderen*]" (*AP* 95; 7:200), in the *Critique of Judgment* it is more demanding: "to think into the place of *everyone* else [*Stelle jedes anderen*]" (*C3* 174; 5:294). We are expected to reflect on our "own judgment from a *universal standpoint*" (*C3* 175; 5:294). The *Anthropology* prompts us to think into the place of the other for the sake of the effective "communication" (*AP* 95; 7:200) of our aims, but the *Critique of Judgment* encourages a broad-minded way of thinking to "make our feeling in a given representation *universally communicable* [*mittheilbar*]" (*C3* 175; 5:295). This communicability involves an engagement with others that makes us mutually receptive to the cosmical perspective.

In the concluding §60 of the "Critique of Aesthetic Judgment," Kant expands on this when he speaks of *humaniora* as the "preliminary modes of cognitive awareness [*Vorkenntnisse*]" that cultivate the mental powers in the direction of our humanity, which he defines as follows:

> *Humanity* means on the one hand the universal *feeling of participation* [*Teilnehmungsgefühl*] and on the other hand the capacity for being able to *communicate* [*mittheilen*] one's inmost self universally, which properties taken together constitute the sociability that is appropriate to humankind, by means of which it distinguishes itself from the limitation of animals. (*C3* 229; 5:355)

The cultivation of our humanity through the model of pure taste thus prepares us for the worldly or cosmical (*weltliche*) capacity to communicate universally and to develop the participatory feelings that define the idea of moral virtue. Then, pointing ahead to how the general idea of aesthetic cultivation must be specified as a teleological theory of culture, Kant alludes to an age of certain model "nations [*Völker*]" in which the drive toward a "lawful sociability" (*C3* 229; 5:355) was able to produce a balance of aesthetic refinement and natural simplicity. These and other concluding remarks of §60 of the "Critique of Aesthetic Judgment" set the stage for how Kant will combine aesthetic ideals and social worldly ends in a theory of human culture, as articulated in §83 entitled "On the Ultimate End of Nature as a Teleological System." There Kant defines the important distinction between ultimate and final purposes that I will use to explain how cosmical philosophy and cosmopolitanism differ. These two kinds of purposes are mentioned again in the *Jäsche Logic*. However, Jäsche does not clarify the distinction between these two kinds of purposes, which has the consequence that the way he relates them to cosmical philosophy and cosmopolitanism is confusing.

Ultimate Purposes and Final Purposes in History

The distinction between ultimate and final purposes or ends becomes important when Kant begins to differentiate between nature and history. In the 1784 essay "Idea for a Universal History with a Cosmopolitan Aim," Kant speaks constantly of nature as spurring the human species to improve itself. Although human beings have "an inclination to become *socialized*" ("IUH" 111; 8:20) and wish for concord, Kant claims that nature "knows better what is good for the species: it wills discord" ("IUH" 112; 8:21). Nature has thus endowed us with an "unsociable sociability" ("IUH" 111; 8:20) that makes us competitive so as to develop our natural predispositions. In this essay, Kant repeatedly speaks of nature compelling us to compete socially as a way of improving ourselves. But because this social antagonism also needs to be reined in, nature providentially compels us to form a "civil society . . . in which freedom under external laws can be encountered" ("IUH" 112; 8:22). Eventually, such states compete among each other in ways that lead to war, so that nature in turn drives them to "enter into a federation of nations" ("IUH" 114; 8:24). Nation-states governed by positive laws and a cosmopolitan federation that will guarantee the rule of law among them serve as the natural "womb in which all original predispositions of the human species will be developed" ("IUH" 118; 8:28). Here it is suggested that the cosmopolitan project is somehow providentially imposed on us.

Six years later, in §83 of the "Critique of Teleological Judgment," most of these speculative, regulative attributions about nature's aim or intent (*Absicht*) for us are reformulated as reflective ascriptions from the human standpoint. Reflective judgment is self-binding and does not objectively attribute purposiveness to us as natural creatures, for no inductive generalizations based on experience can warrant the claim that nature has endowed us with a purpose. It is only by prescribing purposiveness to ourselves that we can reflect on the telos both of nature and of history as they intersect in culture. The hypothetical paradox of the "Idea for a Universal History"—that nature has endowed us providentially with an unsociable sociability to make us the ultimate purpose of nature—is now reflectively reconceived as a conditional characterization that humans can be "the ultimate purpose or end [*letzter Zweck*] of nature" only if they become capable of setting themselves a "final purpose [*Endzweck*]" that is "independent of nature" (*C3* 298; 5:431). We are no longer justified in asserting the objective determinant judgment that we are in fact the ultimate purpose of nature. Nor is Kant claiming that nature has favored human beings "with beneficence above all other animals" (*C3* 298; 5:430). Instead, we find ourselves with many "conflicting natural predispositions" (*C3* 298; 5:430) that are destructive and tend to leave us unsatisfied and make earthly happiness unlikely. Thus Kant writes that

> if nature is regarded as a teleological system, then it is [the human being's] vocation to be the ultimate end of nature; but always only . . . subject to the condition that he has the understanding and the will to give to nature and to himself a relation to an end that can be sufficient for itself independently of nature. (*C3* 298; 5:431)

Although we can make determinant judgments about the final purposes we set for ourselves, we can only consider ourselves as an ultimate purpose of nature as a reflective teleological judgment, that is, to the extent that we locate ourselves as part of human culture. Nature can at best "prepare" (*C3* 298; 5:431) us for what we must do ourselves to cultivate ourselves culturally. We are the ultimate end of nature, not due to any beneficence of nature that would assure our happiness, but only on the condition that we improve ourselves through moral ends that we set for ourselves. When we locate these final ends in human culture as our ultimate end, then we achieve a kind of second nature. What is special about ultimate ends is that they are inherent to our nature as human beings but require wisdom to be attained.

We now have the critical and textual background for assessing the claims in the *Jäsche Logic* about philosophy as scholastic, cosmical, and cosmopolitan respectively. I will briefly recapitulate those claims. Scholastic philosophers were criticized for merely using reason skillfully. Cosmical philosophers, by contrast, use reason legislatively and develop "the idea of perfect wisdom, which shows us the ultimate ends [*letzten Zwecke*] of human reason" (*LL* 537; 9:24). But this is not the end of the progression in the *Jäsche Logic*, for it goes on to say that philosophy "*in senso cosmico*" also relates "all cognition and all use of reason to the final end [*Endzweck*] of human reason" (*LL* 538; 9:24) and that this final end "unifies [*vereinigt*]" the field of philosophy to give it a "cosmopolitan sense or significance [*weltbürgerlichen Bedeutung*]" (*LL* 538; 9:25).

I will argue that even if cosmopolitanism serves to unify philosophy as the *Jäsche Logic* claims, it cannot be the fulfillment of cosmical philosophy. Once we understand the interdependence of Kant's reflectively established ultimate human purpose of culture and the determinant final moral purposes that individuals set themselves, we can see that the relation between cosmical philosophy and cosmopolitanism needs to be considered more carefully. Only the reflective comprehension made possible by the cosmical consideration of human beings as their own *ultimate* purpose can provide the proper cultural framework for understanding what is necessary for the *final* end of cosmopolitanism, which is to develop the political skills to guarantee perpetual world peace.

Culture as the cultivation of our aptitudes can take two forms, the first of which is the culture of skill. Kant claims that because natural human skills are not distributed equally, their development can cause conflict. For him, this means that they must be regulated by the already existing legal and political powers of a civil society (*bürgerliche Gesellschaft*) (*C3* 300; 5:432). And if humans want to also use their skills prudently and in a "sufficiently wise manner [*weis genug*]," they should also "subject themselves willingly to [the] coercion [of] a *cosmopolitan* whole, i.e., a system of all states that are at risk of detrimentally affecting each other" (*C3* 300; 5:432). But this political kind of coercion is a mere means to a higher moral end that only cosmical philosophy can foster.

Because the culture of skill needs to be regulated by civil and cosmopolitan rules of law that impose the conditions for making moral action possible for the human species, it does not suffice to produce moral action per se. The anthropological cosmopolitan ideal may be *oriented* by the final ends of morality and wisdom, but it merely provides the background conditions for these higher ends by establishing the institutions needed to minimize the outbreak of wars. Only individuals can *direct* themselves at the ends inspired by cosmical philosophy and act autonomously and wisely. This is where the second kind of culture discussed in §83 of the *Critique of Judgment* becomes relevant, namely, the culture of discipline. This culture of discipline is conceived broadly to help us as individuals "and make us receptive to higher ends than nature itself can afford" (*C3* 300; 5:433). This starts with the receptivity of aesthetic taste, which is then expanded into a moral receptivity that signals true human wisdom.

The culture of discipline involves a receptivity to final ends that exceed any positive natural goal. It is "negative and consists in the liberation of the will from the despotism of desires" (*C3* 299; 5:432). We recall here that the wisdom we referred to earlier in the *Anthropology* was also negative, but unlike the wisdom of discipline, it was mostly backward-looking in recognizing the follies of earlier stages of our life. The wisdom of the culture of discipline, by contrast, is forward-looking and ultimately morally uplifting. Only the culture of discipline can prepare human beings to establish "a sovereignty in which reason alone shall have power" (*C3* 301; 5:433). For this to be achieved, it is not enough for the human species to be governed by a cosmopolitan confederation. It is also necessary that individuals know their place in the world in accordance with the original idea of cosmical philosophy as expounded in the *Critique of Pure Reason*. Thus, it cannot be the case that Kant would want philosophy according to a world-concept to be superseded by a philosophy that is cosmopolitan, as suggested by the *Jäsche Logic*.[5] The cosmopolitan project is a product of skill, but what differentiates philosophy according to a world-concept is that it strives for a wisdom that goes beyond the skillful use of reason. The proper way to reconcile cosmical philosophy and cosmopolitan theory is for the latter to be encompassed by the former.

It is thus important to more sharply distinguish between cosmical philosophy and cosmopolitan theory than is generally done. Cosmical philosophy may take on a "cosmopolitan significance," which is to choose the weaker translation of *Bedeutung*, but it should not let itself be transformed into cosmopolitan philosophy, which is what the presentational order of the Jäsche text suggests. The strongest evidence for not regarding cosmopolitanism as the culmination of Kant's philosophy comes straight out of *Perpetual Peace: A Philosophical Sketch* (1795). There he writes that the task of establishing a cosmopolitan or politically regulated world "does not involve the moral improvement of man; it only means finding out how much the mechanism of nature can be applied to men in such a manner that the antagonism of their hostile attitudes will make them compel one another to submit to coercive laws, thereby producing a condition of peace within which the laws can be enforced" (*PP* 113; 8:366). Kant admits that a cosmopolitan world can consist of nations "of devils (so long as they possess understanding)" (*PP* 112; 8:366). Whatever the evil attitudes that citizens may harbor privately, laws can be devised by a skillful politician to make it in their interest to behave publicly "as if they did not have such evil attitudes" (*PP* 113; 8:366). Thus, the claim that the human species is moving toward a cosmopolitan state of existence does not by itself entail that it is becoming more moral. The cosmopolitan confederation of states may provide a necessary condition for the development of human morality, but it is not at all a sufficient condition.

As Kant had already pointed out in the "Idea for a Universal History," the cosmopolitan orientation of universal history can begin to civilize us through "all kinds of social decorum and propriety" ("IUH" 116; 8:26). But at this stage "very much is still lacking before we can be held to be already *moralized*" ("IUH" 116; 8:26). The idea of social decorum "comes down only to a resemblance of morals in the love for honor and the external propriety" that define our being *civilized.* The final stage requires "the idea of morality which belongs to *culture*" ("IUH" 116; 8:26).

Philosophy's reference to the ends of man can be thought of as developing either the humanity of individuals or the anthropological nature of the human species. In the former case of individuals, we have the basis for a philosophy in the cosmical sense; in the latter case of the history of the human species, we have a cosmopolitan aim. The scholarship on Kant's social and historical views focuses almost exclusively on his cosmopolitanism, but we also need a philosophy in the worldly or cosmical sense to cultivate the aesthetic openness and human maturity that only individuals can attain. Such a philosophy must produce the comprehensive wisdom to judge what it is reasonable to expect of oneself, as one gauges one's place in the trajectory of the human species from the state of nature by means of a cosmopolitan society to a morally disciplined culture that embodies our second nature.

16

The Obstacles to Be Overcome in Fulfilling the Goals of a World-Oriented Philosophy

Cosmical philosophy and cosmopolitanism have been shown to represent two interrelated but distinct goals for Kant. One has to do with the reflective appropriation of wisdom, and the other with assuring the world peace that provides the most favorable conditions for the human species to progress. We also found that cosmopolitanism depends on the culture of skill, and that cosmical philosophy goes further by also relying on the culture of discipline. In the *Anthropology*, Kant claims that the fulfillment of his worldly goals for the human species requires three levels of effort, which can be correlated with the three levels of intuitive assimilation, cognitive acquisition, and rational-reflective appropriation that were delineated in chapter 1. This is how he formulates the threefold vocation of human beings and their characteristics in the last chapter: "The human being is destined by his reason to live in a society with human beings and in it to *cultivate* himself, to *civilize* himself, and to *moralize* himself by means of the arts and sciences" (*AP* 229–30; 7:324). Whereas in the *Critique of Judgment* Kant simply contrasted the culture of discipline with the culture of skill, now he distinguishes between two kinds of skill, one of which is technical and the other pragmatic (see *AP* 226–28; 7:322–23). Technical skills cultivate us even as solitary beings, whereas pragmatic skills are social in nature and make us behave civilly. The technical skills are rooted in our natural bodily constitution, namely,

> in the form and organization of [our] hand, fingers, and fingertips, partly through their structure, partly through their sensitive feeling. By this means nature has made the human being not suited for one way of manipulating things but undetermined for every way, consequently suited for the use of reason. (*AP* 227–28; 7:323)

The technical skills of cultivating our natural capacities are similar to what we medially assimilate on the intuitive level and clarify by logical analysis, as discussed in the opening chapters. But now these skills are conceived more broadly as behavioral ways for human beings to cultivate their animality in living well. It is important to note that by contrast to other animals, humans are less bodily predetermined and more open to develop themselves technically in accordance with rational choice.

Since there is a limit to what technical skills allow individuals to achieve by themselves, humans also need socially cooperative or pragmatic skills, whereby we "become civilized through culture" (*AP* 228; 7:323). The latter claim might seem strange, since Kant asserted in the "Idea for a Universal History" that we need to become civilized before we can reach the level of culture. However, there are two kinds of culture for Kant, and we need both to be considered as cultured. The kind of culture that civilizes is merely the culture of skill, namely, the pragmatic or socializing skill that corresponds to what was discussed earlier as our predisposition to humanity. Pragmatic social skills are *acquired through* comparison with other human beings and may even allow us to make a limited use of them. In chapter 1, we saw Kant speak of our predisposition to humanity as a competitive use of reason. However, the need to uphold our honor in society also encourages us to cooperate with others. Kant conceives of competition as a positive challenge that should not be allowed to become cutthroat. It is thus compatible with the ends of cosmopolitanism. Pragmatic skills employ reason in prudential ways and can civilize by making us "well-mannered" (*AP* 228; 7:323). However, Kant's cosmical philosophy demands a higher sense of culture.

The "complete formation [*Ausbildung*]" (*AP* 229; 7:324) of human characteristics requires us to also moralize ourselves, and this is not just an acquired skill. This requires what Kant had called the negative culture of discipline in the *Critique of Judgment*, but it is now characterized in more encompassing terms. We are still told to "*actively* struggle with the obstacles" that cling to us because of the crudity of our nature, but we are also reminded that we are "innately predisposed to the good" (*AP* 229; 7:324). To develop moral character is to exhibit one's overall "mode of thinking [*Denkungsart*]" (*AP* 185; 7:285) or what one has made of oneself.[1] At this third level, our reason is expected to be fully self-active to make commitments as moral persons. Here we should be more than socially civil and work to *appropriate* what binds us communally. For Kant, this entails that we must extend what it means to act lawfully or in conformity with universal standards by also adopting a more encompassing standpoint. Laws require us to treat everyone as abstractly equal, but they cannot take account of the specific contexts that individuals find themselves in and make sure that they are treated fairly. We saw Kant claim that to be moral, we must act not only in accordance with the letter of the law, but also as respecting the spirit of the law. Now, if an action initiated in this sincere manner has unintended consequences that harm others, then something must be done to compensate or correct that and restore the spirit of the law. This is where Kant's omnilateral perspective concerning our rights becomes relevant.

Unilateral, Bilateral, and Omnilateral Legitimacy

Because we live in a world with finite material resources, conflicting human claims on them will inevitably arise. Kant attempts to address this problem in his *Metaphysics of Morals* when dealing with property rights. He asserts that the earth is originally possessed in common. This means that human beings have the right "to be wherever nature or chance (apart from their will) has placed them" (*MM* 50; 6:262). The natural right to occupy the contingent habitat (*Aufenthalt*) where we are born or find ourselves on this earthly territory (*Boden*) does not, however, entail the further right to turn it into one's "property [*Besitz*] or lasting residence [*Sitz*]" (*MM* 50; 6:262) and thereby exclude others. The possession of property can only be legitimated by conceiving what is earthly in relation to what is communally worldly. The legitimacy of owning things in this world depends on making sure that it does not deprive others of what they need. How then can one person's right to possess something coexist with the rights of others? There are, for Kant, three contextualizing moments in the process of legitimizing the possession of property which can be correlated with the three predispositions of our species that we have seen him speak of.

The first moment involves the simple "apprehension of an object that belongs to no one" so that it does not "conflict with another's freedom" (*MM* 47; 6:258). This *assimilative* apprehension of property is a unilateral act of grasping it, which can only be considered legitimate if from the limited perspective of my local habitat I am not aware that anyone one else is, or might be, making a claim on it as well. This accords with the level of our animalistic predisposition at which we are primarily concerned to preserve ourselves and our offspring. Our interests at this stage are merely *unilateral* in being indifferent to those who are different. Here indifference is mostly a function of ignorance and need not involve hostility. This primitive unilateral conception of property would seem to support the traditional institution of inheritance based on kinship.

The second contextualizing moment of legitimating property involves "designating [*Bezeichnung*] or declaring] (*declaratio*)" it as mine by "an act of choice [*Willkühr*]" (*MM* 47; 6:258) over against others. This corresponds to the level of the predisposition to humanity whereby I regard myself as coexisting with others. My pragmatic goal here is to defend my standing within the social context that Kant defined as a territory, and when I find myself competing with particular others for something, the solution is to establish a *bilateral* agreement. At this *acquisitive* stage, we learn to curb some of our egoism on the basis of the calculation that our rivals will also curb theirs to attain a mutually beneficial outcome. We establish a social equilibrium that is "*bilateral*" like a "contract of two (or more) persons" (*MM* 48; 6:259) which each is expected to honor. By means of legal contracts, we compromise in order to secure our most important pragmatic interests. Bilateral contracts have the authority of positive laws so that their violation will have negative consequences, such as a public sanction that could cause one to lose honor in the eyes of others, receive a monetary fine, or be imprisoned.

It is the culture of discipline that can move us from the level of humanity to the next level of personality, where we act not only in accordance with the letter of a legal agreement with another person, but also out of respect for all persons. At this third level, we are expected to act autonomously and aim at deeds that can be legitimated "*omnilaterally* [*allseitig*]" (*MM* 48; 6:259). This demands that we consider how our deeds as manifestations of our autonomous decisions affect the freedom of all others. Thus, in examining the right to *appropriate* property, Kant writes that it can only be completely legitimate if it becomes the "will of all [*Willens Aller*]" (*MM* 48; 6:259) who reside on this planet. More generally, any morally appropriative action must be compatible with the freedom of all. Whereas the unilateral act of apprehension and the bilateral act of choice were phenomenal, the omnilateral deed of appropriation is said to produce a "*possessio noumenon*" (*MM* 47; 6:259). This ideal of omnilateral legitimacy assumes that everyone is equally participating (*teilnehmen*) in the moral community. Something can be possessed noumenally or from within only to the extent that the whole community could in principle consent. In chapter 6, I indicated that if we could know a noumenal thing-in-itself as an archetypal intellect, then we would know it from the inside. Now I am suggesting that if we are to possess something noumenally, this must entail a willingness to at least temporarily extend a part of what is within our control to those outside, should the need arise. This is not something that Kant states here, but he moves in that direction with the right of hospitality which he introduces in *Perpetual Peace*, namely,

> the right of a stranger not to be treated with hostility when he arrives on someone else's territory. He can indeed be turned away, if this can be

> done without causing his downfall [*Untergang*], but he must not be treated with hostility so long as he behaves in a peaceable manner in the place he happens to be. (*PP* 105–6; 8:357–58)

This does not mean that the stranger can expect to be received warmly as a guest (*Gast*); it only entails the right to be received civilly as a visitor. All human beings possess this "right to visit [*Besuchsrecht*]" because they are entitled to "present themselves in the society of others by virtue of their right to communal possession of the earth's surface. Since the earth is a globe, they cannot disperse over an infinite area, but must necessarily tolerate one another's company" (*PP* 106; 8:358). Kant attempts to find a middle ground about this right of coexistence, attacking the coastal dwellers on the Barbary coast for "enslaving stranded seafarers" on the one hand and European colonialists for "conquering foreign countries and peoples" (*PP* 106; 8:358) on the other.[2] His hope is that "continents distant from each other [will] enter into peaceful mutual relations which may eventually be regulated by public laws, thus bringing the human race nearer and nearer to a cosmopolitan constitution" (*PP* 106; 8:358).

There has been much debate of late about what Kant's right of hospitality entails. Seyla Benhabib has argued for extending it as a right that "is grounded upon the common humanity of each and every person and his or her freedom of the will."[3] Dilek Huseyinzadegan finds no such ethical basis in Kant and has made the case that 'there is a peculiar political economy tied to the context of Kant's own formulation of the right of hospitality,"[4] namely, a Eurocentric interest in commerce. This interest in commerce is indeed there, but to conceive of hospitality as a mere non-ideal right apart from more ideal ethical considerations would not be proper either. We can see this when Kant comments on the decision of Japan to refuse "access or contact [*Zugang*]" (*PP* 107; 8:359) with all Europeans nations except the Dutch. This contact with the Dutch was a minimal condition that allowed for commercial trade. But even the Dutch were not allowed a more lasting "entrance [*Eingang*]" (*PP* 107; 8:359) that would normally be expected. Kant only accepts this as a temporary policy because the Japanese were rightfully concerned about the way the Europeans had oppressed natives of the territories they had colonized. The limited "access" that the Japanese authorities granted the Dutch was for commerce or trade only. With a cosmopolitan confederation of nation-states a more normal "entrance" into other states would become a right, which would also allow for more extended noncommercial modes of human exchange. This would include the right to seek refuge on foreign soil if the need should arise or circumstances beyond one's control landed you there. We quoted Kant as saying that one should not be turned away as long as that could cause one's "*Untergang*" (8:358). I translated this word literally as "downfall" above, but H. B. Nisbet has translated it as "death." I agree with Pauline Kleingeld that other harms such as torture should be included under the heading of downfall. She explicitly extends the right to entrance to refugees who actively flee war or political oppression. To those who claim that we should not superimpose current problems of refugee migration due to war and oppression back onto Kant's time, Kleingeld points out that in Kant's own time, Prussia accepted many refugees fleeing from "religious intolerance and political oppression."[5] She also puts this in historical context by describing how Johann Heinrich Tieftrunk in his 1798 commentary on Kant's "Doctrine of Right"[6] expands on how cosmopolitan right was defined more generally in the *Metaphysics of Morals*; namely, as the freedom to "interact with all others" in a "thoroughgoing relation" and to offer to enter "into exchange [*Verkehr*] with any other" (*MM* 121; 6:352). Again, as Kleingeld points out, exchange can mean more than commercial trade. Cosmopolitan rights attempt to overcome hard borders in a peaceful manner. A certain amount of access or hospitality should be normalized in order to manage the crossing of borders. Both intentional trade and unintended incursions need to be regulated so borders can be made permeable without losing their protective aspects. This also means that if what a nation does within its borders has a negative effect on "neighboring peoples (or families)," then "resistance" (*MM* 53; 6:266) is appropriate. This problem has become increasingly evident because of widespread pollution emitted from industrial sites and points to an intermediary source of sovereignty over land, namely, corporate ownership.

By allowing for resistance in the above circumstances, Kant is again relating the political issue of hospitality to the general domain of ethics. Huseyinzadegan argues that whereas the inner freedom of morality is bound merely by the ideal universal rules of the categorical imperative, the outer freedom asserted in the rights of hospitality and property is constrained by non-ideal limited contexts that are political and commercial.[7] But this sets up too sharp a split, for we saw in our earlier discussion of moral duties of virtue such as benevolence that local conditions also come into play in deciding how much personal wealth to sacrifice: they require reflective judgment to evaluate what is appropriate. The need for proper contextualization becomes a pervasive feature of Kant's philosophy once one realizes that reflective comprehension as he conceives it is always purposive relative to specific human needs. Although there is something subjective and hypothetical about Kant's regulative use of teleology, there is also a reflective normative dimension to it that makes Kant look for intersubjective consensus. Obviously, some of Kant's political proposals can no longer count on our consensus today, and I can fully endorse Huseyinzadegan when she defends Kant's use of "teleology" in politics "not in terms of the specific claims that it produces in Kant's own thought, but as a hermeneutic invitation to political thought today to take into account" our own "contingent human conditions."[8]

Further Issues and Obstacles

It becomes more difficult to judge what implications Kant's cosmopolitan concern with regulating border issues at the level of nation-states has today when global corporate interests are so much more predominant. Economic inequality has increased to the point that many nations can no longer adequately care for their own citizens and their contingent residents. To what extent must individuals and corporations that own property share in this burden? If people are somehow stranded on land that does not belong to them because of disasters such as war, flooding, or storms, how much support is owed to them by the state and others? To what extent can the expectation of hospitality cross over into the expectation of temporarily sharing some of what is owned with those who have become homeless? Here the sentiments of com-passion and sym-pathy (*Mit-leid*) as passive manifestations of our animality are unreliable, for we tend to be generous mostly to those who are close at hand and familiar to us. Ultimately, sympathy and its civil counterpart of hospitality must be cultivated into a more active mode of "participation [*Teilnehmung*]" that makes us feel committed to everyone else.[9] From the corresponding communal perspective, Kant claims that what makes any acquisition of property a rightful "appropriation [*appropriatio*] is the act of a general will (in idea) giving an external law through which everyone will be bound to agree with my choice" (*MM* 47; 6:259). The acquisition of property is only communally appropriate if it can be legitimated *omnilaterally*, that is, by taking all sides into account.

It turns out, however, that this omnilateral justification of the appropriation of property is merely "provisional" and formal. Kant admits that it can only become "conclusive" by means of governmental determinations that "take place in the civil condition" (*MM* 54; 6:264) of specific nation-states. The related problems of hospitality and human rights that Kant treats on the individual level have become large-scale problems as wars and other destructive forces such as storms and droughts have led masses to migrate and seek asylum. And because this brings groups with different ethnic and racial origins as well as conflicting religious traditions into contact, Kant cannot really help us here. The problem is that Kant's conception of human culture is at best formally universal. This means that it does not do justice to what we have come to know about the richness and complexity of cultures since his time. Indeed, it has become increasingly clear that culture manifests itself in distinctive ethnic configurations. For this reason, we need to make room for another legitimate form of human coexistence that falls between Kant's direct bilateral contract variety and his omnilateral all-encompassing kind.

This would be a more indirect *multilateral* approach to bridge the gap between Kant's cosmopolitanism that projects a confederation of states still based on contractual relations and his cosmical philosophy that aims at an omnilateral worldview. Such a multilateral addition requires us to expand on the contributions of culture. But before we explore this need for a multilateral acknowledgment of human culture, there is an aspect of Kant's views about human differences that has come under severe criticism in the last decades. This relates to the following three essays: "Of the Different Races of Human Beings" (1775), "Determination of the Concept of a Human Race" (1785), and "On the Use of Teleological Principles in Philosophy" (1788). In these works, Kant takes account of the most widely held taxonomic theories about race of his time and responds to some of them. In the last of these essays, he maintains that race is not a descriptive theoretical concept which can be definitively understood and explained. Instead, Kant considers it a hypothetical teleological concept of natural history that attempts to make certain human differences "rationally comprehensible [*begreiflich*]" ("TP" 204; 8:169; see also "CHR" 152; 8:99) by looking for how the races came about over time. The fact that human beings have different skin colors does not mean that there are different species of human beings, according to Kant. He writes that

> races are not characters that are originally distributed through so many phyla [*Stämme*] as species of the same genus [*Gattung*] but rather characters that develop only over the course of generations, hence not different kinds [*Arten*] but variations [*Abartungen*],[10] yet determinate and persistent enough to justify a distinction in terms of classes. ("TP" 199–200; 8:164)

Kant thinks that these variations can be "comprehended" or interpreted as ones that were needed by human beings to adapt to the different climates. "The *Negro race* [*Negerrace*]" ("CHR" 156; 8:103) is thought to have darker skin than whites in order to cope with the large amounts of "phlogiston" released by the "thick forests and swamp-covered regions" ("CHR" 156; 8:103) of Africa. Before oxygen was discovered in the late eighteenth century by Joseph Priestley and found to contribute to combustion, scientists had posited phlogiston to account for things being combustible. Kant cites a report that Europeans found concentrations of phlogiston to be a "deadly peril" ("CHR" 156; 8:103) and speculates that it makes the blood of the African natives turn blackish, just as oxidation makes dried blood turn dark. Nature's "wise" ("CHR" 156; 8:103) recourse was to allow their blood to "*dephlogistize itself* . . . through the skin in a far greater measure than happens in us, where that is for the most part the task of the lungs" ("CHR" 156; 8:103). Kant disagrees with the contemporary naturalist Georg Forster, who thought there is only one racial difference, namely, between the Negro and all other human beings; and Kant writes "I judge still others (those of the Indians and native Americans, in addition to that of the whites) to be equally entitled to figure in the complete classificatory division" ("TP" 204; 8:168). Moreover, he thinks Forster is wrong to "assume two original phyla to explain" his division, and instead considers the then more commonly accepted fourfold division to be "a development of purposive first predispositions implanted in one phylum" ("TP" 204; 8:169).

Kant cites another report to support an equally bold hypothesis to comprehend what he had heard about "the red rust color which distinguishes the skin" ("CHR" 157; 8:104) of native Americans. Here the iron particles in the blood are supposedly aggravated by "aerial acid" ("CHR" 157; 8:104). Finally, what seems to distinguish the people of India is the ability of their bodies to remove "volatile alkali" ("CHR" 157; 8:104) from their blood. This suggests that there are not inherently different kinds of human skin, but that its color is affected by chemical reactions. Although Kant offers no explanation for the white-skinned race, he claims that it too is "only the development of one of the original predispositions" ("CHR" 159; 8:106). He admits that the foregoing has been an exercise in "artificially constructing hypotheses" ("CHR" 158; 8:104) that are plausible at best.

Because of human migration, Kant recognizes that these deviations adapted to different climates are diminished through a mixing of the races, but he claims that there is a limit to this process. He sees this as confirmed by the fact that "the *gypsies* among us, of whom it is established that they are *Indians* in terms of their phyletic origination . . . still have not deviated [*ausgeartet*] in the least from the appearance [*Gestalt*] of their forebears" despite having arrived in Europe more than "three hundred years" ago ("CHR" 158; 8:105). More generally, he writes that "nature seems at least to permit the melting together, although not to favor it, since thereby the creature becomes fit for several climates but not suited to any one of them to the degree achieved by the first adaptation

[*Anartung*] to it" ("TP" 202; 8:166–67). However, if the surrounding air for Africans who move to other regions no longer has a surfeit of phlogiston, why would the first adaptation not disappear? There would be no blackish blood to color the skin. In a review of Johann Herder's *Ideas for a Philosophy of the History of Humanity*, Kant agrees that the human species has the capacity to "appropriately modify itself internally in accordance with differences of the external circumstances" ("RH" 139; 8:62). Yet he qualifies this by returning to his notion of "original predispositions" ("RH" 140; 8:62) that could put a limit to the capacity to evolve. This recalls what was discussed earlier about Kant's efforts to find a balance between preformationism and epigenesis.

Kant's efforts to make racial differences somewhat "comprehensible" may not be regarded as strengthening my case for the cognitive importance of comprehension, but they do illuminate how he thinks comprehension can supplement the kind of functional teleological descriptions discussed in chapter 12 with a more explanatory use of epigenetic natural history. What I would like to suggest in response is that it is important to differentiate the ways in which comprehension can be employed. If comprehension is used regulatively for teleological purposes without critical constraints to rule out conjectural ideas like providence or the claim that nature wills or favors certain tendencies, then it can become purely hypothetical and even dogmatic, as with the concept of race. However, if comprehension is used with reflective restraint for moral or other normative cultural ends, its teleological function is worth taking seriously. Then it can help us to recontextualize and reframe unresolved philosophical issues.

The danger of using racial differences for teleological purposes as part of a natural history that ties us back to the earth becomes especially evident in writings where taxonomists have related them to the four classical temperaments derived from Galen's four humors. Then it becomes clear that some racial variations (*Abartungen*) may be considered as deviations—the more negative way in which this German term can be translated to suggest degeneracy. As Jennifer Mensch points out in the essay "Caught between Character and Race: 'Temperament' in Kant's Lectures on Anthropology,"[11] his fourfold division of races goes back to Linnaeus's classificatory schema for understanding the varieties of human beings in the tenth edition of his *Systema naturae* (1758–59), which aligns them with the so-called temperaments and thus stereotypes human beings as follows:

> Americanus. Rufus, cholericus, rectus [red, choleric, upright]
> Europoeus. Albus, sanguineus, torosus [white, sanguine, muscular]

Asiaticus. Luridus, melancholicus, rigidus [yellow, melancholy, rigid]
Afer. Niger, phlegmaticus, laxus [black, phlegmatic, relaxed][12]

This schema identifies Negroes as phlegmatic and American Indians as choleric, which are generally considered to be the least desirable temperaments. This clear reference back to Linnaeus show that Bernasconi is wrong to suggest that Kant invented or offered original formulations of race theory.[13] He was a monogenist who generally relied on others such as Linnaeus, Buffon, von Haller, and Blumenbach for his classificatory terms, and differed from polygenists such as Hume and Voltaire.

In the early 1764 essay *Observations on the Feeling of the Beautiful and the Sublime,* Kant wrote that "Mr. Hume challenges anyone to adduce a single example where a Negro has demonstrated talents" (*OBS* 59; 2:253), which would seem to confirm the phlegmatic stereotype. But in the *Menschenkunde* anthropological lectures of 1781–82, Kant departs from Linnaeus by characterizing Negroes as concerned with honor and thus as being choleric. Indians or Asians, however, are acknowledged to love the arts and have talents, but not for science. The "serenity [*Gelassenheit*]" (VA-*Menschenkunde,* 25:1187) that Kant assigns to Asians fits well with what he elsewhere calls the sanguine temperament. Now indigenous Americans are said to lack the incentive to accomplish much and are considered as phlegmatic. Finally, the white race is claimed to have "all the incentives and talents" (VA-*Menschenkunde,* 25:1187).[14] Kant made such disparaging comments not only about other races, but also about European nationalities, including the Germans. Since he never traveled even in Europe, I assume these were also based on anecdotal reports he heard and books he read and were thus mostly at the informational level of what is assimilated, rather than at the levels of what is cognitively acquired or critically appropriated. Italians and the French are said to distinguish themselves in their sanguine feeling for beauty, and the English, Spanish, and Germans in their melancholy feeling for the sublime. However, in the Dutch these finer feelings are "fairly unnoticeable" (*OBS* 52; 2:243); the Dutch are also stereotyped as phlegmatic. For someone who warned his students in his lectures on logic about their prejudices, all these racial and national stereotypes are quite remarkable.

There is also a footnote in the *Anthropology* where Kant speaks of Jews as Palestinians and notes that "the great majority of them have earned the not unfounded reputation of being cheaters, on account of the spirit of usury" (*AP* 100; 7:205–6n). He traces this back to their role as merchants in Jerusalem, given the advantageous place this city occupied in the caravan trade routes. This characterization can be put in the context of similar pejorative characterizations that Kant assigns to other nationalities, like the "arrogant rudeness" (*AP* 213; 7:311) of English merchants who are "very unsociable in their assumption of high standing" (*AP* 217; 7:315) relative to other nations. He speaks of the Spanish as having a sense of dignity, but "as the bullfight shows" (*AP* 218; 7:316), they are cruel and resist reform. In her thorough treatment of the prejudices that affect Kant's cosmopolitanism, Kleingeld informs us that in the Kowalewski Dohna-Wundlacken anthropology lectures, which are not included in the Academy edition, Kant is reported to have said that "if a trait is a national characteristic, this does not mean that all members of a people have it in equal measure."[15] The question she poses is whether Kant's comment about Jews being prone to deception is ethnically/racially motivated or more on the order of his stereotypes about nationalities, for which institutional grounds are often given as mitigating factors.

The charge that Kant was antisemitic is of course also rooted in what he says about the Jewish faith. He does indeed criticize Judaism for not being a universal religion like Christianity and writes that the "Jewish faith, as originally established, was only a collection of merely statutory laws supporting a political state; for whatever moral additions that were appended to it, whether originally or only later, do not in any way belong to Judaism as such. Strictly speaking Judaism is not a religion at all" (*R* 130; 6:125). But later he does admit that subsequently moral doctrines "gained public acceptance within it" (*R* 132; 6:128), which would allow people like Moses Mendelssohn, whose philosophical importance he recognized, to also merit moral standing. Manfred Kuehn reports that Kant "had many Jewish students whom he considered to be talented and capable."[16] The most important of them was Marcus Herz, who remained in correspondence with Kant after he moved back to Berlin. He wrote Kant: "It is you alone whom I have to thank for the happy change in my circumstances. . . . Had it not been for you I would even now, like so many of my brethren, drag a burden of prejudice, lead a life inferior to that of a beast . . . I would be nothing."[17]

There is no doubt that Kant thought that Europeans were the most civilized peoples. It is interesting that he places Germans beneath the French and English peoples on this score. Despite this, he has many reservations about the English, especially for the lack of hospitality they show foreigners. He is most kind to the French and calls them "lovable" (*AP* 215; 7:313). They have a taste for conversation and are "courteous, especially toward foreigners who visit France" (*AP* 215; 7:313). Especially important is the claim that they possess "an infectious *spirit of freedom*, which probably also pulls reason itself into its play" (*AP* 216; 7:313). Germans do not exhibit the wit and artistic taste of the French, English, and

Italians, but they do have as much of the talents of "correct understanding" and a "deeply reflective reason" as can be expected from "any other people capable of the highest culture" (*AP* 220; 7:318). While Kant touts the so-called "modesty" (*AP* 220; 7:318) of the Germans, these claims about how they have cultivated their talents are not so modest, for Kant's worldview prizes culture more than civilization. While the most civilized peoples manifest excessive national pride, the average German is "too cosmopolitan to be deeply attached to his homeland" (*AP* 221; 7:318). The main unflattering qualities that are attributed to Germans are a mania for method and an obsession with rank and titles. If we were to define Kant's worldview on the basis of this impressionistic survey of human characteristics, we could start by regarding the French spirit of freedom and the reflective use of reason that I have stressed as being essential for our German philosopher. The former is socially expansive, and the latter is thoroughgoing and comprehensive.

Of course, we have to remove any association of nationality from these characteristics for the obvious reason that much of what Kant has written about the character of peoples and races is questionable. He is especially harsh about the "not yet developed" (*AP* 221; 7:319) and more remote peoples of Russia and Turkey. Although we could explain some of Kant's prejudices about these matters as the result of assimilating the secondhand information available to him, they are also the product of a dogmatic use of his three levels of human awareness, namely, the mere animate life of the soul, the reactive life of the mind, and finally the self-active life of spirit. Instead of allowing a continuity there, as when Kant considers the cognitive processes purely theoretically, he chooses to apply these levels more rigidly when evaluating the worth of animals and other human races. Animals are assumed to be merely animate at the level of soul and therefore sentient without the judgmental powers needed to be conscious. Other human races are stereotyped in terms of temperaments that accentuate the reactive aspects of the level of mind, thereby raising doubts about their full spiritual potential. This makes it clear that despite Kant's call for overcoming prejudices, this is easier to accomplish in theoretical matters than in the normative issues that arise in interpreting history. We see this in Kant's review of Herder's *Ideas*, where he asks, "Does the author really mean that if the happy inhabitants of Tahiti had never been visited by more civilized [*gesitteten*] nations and would have been destined to live for thousands of centuries in their tranquil indolence, one could give a satisfying answer to the question why they exist at all, and whether it would not have been just as good as having the island populated with happy sheep . . . ?" ("RH" 142; 8:65). As if to justify these contemptuous remarks, Kant prefaces them by stating that human history and its progress should be measured by "concepts of human rights" ("RH" 141; 8:64) rather than by concerns about happiness.

In the same review, Kant again shows his prejudices about other races, yet makes a distinction between their mental and natural predispositions that would become important for his project of cosmopolitanism and lead him to attack colonial exploitation:

> Now from a multiplicity of descriptions of countries one can prove, if one wants to, that . . . Americans and Negroes are each a race, sunk beneath the remaining members of the human species in their spiritual [*geistige*] predispositions, but on the other side, according to reports that are just as plausible regarding their natural predispositions, they are to be estimated equal to every other inhabitant of the world; so it remains to the choice of the philosopher whether he wants to assume differences of nature or wants to judge everything in accordance with the principle that everything is as it is with us [*tout comme chez nous*]. ("RH" 139; 8:62)

The admission here that we have a "choice" suggests the pragmatic option to move beyond his genetic natural history based on climatic and temperamental differences and make an epigenetic shift toward a cosmopolitan history based on more general natural predispositions. The natural predispositions of human beings pertain to their rights to life and liberty in the civil world, and this allows Kant to move on to the more important task of assessing what human beings can make of themselves in conjunction with each other as part of his political cosmopolitan project. If only pragmatic considerations about human relations are in play, as in the *Anthropology* of 1798, racial differences can be overlooked, and this is now done. Surprisingly, Kant now claims that nature favors the "convergence [*Verähnlichung*]" or the "melting together of different races," but aims at "varieties or modifications . . . in one and the same race" (*AP* 223; 7:320) as well as in the same family bloodline. The fact that "human regeneration" requires the "heterogeneity of individuals" (*AP* 223; 7:321) will make stereotyping the races more difficult. Kleingeld points out that here Kant develops a position intermediate between Herder, who prized ethnic diversity as worth preserving in its original form, and Forster, who prized it as a source of "intercultural learning and exchange."[18] There is a sense in which she is correct, namely, Kant is committed to human exchange to expand our acquaintance with the world, but this is not necessarily for the sake of intercultural learning. He argues for an abstract right of all to "visit" throughout the world, but not for regarding foreigners of any race as more permanent "guests" to be appreciated for who they are.

Kleingeld seems to give a final moral defense of Kant based on tolerance. She argues that whereas Herder saw diversity as an intrinsic value and Forster appreciated it for its edificatory value, Kant saw it as expressing individual freedom "as long as these choices are compatible with the principles of morality and right."[19] It is true that individual freedom for Kant takes human multiplicity (*Vielheit*) into account, but this does not explicitly address the problems of racial, ethnic, and cultural diversity (*Verschiedenheit*) that Herder and Forster championed. We saw in chapter 7 that Kant's formulations of the categorical imperative moved from the *unity* of one's own assent to the moral law, to the *multiplicity* that respects others, to an *allness* (*Allheit*) of communal consent, and that Dilthey's moral theory departed from this by moving from the *unity* of the commitment to equal justice and the *multiplicity* of benevolent inclusion to the *plurality* (*Mehrheit*) of culturally articulated moral systems, each with its own inner worth. As was made clear earlier, multiplicity acknowledges undifferentiated otherness, whereas plurality recognizes differentiated otherness. Now we can add that multiplicity involves a particularized mode of differentiation, whereas plurality introduces an individuating mode of differentiation that respects diversity and stops short of an all-subsuming totality. Dilthey's conception of plurality made room for culturally diverse moral systems, but it is not clear that Kant would have approved of such cultural variations.

The fact that Kant does not focus on racial differences in the brief section on "The Character of the Races" of the final *Anthropology* is fortunate. But we cannot be sure as Kleingeld claims that it means that he "gave up the hierarchical view of the races"[20] which he had formulated earlier. What is important is that Kant decided that the supposed racial differences he had delineated should have no bearing on his cosmopolitan project, which is based on the limited cultural skill of learning to coexist peacefully. However, it is likely that he would still have regarded some racial or ethnic groups as not yet ready to participate in his cosmical project of communal cooperation, which I have argued is more demanding and requires the culture of discipline. The consideration of cosmopolitan rights and laws can abstract from specific cultural and ethnic differences and proceed directly from unilateral and bilateral legitimacy to the final level of omnilateral legitimacy. But when Kant's philosophy according to a world-concept comes back into focus, it will be useful to interpolate a level of multilateral legitimacy that can do justice to cultural and ethnic pluralism. We can now resume our discussion of what culture should strive for.

The Multilateral Legitimacy of Cultures

Up until now, I have mostly discussed the Kantian sense of culture which the neo-Kantians revived at the end of the nineteenth century and which they used to argue that the post-Hegelian conception of the human sciences or *Geisteswissenschaften* should be rethought as the cultural sciences, or *Kulturwissenschaften.* I will make the case that the human sciences can better integrate culture with historical life so that its multiple functions can be more fully understood. The human sciences are also more comprehensive in scope than the cultural sciences. One of the striking differences is that whereas Dilthey included psychology among the human sciences, the neo-Kantians excluded it from the cultural sciences. For them, psychology should model itself on the natural sciences.

In his *Ideas for a Descriptive and Analytic Psychology* of 1894, Dilthey reconceived psychology in ways that took Kant's critique of introspection into account. Like Kant's anthropology, Dilthey's descriptive psychology is directed at the world. It examines the structures of our experience of the human world, and as such it provides an orientational background for the other human sciences. Instead of starting with hypotheses about how the body determines mental processes, the first task of a descriptive psychology is to gain some understanding of how we experience what we see, feel, and do.[21] In this Dilthey is closer to Kant than the neo-Kantians are. Both Kant and Dilthey worried about untestable psychological hypotheses. As a human science, Dilthey's psychology is expected to delineate the basic intentional structures that give meaning to human experience and only gradually introduce causal explanations about how we are conditioned—not only by our physiology, but also by the sociocultural systems that we participate in. Only when hypotheses are contextually delimited in this way can they be adequately tested. Dilthey's contextualizing approach to the human sciences was not explicitly based on the way I have analyzed the kinds of judgmental contexts delineated by Kant. Dilthey's contexts are conceived as cultural systems that focus what happens in the sociohistorical world, but they do appeal to Kant's idea of immanent purposiveness.

The neo-Kantian Wilhelm Windelband rejected Dilthey's new approach to the human sciences and assumed that experimental psychologists such as Wilhelm Wundt could raise psychology to the level of an explanatory natural science. Windelband insisted on a sharp distinction between natural sciences that are law-based or *nomothetic* and cultural sciences that are like history in being *ideographic* and focusing on what is singular. Dilthey rejected this rigid distinction and argued that the human and natural sciences merely pursue different ways of relating particulars to what is universal. The human sciences are able to articulate structural patterns of human experience that allow us to understand the individuality of particular actions and interactions in relation to more general social and cultural systems.[22] It is only within such organizational contexts that Dilthey expects to discover the kinds of causal modes of correlation that the explanatory natural sciences aim at. Although there can be explanatory laws in the human sciences, they will never have the scope that the laws of physics and chemistry have. If laws of historical development are to be found, they will be limited to specific sociocultural systems, such as the advancement of scientific institutions and the organization of production in different economies. This kind of regional and historical contextualization of the human sciences brings out not only the formal refinement produced by the culture of skill and discipline, but also the more concrete aspects of what cultural systems assimilate from everyday life and its customs. This allows the human sciences to attend to the shared medial and organizing characteristics of culture that factor in its ethnic variations.

Of all the neo-Kantians, Ernst Cassirer was the most successful in expanding Kantian assumptions about the role of culture and bringing them closer to the human science approach. Cassirer greatly advanced what Kant proposed about the indicative functions of symbolic analogies in order to develop a theory of symbolic forms that can do justice to the medial and organizing functions of human cultures. Recognizing what cultural systems medially assimilate from everyday life allows for a more deeply rooted notion of culture that is content-based and refers back to the cultivation of one's native soil or habitat. There is therefore something inherently local and situated about the way that cultures organize people. Although cultures relate people to their regional context, through trade and other modes of contact this can gradually transcend strict ethnic and national identities and become encompassing enough to emulate the kind of participatory stance that Kant considered to be essential to his omnilateral ideal. Even though cultures represent the intersection of various influences, they can foster an involvement that approximates Kant's ideal of communal participation without its commitment to total judgmental consent and univocal consensus. Multicultural analogues of Kant's communal participation would have to leave room for a measure of difference.

Kant seems to attribute most cultural differences of people to their level of historical advancement. He assumed that as we advance from the level of animality to humanity and personality, the former levels remain operative merely in terms of biological and functional needs. But much of the actual content of what is assimilated as we move from the animality of our youth to our humanity remains as a residue. Kant is right to expect us to move from local prejudices of taste to more universal judgments of taste. However, experience teaches us that the gradual realization that certain foreign artworks have greater aesthetic value than the work of local artists, does not entail that we will not continue to appreciate and enjoy the latter as part of our own history. Accordingly, it is more realistic to think that most people will at best shift from a narrow cultural perspective to one that is more accommodating without being universal. While continuing to strive for an omnilateral consensus about standards of justice and morality, it is important to cherish the value of a multilateral cultural perspective that leaves some, but not all, alternatives open. Making room for a multilateral understanding of the cultural world can also serve self-understanding if it continues to draw on all three levels of our being. What is most important about multilateralism is the ability to recall aspects of ourselves that can link us to others whose current interests differ from ours. Whereas Kant's omnilateralism champions an ideal of full engagement based on an overall consensus, multilateralism involves a willingness to probe how far different perspectives rooted in divergent contextual conditions can be made to intersect so as to make a modicum of understanding possible even without achieving convergence.

Although these ideas about the need for multilateral understanding are not Kant's own, they can be seen as an extension of the *Critique of Judgment* if we do not insist on framing it only in its immediate Enlightenment context. And if we historicize Kant's insights into teleology, we need to acknowledge that the same omnilateral goal may be capable of diverse instantiations. As was already indicated in chapter 7, the very project of fulfilling Kant's ideal of the kingdom of ends on earth can produce a plurality of sociocultural instantiations that compete with one another. Similarly, we saw that the personal ideal of achieving inner worth can take on various forms in different societies. This led Dilthey to extend Kant's idea of immanent purposiveness from organic life to historical development. Given different worldly background conditions, the same overall goal may produce distinctive sociocultural systems, each with its own immanent purposiveness. This can be seen as a historical relativization of Kant. But there is also a more fundamental reason why cultural systems cannot be merged omnilaterally. This is because cultures as social attempts at human cultivation aim at a kind of perfection that strives for completion. Dilthey, who saw philosophy as having an important cultural function, points to this goal of completeness in the way it articulates worldviews. But no effort to bring together everything we think and value can do so without prioritizing certain aspects over others. The same is true for metaphysical attempts to formulate an all-encompassing worldview that can satisfy all the cognitive, evaluative, and volitional aspirations of human experience. The very attempt to totalize produces a plurality of solutions, each of which prioritizes one of these three aspirations. Thus, Dilthey's analysis of worldviews in the Western tradition points to three recurring types: (1) a naturalism that prioritizes our intellectual demands but regards our overall aspirations as contingent, (2) an idealism of freedom that sets our volitional purposes above all else, and (3) an objective idealism that ultimately prizes our evaluative expectations for an overall harmonious order.

Naturalism goes back to philosophers such as Democritus and Epicurus, was further refined by Hobbes and Hume, and has many contemporary adherents. Whereas Dilthey characterizes naturalism as deterministic but pluralistic, the idealism of freedom is considered dualistic because it limits the extent to which we are determined from without. The idealism of freedom was upheld by such lofty figures as Plato, Kant, and Fichte, and we can still find remnants of it in subsequent thinkers such as Sartre, Rawls, and Habermas. Objective idealism has its origins in monists like Parmenides and Spinoza, also applies to Schelling and Hegel, and still resonates in some contemporary hermeneutical and environmental philosophies. This Diltheyan analysis of three incommensurate worldview perspectives at the level of philosophy exposes the Enlightenment illusion that universalization always leads to increasing uniformity. Indeed, all three types are complex enough to survive the more simplistic optimistic worldview of rationalism and its counterpart of Schopenhauerian pessimism. The enduring quest for worldviews that aim at theoretical and practical comprehension and the inner worth of a "deeply reflective reason" will undoubtedly produce other types. A single totalizing comprehension of the world is not humanly available, only perspectival overarching viewings.

Conclusion

Kant's Multifaceted Worldview

Dilthey's typology of worldviews pointed to Kant as a prime exemplar of a dualistic idealism of freedom, and this does indeed capture a core tenet of his philosophical stance. But the freedom we humans are claimed to possess is not fully understood, according to Kant, and can only be comprehended in terms of how we respond to the world. Our freedom expresses itself theoretically in terms of the formal transcendental conditions we bring to the process of acquiring cognition. But there are severe external limits to what we can understand about the world, and even though pure reason has broader powers, it produces antinomies that force us to set inner bounds to what we can claim to know. Practical reason is superior in allowing us to know what we should do, but it sets ideal ends that even Kant does not believe we can achieve in this life. Kant's idealism of freedom represents a challenge that sets the stage for how we should judge the world and our place in it. Thus, more needs to be said to characterize Kant's worldview.

To be sure, Kant is closer to the idealism of freedom than to Dilthey's two other worldview types. It is very clear that Kant is not a naturalist. Although he takes empirical inquiry seriously, its results have to be framed by transcendental self-reflection to demonstrate its boundary conditions. Nor is he an objective idealist who regards everything in the world as internally related and part of some overall harmonious order. Kant does not rule out contingency in this world, and he discerns tensions such as unsocial sociability in human nature. If harmony is to be discerned in the world, it will be because we have found a way to delineate distinct spheres in which it can be elicited or produced.

One could say that naturalism only applies to what I have called the assimilative level of Kant's account of experience and that his idealism of freedom sets the boundaries of the determinate knowledge produced as the acquisitive level. Accordingly, objective idealism could at best have some relevance to how Kant tried to reflectively appropriate our experience by exploring symbolic analogies. This way of relating Dilthey's types to Kant's overall worldview leads to the recognition that they provide mere schemata for further reflection. Thus Kant's idealism of freedom is quite different from that of Fichte, who goes much further by positing a foundational "*self-in-itself*"[1] that is "absolutely self-active."[2] Fichte expands

Kant's idea of moral self-determination into the power to fully determine things and to not be determined by them. From this standpoint, the sensible world becomes "that which stands opposed to my action," and what "is to come about through my action is the intelligible world."[3] This sets up the kind of sharp oppositions that Kant tried to at least partly overcome. Nor is Kant the kind of extreme voluntarist that Richard Kroner makes him in his book *Kant's Weltanschauung*, originally published in German in 1914 and translated into English in 1956. Kroner claims that Kant's worldview is rooted in an ethical subjectivity that "illuminates another world, the world of absolute values."[4] This creates an even starker opposition than Fichte and makes theoretical reason completely subordinate to practical reason. We find Kroner making the startling assertion that for Kant "the world cannot be grasped in its reality by any theoretical means."[5] Reality for Kroner refers to a "supersensible and eternal world" that is "accessible only through moral activity."[6] What Kant's worldview does according to this reading—probably inspired by Hermann Lotze's value theory—is to replace theoretical metaphysics with a perspective that affirms "the non-theoretical but metaphysical validity of the moral life."[7] Whereas Fichte attempted to radicalize Kant's ideals by locating them in an intelligible world that is not transcendent, Kroner etherealizes Kant's ideals by transposing them into a transcendent world of values. The idealism of freedom that I see as inherent in Kant's worldview is not absolutist in either Fichte's or Kroner's sense, but is powerful enough to critically assess the world we live in and comprehend it for our purposes to begin to reform it.

The *Weltanschauung* that Kroner attributes to Kant is intensely religious. Although it is true that Kant took religion seriously, his attempts to give it moral relevance were never doctrinal. His claim that we cannot prove the existence of God means that religion should have no metaphysical validity. Kant's religion was in the more modest spirit of his Pietistic background and focused on personal belief. Philosophically, he denies knowledge of God in order to make room for a faith that encompasses a symbolic religious cognition based on aesthetic analogies. Kant's preference is for non-institutional religion and for a theodicy that is authentically felt rather than doctrinal (see "MTT" 24; 8:264).[8] He rejects the doctrinal interpretation that Job's suffering can be explained as a divine punishment that needs to be atoned for (see "MTT" 25; 8:265). The significance of a religious outlook should be interpreted authentically in this-worldly terms and not rely on doctrinal pseudo-explanations appealing to some higher authority or the otherworldly absolute values posited by Kroner.

I have attempted to show that Kant's strategy was to defuse the oppositions that stem from the legislative faculties of understanding and reason of the first two *Critiques* by turning to judgmental mediation. Accordingly, one of the most important contributions that Kant made to philosophical idealism is to rid it as much as possible of absolutism. There are indeed core absolutes such as the principle of noncontradiction and the categorical imperative. But transcendental idealism as an overall worldview is a conditional idealism that must constantly be subjected to critique and judgmental refinement. From the very beginning, we saw Kant argue that human attempts at comprehension can never be absolute. Even when Kant comes closest to being absolutist, as in his moral philosophy, he increasingly supplements his subordinative determinant approach with a reflective correlative approach. We see this most clearly in the final way he relates our empirical character to our intelligible character in *Religion within the Boundaries of Mere Reason.* This passage comes roughly ten pages after he introduced the incorporation thesis that was considered earlier, and sheds further light on the question of whether respect for the law must be the sole determining ground of moral action or merely the first among several incentives. The demand that respect for the law be the sole ground is now related to our intelligible character, and the lesser demand that respect be the most important incentive is related to our empirical character. The act of deciding what maxim to act on would involve an instantaneous, nontemporal "revolution in disposition" or a "revolution in mode of thought" (*R* 68; 6:47). But the act of thought that "incorporates the purity [of holiness] into its maxims" is not yet tantamount to the deed of attaining holiness, for as Kant admits, "between maxim and deed there still is a wide gap" (*R* 67; 6:47). A revolution in thought on the level of intelligible character must be translated into a "gradual reformation in the mode of sense" (*R* 67; 6:47). It is at this phenomenal level of dealing with empirical obstacles to our being good or virtuous that we could still take other incentives into consideration, as long as they do not override our respect for the moral law. And some of these incentives may be informed by theoretical considerations.

Kant now compares his revolution in thought to a religious conversion. Accordingly, he alludes to Colossians 3:9–10 in his recapitulation:

> If by a single and unalterable decision a human being reverses the supreme ground of his maxims by which he was an evil human being (and thereby puts on a "new man"), he is to this extent, by principle and attitude of mind, a subject receptive to the good; but he is a good human being only in incessant laboring and becoming. (*R* 68; 6:48)

This is a noteworthy passage because it indicates that however important the supreme ground of a person's maxims may be for the determination of whether he or she is good, this index of intelligible character is not sufficient. It is just as important to consider the empirical trajectory of individuals in the timeline of their existence. The revolution of thought is really an attitude of mind or resolve by which we first become "receptive to the good" (*R* 68; 6:48). The further test is how we carry out this initial attitude of openness to the good and actively struggle to overcome empirical obstacles and pathological temptations. Here again we do not have the compatibilist problem of reconciling two modes of agency or causality. The intelligible character is for us humans a mode of receptivity and by itself remains a sublime presentation (*Darstellung*) that evokes a feeling, but it is not a representation (*Vorstellung*) of any concrete action. We can abstractly conceive of the change from evil to goodness as a conversion, but we can ascertain it only by "a gradual reformation" (*R* 68; 6:47) and by a consideration of the various incentives still at work in empirical beings after they have resolved to be good. Therefore, a resolve with no subsequent reformative confirmation of improvement is to be doubted. Usually Kant is thought to judge the morality of human beings merely by the goodness of their intentions. In contrast to utilitarians, he is regarded as a philosopher who does not care much about the consequences or results of actions. We can now see that Kant is not indifferent to the working out of our moral decisions. Empirical reformative progress is relevant to the determination of whether we really did resolve to make a revolutionary break with self-love. It is only through the correlation of intelligible and empirical character that we can judge virtue. In itself, the idea of intelligible character makes sense only "for him who penetrates the intelligible ground of the heart . . . , i.e., for God" (*R* 68; 6:48). For us, it is a regulative idea for measuring all reformative activity by a standard of holiness. Here religion can be seen as a supplement to morality to encourage us to persevere in the long road to self-reformation.

However, when it comes to deciding where to start on the road to reform, reflection becomes essential. Any regulative idea of progress remains an empty promise until it is matched by a reflective diagnosis that assesses what needs to be done first. It is thus interesting that Kant speaks of a "reflective faith" in the context of his discussion of the "*parerga* to religion within the boundaries of pure reason" (*R* 72; 6:52). A *parergon* of faith does not fall strictly within the religion of pure reason, "yet borders on it" (*R* 72; 6:52). Such a borderline supplement is not merely external because we feel the need to draw on it for support. Kant admits that we tend to project beyond the intrinsic work (*ergon*) of reason when we become "conscious of its impotence to satisfy its moral needs" (*R* 72; 6:52). The traditional *parerga* Kant has in mind involve the belief and hope that we can rely on God's grace or some providential concurrence of forces to support us in realizing our moral ends. But it is important to recognize that we may "not incorporate" our faith in the effect of such providential aid "into the maxims of reason" (*R* 72; 6:53) themselves. This would be to sit back and expect a higher or divine power to take over. Instead, Kant makes it clear that we must first institute "a rule concerning what good *we ourselves must do* (with a particular aim in mind) in order to achieve something" (*R* 73; 6:53). Our faith in providential aid can only become reflectively warranted if we have already incorporated our own subjective incentives into the maxim of action we have adopted. *Parerga* are contextually relevant, but only marginally.

Instead of directing all reformative activity towards one transcendent goal—holiness—a reflective use of the idea of intelligible character allows a person to orient specific reforms immanently, that is, within himself through a concern with virtue. Here goodness lies not in extirpating incentives other than respect, but in making sure that respect for the moral law remains first among the incentives. This reflective interpretation is supported by an even later discussion of the revolution-reformation contrast in *Religion within the Boundaries of Mere Reason*, where Kant warns about the violence of revolution. He replaces his earlier language of a revolution in thought with that of revelation when he writes:

> The basis for the transition to the new order of things must lie in the principle of the pure religion of reason, as a *revelation* (though not an empirical one) unchangingly [*beständig*] taking place within all human beings, and this basis, once grasped after mature reflection [*Überlegung*], will be carried to effect, inasmuch as it is to be a human work, through gradual *reform*. (*R* 128; 6:122)

An intellectual revelation does not change over time, and being instantaneous, is not an integral part of time, and therefore will not magically wipe away all our earlier beliefs and habits empirically accumulated over time. That would require a time-demanding and laborious effort of reflection about our prejudices and inclinations. Some of these may stand the test of time, while others will have to be overthrown or revised. Thus a noumenal revelation can, upon mature reflection, serve as the overall principle of orientation for all our judgments about the relative worth of specific deeds done from a variety of empirical incentives. Respect for law as the sole incentive of our moral maxims would have us seek a purity of incentives and regulate everything by the standard of holiness; respect for law as the primary incentive allows us to accept a plurality of other incentives and reflect on which among those should take precedence as we gradually reform ourselves. Historical, cultural, and moral progress will inevitably be gradual.

Coordinative Comprehension and the Application of Reflective Judgment to Human Practices

Although Kant was criticized for not considering a multilateral mode of legitimacy that could make room for cultural pluralism, we have seen that he does have a multilevel approach both in accounting for knowledge and in assessing our moral development pertaining to the culture of discipline. Better coordinating the levels of our awareness could be considered the final task of comprehension that is both rational and reflective. Thus, the idea of an intelligible act of conversion whereby we effect a shift in our *Denkungsart* or mode of thinking can be made an orientational principle whereby the empirical *Sinnesart* of our life-course is purposively ordered. The little reforms we make here and there can then be judged reflectively and assessed in terms of how much they contribute to the overall telos of character formation. We know from the *Critique of Judgment* that teleological judgments cannot be objective determinant judgments. Claims about purposes or final causality are not constitutive for experience—only claims about efficient causality are. When Kant speaks of teleological judgments as both regulative and reflective, it is commonly assumed that these predicates mean the same thing,[9] but this cannot be because Kant considers aesthetic judgments as reflective without being regulative. Aesthetic judgments are "constitutive" (*C3* 82; 5:197) for human feeling. Only teleological judgments are both regulative and reflective. They are regulative in that they apply concepts hypothetically beyond their experiential bounds and reflective in that they are valid only "for us (human beings in general)" (*C3* 327; 5:462). They reflect our human mode of thinking and can therefore be intersubjectively valid without determining what an organism "is in itself" (*C3* 327; 5:462). Similarly, we saw that judgments about moral character are *regulative* for Kant insofar as they project an infinite telos of holiness or purity of motive. But they are also *reflective* insofar as they acknowledge the coexistence of multiple incentives and aim at the more limited virtue of setting the right priority among them when deciding to act. In saying this, I may be thought to extend reflective judging more into the domain of practical philosophy than is proper. This seems to be the view of Onora O'Neill, who is only willing to allow "reflective judging" to do preparatory work for practical judgments in "describing, articulating, or interpreting cases"[10] where our moral duty or course of action cannot be directly determined.

O'Neill considers reflective judgments to be primarily descriptive and comparative in an effort to "consider more openly what *sort*"[11] of situation we are facing when familiar concepts, labels, and rules do not suffice. But reflective judgments are not merely theoretical as she claims because as in the case of judgments of taste, they are clearly normative. When we need to make a practical decision, reflective judgments can evaluate the relevant situation and discern likely conflicts that need to be resolved. Reflective judgments also possess another characteristic that O'Neill assigns to practical judgments, namely, the capacity of "limiting one maxim by another."[12] Nevertheless, she thinks that reflective judgments do not achieve what a practical judgment goes on to do:

> Practical judgement is *always* a matter of finding a way of *achieving* a range of aims and objectives while conforming to a plurality of principles of duty, and of doing so while taking account of the varied realities and vulnerabilities of human life.[13]

If practical judgments are about "finding a way of achieving a range of aims" as described above, then reflective judgments can also fill the bill. According to O'Neill, reflective judgments are about what is given, whereas practical judgments project into the future. But this contrast is too stark, for as she herself admits, many decisions are prepared for by an assessment of a problematic situation that needs to be addressed. To reflectively assess the unusual symptoms that a diseased patient manifests is to already consider alternative diagnoses that anticipate possible treatments. A practical judgment only goes further if it also executes the decision of which alternative to enact. But to define a practical judgment as only projecting into the future and detach it from the given would seem to make room for arbitrary and irrational choices. Nor is it sufficient to say that reflective judgments are merely preparatory, for once a decision about action has been made, many more adjustments in the course of action are likely to be called for. If a patient does not respond to the chosen treatment, a reflective reassessment becomes necessary. And when medical matters become more directly moral as they could affect the dignity of the patient being treated, it is crucial that practical judgments be made as part of an overall evaluative and attitudinal context that is informed by both determinant and reflective judgments. Practical judging thus fits into the framework of what I have called reflective comprehension. And on the personal level, this occurs at the third or appropriative dispositional level of moral character.

These final considerations about what a morally developed and world-oriented human character should strive for allow me to reinforce the claim made earlier that cosmical philosophy and cosmopolitanism are not to be conflated. The important issues dealt with by O'Neill's approach to practical judgment apply much more to the level of cosmical philosophy than to that of cosmopolitanism. This raises the question of whether it was sufficient for Kant to regard the cosmopolitan project as a mere pragmatic goal. If we regard the pragmatic cosmopolitan skill of containing our aggressive tendencies as one of cleverly regulating the instincts and self-interests even of a race of devils, then we are legislating at the lowest levels of our animality and humanity. This reduces cosmopolitan legislation to a negative project that short-circuits both the judgmental processes that Kant's cosmical philosophy makes essential for the spiritual level of moral personality and the important project of comprehending the relation between our intelligible and empirical character.

Cosmopolitanism needs to be rethought as a more positive project that can reconcile different cultures through the multilateral approach that was recommended earlier. The cosmopolitanism of *Perpetual Peace* was based on cultivating our technical and pragmatic skills for human coordination, but it does not engage the next level of our mental life. This middle ground for cultivating human engagement was explored in §40 of the *Critique of Judgment* by establishing that good taste is consensus-building without insisting on the teleological univocity aimed at in §60 and §83. Kant's final demand for total consensus is itself an illusory prejudice associated with the Enlightenment assumption that universality is about uniformity. He was right to question the prejudices that we assimilate in life and that encourage many to prefer what is local and familiar over what is strange and foreign. But the reason why Kant's own universalism is also prejudiced is his acquired conviction that one branch of the human race can legislate what counts as universal for the race as a whole.

This allows us to see that prejudices are more than untested or erroneous beliefs. They are beliefs that tend to infect other beliefs. Even when an obviously parochial prejudice is corrected, it may already have generated other, less obvious associated misjudgments that creep into the higher levels of cognitive acquisition and reflective appropriation to produce illusions and delusions that stand in the way of an adequate worldview. Philosophy according to a world-concept must thus constantly reexamine itself if it is to be truly critical. Kant recognized that one of the greatest challenges to his idealism of freedom is our failure to test the beliefs and views we assimilate. This includes not only the provincial attitudes of those who support and surround us in our youth, but also the obscure contents that we absorb in inner sense throughout our life and which can distract us. Assimilative distortions can be as harmful to us as ignorance. At the next level, that of conceptual acquisition, one of the greatest dangers is the assumption that because phenomenal natural occurrences and human events are in principle causally explainable, we can thereby fully comprehend their significance. To explain something is to cognize its necessary and sufficient conditions. This involves tracing clear and distinct lines of dependence. But when we reach the limits of this kind of world-concept understanding, we can turn to worldview comprehension to further appropriate what has been cognized. Although Kant has been touted for his architectonic systematic aspirations, this should not lead us to assume that he believes in the kind of overall harmonious solution that objective idealists aim at. Increasingly, he came to the realization that reflective judgment gives us the tectonic power or freedom to demand contextual specification in order to better make sense of the world and to orient ourselves within it. This makes his worldview, if not pluralistic in the sense of fully appreciating human and cultural diversity, sufficiently multifaceted so as to provide some checks on prejudices getting out of hand. One of the best ways of using the tectonic power of reflective judgment to test for possible prejudices is to make use of the contextual shifts in thinking that were uncovered in Kant's aesthetics.

It is a common assumption that as an Enlightenment thinker, Kant thought we could overcome all our prejudices, and therefore he is criticized for not being able to overcome what we see to be his own prejudices. But as I already said earlier, Kant's own motto was that the process of enlightenment involves the liberation from superstition, by which he means our greatest or preeminent prejudices (see *C3* 174–75; 5:294). Kant never thought that individuals could overcome all their prejudices, and that is why he increasingly became a contextualizing thinker, the virtue of which is to mitigate the bad effects of possible prejudices. One way to accomplish this is to limit the excesses of one contextual mode of thinking (*Denkungsart*) by another and let them intersect. Of course, this still leaves us with the reflective hermeneutical task of deciding which perspective should take precedence on a given issue. This is the way in which Kant's multifaceted worldview can still provide meaningful parameters for further critical inquiry today.

By comprehending Kant's philosophy as oriented to the human world, I have minimized talk of a transcendent noumenal world. There are many things that surpass our experience that do not need to be projected onto a transcendent world. Kant shows this in his account of the sublime as a confrontation with the infinite beyond us, which is to be comprehended in terms of the infinity of our own moral potential. And I have pointed to the way Kant brings the noumenal into this world, as when we are said to possess things noumenally when they satisfy the ideal standards of omnilateral legitimacy. Similarly, we can be said to cognize something "noumenally" to the extent that we have reflective comprehensive insight into it. And if we regard the suggestions Kant made in his religious writings about correlating an instantaneous conversion of thought with temporal reformative efforts of judgment, then we have another application of rational comprehension that is relevant to this life.

Kant's search for the transcendental foundational conditions of what is objectively possible focuses mostly on the faculties of understanding and reason. But as we have seen, it is the power of judgment that frames the categories of the understanding and guides the imagination in schematically relating these a priori concepts to actual objects of cognition. And in order to validate cognition as certain knowledge by the standards of reason, we need the judgmental consent of the community of investigators. The capacity to judge is essential for being fully conscious and was said by Kant to differentiate the human species from other animals. Whereas the faculties of understanding and reason are largely a function of our endowment, judgment is a power that humans must fully fashion for themselves.

Transcendental philosophy is ultimately about establishing judgmental priorities among the conditions of theory and practice. In those spheres where we do not have certain knowledge and univocal consent about normative standards, comprehension sets the bounds of what is intelligible relative to what is judged to be purposive for us humans. Rational comprehension and reflective judgment thus serve similar purposes. Together they can orient us among the various contexts of the world and make sense of Kant's multifaceted worldview. The transcendental orientational principle of judgment that applies here provides the conditions, not only for the communication of what is *objectively possible,* but also for a communicability about larger issues where *intersubjective feasibility* is at issue.

From Antinomies to Amphibolies

As was suggested at the start of chapter 7, it is possible to see Kant's worldview as rooted in his efforts to dissolve metaphysical antinomies into contextual amphibolies that are at least partly soluble if we apply transcendental reflection. In the *Critique of Pure Reason,* Kant still defended a separate transcendent world and proposed that we can avoid falling into metaphysical confusions if we neither sensitivize what is noumenal nor intellectualize what is phenomenal. Kant first defined such a confusion as an amphiboly when he accused Leibniz of intellectualizing appearances and not recognizing that the phenomena of sense can only be approached from the outside—meaning that formal considerations must precede our understanding of objective intuitive content. For us, any purely intellectual way of intuiting objects from the inside is impossible.

Whatever we think about noumenal ideals will always remain theoretically abstract and empty of content.

But when we turn to practical reason, there is only one world to think about: the community of human spirit.[14] In this world of intersubjective relations which have been instituted by us humans among ourselves as moral agents, it becomes possible to assess our phenomenal affairs by means of noumenal or intelligible norms.[15] But success here presupposes a careful delimitation of the world by specifying it into the contextual spheres that can be defined on the basis of the *Critique of Judgment.* This kind of reflective specification is central to Kant's worldview and allows him to think that although the world is not understandable or explainable as one complex whole (mechanism leads us only so far), we can at least comprehend it for our purposes by delineating it into modal contexts, such as a general territory or a universal lawful domain. And to the extent that each of us relates to these objective contexts differently, we also depend on the intersubjective forms of medial transmission and access that Kant opened up in his aesthetics. Similarly, as a geographer of human reason, he imagined the world in terms of different topological terrains, which allows for what is today called an orientational hermeneutics of place.[16] Whereas some biological species are naturally amphibious by being equally comfortable on land and in water, we humans who are most comfortable on land can nevertheless learn to navigate a wider range of earthly and conceptual worldly regions. To ignore the different status of these regions and generalize on the basis of the one we are most familiar with is to subject ourselves to the contextual confusions that Kant calls amphibolies. This entails that to be a good philosopher, one must have a discerning contextual awareness. This was made especially clear when Kant added moral amphibolies to theoretical ones.

Moral amphibolies amount to normative confusions. In chapter 8, we saw Kant claim that human beings have *direct* duties only to other human beings. Even when we orient our conscience to what a higher, purely rational being like God would think of our actions, we must not regard any of our moral duties as direct "*duties to* [*gegen*]" (*MM* 192; 6:442) God. To do so would be to cede our autonomy to a higher being where fear could be mixed with respect. At most we can speak of an indirect duty "in reference [*in Ansehung*]" (*MM* 192; 6:442) to God. Similarly, Kant considers our duties to nonrational animals as indirect. These animals should not be subjected to "violent and cruel treatment" (*MM* 192; 6:443) because that is "opposed to a human being's duty to himself" (*MM* 192; 6:443). To mistreat an animal is wrong because it erodes our capacity to feel the suffering of our fellow human beings. If animals are to be killed, this should be done "quickly (without pain)," and when they are put to work for us they should "not be strained beyond their capacity" (*MM* 193; 6:443).

To worry about the mistreatment of animals on the basis of concern over the erosion of our own humanity has been criticized as showing insufficient respect for animals as such. Kant has been compared unfavorably with Schopenhauer's more deeply felt appeal to treat animals with compassion. A contemporary Kantian, Christine Korsgaard, goes even further in thinking that we have a direct duty to animals because all living conscious beings should be equally valued. She does acknowledge Kant's point that our duty to respect other human beings as ends in themselves differs from our duties to nonrational animals as ends in themselves because only humans can be co-legislators of moral laws. Whereas Kant thought that we have direct duties only to our human co-legislators, Korsgaard thinks that we have direct duties both to human beings as ends in themselves in an "active sense" and to nonrational animals as ends in themselves in a "passive sense."[17] As one part of her effort to justify this claim, she reconstructs Kant's account of what it means to form a maxim of action by arguing that human decisions have two moments or aspects: the first is that when I desire what is "good-for me, I decide to pursue it *as if it were good absolutely*. The second aspect is that I embody that decision in a law that I make for everyone, including myself."[18] Because the second aspect builds on the first, we are as moral agents also "affirming the value of animal nature itself," according to Korsgaard. "The claim of the other animals to the standing of ends-in-themselves has the same ultimate foundation as our own claim does, the same ultimate foundation as morality—the essentially self-affirming nature of life itself."[19] While I fully agree with the conclusion that all life is self-affirming and should be valued, I am not convinced by Korsgaard's assertion that the first, animal-based aspect of our decisions already posits what she considers an "as-if absoluteness." Certainly, as a reconstruction of Kant, one would have to insist that only after a desired good has been found worthy of being co-legislated can it make any claim to being universally valid and legitimate based on consensus. And I have already expressed doubts about whether even that counts as absoluteness.

Based on her book as a whole, we see that Korsgaard's claim for the absoluteness of holding something to be good is not based on universal consent. She attaches absoluteness not only to rational moral goods, but also to all the goods that are basic to life, namely, the desire for food and sex as much as the desire for mutual cooperation. Although Korsgaard says that something which is "absolutely important" means that "it is important to . . . every sentient creature,"[20] she also claims that "there's no difference between being absolute, and being relative to everyone."[21] This reduces the meaning of absoluteness to something incomparable, which Korsgaard seems to admit when she writes:

> If everything that is important is important to someone—to some person or animal—there is no place to stand and make a comparative judgment, or at least with any plausibility, about the comparative importance of people and animals themselves.[22]

It is in this neutral sense that we can be said to have a direct duty to other animals, but it remains an imperfect duty in that there are many ways in which we interact with animals, ranging from the most egregious one of factory farming chickens, to the unavoidable one of protecting ourselves from dangerous animals and pests, to the more benign practice of keeping dogs and cats as pets. Each of these relations poses problems that demand a different contextual response.

Kant's otherwise useful three-level approach leaves animals behind because it is applied too rigidly here. We saw that despite acknowledging that animals can reflect and distinguish things, Kant denied them consciousness because he thought they lacked the judgmental capacity to recognize *how* things differ from each other. But clearly animals have awareness and can remember that certain things are painful, which is evidence for the kind of continuity that we associate with consciousness. We saw that Kant granted animals the life of the soul with only minimal powers of modification, and without the higher activities that come with mind and spirit. He acknowledged that beavers are alive in that they manifest purposive skills, but he considers their acts of "choice" (*MM* 192; 6:442) merely instinctive. Just as Kant had high standards for what constitutes consciousness, he was cautious about assigning life to organisms such as plants because they do not even manifest any soul-like life. Regardless of how Kant would have modified his positions about animate life and the notion of race in light of what we have come to know about biology, it is likely that his moral outlook would still apply some kind of stratified approach to assessing the world. Stratification seems to be inherent in Kant's way of trying to reconcile a genetic or dispositional preformationism with the epigenetic development of life in terms of soul, mind, and spirit.

Stratification also characterizes Kant's duties of virtue, which he subjects to modifiable rules insofar as they deal with people "in accordance with their differences in rank, age, sex, health, prosperity or poverty" (*MM* 214; 6:469). These variables also play themselves out in Kant's extensive reflections on the meaning of friendship. He thinks that true friendship can only exist among those who respect each other as equals. Therefore, philanthropists who engender a generic "mutual love [*Wechselliebe*]" among human beings cannot be considered to be friends of the recipients of their generosity. Their beneficence is admirable because it helps others, but if "the respect owed by each is not equal" (*MM* 217; 6:473), it cannot count as an act of friendship.

Kant starts describing his ideal of personal friendship in Aristotelian terms as a "union of two persons through equal mutual love and respect" (*MM* 215; 6:469) and demands a balance that may be difficult to maintain. Friendship is an intimate, but not a total union like marriage, because love and respect set different demands. Whereas "the principle of love bids friends to draw closer, the principle of respect requires them to stay at a proper distance from each other" (*MM* 215; 6:470). This space between two friends manifests itself in the question of how much one can afford to disclose to the other about one's private thoughts and attitudes. Too much intimacy could diminish the value of human dignity that we saw to be so important for Kant in chapter 8. There can be no perfect or determinate rules about the right degree of intimacy. If the union of friendship is based exclusively on feeling, then it is "something so delicate [*etwas so Zartes*]" (*MM* 216; 6:471) that it can easily be lost if we are not careful. There is something fragile about true friendship. Here again, we see Kant broach the theme of delicateness and the judgmental tact that it calls for. Delicateness and tact are central to his approach to the world and point to the importance of the freedom of reflective judgment to navigate among alternatives. We saw Kant first invoke delicateness, or what I would prefer to call "discernment," when discussing rational comprehension. After urging us to not get lost in the obscurities and confusions of inner sense and to explore what we can learn about ourselves from the outer senses, he adds the proviso that we should replace tender sensitivity with delicate sensitivity. People with tender sensitivity remain too passive and allow their state of mind to be disturbed when their vital sense is negatively affected. People with a delicate sensitivity are more receptive and open. They learn to accept negative influences on their vital sense by focusing on how to preserve their state of mind. Their reflective receptivity allows them to limit the disturbing effects of strong stimuli as much as possible to the lowest level of soul, so that they can recover their mental composure and remain discerning in their judgments. This delicate sensitivity is also an important element in preserving human friendships.

Kant concludes that the fragile balance of genuine friendship can only be preserved if it has a moral core. In an "Appendix" to this discussion of moral friendship, Kant recommends a more general "duty to oneself as well as to others not to isolate oneself" but to participate in "social intercourse. . . . While making oneself a fixed center of one's principles, one ought to regard the *circle drawn around one* as also forming part of *an all-inclusive circle* of those who, in their disposition, are citizens of the world" (*MM* 218; 6:473). Whereas the sociopolitical ideal of cosmopolitanism is to cultivate being a "friend of human beings in general (i.e., of the whole race)" which " takes an affective interest in the well-being of all human beings " (*MM* 217; 6:472), the cosmical counterpart could be the cultivation of a more intimate circle of social intercourse around oneself that would include some friends who are actually respected as equals . This would specify the sphere of active engagement that aesthetic communicability first made possible. Thus, we can fill in the schematic idealism of freedom formulation of the Kantian worldview with a cosmical ideal of wisdom that expects us to assimilate experience receptively, live a life of responsive and responsible self-governance, and interact with the world through participatory communal engagement.

Final Thoughts

This work about Kant's worldview has been an effort to show how Kant continued to reach out to consider whether his philosophical conclusions needed to be extended or qualified in order to deal with unresolved issues. I introduced the term *Weltanschauung* as a limit idea based on its usage in Kant's discussion of the sublime, and have elaborated it in relation to his challenge at the end of the *Critique of Pure Reason* that henceforth philosophy should be conceived cosmically in accordance with a *Weltbegriff.* It turns out that the idea of a worldview stands as a challenge that philosophers must continue to pursue. One could say that everything that Kant wrote after he completed his first two *Critiques* on what could be determinantly known about theoretical and practical matters is worldview philosophizing. It probes beyond the boundaries of what Kant considered to be knowable as true, but in a reasonable and reflective manner whose results would be more comprehensive and therefore somewhat provisional. It would be wrong, however, to think that there is a sharp split here that undermines Kant's core positions. The reason I have differentiated the three levels of experience starting with the first *Critique* is to show that the middle level of cognitive acquisition can stand firm as synthetically determinant for our understanding. What was initially assimilated as intuitive content for scientific cognition was further tested through a logical analysis of prejudicial beliefs and then reexamined for how it is felt and reflectively appropriated through judgments of taste. Finally, the *Anthropology* reexplored sensibility for how it can shape our outlook on the world. These extensions allowed Kant to compensate for the inadequacies of inner sense by rethinking it as an interior sense that takes our pulse in response to the five outer senses. Equally transformative is the way he supplements these organ-based outer senses with a vital sense that holistically pervades our bodies. And because these extensions undergird Kant's efforts to use reflective judgment to attain a more comprehensive worldview, they also enable us to coordinate the first level of what is assimilated more closely with the third level of what is rationally appropriated. Whereas the determinant results of the discursive understanding proceeded acquisitively from part to whole, both the assimilative and appropriative levels of experience function holistically from the start.

The "Dialectic of Pure Reason" had only limited success in answering all the questions we have about what can be known. The antimonies of reason were never definitely resolved. What is rationally systematized as objective knowledge in the "Canon of Pure Reason" is only the sum total of what the community of scientific understanding has agreed on. This is why Kant's claims about rational comprehension as an intersubjective human mode of cognition and about reflective judgment as a mode of discernment are important for the formulation of a worldview that can give further meaning to his world-concept by exploring our proper place in the world.

Kant's cosmical philosophy was initially supported by the main claim of the first *Critique* that our understanding (*Verstand*) is an intellectual faculty that has the capacity to conceive all of nature as an intelligible continuum. But its capacity to lawfully explain natural events turns out to provide a mechanistic mode of causality that still leaves gaps in our conception of the world as a whole. Our human intellect does not allow us to fully explain how organisms function, nor does it give a well-rounded understanding (*Verstehen*) of the life of the mind. Those two regions were opened up for further reflection in the third *Critique*. An even more important limit of *Verstand* is its incapacity to legislate how we should live out our lives in action. This is where Kant calls on the practical reason of the second *Critique* to test whether our maxims of action can be universalized. And when universalization leads to conflicts, the law-giving power of reason becomes juridical. Constitutive rules are supplemented with regulative rules that need judgment to be applied. While Kant's worldview of the idealism of freedom would be in agreement with Hegel that we will only be truly free when we are all free, it provides less confidence that we will reach that goal. Kant clearly thinks that we will always need a court of reason to resolve ongoing moral and social conflicts. Increasingly, his philosophy relies on reflective judgment to orient us to the world in terms of the specific contexts in which we participate. My thesis that Kant's philosophy is ultimately framed by judgment, can also be illustrated by his willingness to allow good sense to trump his own prejudicial comprehension of racial differences so he could at least move on to the more urgent task of gaining cosmopolitan coordination.

Kant provides us with a worldview based on the realization that our earth is a delimited global sphere that forces us to compete for space and resources. But our reason gives us the power to transform some limits imposed on us into boundaries that we can also project beyond. Boundaries are important in defining safe spaces within which we can cooperate and establish communal goals and ideals. But they must leave room for us to cross borders and take account of other, less well-defined regions. Kant was curious about the multiplicity of things, but he was not what we would call a pluralist. He was intellectually inclined to think omnilaterally and in overarching systematic terms, yet his assessment of the limits of what we can actually comprehend leads him to avoid absolutism. His transcendental idealism of freedom is a conditional idealism. It results in a worldview that is ultimately liberal in generating divergent judgmental contexts and coordinating them when possible. It no longer espouses the optimism of a pure rationalist such as Leibniz, but it evokes a forward-looking hope. Kant inspired the dramatic idealism of freedom of Schiller, but his interest in organic analogies also points sideways toward Goethe's more lyrical way of characterizing human life as interconnected. Kant's exploration of symbolic analogies has something in common with Goethe's search for elective affinities. I indicated earlier that if there are any affinities with objective idealism in Kant, they are to be found at the final level of the reflective appropriation of experience. Whereas most idealisms are solely projective and legislate from on high, reflective appropriation in Kant is primarily regulative and must be tested and specified by judgment. Beyond that, I have tried to show that Kant's cosmical program of consensus-building to make possible a better world in which we can equitably and actively participate is supported by a worldview that allows for contingencies that make him open to a much greater degree of self-qualification and flexibility than he is given credit for.

Looking back at Kant from where we are now, it is clear that he was less successful in understanding the complex ways in which history affects our lives and shapes our worldview. History is not just the linear succession of natural forces impelling us and our responsive strivings, as Kant thought. It is more useful to think of history as a kind of cosmic weather system in which there are disparate forces and moving currents that interact. To understand our role in history, we need to focus on certain locations where these forces tend to come together. And by forming sociocultural systems around those points of intersection, we can in turn exert some leverage on these historical forces. I noted that Kant's own idea of organic immanent purposiveness has been applied to these sociocultural systems to make more sense of how they function. To critically assess the historical forces that influence the worldviews that speak more directly to our time, we need to know which of these organizational contexts took precedence in their formation. This application of judgment to self-understanding and historical interpretation further extends Kant's insight that the fundamental task of critical philosophy is to make sure that we set the right priorities in our life. This is the hermeneutic import of our exploration of Kant's worldview. The challenge of the young Marx that we must change rather than interpret the world does not apply to hermeneutics if interpretation is conceived diagnostically and judgment-focused. We need to critically diagnose our situation if change is to be effective.

In the final analysis, we can think of a worldview as a way of compensating for the fact that we do not have archetypal or absolute intellectual powers. Our understanding functions ectypally by proceeding from part to part in building up a systematic approximation of the whole of reality. Because determinant judgment leads us only part of the way in understanding the world, comprehension becomes a necessary supplement that allows us to have the world in a more holistic way. But comprehension is not a purely theoretical accomplishment, for it requires an accommodation with our practical goals. Comprehension was originally conceived in purely rational terms, but I have argued that Kant gradually reconceives it as a task for reflective judgment. This makes comprehension both this-worldly and provisional enough to be an important stimulus for further human inquiry.

Notes

Chapter 1

The epigraph for this chapter is a free elaboration of the following two lines from Goethe's *Faust*: "Was du ererbt von deinen Vätern hast, Erwirb es, um es zu besitzen" (682–83).

1. Throughout, I will refer to the third *Critique* (*C3*) by its traditional title of *Critique of Judgment*, but will be citing the Cambridge edition with the more accurate but cumbersome title *Critique of the Power of Judgment*.

2. The *Merriam-Webster Dictionary* claims that the term *Weltanschauung* was first used in 1868, but Kant coined it in 1790.

3. This awareness that there is a space beyond a boundary also prepares for the kind of contextual differentiation spelled out in the *Critique of Judgment* and allows for multiple spheres where different rules may apply.

4. All the more so now that the issue of multiple pre-given influences has a contemporary analogue in the area of artificial intelligence, where computers are not only programmed with a priori algorithms, but are also fed vast amounts of data which can cumulatively generate unexpected stereotypes that need to be uncovered and guarded against. At certain points, we will also address some of Kant's own prejudices (e.g., about the status of animals and other human races) and what aspects of his own philosophical approach contributed to them.

5. Hubert L. Dreyfus, *Skillful Coping: Essays on the Phenomenology of Everyday Perception and Action*, ed. Mark Wrathall (Oxford: Oxford University Press, 2014).

6. Hannah Arendt was probably the first thinker to challenge this limited view by also extending reflective judgment to political discourse. See Arendt, *Lectures on Kant's Political Philosophy*, ed. Ronald Beiner (Chicago: University of Chicago Press, 1982). I attempted to extend reflective judgments even more widely by characterizing them as interpretive rather than explanatory; see Makkreel, *Imagination and Interpretation in Kant: The Hermeneutical Import of the "Critique of Judgment"* (Chicago: University of Chicago Press, 1990). More recently, Robert Nehring has stressed the various roles of reflective judgment in relation to common sense. See his *Kritik des Common Sense: Gesunder Menschenverstand, reflektierende Urteilskraft und Gemeinsinn—der Sensus communis bei Kant* (Berlin: Duncker & Humblot, 2010). In the present work, I will stress the contextualizing aspects of reflective judgment and their more pervasive effects on Kant's later writings.

7. How far Kant lives up to this expressed expectation will come into focus when the charge against him of Eurocentrism is discussed in chapter 16.

8. The spelling, reading, and interpreting trio was the organizing scheme for my earlier book *Imagination and Interpretation in Kant.* There I correlated these stages with three different functions of the imagination: a pre-critical formative power, a synthetic cognitive power, and a symbolical analogical power. In this work, I will flesh out these stages somewhat differently and more fully to bring out not only how Kant understands and interprets the world, but also how we humans should comprehend our role in this world.

9. "Medial elements" refer to the visible and audible marks (*Merkmale*) that we note in the things around us and the signals that are transmitted to us from others by means of gestures, words, or other symbols. Medial elements can thus shape our beliefs. In chapter 9, the phrase "medial context" will be introduced to designate the shared public sphere that governs the conventional use of those marks and signals, as well as their aesthetic transformation and reconfiguration.

10. This is not unlike the kind of proto-conceptual, linguistically embedded meaning that John McDowell wants to find in our perceptual intake. But I consider "intake" to be a mode of receptivity and to involve more than the passive "impressions" that McDowell focuses on. See his *Mind and World* (Cambridge, MA: Harvard University Press, 1994), 10–13, 125.

11. See Beatrice Longuenesse, *Kant and the Capacity to Judge* (Princeton, NJ: Princeton University Press, 1998), 7. Longuenesse examines this initial level in terms of how we analytically "form general concepts from sensible objects" (10) and shows how this analysis is "*performed with a view to forming judgments*" (11). These processes of concept- and judgment-formation will be discussed in chapter 2. My conception of assimilative intake is more inclusive in order to acknowledge that prejudices can enter into our cognition, and this will be dealt with more in chapters 6 and 16.

12. The distinction between what is assimilated, acquired, and appropriated in consciousness provides an initial estimate of how well we grasp the cognitive content of our experience. Indeed, as one moves from assimilation to acquisition and appropriation, one shifts from common to universal understanding and finally to communal comprehensibity. It is important to recognize that what is rationally appropriated is not a private possession but a legitimate mode of access. I originally introduced this threefold distinction as useful for hermeneutical inquiry in Makkreel, *Orientation and Judgment in Hermeneutics* (Chicago: University of Chicago Press, 2015). See especially pp. 9, 83, and 194–97.

13. See Dilthey's 1902 "Editorial Preface" to volume 1 of the Academy edition of Kant's works (*GS* 1:x).

Chapter 2

1. René Descartes, *Principles of Philosophy*, in *The Philosophical Writings of Descartes*, vol. 1, trans. John Cottingham, Robert Stoothoff, and Dugald Murdoch (Cambridge: Cambridge University Press, 1988) §45, 207–8.

2. Gottfried Wilhelm Leibniz, "Reflections on Knowledge, Truth, and Ideas," in *Leibniz Selections,* ed. Philip Wiener (New York: Charles Scribner's Sons, 1951), 283.

3. See Leibniz, "Reflections on Knowledge," 285.

4. Leibniz, "Reflections on Knowledge," 285.

5. Leibniz, "Reflections on Knowledge," 283.

6. Christian Wolff, *Rational Thoughts on God, the World, and the Soul of Human Beings,* in *Kant's Critique of Pure Reason: Background Source Materials,* ed. and trans. Eric Watkins (Cambridge: Cambridge University Press, 2009), §198, p. 24.

7. Wolff, *Rational Thoughts,* §201, p. 24.

8. See, for example, Christian Wolff, *Vernünftige Gedanken von des menschlichen Verstandes und ihrem richtigen Gebrauche in Erkenntnis der Wahrheit* (Hildesheim: G. Olms Verlag, 1981), 126, §9; and Christian Wolff, *Vernünftige Gedancken von Gott, der Welt und der Seele des Menschen, auch allen Dingen überhaupt* (Hildesheim: G. Olms Verlag, 1983), 115–16, §207.

9. Alexander Gottlieb Baumgarten, *Reflections on Poetry,* trans. Karl Aschenbrenner and William Holther (Berkeley: University of California Press, 1954), 43.

10. Baumgarten, *Reflections on Poetry,* 43.

11. John Zammito, *The Genesis of Kant's Critique of Judgment* (Chicago: University of Chicago Press, 1992), 49.

12. See especially A727/B755–A731/B759.

13. The fact that Kant speaks of "generation" rather than "active production" means that we are still at the level of assimilation here.

14. Longuenesse, *Kant and the Capacity to Judge,* 116

15. Longuenesse, *Kant and the Capacity to Judge,* 123.

16. See chapter 5.

17. Matthew McAndrew suggested to me that *willkürlich* should not be translated as "arbitrary," as in the Young translation I have been using. McAndrew claims that made concepts are "assembled through the *voluntary* combination and separation of other concepts." See Matthew McAndrew, "Kant's Theories of Concept Formation and Definition," unpublished manuscript.

Chapter 3

1. When the term "*Kenntnis*" is used by itself, I will translate it as "acquaintance" or "cognizance" to distinguish it from *Erkenntnis,* or conceptual cognition. Neither term will be translated as "knowledge," as is often done. The word "knowledge" will be reserved for *Wissen.*

2. This is one of the passages that provides strong evidence for differentiating between an assimilative and an acquisitive level of cognizing the world, as was delineated in chapter 1.

3. This is my example, not Kant's.

4. Colin McClear argues that Kant allows animals to be "aware of objects"

in a perceptual but not conceptual way that is compatible with what is today called "access consciousness." See his "Kant on Animal Consciousness," *Philosophers' Imprint* 11, no. 15 (2011): 1–16.

5. The Warschauer set of logic notes was not included in the Academy edition but was subsequently made available. See Immanuel Kant, *Logik-Vorlesungen; Unveröffentliche Nachschriften*, vol. 2, ed. Tillmann Pinder (Hamburg: Felix Meiner Verlag, 1998), 567.

6. Kant, *Logik-Vorlesungen; Unveröffentliche Nachschriften*, 2:567. I was referred to the Warschauer text by Patrick Leland. For an excellent account of the reasons given by the early Kant for denying nonrational animals consciousness, see Leland's "Kant on Consciousness in Animals," *Studi Kantiani* 31 (2018): 75–107.

7. This will be made more evident in chapter 5.

Chapter 4

1. Clinton Tolley claims that the activity of imagination serves "to make perception possible by acting on already-formed intuitions in order to bring about the consciousness of them," and "this synthesis of intuitions should be kept distinct from the activity of understanding." Tolley, "Kant on the Role of the Imagination (and Images) in the Transition from Intuition to Experience," in *The Imagination in German Idealism and Romanticism*, ed. Gerad Gentry and Konstantin Pollok (Cambridge: Cambridge University Press, 2019), 29. Tolley's concern is to focus on what the imagination can do by itself apart from the understanding. My main concern, however, is to show what the imagination can also do to supplement the categories of the understanding, namely, to schematically relate them to objects. There is more on this in the next chapter.

2. Pierre Keller, *Kant and the Demands of Self-Consciousness* (Cambridge: Cambridge University Press, 1998), 105.

3. Keller, *Kant and the Demands of Self-Consciousness*, 104.

4. See Wilhelm Dilthey, *Selected Works, Volume V: Poetry and Experience*, ed. Rudolf A. Makkreel and Frithjof Rodi (Princeton, NJ: Princeton University Press, 1985), 16.

5. See also Rudolf Makkreel, *Dilthey, Philosopher of the Human Studies*, 2nd ed. (Princeton, NJ: Princeton University Press, 1992), 432, where I wrote that "reflexive awareness . . . can potentially accompany every state of consciousness, not unlike Kant's transcendental 'I think.'" Whether or not reflexive awareness is considered to be transcendental, it deserves to be distinguished from reflective consciousness.

6. The nature of Kant's idealism will be discussed again when we examine Kant's moral philosophy and finally when his overall worldview is characterized in the last chapters.

7. The problematic nature of some of Kant's early claims about inner sense will also come back to haunt him in the *Anthropology from a Pragmatic Point of View*, as we will see in chapters 13 and 14.

8. Hermann Cohen, *Kants Theorie der Erfahrung,* 3rd ed. (Berlin: Bruno Cassirer, 1918), 557.

9. Longuenesse, *Kant and the Capacity to Judge,* 305.

10. Whereas an infinite judgment is one that negates only its predicate, as in "the soul is not mortal," now we can say that objects are not just finitely divisible into member parts, but infinitely divisible mathematically. For more on this, see the discussion of infinite divisibility in the antinomies in chapter 7.

Chapter 5

1. See Makkreel, *Imagination and Interpretation in Kant,* for a developmental examination of the shifting functions assigned to the imagination. It changes from its pre-critical function of being a formative imaging power, to a determinant synthetic judgmental power that serves cognition, to a reflective articulative judgmental power that can also be symbolically expressive.

2. When defining pure general logic, Kant spoke of "a canon of the understanding and reason" as a critical standard for cognition. Now we can speak of a canon of the understanding and reason for knowledge.

3. Karin de Boer, "Categories versus Schemata: Kant's Two-Aspect Theory of Pure Concepts and His Critique of Wolffian Metaphysics," *Journal of the History of Philosophy* 54, no. 3 (2016): 441.

4. de Boer, "Categories versus Schemata," 458.

5. de Boer, "Categories versus Schemata," 458–59.

6. Makkreel, *Imagination and Interpretation in Kant,* 30. I also elaborated on Robert Butt's claim that the categories are like syntactical rules and schemata are like semantic rules.

7. Another challenge to de Boer's position comes from Uygar Abaci, who argues that except for the modal categories, we can think of noumena "through 'unschematized' categories" as long as we do not "positively attribute" to them any "properties that instantiate the categories." Abaci, *Kant's Revolutionary Theory of Modality* (Oxford: Oxford University Press, 2019), 250.

8. Samantha Matherne, "Kant and the Art of Schematism," *Kantian Review* 19, no. 2 (2014): 202.

9. See the note on page 271 of the Cambridge translation of the *Critique of Pure Reason.*

10. See Longuenesse, *Kant and the Capacity to Judge,* 246, 12.

11. See Longuenesse, *Kant and the Capacity to Judge,* 12.

12. Eric Watkins and Marcus Willaschek, "Kant's Account of Cognition," *Journal of the History of Philosophy* 55, no. 1 (2017): 86.

13. Watkins and Willaschek, "Kant's Account of Cognition," 100.

14. Watkins and Willaschek, "Kant's Account of Cognition," 92.

15. Cohen, *Kants Theorie der Erfahrung,* 622.

16. Watkins and Willaschek, "Kant's Account of Cognition," 94.

17. For a more extensive treatment of the secondary literature on how

Kant defines sensation, see Apaar Kumar, "Transcendental Self and the Feeling of Existence," *Con-Textos Kantianos* 1, no.3 (2016): 90–121. Kumar distinguishes between durational/referential readings of sensation like that of Lorne Falkenstein and the ephemeral/non-referential readings that he and I think are more definitive.

18. Cohen, *Kants Theorie der Erfahrung*, 621.

19. I first wrote about this progression in "The Cognition-Knowledge Distinction in Kant and Dilthey and the Implications for Psychology and Self-Understanding," *Studies in History and Philosophy of Science*, no. 34 (2003): 149–64. See also my "The Hermeneutics of Attaining Knowledge," in Makkreel, *Orientation and Judgment in Hermeneutics*, 81–99.

20. Andrew Chignell considers conviction to be objective in his essay "Belief in Kant," *Philosophical Review* 116, no. 3 (2007): 323–60. For his reasoning and my arguments against it, see Makkreel, *Orientation and Judgment in Hermeneutics*, 89–90.

21. For more on this, see chapter 11.

22. Desmond Hogan, "How to Know Unknowable Things in Themselves," *NOUS* 43 (2009): 60.

23. Chignell, "Belief in Kant," 345–54.

Chapter 6

1. The distinction between bounds and limits was discussed in chapter 1.

2. Norman Kemp Smith, *A Commentary to Kant's "Critique of Pure Reason"* (New York: Humanities, 1962), 391.

3. Kemp Smith, *A Commentary*, 393.

4. Longuenesse, *Kant and the Capacity to Judge*, 164.

5. I will not pursue the question of pathology here, but have dealt with it to some extent in "Kant's Anthropology and the Use and Misuse of the Imagination," in *Kant und die Berliner Aufklärung: Akten des IX. Internationalen Kant-Kongresses*, vol. IV: Sektionen XI–XIV, ed. Volker Gerhardt, Rolf-Peter Horstmann, and Ralph Schumacher (New York: Walter de Gruyter, 2001), 386–94.

Chapter 7

1. Henry Allison, *Kant's Theory of Freedom* (Cambridge: Cambridge University Press, 1990), 28.

2. Allison, *Kant's Theory of Freedom*, 189.

3. Allison, *Kant's Theory of Freedom*, 189.

4. See Wilhelm Dilthey, *Selected Works, Volume VI: Ethical and World-View Philosophy*, ed. Rudolf A. Makkreel and Frithjof Rodi (Princeton, NJ: Princeton University Press, 2019), 93–94, 127–28.

5. See Dilthey, *Selected Works*, 6:134–35.

6. Dilthey, *Selected Works*, 6:135.

7. Dilthey, *Selected Works*, 6:134.

8. Dilthey, *Selected Works*, 6:136.

9. Dilthey, *Selected Works*, 6:134.

10. Dilthey, *Selected Works*, 6:136.

11. John Rawls, *A Theory of Justice* (Cambridge, MA: Harvard University Press, 1973), 252.

12. Rawls, *A Theory of Justice*, 257.

13. Rawls, *A Theory of Justice*, 256. I think that Rawls goes too far in saying that ultimately Kant attaches more importance to shame and a loss of self-respect than to guilt, but as we will see later, Kant does come to recognize the importance of self-respect and even a sense of public honor.

14. Rawls, *A Theory of Justice*, 256.

Chapter 8

1. We will return to the significance of the instantaneous moment (*Augenblick*) as a limiting point of the timeline when discussing the sublime.

2. See Allen W. Wood, *Kant's Ethical Thought* (Cambridge: Cambridge University Press, 1999), 289–90. For my rejection of this claim and a more detailed discussion of these refined aesthetic feelings, see Makkreel, "Relating Aesthetic and Social Feelings to Moral and Participatory Feelings," in *Kant's Observations and Remarks: A Critical Guide*, ed. Susan Shell and Richard Velkley (Cambridge: Cambridge University Press, 2012), 106–9.

3. *Mitgefühl* is a vague term that could most simply be translated as "feeling-with" and is more general than "sympathy." When discussing Dilthey earlier, we translated *Mitgefühl* as "fellow-feeling" because he links it to the social feeling of solidarity that goes deeper than sympathy. Here I translate it as "shared feeling" to underscore the mutual respect involved.

4. Note that here the term *Empfindung* is not used in a cognitive context and thus is no longer translated as "sensation," but as "feeling."

5. For the sake of thoroughness, I will point out that Kant also sometimes used the term *Theilnehmung* in the *Groundwork*. But there I can accept Mary Gregor's translation as "sympathy" because it is not conceived as being active. Indeed, Kant speaks of sympathy as being "disposed to partake [*theilnehmend gestimmt*]" in the fate of others (*G* 11; 4:398). This early sense of *Theilnehmung* is *schmelzend* (melting) (*G* 13; 4:439) and indicates a passive form of partaking that is very different from the actively cultivated participation called for in the *Metaphysics of Morals*. In the *Friedländer* anthropology lectures, Kant differentiates between *Mitleid* and *Sympathie* by considering the latter as more uplifting (see 25:606). This suggests that *Sympathie* is a kind of intermediary between *Mitleid* and *Teilnehmung* which can be aesthetically cultivated.

6. Jeanine Grenberg makes the case that humility takes a central place in

Kant's ethics. See Grenberg, *Kant and the Ethics of Humility* (Cambridge: Cambridge University Press, 2005).

7. The problem of our duties to nonrational animals will be discussed in the conclusion.

Chapter 9

1. Paul Guyer, *Kant and the Claims of Taste* (Cambridge, MA: Harvard University Press, 1979), 110.

2. Guyer, *Kant and the Claims of Taste,* 111.

3. Guyer, *Kant and the Claims of Taste,* 112.

4. Uygar Abaci, *Kant's Revolutionary Theory of Modality* (Oxford: Oxford University Press, 2019), 203.

5. See Abaci, *Kant's Revolutionary Theory of Modality* 206.

6. Abaci, *Kant's Revolutionary Theory of Modality* 206.

7. Abaci, *Kant's Revolutionary Theory of Modality,* 207.

8. C. Cazeaux, "Kant and Metaphor in Contemporary Aesthetics," *Kantian Review* 8 (2004): 11.

9. I recently found a similar claim by Joseph Tinguely: "The philosophical significance of Kant's aesthetics lies primarily not in the questions it answers but in the one it poses. How does one find the world?" in Tinguely, *Kant and the Reorientation of Aesthetics: Finding the World* (London: Routledge, 2018), 215.

10. Karl Ameriks, "Ginsborg, Nature, and Normativity," *British Journal of Aesthetics* 56, no. 4 (2016): 395.

11. Rachel Zuckert rightly stresses the anticipatory nature of aesthetic judgments and that they are "open to whichever qualitatively nuanced properties there are in the object" being evaluated, and points to the "ways in which such properties may reciprocally contrast with and complement one another." Zuckert, *Kant on Beauty and Biology* (Cambridge: Cambridge University Press, 2007), 306. Since we have seen that anticipation is a general feature of all kinds of schematization, one further way to distinguish what is at stake in aesthetic judgment is to specify it as the expectation of a reciprocal agreement with other human beings.

12. Arthur Danto, "The Art World," in *Philosophy Looks at the Arts,* ed. Joseph Margolis (Philadelphia: Temple University Press, 1978), 132–44.

13. Jacques Rancière, *The Politics of Aesthetics,* trans. Gabriel Rockhill (London: Continuum, 2006), 33.

14. Joseph Tinguely offers an insightful discussion of Kant on tonal modulation as a language of affects. What is being modulated is the "affective state of the listener . . . one's 'mode' of taking in the world." *Kant and the Reorientation of Aesthetics,* 91.

15. See Heinrich Wölfflin, *Principles of Art History: The Problem of the Development of Style in Later Art,* trans. M. D. Hottinger (New York: Dover, 1932).

16. For a more extended account of the role of artistic medial contexts, see

chapter 9 of Makkreel, *Orientation and Judgment in Hermeneutics,* especially the section "The Medial Presentation of the Commonplace in Contemporary Art."

Chapter 10

1. See Abaci, *Kant's Revolutionary Theory of Modality,* 194.

2. Since Kant provides four sets of concepts of reflection in the first *Critique* and lays out four kinds of reflective context in the third *Critique,* I suggest that a field is where we look primarily for either agreement or opposition in what is possible. The territory of what is actual first allows us to distinguish the matter and form of things. Domains that determine the necessity of things serve to bring out their true identity and differences. A contingent local habitat could be defined existentially by what is inside it or familiar and what is outside or strange. Of course, these Kantian polarities can also be applied more extensively.

3. To call comprehension an orientational hermeneutical strategy does not reduce it to a subjective interpretation. But that seems to be the view of Tinguely when he writes: "as much as there is to recommend the hermeneutical interpretation" of orientation ["pioneered by Makkreel"], it is wrong to assume "the nonobjectivity of orienting oneself in the world." Tinguely, *Kant and the Reorientation of Aesthetics,* 189 [187]. I have always differentiated mere subjective and regulative speculation from hermeneutically legitimated reflective judgments based on orientation. Indeed, Kant himself stated that ultimately nature must be interpreted (see chapter 1 above). It should be obvious that in the present work about viewing the world, I can endorse Tinguely's claim that "the process of orienting oneself is one in which a 'feeling' is revelatory of the structure of the world" (200). Our main difference seems to be that I discuss orientation mostly in part 2 about the human and social world where theoretical and practical concerns intersect, whereas Tinguely places more stress on the natural world. Nevertheless, I am sympathetic to his assertion that although orientation "draws on an ineliminable affective and thus subjective state," it is "cognitive in the sense that it gets purchase on and discloses features of the objective world" (207).

4. In *Orientation and Judgment in Hermeneutics,* I make proper contextualization the central task of critical hermeneutics.

5. See, for instance, Henry Allison, *Kant's Theory of Taste* (Cambridge: Cambridge University Press, 2001), 315.

6. The three available translations of the *Critique of Judgment* fail to distinguish between these alternatives, so you will not find the term "worldview" there.

7. In his *Phenomenology of Spirit,* Hegel exploits the ethereal nature of Kant's use of the term *Weltanschauung* when he characterizes the Kantian "moral worldview [*moralische Weltanschauung*]" as an abstract mode of consciousness that is "unfulfilled" and must be actualized in an "ethical world [*sittliche Welt*]." See G. W. F. Hegel, *Phänomenologie des Geistes* (Hamburg: Verlag von Felix Meiner, 1952), 424, 443, 473.

Chapter 11

1. The distinction between what is immediately or reflexively self-referring and a more mediated or reflective self-reference goes back to chapter 4. Whereas I distinguished between an implicit reflexive self-awareness and an explicit or reflective self-consciousness, Pierre Keller spoke of Kant's self-consciousness as "an immediate reflexive awareness" and self-knowledge as reflective.

2. For a more detailed clarification of the issues at stake here, see Makkreel, *Imagination and Interpretation in Kant*, chapter 4.

3. Kant notes that when children begin to speak, they refer to themselves in the third person. About a year later "a light seems to dawn" and they start to "speak by means of 'I.'" Merely feeling themselves is replaced by thinking themselves. See *AP* 15; 7:127.

4. The English word "animus" intensifies this human state of mind into a hostile attitude against someone.

5. This passage about animals lacking judgment is important in that it spells out Kant's main reason for denying that an ox can consciously distinguish representations.

6. In light of all the research currently being done on animal behavior, it is unnecessary to deny animals consciousness in the way we think of it. And the fact that capuchin monkeys react negatively when they receive a less favorable reward than their partners for the same task indicates that they have some kind of self-consciousness as well. The only claim about animals by Kant that still has relevance is the one about them lacking judgment.

7. Angelica Nuzzo, *Ideal Embodiment: Kant's Theory of Sensibility* (Bloomington: Indiana University Press, 2008), 51, 376n113.

8. Nuzzo, *Ideal Embodiment*, 376n113. See also Makkreel, *Imagination and Interpretation in Kant*, 98–101.

Chapter 12

1. Dilek Huseyinzadegan's less idealistic and hypothetical formulation of the role of teleology in Kant avoids my appeal to transcendental reflection, but she still acknowledges that we have here a "critical and regulative principle" according to which we "must judge" the "interrelatedness of the parts of the whole" of an organism as purposive. See her *Kant's Nonideal Theory of Politics* (Evanston, IL: Northwestern University Press, 2019), 72–73.

2. Although I am not in a position to assess the heuristic import of Kant's reflections on the organizational order of organisms for subsequent biological developments, I found it interesting to note what a reviewer of John Zammito's book *The Gestation of German Biology* wrote in the August 2018 *Notre Dame Philosophical Reviews*: "Many of the foremost advances in cellular biology have, for all intents and purposes, followed Kant's heuristic playbook. The heuristics of the stock of the *Keime und Anlagen* model, explicitly or otherwise, have served as pro-

ductive alternatives to informational reductionisms in investigations of cancer, adaptive phenotypic plasticity, and evolutionary developmental constraints."

3. Using Kant's delineation of contexts, an organism can be said to be a system that must contend with its contingent "habitat." But to the extent that we can discover certain necessary laws governing its behavior, we can regard an organism as a system that is also partly domain-like. See Makkreel, *Orientation and Judgment in Hermeneutics*, 72–78, for how this approach can be extended to social systems and disciplinary contexts.

4. For more details about *Gegenbildung* as one of the many formative powers of the imagination, see Makkreel, *Imagination and Interpretation in Kant*, 13–15, 19, 123.

5. Hannah Ginsborg, *The Normativity of Nature* (Oxford: Oxford University Press, 2015), 299–303.

6. Ginsborg, *The Normativity of Nature*, 241.

7. Ginsborg, *The Normativity of Nature*, 276.

8. Ginsborg, *The Normativity of Nature*, 242.

9. To be sure, Kant had personal doubts that there would ever be a Newton who could explain a blade of grass in the way that the motions of the planets have been explained through the mere mechanism of nature. (See *C3* 271; 5:400). On the other hand, he thought it presumptuous to rule out partial mechanistic explanations.

10. For more on this, see the chapter on "System and Organism in the *Critique of Pure Reason*" in Jennifer Mensch, *Kant's Organicism: Epigenesis and the Development of Critical Philosophy* (Chicago: University of Chicago Press, 2013).

11. Dilthey distinguishes between subjective and objective modes of immanent purposiveness. See Wilhelm Dilthey, *Selected Works, Volume II: Understanding the Human World*, ed. Rudolf A. Makkreel and Frithjof Rodi (Princeton, NJ: Princeton University Press, 2010), 183–96.

12. See Wilhelm Dilthey, *Selected Works, Volume III: The Formation of the Historical World in the Human Sciences*, ed. Rudolf A. Makkreel and Frithjof Rodi (Princeton, NJ: Princeton University Press, 2002), 172–84.

Chapter 13

1. For a more detailed exploration of how Kant's conception of anthropology relates to the rise of the human sciences, see Makkreel, "Kant on the Scientific Status of Psychology, Anthropology, and History," in *Kant and the Sciences*, ed. Eric Watkins (Oxford: Oxford University Press, 2001), 185–201; and Makkreel, "Kant and the Development of the Human and Cultural Sciences," *Studies in History and Philosophy of Science* 39 (2008): 546–53. See also Alix Cohen, *Kant and the Human Sciences: Biology, Anthropology, and History* (London: Palgrave Macmillan, 2009).

2. *Animadvertere* means "to turn the mind to." See also *AP* 95; 7:201, where taking note is assigned to judgment.

3. Since *Empfindung* is normally translated as "sensation," I am translating

the Latinate German "*Sensation*" as what strikes us as "sensory" in a lively sense. For more on this unusual term, see below when Kant introduces his idea of a vital sense. We can thus distinguish between the *sensible (sinnliche)* representation of a perceived object, the *sensuous* pleasure associated with its symmetrical form, and the *sensory* impression of its catching fire.

4. Wilhelm Dilthey, *Selected Works, Volume I: Introduction to the Human Sciences,* ed. Rudolf A. Makkreel and Frithjof Rodi (Princeton, NJ: Princeton University Press, 1989), 247.

5. Melissa Merritt, *Kant on Reflection and Virtue* (Cambridge: Cambridge University Press, 2018), 37.

6. See Merritt, *Kant on Reflection and Virtue,* 43.

7. Merritt, *Kant on Reflection and Virtue,* 15–16.

8. Kant's term *Chorographie* seems to refer back to the ancient Greek *chora* (χώρα), which was the territory of the ancient Greek polis outside the city proper.

9. The Cambridge translation of the *Anthropology* renders Kant's term "*Blendwerk*" as "delusion." I will instead follow the translation of the *Critique of Pure Reason* and translate it as "semblance." "Delusion" comes too close to "deception" and is not an adequate covering term to encompass illusion.

10. See Susanne Langer, *Feeling and Form (*New York: Charles Scribner's Sons, 1953), which aligns each of the arts with a distinctive virtual mode of semblance. See also Makkreel, "Cassirer, Langer, and Dilthey on the Distinctive Kinds of Symbolism in the Arts," *Journal of Transcendental Philosophy,* 2, no.1 (2021), 7–20.

Chapter 14

1. As we saw earlier, life, as Kant comprehends it, is essentially mental and may never fully pervade the body, since he regards matter as inert.

2. Heidegger's "a priori" characterization t of our "*being-in-the-world*" is anticipated by Kant's own worldview. See Martin Heidegger, *Being and Time,* Translated by Joan Stambaugh (Albany: State University of New York Press, 2010, 53.

3. Merritt, *Kant on Reflection and Virtue,* 181.

4. Merritt, *Kant on Reflection and Virtue,* 16.

5. These differences here and in the following pages are discussed more fully in Makkreel, "Baumgarten and Kant on Clarity, Distinctness, and the Differentiation of Our Mental Powers," in *Baumgarten and Kant on Metaphysics,* ed. Courtney Fugate and John Hymers (Oxford: Oxford University Press, 2018), 94–109.

6. See Makkreel, *Imagination and Interpretation in Kant,* chapter 1.

7. Perhaps Kant omits Baumgarten's notion of perspicuous recollection because his theory of apperception is a productive version of it. To apperceive is to recognize that what is being perceived is identical to what was already perceived.

8. This term "*Vergegenwärtigung*" was revived by the phenomenologist Edmund Husserl. Not enough attention has been paid to the phenomenological import of Kant's lectures on anthropology.

9. The primacy that listening has over perceiving for understanding became one of the hallmarks of Heidegger's thought. See Heidegger, *Being and Time*, 157–58.

10. For more on the relation between character and characterization, see Makkreel, "Kant on the Scientific Status of Psychology," 197–99.

11. Modern literary critics like Lionel Trilling have distinguished more sharply between authenticity and sincerity. Kant, however, seems to think that sincerity is a surface manifestation of a more deeply felt authentic attitude.

Chapter 15

1. The translations of *letzer Zweck* and *Endzweck* have been revised to be consistent with how the terms have been used in both the Pluhar and Guyer/Matthews translations of the *Critique of Judgment*.

2. Robert Louden, "Anthropology from a Kantian Point of View," *Studies in History and Philosophy of Science* 39, no. 4 (December 2008): 520.

3. Otfried Höffe, *Kant's Cosmopolitan Theory of Law and Peace*, trans. Alexandra Newton (New York: Cambridge University Press, 2006), 223–24.

4. Höffe, *Kant's Cosmopolitan Theory of Law and Peace*, 206.

5. It is generally thought that Kant was too old and senile to have proofed the Jäsche edition.

Chapter 16

1. See G. Felicitas Munzel, *Kant's Conception of Moral Character: The "Critical" Link of Morality, Anthropology, and Reflective Judgment* (Chicago: University of Chicago Press, 1999), for more on this link between moral character and our mode of thinking.

2. Although Kant is critical of colonialism here, he seems to condone at least some forms of colonialism when he praises Germans for not being passionately bound to their fatherland and being willing to emigrate. He adds that when a German "goes to a foreign country as a colonist, he soon contracts with his compatriots a kind of civil union. . . . So goes the praise that even the English give the Germans in North America" (*AP* 220; 7:317).

3. Seyla Benhabib, *The Rights of Others: Aliens, Residents, and Citizens* (Cambridge: Cambridge University Press, 2004), 20.

4. Huseyinzadegan, *Kant's Nonideal Theory of Politics*, 150.

5. Pauline Kleingeld, *Kant and Cosmopolitanism: The Philosophical Ideal of World Citizenship* (Cambridge: Cambridge University Press, 2012), 77.

6. Kleingeld, *Kant and Cosmopolitanism*, 82.

7. See Huseyinzadegan, *Kant's Nonideal Theory of Politics*, 139.

8. Huseyinzadegan, *Kant's Nonideal Theory of Politics*, 162–63.

9. Kant calls this feeling the love of human beings. Unfortunately, Mary Gregor translated *Teilnehmung* as "sympathy," which makes it hard for the English reader to recognize how Kant moved beyond his well-known earlier views about sympathy as *Mitleid.* I trace this development in Makkreel, "Relating Aesthetic and Sociable Feelings to Moral and Participatory Feelings: Reassessing Kant on Sympathy and Honor," in *Kant's Observations and Remarks; A Critical Guide,* ed. Susan Shell and Richard Velkley (Cambridge: Cambridge University Press, 2012), 101–15.

10. *Abartung* can also be translated as "deviation," as we will see later.

11. Jennifer Mensch, "Caught between Character and Race: 'Temperament' in Kant's Lectures on Anthropology," *Australian Feminist Law Journal* 43, no. 1 (2017): 125–44.

12. Carolus Linnaeus, *Systeman naturae per regna tria naturae,* vol. 1 (Uppsala: Laurentii Salvi Holmiae, 1758–59), 20–22.

13. Robert Bernasconi, "Who Invented the Concept of Race?—Kant's Role in the Enlightenment Construction of Race," in *Race,* ed. R. Bernasconi (Oxford: Blackwell, 2001), 11–36.

14. See also table 7.7 in Alix Cohen, "Kant's 'Curious Portrait of Human Frailties' and the Great Portrait of Nature," in *Kant's Observations and Remarks: A Critical Guide,* ed. Susan Shell and Richard Velkley (Cambridge: Cambridge University Press, 2012), 155.

15. Kleingeld, *Kant and Cosmopolitanism,* 118.

16. Manfred Kuehn, *Kant: A Biography* (Cambridge: Cambridge University Press, 2001), 333.

17. Kuehn, *Kant: A Biography,* 162.

18. Kleingeld, *Kant and Cosmopolitanism,* 109.

19. Kleingeld, *Kant and Cosmopolitanism,* 122.

20. Kleingeld, *Kant and Cosmopolitanism,* 116.

21. See Wilhelm Dilthey, *Ideas for a Descriptive and Analytic Psychology,* in *Selected Works, Volume II: Understanding the Human World,* ed. Rudolf A. Makkreel and Frithjof Rodi (Princeton, NJ: Princeton University Press, 2010), 119–28, 143–55.

22. See Wilhelm Dilthey, *Contributions to the Study of Individuality,* in *Selected Works, Volume II: Understanding the Human World,* ed. Rudolf A. Makkreel and Frithjof Rodi (Princeton, NJ: Princeton University Press, 2010), 225–27.

Conclusion

1. J. G. Fichte, *The Science of Knowledge,* ed. Peter Heath and John Lachs (Cambridge: Cambridge University Press, 1982), 10.

2. Fichte, *Science of Knowledge,* 41.

3. Fichte, *Science of Knowledge,* 41.

4. Richard Kroner, *Kant's Weltanschauung,* trans. John Smith (Chicago: University of Chicago Press, 1956), 22.

5. Kroner, *Kant's Weltanschauung,* 2.

6. Kroner, *Kant's Weltanschauung*, 2–3.

7. Kroner, *Kant's Weltanschauung*, 4.

8. For a more detailed treatment of Kant's distinction between doctrinal and authentic interpretation and its hermeneutical relevance for religion, see Makkreel, *Imagination and Interpretation in Kant*, 141–53.

9. See Michael Friedman, "Regulative and Constitutive," in "*System and Teleology in Kant's 'Critique of Judgment,'*" ed. Hoke Robinson, Supplement, *Southern Journal of Philosophy*, vol. 30 (1991): 74.

10. Onora O'Neill, *From Principles to Practice: Normativity and Judgement in Ethics and Politics* (Cambridge: Cambridge University Press, 2018), 123.

11. O'Neill, *From Principles to Practice*, 124.

12. O'Neill, *From Principles to Practice*, 99.

13. O'Neill, *From Principles to Practice*, 95.

14. According to Yirmiahu Yovel, Kant's highest good changes from being about the next world to a this-worldly historical goal. See his *Kant and the Philosophy of History* (Princeton, NJ: Princeton University Press, 1980), 72.

15. We saw Kant speak of omnilateral legitimate appropriation as a "*possessio noumenon*" (*MM* 47; 6:259).

16. See Jeff Malpas, "Place and Situation," in *The Routledge Companion to Hermeneutics*, ed. Jeff Malpas and Hans-Helmuth Gander (London: Routledge, 2015), 354–66.

17. Christine Korsgaard, *Fellow Creatures: Our Obligations to the Other Animals* (Oxford: Oxford University Press, 2018), 141.

18. Korsgaard, *Fellow Creatures*, 144.

19. Korsgaard, *Fellow Creatures*, 146.

20. Korsgaard, *Fellow Creatures*, 10.

21. Korsgaard, *Fellow Creatures*, 10.

22. Korsgaard, *Fellow Creatures*, 15.

Bibliography

Kant's Works

Kant's gesammelte Schriften. Edited by the Prussian Academy of Sciences in Berlin. 29 vols. Berlin: Walter de Gruyter, 1902–97. This work is cited parenthetically in the text by volume and page number.

Allgemeine Naturgeschichte und Theorie des Himmels. In *Kant's gesammelte Schriften,* vol. 1. Berlin: Walter de Gruyter.

"An Answer to the Question: 'What Is Enlightenment?'" Translated by H. B. Nisbet. In *Political Writings,* edited by Hans Reiss. Cambridge: Cambridge University Press, 1991.

Anthropology from a Pragmatic Point of View. Translated by Robert B. Louden. Cambridge: Cambridge University Press, 2006.

Bemerkungen zu den Beobachtungen über das Gefühl des Schönen und Erhabene. In *Kant's gesammelte Schriften,* vol. 20. Berlin: Walter de Gruyter.

Critique of Practical Reason. Translated and edited by Mary Gregor. Cambridge: Cambridge University Press, 1997.

Critique of Pure Reason. Translated and edited by Paul Guyer and Allen W. Wood. Cambridge: Cambridge University Press, 1998.

Critique of the Power of Judgment. Translated and edited by Paul Guyer and Eric Matthews. Cambridge: Cambridge University Press, 2000.

"Determination of the Concept of a Human Race." Translated by Holly Wilson and Günter Zöller, in Kant, *Anthropology, History, and Education,* Edited by Günter Zöller and Robert Louden. Cambridge: Cambridge University Press, 2007.

"The False Subtlety of the Four Syllogistic Figures." In *Theoretical Philosophy 1755–1770,* edited by David Walford and Ralf Meerbote. Cambridge: Cambridge University Press, 1992.

"First Introduction to the *Critique of the Power of Judgment.*" In *Critique of the Power of Judgment,* translated and edited by Paul Guyer and Eric Matthews. Cambridge: Cambridge University Press, 2000.

Groundwork of the Metaphysics of Morals. Translated and edited by Mary Gregor. Cambridge: Cambridge University Press, 1997.

"Idea for a Universal History with a Cosmopolitan Aim." In *Anthropology, History, and Education,* edited by Günter Zöller and Robert Louden. Cambridge: Cambridge University Press, 2007.

"Inquiry concerning the Distinctness of the Principles of Natural Theology and

Morality." In *Theoretical Philosophy 1755–1770*, edited by David Walford and Ralf Meerbote. Cambridge: Cambridge University Press, 1992.

Lectures on Logic. Edited by J. Michael Young. Cambridge: Cambridge University Press, 1992.

Metaphysical Foundations of Natural Science. Translated by James Ellington. Indianapolis, IN: Bobbs Merrill, 1970.

The Metaphysics of Morals. Translated by Mary Gregor. Cambridge: Cambridge University Press, 1996.

Observations on the Feeling of the Beautiful and the Sublime. Translated by Paul Guyer. In *Anthropology, History, and Education.* Cambridge: Cambridge University Press, 2007.

On the Form and Principles of the Sensible and Intelligible World. In *Theoretical Philosophy 1755–1770*, edited by David Walford and Ralf Meerbote. Cambridge: Cambridge University Press, 1992

"On the Miscarriage of All Philosophical Trials in Theodicy." In *Religion within the Boundaries of Mere Reason and Other Writings*, translated and edited by Allen Wood and George di Giovanni. Cambridge: Cambridge University Press, 1998.

"On the Use of Teleological Principles in Philosophy" Translated by Günter Zöller. In Kant, *Anthropology, History, and Education*, edited by Günter Zöller and Robert Louden. Cambridge: Cambridge University Press, 2007.

Opus postumum. In *Kant's gesammelte Schriften*, vol. 22. Berlin: Walter de Gruyter.

Perpetual Peace: A Philosophical Sketch. Translated by H. B. Nisbet. In Kant, *Political Writings*, edited by Hans Reiss, Cambridge: Cambridge University Press, 1993.

Physische Geographie. In *Kant's gesammelte Schriften*, vol. 9. Berlin: Walter de Gruyter.

Prolegomena to Any Future Metaphysics. Translated by Paul Carus, edited by Beryl Logan. London: Routledge, 1996.

Reflexionen zur Anthropologie. In *Kant's gesammelte Schriften*, vol. 15. Berlin: Walter de Gruyter.

Reflexionen zur Logik. In *Kant's gesammelte Schriften*, vol. 16. Berlin: Walter de Gruyter.

Reflexionen zur Metaphysik. In *Kant's gesammelte Schriften*, vols. 17 and 18. Berlin: Walter de Gruyter.

Reflexionen zur Moralphilosophie. In *Kant's gesammelte Schriften*, vol. 19. Berlin: Walter de Gruyter. 1984.

Religion within the Boundaries of Mere Reason and Other Writings. Edited by Allen Wood and George di Giovanni. Cambridge: Cambridge University Press, 1998.

"Review of J.G. Herder's *Ideas for the Philosophy of the History of Humanity.* Parts 1 and 2." Translated by Allen W. Wood. In Kant, *Anthropology, History, and Education*, edited by Günter Zöller and Robert Louden. Cambridge: Cambridge University Press, 2007.

Vorlesungen über Anthropologie. In *Kant's gesammelte Schriften*, vol. 25. Berlin: Walter de Gruyter.

Vorlesungen über Rationaltheologie. In *Kant's gesammelte Schriften*, vol. 28. Berlin: Walter de Gruyter.

"What Does It Mean to Orient Oneself in Thinking?" In *Religion within the Boundaries of Mere Reason and Other Writings*, edited by Allen Wood and George di Giovanni. Cambridge: Cambridge University Press, 1998.

Other Relevant Works

Abaci, Uygar. *Kant's Revolutionary Theory of Modality*. Oxford: Oxford University Press, 2019.

Allison, Henry. *Kant's Theory of Freedom*. Cambridge: Cambridge University Press, 1990.

———. *Kant's Theory of Taste*. Cambridge: Cambridge University Press, 2001.

———. *Kant's Transcendental Idealism: An Interpretation and Defense*. New Haven, CT: Yale University Press, 2004.

Ameriks, Karl. "Ginsborg, Nature, and Normativity." *British Journal of Aesthetics* 56, no. 4 (2016): 389–95.

———. *Interpreting Kant's Critiques*. Oxford: Clarendon, 2003.

Arendt, Hannah. *Lectures on Kant's Political Philosophy*. Edited by Ronald Beiner. Chicago: University of Chicago Press, 1982.

Baumgarten, Alexander Gottlieb. *Aesthetica*. Hildesheim: Georg Olms, 1961.

———. *Metaphysics: A Critical Translation with Kant's Elucidations, Selected Notes, and Related Materials*. Translated and edited by Courtney Fugate and John Hymers. London: Bloomsbury, 2013. Citations of this work in text are abbreviated as *M*, followed by the paragraph and page numbers.

———. *Reflections on Poetry*. Translated by Karl Aschenbrenner and William B. Holther. Berkeley: University of California Press, 1954.

Benhabib, Sheila. *The Rights of Others: Aliens, Residents, and Citizens*. Cambridge: Cambridge University Press, 2004.

Bernasconi, Robert. "Who Invented the Concept of Race? Kant's Role in the Enlightenment Construction of Race." In *Race*, edited by Robert Bernasconi, 11–36. Oxford: Blackwell, 2001.

Brandom, Robert. *Making It Explicit: Reasoning, Representing, and Discursive Commitment*. Cambridge, MA: Harvard University Press, 1994.

Cassirer, Ernst. *Kant's Life and Thought*. Translated by James Haden. New Haven, CT: Yale University Press, 1981.

Cazeaux, C. "Kant and Metaphor in Contemporary Aesthetics." *Kantian Review* 8 (2004): 1–37.

Chignell, Andrew. "Belief in Kant." *Philosophical Review* 116, no. 3 (2007): 323–60.

Cohen, Alix. *Kant and the Human Sciences: Biology, Anthropology, and History*. New York: Palgrave Macmillan, 2009.

———. "Kant's 'Curious Portrait of Human Frailties' and the Great Portrait of Nature." In *Kant's Observations and Remarks: A Critical Guide*, edited by Susan Shell and Richard Velkley. Cambridge: Cambridge University Press, 2012.

Cohen, Hermann, *Kants Theorie der Erfahrung.* 3rd ed. Berlin: Bruno Cassirer, 1918.

Danto, Arthur. "The Artworld." In *Philosophy Looks at the Arts,* edited by Joseph Margolis, 132–44. Philadelphia: Temple University Press, 1978.

———. *The Transfiguration of the Commonplace: A Philosophy of Art.* Cambridge, MA: Harvard University Press, 1981.

De Boer, Karin. "Categories versus Schemata: Kant's Two-Aspect Theory of Pure Concepts and His Critique of Wolffian Metaphysics." *Journal of the History of Philosophy* 54, no. 3 (2016): 441–68.

Descartes, René. *Principles of Philosophy.* In *The Philosophical Writings of Descartes,* vol. 1, translated by John Cottingham, Robert Stoothoff, and Dugald Murdoch, Cambridge: Cambridge University Press, 1988.

Dilthey, Wilhelm. *Contributions to the Study of Individuality.* In *Selected Works, Volume II: Understanding the Human World,* edited by Rudolf A. Makkreel and Frithjof Rodi. Princeton, NJ: Princeton University Press, 2010.

———. *Ideas for a Descriptive and Analytic Psychology.* In *Selected Works, Volume II: Understanding the Human World,* edited by Rudolf A. Makkreel and Frithjof Rodi. Princeton, NJ: Princeton University Press, 2010.

———. *Selected Works, Volume I: Introduction to the Human Sciences.* Edited by Rudolf A. Makkreel and Frithjof Rodi. Princeton, NJ: Princeton University Press, 1989.

———. *Selected Works, Volume II: Understanding the Human World.* Edited by Rudolf A. Makkreel and Frithjof Rodi. Princeton, NJ: Princeton University Press, 2010.

———. *Selected Works, Volume III: The Formation of the Historical World in the Human Sciences.* Edited by Rudolf A. Makkreel and Frithjof Rodi. Princeton, NJ: Princeton University Press, 2002.

———. *Selected Works, Volume V: Poetry and Experience.* Edited by Rudolf A. Makkreel and Frithjof Rodi. Princeton, NJ: Princeton University Press, 1985.

———. *Selected Works, Volume VI: Ethical and World-View Philosophy.* Edited by Rudolf A. Makkreel and Frithjof Rodi. Princeton, NJ: Princeton University Press, 2019.

Dreyfus, Hubert L. *Skillful Coping: Essays on the Phenomenology of Everyday Perception and Action.* Edited by Mark Wrathall. Oxford: Oxford University Press, 2014.

Forster, Michael. *Kant and Skepticism.* Princeton, NJ: Princeton University Press, 2010.

Friedman, Michael. "Regulative and Constitutive." In "System and Teleology in Kant's *Critique of Judgment,*" edited by Hoke Robinson. Supplement, *Southern Journal of Philosophy,* vol. 30 (1991): 72–102.

Gasché, Rodolphe. *The Idea of Form: Rethinking Kant's Aesthetics.* Stanford, CA: Stanford University Press, 2003.

Ginsborg, Hannah. *The Normativity of Nature.* Oxford: Oxford University Press, 2015.

———. "Thinking the Particular as Contained under the Universal." In *Aesthetics and Cognition in Kant's Critical Philosophy*, edited by Rebecca Kukla. Cambridge: Cambridge University Press, 2006.

Grenberg, Jeanine. *Kant and the Ethics of Humility*. Cambridge: Cambridge University Press, 2005.

Guyer, Paul. *Kant and the Claims of Knowledge*. Cambridge: Cambridge University Press, 1987.

———. *Kant and the Claims of Taste*. Cambridge, MA: Harvard University Press, 1979.

———. *Kant and the Experience of Freedom*. Cambridge: Cambridge University Press, 1996.

Habermas, Jürgen. *Between Facts and Norms: Contributions to a Discourse Theory of Law and Democracy*. Cambridge, MA: MIT Press, 1996.

———. *Knowledge and Human Interests*. Translated by Jeremy J. Shapiro. Boston: Beacon, 1972.

Hegel, Georg Wilhelm Friedrich. *Enzyklopädie der philosophischen Wissenschaften im Grundrisse* (1827). Vol. 19 of *Gesammelte Werke*. Hamburg: Felix Meiner Verlag, 1989.

———. *Phenomenology of Spirit*. Translated by A. V. Miller. Oxford: Oxford University Press, 1979.

———. *Science of Logic*. Translated by W. H. Johnston and L. G. Struthers. London: Allen and Unwin, 1961.

Heidegger, Martin. *Being and Time*, Translated by Joan Stambaugh. Albany: State University of New York Press, 2010.

Henrich, Dieter. *Aesthetic Judgment and the Moral Image of the World: Studies in Kant*. Stanford, CA: Stanford University Press, 1992.

Herman, Barbara. *The Practice of Moral Judgment*. Cambridge, MA: Harvard University Press, 1993.

Hogan, Desmond. "How to Know Unknowable Things in Themselves." *NOUS* 43 (2009): 60.

Höffe, Otfried. *Kant's Cosmopolitan Theory of Law and Peace*. Translated by Alexandra Newton. New York: Cambridge University Press, 2006.

Huseyinzadegan, Dilek, *Kant's Nonideal Theory of Politics*. Evanston, IL: Northwestern University Press, 2019.

Keller, Pierre. *Kant and the Demands of Self-Consciousness*. Cambridge: Cambridge University Press, 1998.

Kemp Smith, Norman. *A Commentary to Kant's "Critique of Pure Reason."* New York: Humanities, 1962.

Kleingeld, Pauline. *Kant and Cosmopolitanism: The Philosophical Ideal of World Citizenship*. Cambridge: Cambridge University Press, 2012.

Kneller, Jane. *Kant and the Power of Imagination*. Cambridge: Cambridge University Press, 2007.

Korsgaard, Christine. *Fellow Creatures: Our Obligations to the Other Animals*. Oxford: Oxford University Press, 2018.

———. "Reflective Endorsement." In *The Sources of Normativity*, edited by Onora O'Neill, 49–89. New York: Cambridge University Press, 1996.

Kroner, Richard. *Kant's Weltanschauung*. Translated by John Smith. Chicago: University of Chicago Press, 1956.

Kuehn, Manfred. *Kant: A Biography*. Cambridge: Cambridge University Press, 2001.

Kukla, Rebecca, ed. *Aesthetics and Cognition in Kant's Critical Philosophy*. Cambridge: Cambridge University Press, 2006.

Kumar, Apaar. "Transcendental Self and the Feeling of Existence." *Con-Textos Kantianos* 1, no. 3 (2016): 90–121.

Langer, Susanne. *Feeling and Form*. New York: Charles Scribner's Sons, 1953.

Leibniz, Gottfried Wilhelm. "Reflections on Knowledge, Truth, and Ideas." In *Leibniz Selections*, edited by Philip P. Wiener. New York: Charles Scribner's Sons, 1951.

Leland, Patrick. "Kant on Consciousness in Animals." *Studi Kantiani* 31 (2018): 75–107.

Lessing, Hans-Ulrich, Rudolf Makkreel, and Riccardo Pozzo, eds. *Recent Contributions to Dilthey's Philosophy of the Human Sciences*. Stuttgart-Bad Cannstatt: Problemata, Frommann-Holzboog, 2011.

Linnaeus, Carolus. *Systema naturae per regna tria naturae*, vol. 1. Uppsala: Laurentii Salvi Holmiae, 1758–59.

Longuenesse, Beatrice. *Kant and the Capacity to Judge: Sensibility and Discursivity in the Critique of Pure Reason*. Princeton, NJ: Princeton University Press, 2001.

Louden, Robert. "Anthropology from a Kantian Point of View." *Studies in History and Philosophy of Science* 39, no. 4 (December 2008): 515–22.

Makkreel, Rudolf A. "Baumgarten and Kant on Clarity, Distinctness, and the Differentiation of Our Mental Powers," In *Baumgarten and Kant on Metaphysics*, edited by Courtney Fugate and John Hymers, 94–109. Oxford: Oxford University Press, 2018.

———. "Cassirer, Langer, and Dilthey on the Distinctive Kinds of Symbolism in the Arts," *Journal of Transcendental Philosophy* 2, no.1 (2021).

———. "The Cognition-Knowledge Distinction in Kant and Dilthey and the Implications for Psychology and Self-Understanding." *Studies in History and Philosophy of Science* 34 (2003): 149–64.

———. "The Confluence of Aesthetics and Hermeneutics in Baumgarten, Meier, and Kant." *Journal of Aesthetics and Art Criticism* 54, no. 1 (1996): 64–75.

———. *Dilthey, Philosopher of the Human Studies*. Princeton, NJ: Princeton University Press, 1975. Expanded with a new afterword, 1992.

———. *Imagination and Interpretation in Kant: The Hermeneutical Import of the "Critique of Judgment."* Chicago: University of Chicago Press, 1990; revised 1994.

———. "Kant, Dilthey, and the Idea of a Critique of Historical Judgment." *Dilthey-Jahrbuch für Philosophie und Geschichte der Geisteswissenschaften* 10 (1996): 61–79.

———. "Kant on Cognition, Comprehension, and Knowledge." In *Natur und Freiheit. Akten des XII. Kant-Kongresses 2015*, edited by Violetta Waibel & Margit Ruffing, 1297–1304. Berlin: Walter de Gruyter, 2018.

———. "Kant on the Scientific Status of Psychology, Anthropology, and History."

In *Kant and the Sciences*, edited by Eric Watkins. Oxford: Oxford University Press, 2001.

———. "Kant's Anthropology and the Use and Misuse of the Imagination." In *Kant und die Berliner Aufklärung: Akten des IX. Internationalen Kant-Kongresses*, vol. 4, Sektionen XI–XIV, edited by Volker Gerhardt, Rolf-Peter Horstmann, and Ralph Schumacher, 386–94. New York: Walter de Gruyter, 2001.

———. *Orientation and Judgment in Hermeneutics*. Chicago: University of Chicago Press, 2015.

———. "Reflection, Reflective Judgment, and Aesthetic Exemplarity." In *Aesthetics and Cognition in Kant's Critical Philosophy*, edited by Rebecca Kukla, 223–44. Cambridge: Cambridge University Press, 2006.

———. "Relating Kant's Theory of Reflective Judgment to the Law." *Washington University Jurisprudence Review* 6, no. 1 (2013): 147–60.

Malpas, Jeff. "Place and Situation." In *The Routledge Companion to Hermeneutics*, edited by Jeff Malpas and Hans-Helmuth Gander, 354–66. London: Routledge, 2015.

Matherne, Samantha. "Kant and the Art of Schematism." *Kantian Review* 19, no. 2 (2014): 181–205.

McAndrew, Matthew. "Healthy Understanding and *Urtheilskraft*: The Development of the Power of Judgment in Kant's Early Faculty Psychology." *Kant-Studien* 105, no. 3 (2014): 394–405.

———. "Kant's Theories of Concept Formation and Definition," unpublished manuscript.

———. "Kant's Theory of Inductive Reasoning: The Reflecting Power of Judgment in Kant's *Logic*." *Kantian Studies Online* 43 (2014): 43–64.

McClear, Colin. "Kant on Animal Consciousness," *Philosophers' Imprint* 11, no. 15 (2011): 1–16.

McDowell, John. *Mind and World*. Cambridge, MA: Harvard University Press, 1994.

McQuillan, Colin J. *Immanuel Kant: The Very Idea of a Critique of Pure Reason*. Evanston, IL: Northwestern University Press, 2016.

Meier, Georg Friedrich. *Anfangsgründe aller schönen Wissenschaften*, vol. 1. Halle, 1755; Hildesheim: Georg Olms, 1976.

———. *Auszug aus der Vernunftlehre*. Halle: Johann Justinus Gebauer, 1752. Reprinted in *AA* 16.

———. *Versuch einer allgemeinen Auslegungskunst*. Düsseldorf: Stern-Verlag Jannsen, 1965.

Mensch, Jennifer. "Caught between Character and Race: 'Temperament' in Kant's Lectures on Anthropology." *Australian Feminist Law Journal* 43, no. 1 (2017): 125–44.

———. *Kant's Organicism: Epigenesis and the Development of Critical Philosophy*. Chicago: University of Chicago Press, 2013.

Munzel, G. Felicitas. *Kant's Conception of Moral Character: The Critical Link of Morality, Anthropology, and Reflective Judgment*. Chicago: University of Chicago Press, 1999.

Nagel, Thomas. *The View from Nowhere.* Oxford: Oxford University Press, 1986.

Nehring, Robert. *Kritik des Common Sense: Gesunder Menschenverstand, reflektierende Urteilskraft und Gemeinsinn—der Sensus communis bei Kant.* Berlin: Duncker & Humblot, 2010.

Nelson, Eric, ed. *Interpreting Dilthey: Critical Essays.* Cambridge: Cambridge University Press, 2019.

Nietzsche, Friedrich Wilhelm. *Beyond Good and Evil.* Translated by Walter Kaufman. New York: Vintage Books, 1989.

———. *On the Genealogy of Morals.* Translated by Walter Kaufman and R. J. Hollingdale. New York: Vintage Books, 1967.

———. *Untimely Meditations.* Translated by R. J. Hollingdale. Cambridge: Cambridge University Press, 1986.

Nuzzo, Angelica. *Ideal Embodiment: Kant's Theory of Sensibility.* Bloomington: Indiana University Press, 2008.

O'Neill, Onora. "Experts, Practitioners, and Practical Judgement." *Journal of Moral Philosophy* 4, no. 2 (2007): 154.

———. *From Principles to Practice: Normativity and Judgement in Ethics and Politics.* Cambridge: Cambridge University Press, 2018.

Pasternack, Lawrence. "The Development and Scope of Kantian Belief." *Kant-Studien* 102 (2011): 290–315.

———. "Kant's Doctrinal Belief in God." In *Rethinking Kant,* edited by Oliver Thorndike, 200–218. Newcastle upon Tyne, UK: Cambridge Scholars, 2011.

Paton, H. J. *Kant's Metaphysic of Experience.* London: George Allen and Unwin, 1936.

Pippin, Robert. *Hegel's Idealism: The Satisfactions of Self-Consciousness.* Cambridge: Cambridge University Press, 1989.

Prauss, Gerold. *Erscheinung bei Kant: Ein Problem der "Kritik der reinen Vernunft."* Berlin: Walter de Gruyter, 1971.

Rancière, Jacques. *The Politics of Aesthetics.* Translated by Gabriel Rockhill. London: Continuum, 2006.

Rodi, Frithjof. *Das strukturierte Ganze: Studien zum Werk von Wilhelm Dilthey.* Weilerwist: Velbrück Wissenschaft, 2003.

Sgarbi, Marco. *Kant on Spontaneity.* London: Continuum International, 2012.

Shell, Susan Meld, and Richard Velkley, eds. *Kant's Observations and Remarks: A Critical Guide.* Cambridge: Cambridge University Press, 2012.

Strawson, P. F. *The Bounds of Sense: An Essay on Kant's Critique of Pure Reason.* London: Methuen, 1966.

Thompson, Michael L., ed. *Imagination in Kant's Critical Philosophy.* Berlin: Walter de Gruyter, 2013.

Tinguely, Joseph J. *Kant and the Reorientation of Aesthetics: Finding the World.* London: Routledge, 2018.

Truwant, Simon. "Kant's Transcendental Reflection: An Indispensable Element of Philosophy of Culture." In *Critical Studies in German Idealism.* Leiden: Brill Academic Publishing, 2014.

Watkins, Eric, ed. *Kant and the Sciences.* Oxford: Oxford University Press, 2001.

———, ed. and trans. *Kant's Critique of Pure Reason: Background Source Materials.* Cambridge: Cambridge University Press, 2009.

Watkins, Eric, and Marcus Willaschek. "Kant's Account of Cognition." *Journal of the History of Philosophy* 55, no. 1 (2017): 83–112.

Wolff, Christian. *Rational Thoughts on God, the World, and the Soul of Human Beings.* In *Kant's Critique of Pure Reason: Background Source Materials,* edited and translated by Eric Watkins, §198. Cambridge: Cambridge University Press, 2009.

Wölfflin, Heinrich. *Principles of Art History: The Problem of the Development of Style in Later Art.* Translated by M. D. Hottinger. New York: Dover, 1932.

Yovel, Yirmiahu. *Kant and the Philosophy of History.* Princeton, NJ: Princeton University Press, 1980.

Zammito, John. *The Genesis of Kant's "Critique of Judgment."* Chicago: University of Chicago Press, 1992.

———. *The Gestation of German Biology: Philosophy and Physiology from Stahl to Schelling.* Chicago: University of Chicago Press, 2017.

Zuckert, Rachel. *Kant on Beauty and Biology: An Interpretation of the "Critique of Judgment."* Cambridge: Cambridge University Press, 2007.

Index

Abaci, Uygar, 115–16, 125–27, 251n7
absolutism, 229–30
abstraction, 29, 35; in general logic, 48
acquisition, 23–24, 46; active, 82; conceptual, 5, 24; of objective cognition, 47–58. *See also* cognition
Adickes, Erich, 159
aesthetic ideas: in an artistic genius, 121; and determinant concepts of the understanding, 121; and music, 139, 180; as representations of the imagination, 145. *See also* aesthetics; art; music
aesthetics, 7–8, 54, 111–14, 236; artistic creativity and, 121–22; the artistic relevance of Kant's, 122–24; modern, 27; morality and, 109; tradition of, 173. *See also* aesthetic ideas; art; beauty; *Critique of Judgment*; life; philosophy; *sensus communis*; sublime, the; symbolization; taste
affect, 169
affectedness: as a level of awareness, 82; passive, 82
Allison, Henry, 89, 91
Ameriks, Karl, 119
amphibolies, 9, 34–35; moral, 238; reflective, 87; theoretical, 238
analysis: distinctness of a concept through formal, 36; logical analysis of our mental representations, 36. *See also* analytic/synthetic
analytic/synthetic, 6; distinctness of, 35–36, 47–48. *See also* analysis; synthesis
animals, 42–43, 141–42, 159; denial of consciousness to, 42, 240, 250n6, 256n6; human beings and, 205, 210, 237–40; soul of, 141; mistreatment of, 238–39; the worth of, 221
anthropology: Kant's pragmatic, 16, 140–41, 165–67, 171–72, 186, 202; Kant's writings on aesthetics and, 54; as the new science that can provide empirical cognizance of humankind, 199; physiological, 140; and strategies for moving beyond the inner sense of psychology, 161–75. *See also* human nature
antinomies, 7, 86–87; metaphysical, 87–91. See also *Critique of Pure Reason*
apperception: all appearances, as contained in a possible experience, must stand in a community of, 57; the category of causal action allows us to read the perception as the, 57; conceptual acquisition of, 5; perceptual constituents of cognition as aspects of, 21; synthetic unity of, 62; transcendental unity of, 51–58, 66, 81, 144–45. *See also* categories
appropriation, 24, 95, 243; communal, 114; rational, 5, 20; reciprocal, 82. *See also* experience
Arendt, Hannah, 247n6
arithmetic, 55. *See also* mathematics
art: contemporary conceptions of, 123; expression theory of, 122; figurative form in visual, 118; modern, 123. *See also* aesthetic ideas; aesthetics; art history; sublime, the
art history, 123. *See also* art
assessment: appropriatively shared, 46; and comprehension, 46; of knowledge in the context of Kant's treatment of reason, 65; of objective meaning claims for their truth, 65–66. *See also* comprehension; epistemology

assimilation, 18–20, 23–24, 46–48, 80, 95, 243; intuitive, 5; perceptual, 54; receptive and selective, 82; of sensible intuition in space and time, 66. *See also* experience
attention, 35

Baumgarten, Alexander Gottlieb, 6, 24, 26–27, 31–36, 112; account of imagination of, 183–85; account of memory of, 185; list of eight distinct sensible faculties of, 183–84; metaphysically informed empirical psychology of, 186; notion of perspicuous recollection of, 258n7
Baumgarten, Alexander Gottlieb, works of: *Aesthetica,* 29; *Metaphysics,* 28, 164, 183; *Reflections on Poetry,* 27–28
Beattie, John, 162
beauty: the appreciation of, 104, 119, 160; normative ideal of, 120; produces aesthetic pleasure, 112, 118–19; reflective judgments about, 7; sympathy and, 107; universal communicability of aesthetic, 118. *See also* aesthetics
belief: assertoric, 46, 70; contingency of, 5; conviction of, 66; knowledge and, 196; moral certainty as a mode of, 93–94; opinion and, 66–70; of prejudice, 75. *See also* knowledge
benevolence, 110–11. *See also* feeling
Benhabib, Seyla, 213
Bernasconi, Robert, 219
Blumenbach, Johann Friedrich, 154, 219
boundary vs. limit: boundaries as internal positive constraints on reason, 14; boundaries of rational comprehension, 20; distinction of, 14; limits of experience, 14; limits to what we can know with certainty, 24, 39, 46. *See also* epistemology
Buffon, Comte de, 219

Cassirer, Ernst, 140, 225
categorical imperative, 94–96, 103, 173, 214, 223; principle of noncontradiction and the, 230; second formulation of the, 98; third formulation of the, 98; three formulations of the, 94–97. *See also* duty; maxims; moral law; practical reason; will
categories: as a priori, 59, 100; dynamical, 56, 64, 71; mathematical, 56, 64; modal, 58, 71–83, 115, 125; and objective experience, 5; the postulates of empirical thinking as, 6, 71; qualitative, 55–56; quantitative, 54–56; relational, 56; transcendental function of the, 60; of the understanding, 3–6, 51, 59, 91, 100; as universal concepts, 61. *See also* apperception; *Critique of Pure Reason*
causality, 56–57, 62, 64, 88–89, 148; agency and, 231; and freedom, 88–90; of the laws of nature, 88; mechanical, 148; natural, 131; noumenal, 91, 93; phenomenal, 91, 93; reciprocal, 149–50; transcendental, 90
Cazeaux, Clive, 116
character: determination of, 190; developing the, 183–90; empirical, 90–91, 230–31, 235; the ideal of inner worth in individual, 98; intelligible, 90, 93, 230–31, 235; moral, 103, 183, 191, 210, 233; temperament and, 170; as a way of thinking, 189–90. *See also* morality; virtue
Chignell, Andrew, 69–70, 252n20
Christianity, 200, 220. *See also* religion
clarity, 26–27, 38; aesthetic, 29, 31–32; extensive, 27–29, 36; intensive, 27–29. *See also* distinctness
cognition: acquisitive level of, 36, 43, 47–58, 82–83, 242; aesthetic, 36; and apperception, 22, 24; assimilative level of, 79, 82–83; the boundaries of, 46; vs. knowledge, 20, 39–46, 65–70, 237; objective, 44–58, 63–64; perceptual constituents of, 21; rational, 47–58, 156; scientific, 78, 242; sensible, 29; sources of, 47–48; symbolic religious, 229; synthetic conceptual, 38; as a system, 45; theoretical, 114; transcendental conditions of, 78, 228; universally valid, 68. *See also* acquisition; comprehension; epistemology; knowledge
Cohen, Hermann, 55, 63–64
comparison, 29, 35, 74, 130

comprehension, 40–41, 159, 218, 230, 245, 255n3; absolute, 41; aesthetic, 132–33; as cognition that is in some way normative, 45; coordinative, 233–37; human cognitive comprehension, 47; imaginative comprehension, 138, 160; logical, 132–33; Meier on, 39–46; the paradox of, 46; progressive account of representational, 143–44; rational, 6, 20, 39–46, 132, 157, 237, 241–43; reflective, 46, 70, 130, 179; speculative, 134; teleological function of, 218. *See also* assessment; cognition; judgment; knowledge; reason
concept: abstract common, 30–31, 35; a posteriori, 37; a priori, 37, 130, 237; clear and distinct, 32, 189; cosmical, 199; determinate, 130; empirical, 30; general scientific, 37–38; and perception, 188; and representation, 32–35, 197; schematizing the objective meaning of a distinct, 37; synthetic, 49; understanding by means of, 43–44; universally distinct or rule-giving, 35. *See also* concept-formation; conceptual acquisition; representation
concept-formation: empirical, 52; logic of, 37; operations involved in, 33; reflection and comparison in, 32–35. *See also* concept
conceptual acquisition, 5; empirical, 29. *See also* concept
conscience, 110–11, 178–79; reflective, 193–97; and self-assessment, 191–97; unerring, 195. *See also* feeling; morality
consciousness: aesthetic, 116; atemporal unity of, 34; the brain as it conditions our consciousness, 79; denied to nonrational animals, 42, 240, 250n6; identity of, 35; the level of objective, 43; many representations in one, 33; perceptual, 43; phenomenal, 93; the power of judgment is essential for cognitive consciousness, 143; reflexive awareness of, 166–67; of representations, 34, 179; representing something to oneself with, 40; spirit as the "principle" of consciousness, 22; temporal continuum of, 50, 188. *See also* mind
contingency, 116, 228
Copernican revolution, 24, 77
cosmopolitanism, 4, 9, 82, 128, 209–27, 235; anthropological, 201–4; and colonial exploitation, 222; confederation of states of, 208–16; and cosmical philosophy, 198–210, 234–35; and economic inequality, 215; justice and, 200; prejudice and, 220–22; religion and, 200; rights of, 214. *See also* morality
critique: as an inquiry into all the cognitions after which reason might strive independently of all experience, 47; and judgmental refinement, 230; as a tribunal of reason that looks for justification, 47. *See also* practical reason; pure reason; reason
Critique of Judgment, 3–8, 17, 57–62, 72–78, 112–60, 177, 180, 188–93, 202–9, 226, 233–38, 247n1; "Critique of Aesthetic Judgment," 114, 139, 152, 156, 160, 175, 204; "Critique of Teleological Judgment," 114, 139, 145–46, 151–52, 156–57, 205; the human relation to God in the, 196; "Introduction" to the, 33, 43, 114, 117, 130, 142, 151. *See also* aesthetics; judgment; Kant, Immanuel; sublime, the; teleology
Critique of Practical Reason, 99–102, 111, 133–34, 136; conclusion of the, 133–34; duty in the, 102–3; feeling of self-love in the, 103–4; and *Groundwork of the Metaphysics of Morals*, 94–96, 98–99; idea of life in the, 136; legislation and moral law in the, 100–102; the noble sublime in the, 133–34; respect for the moral law in the, 100–104, 111. *See also* Kant, Immanuel; practical reason
Critique of Pure Reason (*CPR*), 3–8, 13–19, 23, 31–39, 44–63, 69–83, 112–15, 122–39, 143, 155–57, 184; "Analytic of Principles," 126; applied general logic in the, 172; "Canon of Pure Reason," 45, 68–69, 72, 243; "Dialectic of Pure Reason," 243; epigenesis of pure reason in the second edition of the, 78; ethical self-comprehension in the, 191; the idea of cosmical philosophy in the, 207; knowledge and belief in the,

Critique of Pure Reason (*CPR*) (*continued*) 196; natural optical illusions in the, 173; practical theistic belief defended in the, 70; "Preface" (1781) to the, 31, 47; "Preface" (1787) to the, 167; the sources of cognition in the, 47–48; the task of the imagination in the, 117; "Transcendental Aesthetic," 18–19, 21, 31, 112; "Transcendental Analytic," 6, 18–19, 68; "Transcendental Dialectic," 13, 60, 86; transcendental sources of the, 6. *See also* analytic/synthetic; antinomies; categories; dialectical antinomies; imagination; Kant, Immanuel; objective deduction; pure reason; subjective deduction
culture: civilizing power of, 210, 221; of discipline, 207–12, 233; Kant's conception of human, 216; the multilateral legitimacy of, 224–27; of skill, 206–10
custom, 75–76. *See also* prejudice

Danto, Arthur, 123
de Boer, Karin, 61–62
Democritus, 227
Descartes, René, 24, 26; *Principles of Philosophy*, 26
determinant judgment, 7, 75, 111–17, 125–28, 131, 205–6, 230–34, 245, 251n1. *See also* judgment
determinism: natural, 7; phenomenal, 89. *See also* freedom
dialectical antinomies, 5, 7, 18. See also *Critique of Pure Reason* (*CPR*)
Dilthey, Wilhelm, 23–25, 48, 52, 96–98, 158–59, 166–67, 223–28, 257n11; *Ideas for a Descriptive and Analytic Psychology*, 224; Inaugural Dissertation, 96; *System of Ethics*, 96
distinctness: aesthetic, 27–32, 38, 42; analytic, 35–38; comparative, 32, 40; coordinative, 29–32; explication of, 38; extensive, 36; intelligible or judgmental, 43; intuitive, 30–31; logical, 27–29; qualitative cognitive perfection of, 45; sensible, 43; subordinative, 29–32; synthetic, 35–38, 45. *See also* clarity
doubt: negative, 75; skeptical, 75
Dreyfus, Hubert, 16–17
dualism: Cartesian mind-body, 147; idealism of freedom that is, 228
Duchamp, Marcel, 123
duty: categorical imperative of, 173; direct, 238–40; imperfect, 110–11, 194, 240; indirect, 110–11, 238; to non-rational animals, 238–39; obedience to, 102–3; perfect, 110, 194. *See also* categorical imperative; morality

education, 172
England, 220
Enlightenment, 97, 226–27, 235–36
Epicurus, 153, 171, 227
epigenesis, 78–79; mental, 154–56; organic, 154–56; preformationism and, 218; of pure reason, 79
epistemology: the development of Kant's, 26–38; the power of judgment in Kant's, 17; the three-level approach of Kant's, 167; transcendental judgmental, 21. *See also* assessment; boundary vs. limit; cognition; knowledge; philosophy; truth
ethics. *See* morality
experience: aesthetic, 113; analogies of, 56–57, 64, 71; a priori conditions of, 16, 56–59; assimilative aspects of, 21–22, 38, 47; epistemic logic that can judgmentally relate concepts to the objects of, 37; inner, 93, 167; judgmental conditions of experience in transcendental logic, 48, 78; layered approach to, 21–24, 46; levels of awareness in human, 82; medial recontextualization of, 112–24; perceptual level of, 38; reflective appropriation of, 144; relevance of comprehension for, 13; sequence of spatially definable things in outer, 53; succession of representations in the time-flow of inner, 53; theory of, 166; three levels of, 167, 242; universals of scientific, 18. *See also* appropriation; assimilation; imagination; intuition

feeling: aesthetic, 7, 104–7, 111–13, 135–47, 253n2; aesthetic moral, 109–10, 192–94; a priori, 102, 146; cognitive perfection as determined aestheti-

cally in relation to the interests of, 44; empirical, 104; for honor, 105–9; the interior state of, 180; intuition and, 133; and moral law, 100–111; participatory, 107–10; private, 113; of self-esteem, 111; sensuous, 176–77; shared, 107, 253n3; social, 104; of sympathy, 102, 107–8. *See also* benevolence; conscience; honor; love; morality; passion; pleasure; respect; sympathy; temperament
Fichte, Johann Gottlieb, 227–29
formalism, 122–23
Forster, Georg, 217, 222–23
France, 220–21
freedom, 7, 9, 69; anthropology and, 162; causality and, 88–90; idealism of, 227–29, 235, 243–44; incompatibilist conception of, 89–90; inner, 193–94, 214; noumenal, 89; outer, 193–94; practical, 90–92; and rights, 23; spirit of, 220–21; transcendental, 89–91, 244. *See also* morality; will
Freud, Sigmund, 42
friendship, 240–41

Galen, 218
geometry, 31, 156; axioms of, 54–55; Euclidean, 77; spatial mode of coordination of, 31. *See also* mathematics
Germany, 220–21
Ginsborg, Hannah, 150–52
God: attention of, 29; comprehensibility of, 94; existence of, 67, 70, 93–94, 229; grace of, 231; as an ideal judge, 193; omniscience of, 192; speculative thought cannot know that there is a, 129; theoretical certainty of universally valid metaphysical knowledge of, 196; the voice of conscience and, 110. *See also* religion; theism; theodicy
Goethe, Johann Wolfgang von, 244; *Faust*, 13, 247
Greenberg, Clement, 123
Gregor, Mary, 195, 260n9
Grenberg, Jeanine, 253n6
Guyer, Paul, 113

Habermas, Jürgen, 227
happiness, 95, 206, 222. *See also* morality
hearing, 180. *See also* music; sense
Hegel, Georg Wilhelm Friedrich, 227; *Phenomenology of Spirit*, 5, 158, 243, 255n7
Heidegger, Martin, 258n2
Herder, Johann Friedrich, 9, 222–23; *Ideas for a Philosophy of the History of Humanity*, 218, 221
Herz, Marcus, 220
history, 244–45; cosmopolitan, 208, 222; final purposes in, 204–8; ultimate purposes in, 204–8
Hobbes, Thomas, 227
Höffe, Otfried, 200
Hogan, Desmond, 69–70
honor: feeling for, 105–9; inner, 106–7; love of, 106, 109, 111; public, 253n13. *See also* feeling; virtue
human nature: the dignity of, 104–6, 109, 111; unsocial sociability in, 228; weakness of, 105. *See also* anthropology; psychology
human rights, 6, 97; concepts of, 222; hospitality and, 215
human sciences: Cassirer on the role of culture and the approach of the, 225; Dilthey's psychology as a, 224; Dilthey's writings on the methodology of the, 158, 224–25; Kant's anthropology and the rise of the, 16, 162, 257n1; post-Hegelian conception of the, 224
Hume, David, 14, 96, 219, 227
humility, 109, 253n6. *See also* virtue
Huseyinzadegan, Dilek, 213–15, 256n1
Husserl, Edmund, 258n8
hypotyposis, 121

idealism: of freedom, 227–29, 235, 243–44; the nature of Kantian, 96, 250n6; objective, 228, 236; philosophical, 230; psychological assumptions of traditional, 53, 80; redefining, 53–54; transcendental, 53, 80, 93, 230, 244
imagination: aesthetic idea as a representation of the, 121, 145; the beautiful and the sublime enliven the imagination, 132–33; the formative productivity of the, 184; in Kant's epistemology, 59, 76; perceptual, 138, 143–44; the power of, 184; schematization as a

imagination (*continued*)
judgmental function of, 6, 63; schematization of the objective meaning of a distinct concept through, 37; schematization without a concept, 117–19; shift from spelling to reading of the, 59; synthesis of the, 49–50; transcendental synthesis of the, 61. *See also* experience; memory
imitation, 75, 77; in youth, 75. *See also* prejudice
inclination, 75. *See also* prejudice
India, 217
intuition, 30, 50; acquires a perceptible objectivity, 56; as a posteriori, 59; axioms of, 54–55; and feeling, 133; manifold of, 49–50, 59; sensible, 31; synthetic act that requires, 37. *See also* experience
Italy, 221

Japan, 213
Jäsche, Gottlob Benjamin, 32–35
Jenisch, Daniel, 174
Johns, Jasper, 123
Judaism, 219–20. *See also* religion
judgment, 3, 7, 230; aesthetic, 111–24, 136, 233; categorial, 61, 148; comprehension as a mode of reflective assessment that is a function of, 46; deferral of, 73, 75; epistemic, 37, 48; good, 190–91; maxim at the level of, 190; the modality of a, 125–26; powers of, 162; practical, 233–34; preliminary, 72–75; and the pure concepts of the understanding, 49; reflective, 178, 183, 196, 205, 233–37; the role of judgment in appropriating knowledge as true, 59–70; the role of judgment in validating cognition as meaningful, 59–70; the role of judgment to bridge the divide between the phenomenal and the noumenal, 91; schematization as an imaginative use of, 60–66; subjective maxim of, 88; synthetic, 54, 63; of taste, 113–14, 119, 162, 175, 234, 243; teleological, 233; traditional infinite, 55. *See also* comprehension; *Critique of Judgment*; determinant judgment; reflective judgment

Kant, Immanuel: on Baumgarten and logic, 26–38; the idealism of freedom of, 227–28; pragmatic approach to anthropology of, 16, 140–41, 165–67, 171–72, 186; on the relation of comprehension to cognition and knowledge, 39–46; right of hospitality of, 213–15; theory of experience of, 166. *See also* aesthetics; epistemology; idealism; metaphysics; morality; philosophy; practical reason; pure reason; religion; worldview
Kant, Immanuel, works of: *Anthropology from a Pragmatic Point of View*, 22, 38, 41, 140, 145, 161–91, 202–3, 207–10, 219–23, 243; *Anthropology Parow*, 168; *Blomberg Logic*, 35, 39, 75; *Busolt* anthropology lectures, 189; *Collins* anthropology lectures, 21–22, 140–42, 161, 164, 168, 181; "Determination of the Concept of a Human Race," 216–17; "Doctrine of Right," 214; *Dohna-Wundlacken* lectures on anthropology, 220; *Dohna-Wundlacken Logic*, 32, 41; "Dreams of a Spirit-Seer," 135; essay on Enlightenment, 15; "The False Subtlety of the Four Syllogistic Figures," 142; *Friedländer* lectures on anthropology, 42, 163–66, 170–76, 183, 253n5; *Groundwork of the Metaphysics of Morals*, 94, 98–102, 106–7, 253n5; "Idea for a Universal History with a Cosmopolitan Aim," 204–5, 208–10; *Jäsche Logic*, 32–37, 41–43, 67, 73–74, 156, 199, 201, 204–7; lectures on anthropology, 6–8, 16, 21, 83, 140–42, 161–91; lectures on geography, 187; lectures on logic, 3–7, 13–15, 19–24, 29, 47–52, 63, 69–74, 78; *Logik Busolt*, 33; *Logik Pölitz*, 34–35, 37; *Menschenkunde* lectures on anthropology, 164, 219; *Metaphysical Foundations of Natural Science*, 135, 139; *The Metaphysics of Morals*, 6, 23, 107–11, 192–95, 211–15, 240–42; *Metaphysik L1*, 141; *Metaphysik Volckmann*, 159; *Mrongovius* lectures on anthropology, 163, 170–71, 176, 179; *Observations on the Feeling of the Beautiful and the Sublime*, 104–10, 219; "Of the Different Races of Human Beings," 216; *On the Form and Principles*

of the Sensible and the Intelligible World, 30; "On the Miscarriage of All Philosophical Trials in Theodicy," 195; "On the Use of Teleological Principles in Philosophy," 216–18; *Opus postumum*, 145–46; *Perpetual Peace*, 4, 208, 212–13, 235; *Pillau* anthropology lectures, 161, 199; *Prolegomena to Any Future Metaphysics*, 14, 162; *Reflexionen zur Anthropologie*, 30, 176, 178–79; *Reflexionen zur Logik*, 28, 33–34, 40, 74, 112, 116; *Reflexionen zur Metaphysik*, 145; *Religion within the Boundaries of Mere Reason*, 6, 22, 91, 141–42, 200, 230–32; *Vienna Logic*, 33, 46, 156; *Warschauer Logic*, 43–44, 250n5; "What Does It Mean to Orient Oneself in Thinking?," 129. *See also Critique of Judgment*; *Critique of Practical Reason*; *Critique of Pure Reason*; *Kant's gesammelte Schriften*
Kant's gesammelte Schriften, 25
Keller, Pierre, 52, 256n1
Kemp Smith, Norman, 71–72, 125
Kleingeld, Pauline, 214, 220, 222–23
knowledge: on the basis of the empirical understanding, 14, 18; and belief, 196; certainty of, 6, 15, 24, 39, 45–46, 66–70, 73; claims of, 6, 14; vs. cognition, 20, 39–46, 65–70, 237; cognitive perfection and, 44–46; comprehension falls short of, 39; distinctness the central cognitive standard according to Leibniz, 26–27; empirical certainty of, 73; experiential cognition as scientific, 60; judgmental act of providing objective knowledge, 59; knowledge that aims to deliver the certainty of an intersubjective consensus, 5; the limits of, 71–83; objective determinate knowledge of the inner disposition, 192; practical, 69; rational appropriation of, 66; rational certainty of, 73; system of, 115; terminology of, 249n1. *See also* belief; cognition; comprehension; epistemology; truth; understanding
Korsgaard, Christine, 239–40
Kroner, Richard: *Kant's Weltanschauung*, 229
Kuehn, Manfred, 220

Langer, Susanne, 173
language: aesthetically lively, 28; of clarity and distinctness, 30; as a signification of thought, 189; and symbols, 189
laughter, 139
law: judicial, 100; natural, 100. *See also* moral law
Leibniz, Gottfried Wilhelm, 26–27, 31, 41, 80–81, 237, 244
Lessing, Gotthold Ephraim, 97
life: aesthetic feeling of, 135–47; biological, 136; naturalistic definition of, 135; the shifting meaning of the term "life," 135–40; soul, mind, and spirit as three levels of, 140–47
limit vs. boundary. *See* boundary vs. limit
Linnaeus, Carl, 9; *Systema naturae*, 218–19
logic: applied general, 172; epistemic, 37, 45, 48; general, 48–49, 60; transcendental, 48–49, 60–61, 65; transcendental categories of the understanding in general, 37, 48–49
Longuenesse, Beatrice, 19; *Kant and the Capacity to Judge*, 32, 34, 55, 62–63, 74, 248n11
Lotze, Hermann, 229
Louden, Robert, 199–200
love: duty to, 110; of honor, 106, 109–11; mutual, 241; passion of, 174. *See also* feeling

Makkreel, Rudolf: *Imagination and Interpretation in Kant*, 61–62, 248n8, 257n4; *Orientation and Judgment in Hermeneutics*, 248n12, 252n20, 254n16, 255n4, 257n3
Marx, Karl, 245
mathematics, 16; arithmetic and number theory, 31; determinacy of, 24; direct intuitive demonstrative power of constructions of, 122; objects of, 27. *See also* arithmetic; geometry
Matherne, Samantha, 72
maxims, 94–95, 98, 101–3, 110–11, 239; of reason, 183; respect for the law as the sole incentive of our moral, 232; of thinking, 190–91, 203. *See also* categorical imperative; morality
McAndrew, Matthew, 249n17
McClear, Colin, 42, 249n4

McDowell, John, 248n10
Meier, Georg Friedrich, 4, 6–7, 24, 36, 39–46; *Auszug aus der Vernunftlehre*, 35, 39–40
memory, 185–87; and foresight, 186–87; mechanism of, 186. *See also* imagination; mind
Mendelssohn, Moses, 220
Mensch, Jennifer: "Caught between Character and Race: 'Temperament' in Kant's Lectures on Anthropology," 218
Merkur (journal), 174–75
Merritt, Melissa: *Kant on Reflection and Virtue*, 169–70, 182
metaphysics: dialectical antinomies of, 18, 87–91, 237; real use of the understanding by, 30; speculative, 152. *See also* phenomenal/noumenal; phenomenal world; philosophy; universals
Mill, J. S., 48, 92
mind: conscious, 42; as an immaterial substance, 135–36; and the predisposition to humanity, 22; responsive level of, 181; and spirit, 240; vocation of the, 177. *See also* cognition; memory; soul; spirit; unconscious; understanding
moral decision, 91–94
morality: abstract view of, 99; and aesthetics, 109; feelings of sympathy in, 102; inner freedom of, 214; philosophy of, 98, 230; plurality of ethical systems of, 97–98; religion as a supplement to, 231; social feelings and, 104; subjective conditions of receptiveness to, 194; universally valid, 97–98; and wisdom, 207–8. *See also* character; conscience; cosmopolitanism; duty; feeling; freedom; happiness; moral law; philosophy; pluralism; practical reason; religion; virtue; wisdom
moral law: domain of the, 115; duty to obey the, 102–3; holiness of the, 109–10; inner commitment to the, 191; and the kingdom of ends, 95–97; as legislative, 100–111; as legitimating, 100–111; recognition of the, 92–93; respect for the, 142, 144, 194–96, 230–32; as self-legislative, 7, 95–96, 239. *See also* categorical imperative; law; morality; practical reason
moral philosophy. *See* morality
music, 118, 123, 138–39; enjoyment of, 146 as a language of sheer sensations, 180; and listening to sounds in terms of their tonal qualities, 180. *See also* aesthetic ideas; hearing

nationalism, 221
natural history, 216–18; epigenetic, 218; genetic, 222
natural sciences, 16, 81, 162; explanatory, 224–25; psychology and the, 224
nature: distinction between inorganic and organic nature, 131; experience of beautiful forms in, 201; humanity as the ultimate end of, 206; mathematical conception of, 77; rational access to, 116; scientific principles governing the necessary domain of, 121; state of, 208; tectonic of, 153; theoretical laws of, 115
Nehring, Robert, 247n6
Newtonian physics, 55–56
Nietzsche, Friedrich, 92
Nisbet, H. B., 214
Nuzzo, Angelica: *Ideal Embodiment: Kant's Theory of Sensibility*, 146–47

objective deduction, 51–54, 144. See also *Critique of Pure Reason*
O'Neill, Onora, 233–34

Parmenides, 227
passion, 169; of love, 174. *See also* feeling
Paton, H. B., 61
perception: anticipations of, 55; Cartesian cognitive judgments based on clear and distinct, 26; concept and, 188; objective perception that is cognitive, 143; outer, 177–79; as representing something to oneself with consciousness, 41; of subjective successive representations, 57; touch as the only sense that gives an immediate external, 179–80. *See also* sensations; sense
phenomenal/noumenal, 82, 87–91, 236. *See also* metaphysics; phenomenal world

phenomenal world, 30; inner determinations of the, 80–81; systematic relationships among our phenomenal experiences in the, 92. *See also* metaphysics; phenomenal/noumenal
philosophy: academic, 60, 198; contributions of Kant to modern, 140; cosmical, 4, 9, 198–210, 216, 234–35, 243; cosmopolitan, 206–8; environmental, 227; hermeneutical, 227; moral, 170; practical, 15, 171; scholastic, 206; of science, 146; theoretical, 15, 171; traditional academic, 14; transcendental, 92, 237; world-oriented, 209–27. *See also* aesthetics; epistemology; metaphysics; morality; reason; worldview
photography, 123
Plato, 59, 227
pleasure: aesthetic, 28, 62, 112–14, 118–19, 136; and displeasure, 180; in the moral context, 136; pure, 175; reflective, 118, 166; sensuous, 7, 112, 175; in the way sensations as sense impressions affect us, 112. *See also* feeling; sensations
pluralism, 98, 244; cultural, 223, 233. *See also* morality
point of view, 67, 169–70
practical reason, 7, 60, 86–101, 114, 129, 144, 173, 190–94, 238; ideal ends of, 228; pure, 194. *See also* categorical imperative; *Critique of Practical Reason*; morality; moral law; reason
prejudice, 75–78, 235–36, 247n4; of antiquity, 77; beliefs of, 242; of Kant's cosmopolitanism, 220–22; of taste, 226. *See also* custom; inclination; race
Priestley, Joseph, 217
property rights, 23, 211–12
Prussia, 214
Prussian Academy of the Sciences, 25
psychology, 48, 141, 198–99, 224; descriptive, 224; empirical, 164; the inner sense of, 161–75. *See also* human nature
pure reason, 7, 87, 193, 237; antinomies of, 228; the architectonic of, 198. See also *Critique of Pure Reason*; reason
purposiveness, 134–35; 148–60, 257n11; aesthetic, 149–52; geometrical, 157; immanent purposiveness of organisms, 149–55, 245; reflective comprehension of, 156–60; teleological, 157, 160. *See also* teleology

race, 216–23; animate life and the notion of, 240. *See also* prejudice
Rancière, Jacques, 123
rationalism, 31, 173, 227, 244
Rawls, John, 23, 98, 101, 227, 253n13
reading, 42
realism, 53
reality: exhaustive knowledge of, 47; familiar regions of, 24; of space and time, 55; systematic approximation of the whole of, 245
reason: Baumgarten's definition of, 44; comprehension involves tactfulness or reflective discernment in the use of human, 46; comprehensive aims of, 59; concepts of, 13; demands of, 23; dialectical, 7, 20; epigenesis of, 155; government of, 200; maxim at the level of, 190; moral aesthetic receptivity is not passive but involves an openness to our, 109; and the power of choice, 92, 144; as "pragmatic," 22; reflective use of, 221; self-determination of, 92–94; theoretical, 60, 94, 100–101, 229; theoretical and practical, 6, 94, 193; tribunal of, 47, 100; the ultimate ends of, 206; and understanding, 92, 237; unified nature of, 47; and wisdom, 202. *See also* comprehension; critique; philosophy; practical reason; pure reason
reflection, 29, 35, 169–70; concepts of, 126; on the meaning-content of a prejudice, 73; Merritt's normative definitive of, 182; subjective comparison of preliminary, 75; symbolic elaboration of a kind of, 122; transcendental, 127. *See also* reflective judgment
reflective judgment, 4, 21–23, 72–75, 101, 111–34, 146, 155–58, 230–37, 243–45, 247n6, 251n1; freedom of, 241; rational comprehension and, 237; teleological, 116, 206; transcendental principle of, 130. *See also* judgment; reflection
reflexivity, 51–54; as transcendental awareness, 52

refugees, 214–15
Reid, Thomas, 162
religion: conversion of, 230; and cosmopolitanism, 200; Dilthey's ideal of perfection and, 97; distinction between doctrinal and authentic interpretation in its hermeneutical relevance for, 261n8; idea of hope of, 201; morally informed awareness of, 93, 196; non-institutional, 229; of personal belief, 229. *See also* Christianity; God; Judaism; morality
representation: comparison of, 34; concept and, 32–35; consciousness of, 34; of inner sense, 163–64; as judged in relation to objects in the world, 112; logical analysis of mental, 36; perceptual, 30, 142–43; spontaneous aesthetic, 117; subjective, 55; temporal manifold of, 51; transcendental logic teaches how to bring under concepts the pure synthesis of, 49. *See also* concept
representationalism, 16–19
respect, 111. *See also* feeling
Rickert, Heinrich, 48
Russia, 221

Sartre, Jean-Paul, 227
Schelling, Friedrich Wilhelm Joseph, 227
Schiller, Friedrich, 173, 244
Schopenhauer, Arthur, 227, 239
science, 41, 78
self: and the kingdom of ends, 98; noumenal, 98; true, 173
self-assessment, 176–97; cognitive, 197; conscience and, 191–97; judgmental, 182; morally informed religious awareness in orienting, 196; pragmatic, 182; sensibility and reflexive, 179–83
self-consciousness, 51–52, 167, 171; apperceptive, 163; and self-awareness, 171–72, 178; and self-feeling, 178; transcendental mode of, 52
self-love, 92–93, 103–4, 141–42; subjective principle of, 142
sensations: as conscious representations, 63–64, 174; as mere momentary modifications of the state of the subject, 49, 143; music as a language of sheer, 180; obscure, 174; as physical impressions at the lower limit of consciousness, 173; a play of, 42; as sense impressions in terms of pleasure or pain, 112; as sensory effect, 175; subjective aspects of, 174; the subjective reality of, 55; as synthetically acquired, 50. *See also* perception; pleasure
sense: communal, 175; contribution to human comprehension of, 162; earthly limits that confine the, 14; inner, 51–54, 61, 93, 117–18, 161–72, 175–97, 243, 250n7; intuitive, 165–66; outer, 53–54, 93, 126, 161–73, 180, 243; passivity of, 146; perception of, 5, 179; reflexive, 182; space as the form of outer, 54; synopsis of sense that is merely assimilated, 49; time as the form of inner, 53; vital, 176–97. *See also* hearing; perception; sight; smell; taste; touch
sensus communis, 7, 119. *See also* aesthetics
sight, 180. *See also* sense
signs: Baumgarten on, 187–88; Kant on, 187–89
smell, 180–81. *See also* sense
Smith, Adam, 96
social order: civilization as the pragmatic acquisition of, 6
soul: of animals, 141; life of, 21–22, 160, 168; lower function of, 141; obscurity of, 42, 177; as the organ of inner sense, 165; passive level of mere, 181. *See also* mind; spirit
space: concept of, 31; geometry contemplates relations of, 31; representations in, 18–19; synthetic a priori subjective form of, 21. *See also* time
Spinoza, Baruch, 153, 227
spirit: the community of human spirit, 238; mind and, 240; as the "principle" of consciousness, 22; self-activating level of, 144, 181; in thinking about life, 144–45; wholly rational level of, 22–23. *See also* mind; soul
Stoicism, 168–71
Strawson, Peter, 59
subjective deduction, 49–52, 54, 143. See also *Critique of Pure Reason*

sublime, the, 4, 20, 242; the challenges of, 131–34; dynamical, 134, 137, 175; experience of the, 8, 105, 160; mathematical, 57, 132–34, 137, 143–44; as a state of mind, 177; the sublime magnificence of great art, 104; two kinds of, 133. *See also* aesthetics; art; *Critique of Judgment*
substance: and attribute, 64; principle of no self-alteration of, 57; principle of the persistence of, 56
symbolization, 122; aesthetic judgment and, 123. *See also* aesthetics
sympathy, 15, 111; charitable acts based on, 101; Kant's attack on, 102–3; reactive, 96; social feeling of, 104. *See also* feeling
synthesis: of apprehension, 50; distinctness that arises from, 35–38; judgmental, 63; of recognition, 22, 51; transcendental unity of apperception as the source of all, 51. *See also* analytic/synthetic

taste: aesthetic, 17, 111, 181; judgments of, 113–14, 119, 162, 175, 234, 243; rational guidelines for good, 119–20; as a subjective sense, 180–81. *See also* aesthetics
teleology: Kant's regulative use of, 214–15; purposiveness of, 134–35; reflective judgments of, 116, 122. See also *Critique of Judgment*; purposiveness
temperament, 170. *See also* feeling
theism, 153. *See also* God
theodicy, 195, 229. *See also* God
Tieftrunk, Johann Heinrich, 214
time: the a priori form of, 54; of inner sense, 51–53, 177; linear, 177; phenomenal effect in, 7; representations in, 18–19; synthetic a priori subjective form of, 21. *See also* space
Tinguely, Joseph, 254n14, 255n3
Tolley, Clinton, 250n1
touch, 179–80. *See also* sense
Trilling, Lionel, 259n11
truth: as agreement with the object, 81; as a cognitive perfection, 45; conscience and, 195; knowing or ascertaining, 24; positive standard for, 45; transcendental truth conditions, 48–49; and virtue, 196. *See also* epistemology; knowledge
Turkey, 221

unconscious: inner sense need not be, 163; separate region of the, 42. *See also* mind
understanding: categories of the, 3–6, 51, 59, 91, 100; certainty of the knowledge of the, 46; determinant concepts of the, 121; determinate understanding of the mechanisms of nature, 146; discursive, 243; general use of the, 48; intellectual, 159; maxim at the level of, 190; the mental capacity of, 51; particular use of the, 48; pure concepts of the, 49–51; reason and, 92, 237; relational concepts of the, 5; theoretical, 129; world-concept, 236. *See also* knowledge; mind
universals, 3; abstract, 28. *See also* metaphysics
utilitarianism, 231

violence: to the inner sense, 177; of revolution, 232
virtue: adopted, 105; assessment of, 196; duties of, 111, 194, 240; love of honor as a, 109; moral, 110–11, 194; moralization as the rational and reflective appropriation of, 6; sympathy and agreeableness as supplements for, 105; truth and, 196. *See also* character; honor; humility; morality
Voltaire, 219
von Haller, Albrecht, 219

Watkins, Eric, 63–64
will: as conditioned but not always necessitated, 90; determining grounds of the, 94; intelligible, 90; practical freedom of the, 94; producing an enlivening of the, 170; rational, 91. *See also* categorical imperative; freedom
Willaschek, Marcus, 63–64
Windelband, Wilhelm, 224

wisdom: cosmical ideal of, 242; morality and, 207–8. *See also* morality; worldview
Wolff, Christian, 26–27
Wood, Allen, 106
worldview, 4–5, 221, 228–45; comprehensive, 243; of the idealism of freedom, 143; as intuition of the world, 132; moral, 5; normative, 24. *See also* philosophy; wisdom
Wundt, Wilhelm, 224

Zammito, John, 30–32, 256n2
Zuckert, Rachel, 254n11